AMERICA'S MILITARY TODAY

Also by Tod Ensign

Military Life: The Insider's Guide
GI Guinea Pigs: How the Pentagon Exposed Our Troops to Hazards Deadlier than War
(with Michael Uhl)

AMERICA'S MILITARY TODAY

The Challenge of Militarism

Tod Ensign

THE NEW PRESS

NEW YORK
LONDON

Published in the United States by The New Press, New York, 2004
Distributed by W. W. Norton & Company, Inc., New York

LIBRARY OF CONGRESS CATALOGING-IN-PUBLICATION DATA

Ensign, Tod.
America's military today : the challenge of militarism / Tod Ensign.
p. cm.
Includes bibliographical references and index.
ISBN 1-56584-883-7 (hc.)
1. United States—Armed Forces. 2. United States—Military policy.
3. Militarism—United States. 4. United States—History—21st century.
5. World politics—21st century. I. Title.
UA23.E62 2004
355'.033073—dc22 2004049879

The New Press was established in 1990 as a not-for-profit alternative to the large, commercial publishing houses currently dominating the book publishing industry. The New Press operates in the public interest rather than for private gain, and is committed to publishing, in innovative ways, works of educational, cultural, and community value that are often deemed insufficiently profitable.

www.thenewpress.com

Composition by dix!

Printed in the United States of America

2 4 6 8 10 9 7 5 3 1

Dedication

For Rachel Ensign, my treasure

&

to the memory of

W. Scott and Gretchen Ensign

who taught me about justice

Contents

Preface

Tod Ensign

America's military is approaching a crisis that could rival the one it faced at the end of the Vietnam War. George Bush's reckless invasion of Iraq and the resulting occupation have stretched our armed forces to the breaking point. As some predicted, 135,000 U.S. troops are now bogged down in a guerrilla-type conflict that could drag on for years. As the toll of dead and injured mounts and more Iraqis come to oppose America's domination, moderate voices at home are beginning to call for withdrawal.

Our armed forces are stretched so thin by the Iraq war that the Pentagon had to break its promise to limit combat tours to one year. Nearly half of the Army's thirty-three combat brigades are now serving in the Persian Gulf. If the Army replaced them with fresh units, it would be very difficult to meet its obligations in other parts of the world. At present, there are 368,000 U.S. troops serving in 120 countries. Congress has authorized the Army to add six combat brigades, at a cost of $20 billion. I question whether an additional 40,000 GIs can be recruited into the combat arms without at least a partial return to a draft.

Reservists who signed up thinking they would perform part-time duty are being forced to assume an increasing share of the combat burden. In May 2004, reservists constituted 40 percent of all troops in Iraq and this ratio is likely to hold steady. The strain on these weekend warriors is even greater than for active-duty GIs. Since Bush has driven away potential European allies with his contempt for multinational cooperation, there is little prospect of help in the future. This leaves our military to soldier on, pretty much alone.

Some of the problems confronting our military today could have been foreseen when Congress adopted the all-volunteer-force concept (AVF) at the end of the disastrous Vietnam War. AVF planners thought that an active force of at least two million GIs could be recruited without resort to conscription. Their blueprint relied on sharp increases in pay and benefits, recruiting women for most military jobs, and incorporating the National Guard and Reserves into the active-duty force for war fighting.

For over thirty years, most of the plan worked fairly well. Although the AVF attracted sufficient numbers of volunteers, there were high rates of attrition. However, the military wasn't really tested since it fought only one brief war in the Persian Gulf in 1991 over the entire period.

The Pentagon was forced to recognize that the financial benefits needed to attract volunteers cost much more than had been anticipated. Generous pay hikes, robust bonuses, college aid and loan repayment all fed an escalating military budget. Since Congress insisted on continuing to buy expensive weapons systems from politically connected contractors, something had to give.

The Pentagon cut the active-duty force from 2.1 million in 1989 to a current 1.4 million. Since the Pentagon's far-flung military obligations continue as before, this enormous reduction in troop strength has affected readiness and deployability.

Prior to invading Iraq, Defense Secretary Donald Rumsfeld castigated then–Army Chief of Staff Eric Shinseki for estimating that at least 300,000 troops would be needed to occupy Iraq. Shinseki was also ridiculed for urging large increases in the number of armored vehicles to be sent to Iraq. Bush's refusal to heed his advice led to many deaths and injuries among American GIs.

In order to bridge the manpower gap, Bush and Rumsfeld have tried to squeeze more juice out of a shrunken Pentagon by using "private soldiers" supplied by their corporate cronies. There are now 10,000 of these security consultants just in Iraq. These mercenaries play an active role in war fighting while pretending that they are not military. They perform a range of military jobs, such as acting as security forces and body guards, interrogating detainees, and hauling military equipment and supplies. In fact, special-forces units like the Rangers and Green Berets complain that their ranks are being thinned by corporate recruiters who hire away their most experienced people.

Bush and his generals have also imposed "stop loss" orders, which keep more than 50,000 GIs on active duty past their discharge dates. These "band aid" measures may be effective in the short run, but they can only stave off deeper problems for so long. Troops who are subjected to extra-long combat tours or kept on active duty beyond their contract date will be less likely to reenlist, and these measures may have a chilling effect on new recruits as well.

The "Voices from Iraq" letters reprinted in chapter 3 reveal the low morale felt by most combat troops in Iraq today.

Defense Secretary Rumsfeld's commitment to accelerate the pace of "privatization" by shifting jobs formerly performed by civil servants to private contractors has also had a negative impact on military readiness and security. For example, his campaign has resulted in low-wage security guards without weapons having primary responsibility for guarding important military bases such as Ft. Bragg, North Carolina.

WOMEN: SECOND-CLASS SOLDIERS?

One in every six GIs (one in five in the Air Force) on active duty today is female. Surveys of women GIs in all branches consistently report elevated rates of sexual harassment and assault from male soldiers. Yet military commanders seem unable (or unwilling) to use military laws to punish offending males.

This may be partially due to a clash of values between a patriarchical military institution and women who demand equal treatment. When thousands of GIs are being prepared for combat, it's not surprising that ancient "warrior values" with their ingrained machismo gain new currency.

As the Bush administration expands its "war on terror" in Afghanistan and

Iraq, the dark arts of our "special ops" soldiers gain new status and influence within the military rank and file. Elite units like the Rangers, SEALs, Green Berets, and the secretive Delta Force all stoke a robust machismo within their closed fraternity. For these soldiers, any label that suggests femininity is the grossest of insults. It remains to be seen whether an institution so steeped in male-chauvinist thinking can ever accept women soldiers as equals.

AGAINST THE CURRENT: MILITARY GAYS AND LESBIANS STILL REPRESSED

Gays and lesbians have made enormous strides in their struggle to end discrimination based on sexual orientation. Unfortunately, the US military seems immune to the changes that have occurred in the rest of society. While military commanders will spout rhetoric about racial or sexual equality, this doesn't extend to non-hetero GIs. The military's "Don't Ask, Don't Tell" rules, which mandate discriminatory treatment of homosexuals, enjoy the silent support of George Bush and his "moral majority" supporters.

ASYMMETRICAL WARFARE OR AIMING AT A MOVING TARGET

Richard A. Clarke, one of the Bush administration's former experts on terrorism, recently published a book, *Against All Enemies,* in which he alleges that the day after September 11th Bush began demanding evidence of Saddam Hussein's involvement in the attacks. Clarke also recalls Defense Secretary Donald Rumsfeld's complaint "that there were no decent targets for bombing in Afghanistan . . . and that we should consider bombing Iraq." Most important, Clarke concludes that Bush's decision to invade Iraq "launched an unnecessary and costly war . . . that strengthened the fundamentalist, radical Islamic terrorist movement worldwide."

It appears that Rumsfeld didn't understand the kind of asymmetrical warfare that is being waged by our terrorist opponents. A month after September 11th he proclaimed, "Victory means liquidating the terrorist network and putting them out of business." He apparently thought that if we just applied enough military force against a conspiracy called Al Qaeda we could somehow wipe it out.

The continued ability of the shadowy Al Qaeda network to carry out a devastating series of bombings in Bali, Indonesia, Morocco, Saudi Arabia, Turkey, and most recently Spain underscores the fact that conventional military operations will have little, if any, effect on a decentralized network of highly motivated and disciplined terrorists. As Bruce Hoffman, a terrorist consultant at RAND, recently wrote, "While America has been tied down in Iraq, the international terrorist network has been busy elsewhere with suicide bombings."

Military analyst Jeffrey Record, of the Air War College, has also published a stinging critique of Bush's handling of the war on terrorism. In a lengthy article published by the Army War College's Strategic Studies Institute, he argues that the invasion of Iraq was "unnecessary" and warns that it has brought the Army "near the breaking point." Author of six books on military strategy and a former aide to the Senate Armed Services Committee, Record concludes, "The global war on terrorism . . . is dangerously indiscriminate and ambitious; its parameters should be readjusted." Record adds that Bush's antiterror campaign "promises more than it can deliver and threatens to dissipate military resources in a . . . hopeless search for absolute security."

IRAQ AND AFGHANISTAN: WAR WITHOUT END?

Secretary Rumsfeld has played a crucial role in shaping the administration's response to the September 11th attacks. According to the book *Rumsfeld's Way,* he had just predicted at a Pentagon meeting that a "shocking event" would soon occur when one of the hijacked commercial jets crashed into the Pentagon, killing 180 people.

Prior to September 11, a group of Bush intimates, including Vice President Dick Cheney, Paul Wolfowitz, and Richard Perle, as well as Rumsfeld, had hatched a plan to rebuild a military they believed President Bill Clinton had allowed to deteriorate. Their plan, *Rebuilding America's Defenses,* is a blueprint for ensuring that America remains militarily dominant in the world. In its preface, the report summarizes its main goal as follows: "At present, the United States faces no global rival. America's grand strategy should aim to preserve and extend this advantageous position as far into the future as possible."

As President, George Bush has implemented a number of the recommendations contained in the plan. He dropped the Comanche helicopter and placed the accident-plagued V-22 "Osprey" heli-plane on hold. He has vigorously pushed the "Star Wars" missile-shield project, which will cost billions if fully deployed. By skillfully exploiting the fear and anger arising from the September 11 attacks, he has won congressional support for increasing military spending by $15–20 billion each succeeding year.

RUMMY'S DREAM SHEET

Secretary Rumsfeld has been a tireless advocate for the following "reforms":

• Transforming the Army into a lighter and more mobile fighting force. He chose General Peter Schoomaker, who spent his entire career with the lightly armed Special Forces, to be his Army Chief of Staff.

• Increasing combat capability by retraining and transferring up to 300,000 GIs from administrative jobs to combat-related assignments. (One question: will the military be able to attract sufficient numbers of volunteers who don't want to serve in active combat roles?)

• Speeding the privatization of many military jobs that are currently performed by civil-service workers who enjoy federal benefits. This affects thousands of employees who perform clerical tasks, food service, building maintenance, laundry, etc. Private corporations that bid on these contracts often try to increase their profits by paying workers rock-bottom wages with few, if any, fringe benefits.

- Encouraging the service branches to conduct joint operations and to share resources.
- Rethinking our current troop commitments in foreign countries, notably Germany and South Korea.
- Continuing base closings both in the United States and abroad to reflect the continuing shift away from defensive alignments of the Cold War era.

GOLD-PLATED WEAPONS/SHORTAGES OF ARMORED VESTS AND DRINKING WATER

As mentioned, civilian defense contractors still wield great influence over congressional decisions on military spending. When a lot of money's at stake, the congressional budget process will often trump sound military planning. A Newhouse News Service analysis found that three out of four DOD budget dollars in 2004 are being spent on the same categories as before September 11.

Billions are still squandered on developing high-tech weapons like the supersonic F/A 22 "Raptor" jet, which flies so fast it can't identify ground targets visually. Another example is the Navy's decision to build yet another $1.5 billion Virginia-class attack submarine. This was designed in the 1980s to hunt down Soviet subs. Meanwhile, U.S. troops in Iraq go without metal plates for their Kevlar armored vests, night-vision goggles, or purified bottled water.

THE TRAGEDY OF THE UNARMED HUMVEES

Sometimes purchasing decisions by the Pentagon or Congress don't just waste gobs of tax dollars, they also cost GIs their lives or limbs. Such is the case with thousands of Humvees that were shipped to Iraq with no armor plating. A *Wall Street Journal* article in March 2004 disclosed that only 2 percent of the

Army's vast fleet of 110,000 Humvees had such plating. This meant that the GIs were sent into the mean streets of Iraq riding in vehicles that are vulnerable to small-caliber bullets and shrapnel.

Belatedly, the Army rush-ordered armor plating, which can prevent at least some of these injuries. The article concluded, "The Army failed to buy more [armored units] because it was preparing for major wars with other large armies—rather than low end guerilla conflicts."

MILITARY VETERANS: A FORGOTTEN MINORITY

As chapter 6 documents, America has a lamentable history when it comes to caring for her injured veterans. In its 2004 budget request, the Bush administration initially proposed a $3 billion cut for VA healthcare, despite 18,000 medical evacuations from Iraq so far. Veterans already must wait for months to see specialists and travel greater distances as the VA closes more hospitals and clinics.

A new policy of restricting access to patients by veterans-service organizations, such as the Disabled American Veterans (DAV) at Walter Reed Medical Center, has led to protests from these groups. There have also been serious allegations about deficient medical care provided to soldiers returning from Iraq at several Army bases, including Fort Stewart, Georgia, and Fort Knox, Kentucky. In October 2003, reporters found that several hundred GIs at Fort Stewart, some wounded and some on "medical hold," were being housed in decrepit barracks without bathrooms or running water. They had been waiting weeks for evaluation and/or medical treatment.

CONTEMPT FOR INTERNATIONAL LAW AND THE OPINION OF OTHER NATIONS

One of the worst legacies of Bush's war in Iraq is the damage it has done to America's standing in the world community. When Bush thumbs his nose at the International Criminal Court or the Landmine Treaty he undermines respect for international standards of conduct. The recent disclosure of systematic torture of Iraqi detainees by US military personnel has dealt another body blow to our country's reputation. These abuses have their origin in Rumsfeld's order in early 2002 that labeled fighters we captured in our war on terror as "unlawful combatants" instead of prisoners of war who would be entitled to protection under the Geneva Conventions. In response to protests of this decision, Bush announced that such prisoners could expect humane treatment "consistent with the Geneva Convention." This, however, left the door open to unlimited interrogation and denial of any right to legal counsel.

BOOTS ON THE GROUND: WHO PAYS?

The low-intensity conflicts currently being fought in Iraq and Afghanistan demonstrate once again that "smart bombs" and strategic bombing by B-52s have little value in densely settled cities or remote mountains. As always, success or failure in such a war will come down to the skill and courage of ordinary foot soldiers employing age-old small-unit tactics. Air power alone will not win wars, nor can we hope to impose democracy at the point of a bayonet.

Rumsfeld's vaunted "vision" resulted in sending too few troops with deficient equipment. Clearly, his priority was to take care of his corporate chums, including his new pals in the "private Army" business.

As Richard Clarke recently wrote in the *New York Times,* "We are seriously threatened by an ideological war within Islam. Radical Islamist(s) are striking out at the West and at moderate Muslims. It is a battle not only of bombs and bullets but chiefly of ideas. It is a war that we are losing as more and more of the Islamic world develops antipathy toward the United States."

If our troops are withdrawn, bloody civil war could possibly follow. Terrorists might now find a haven in Iraq where none existed before. But lacking any other strategy for a phased withdrawal under international sponsorship, the American people may soon conclude that this war must be brought to an end.

Acknowledgments

No book of this scope and breadth could be written without the assistance of many people. My longtime friend and legal colleague Louis Font continued to help educate me on many military matters—legal and otherwise. My editor at The New Press, Colin Robinson, has my gratitude for first raising the possibility of this book and then helping me see it through to completion. Thanks is also due Abby Aguirre and Maury Botton of The New Press for their editorial assistance.

Within the military, I must acknowledge Master Sgt. Russell C. Schmidt for patiently helping me understand the world of military recruiting. As always, Bruce Zeilsdorf of the Army's New York public affairs office ran down answers to questions large and small. Navy public affairs NCO James R. Stilipec was equally willing to help me understand military training today.

I also must thank the following friends for their important help at various points in the process: Steve Robinson, Dave Cline, Judith Rew, Abdeen Jabara, Neil Belton, Victor Sidel, Michael Uhl, Steve Ralls, and Michael Smith.

Finally, a special thanks to Francine Smilen for her steadfast support for this sometimes-taxing project. Her editorial contributions shine forth from every page.

1

Military Recruiting: Making Mission

Tod Ensign

That's the driver—the economy. The chaotic conditions in Iraq have yet to hurt recruiting.[1]

—Major Gen. Michael Rochelle
CO, Army Recruiting Command

As our country's largest public employer, the military has almost three million people on its payroll. Over 1.4 million are serving on active duty, with a third of these normally deployed outside the United States. Another 867,000 serve in the active reserves and in the National Guard as "weekend warriors." However, lately, because of President Bush's unilateral invasion of Iraq, 163,000 of these reservists are currently on active duty.[2] About 654,000 civilian employees round out the workforce. Given Defense Secretary Rumsfeld's plan to accelerate base closings and to privatize many military tasks such as food service, maintenance, and base security this workforce will likely shrink further.

Because active-duty units are stretched thin by the occupation of Iraq, the proportion of reservists in the total US force there will climb to 40 percent in

2004.[3] The Army has been enlisting soldiers for almost 200 years. However, it wasn't until 1964, when the Recruiting Command was established, that the Army began using sophisticated recruiting techniques. In 1973, the year that the draft ended, the total Pentagon advertising budget for recruiting was $7 million. Recruiters relied primarily on printed brochures, and stations donated any TV or radio ads as "public service." Compare this to the $340 million that the services will spend just for advertising in 2004.[4]

In the early years of the all-volunteer force, recruiting was a very small item in the Pentagon's budget. Three years after the draft ended, the armed forces were still spending only $67 million on all its recruiting programs. Contrast this with fiscal 2003, in which the military spent nearly $3 billion to recruit a much smaller military. The Army's first recruiting slogan was "Today's Army Wants to Join You." In 1981, this gave way to "Be All You Can Be." This slogan had such impact, *Advertising Age* picked it as one of the top ten ad jingles of the twentieth century.[5]

Twenty years later, this tagline had grown stale and was replaced with "An Army of One." Joseph Anthony, an advertising consultant, explained to *Salon* magazine, "It's becoming really difficult to establish brand loyalty, because these kids are bombarded with multiple messages." American demographics magazines estimate that the average teen sees 3,000 marketing messages a day.[6] Some military critics feel that the new slogan undermines a key military concept—teamwork.

A CHANGE IN PHILOSOPHY

In the draft era, recruiting duty went by default to older GIs who were nearing the end of their careers, since it mostly involved writing enlistment contracts. However, in today's competitive environment, each service branch selects its most motivated and energetic GIs for recruiting duty. Although most recruiters find that the transition to working entirely in civilian society is a challenge, success at recruiting pays off big time for them in terms of their military careers.

MYTHS VERSUS REALITY

Because the all-volunteer military has changed immensely from its earlier form, many Americans, especially parents of potential recruits, have a number of misconceptions. Since the military workforce is no longer representative of all levels of American society, prospects and their parents now have fewer relatives or friends who are recent veterans and can offer independent perspectives on service.

The American military and its wars are the subject for thousands of TV shows, movies, video games, and books. By the time an American teenager reaches enlistment age, he or she will have watched hundreds of such programs. While these media display compelling scenes of bloody combat, fighting and wars represent only one aspect of the military experience.

This chapter will take the reader behind the scenes to reveal how military recruiters perform the difficult job of convincing today's youth to commit to three or four years of military service.

THE CHALLENGE

Each year, 185,000 new recruits must be sworn onto active duty to replace those whose hitches are ending. In addition, the Reserves and National Guard must also enlist thousands of new soldiers each year. Most people who join today do so for one or more of the following reasons: they need money for college or to repay college loans; they're seeking vocational skills training; or they're looking for travel, adventure, or simply a ticket out of the old hometown. Only a small minority actively pursue the rigors of training for war fighting as a Marine, Airborne parachutist, Ranger, or Navy SEAL.

Myth: GIs live in dreary barracks, sleep in bunk beds, eat starchy food in dingy chowhalls, and venture off base only on Saturday night to drink in basetown taverns.

Reality: About half of all enlisted people today are married and almost half have one or more children. After initial training, they live with their families in apartments and houses, on base and off. Single GIs who live on base reside in modern brick apartment-style barracks, where they share semiprivate quarters with one or two other soldiers. An Army private today earns about $1,300 per month compared with $342 when the draft ended. Add to this free health care, room, and board. GIs who live off base often spend nearly as much time with civilians as with military personnel.

Myth: Military people, especially in the Army and Marines, spend much of their time training for or fighting wars.

Reality: Even though 175,000 GIs are currently deployed to Iraq, Afghanistan, and Kuwait, most service members have little or no involvement with war fighting. They work regular hours on military bases in the United States and abroad. GIs perform a wide variety of jobs, from computer programmers to dental hygienists. Some GIs receive job-skills training that they can use later with civilian employers. However, there are many military jobs, particularly in the "combat arms" such as firing artillery or driving tanks, which have little application to the civilian job market.

Myth: Military units are still composed predominantly of white men, as depicted in popular films like *Black Hawk Down.*

Reality: Special combat units, like the Rangers or Delta Force (featured in *Black Hawk Down*), are still entirely male and largely white. Today, only one service branch, the Marines, which is 68 percent white and 94 percent male, still looks somewhat like units depicted in war movies. The bulk of the military is actually more diverse than the civilian workplace. As military sociologist Charles Moskos has commented, "The American military is one of the few places where you're likely to see blacks bossing whites around." Blacks account for one in four in the Army today and are more likely to reenlist than whites because they reportedly feel that the equal-opportunity climate is better than it is in the civilian world.

Myth: Serving in today's all-volunteer military is pretty much like any other job, except you wear a uniform and have to salute officers.

Reality: The military still functions as a separate society. It has its own rules and its own legal system. Some of its rules have no equivalent in civilian life. Military commanders have a lot more authority over subordinates than civilian employers do. The military claims the right to monitor and punish GIs for things they do off base and off duty. For instance, if a GI writes a check that bounces or fails to make child-support payments, his commanders can punish him. "Don't Ask, Don't Tell" rules (see chapter 5) mean that gay or lesbian GIs can be punished for off-base sexual contact with nonmilitary same-sex partners. Military police can search a GI's footlocker or his car in situations where civilian police could not.

WELCOME TO THE ALL-VOLUNTEER MILITARY

The last American draftee entered the Army on June 30, 1973. Anti–Vietnam War protests by millions of Americans were instrumental in ending the draft (see chapter 8). Since then, the active-duty military has consisted entirely of volunteers. Recruiting over 225,000 volunteers each year is a big challenge. Imagine: at the start of World War Two, America's entire military was smaller than its current annual recruiting quota!

UNIQUE ASPECTS OF MILITARY LIFE

The Chain of Command: A Key Concept

"Respect the uniform—not necessarily the person wearing it" is an expression sometimes heard in the military. It means that you obey an order because you respect the rank of the person giving it, not necessarily the person himself. Where one stands on the totem pole of rank is very important in the military.

The Navy's bible for new sailors, *The Bluejacket's Manual,* explains the concept: "The Navy is organized like a pyramid, with the President at the top as commander in chief. There are just as many levels below the President, leading eventually to you. Just as you must follow the orders . . . of your drill instructor, they must likewise follow the orders of the ship's chief petty officer . . . and so on."[7]

There is really nothing like this concept of rank in civilian society, except perhaps the hierarchy and discipline found in police and fire departments. If your superior officer gives you an order that you think may be improper or illegal, you are in a difficult spot. If you obey, you may bring future trouble down on yourself. If you refuse, however, you will certainly be called to account immediately. The military does provide mechanisms for questioning orders but only within your immediate chain of command. For more serious issues, GIs are told to lodge complaints with the inspector general (IG). Some observers have questioned the independence of the IG, especially when the complaint focuses on conduct of high-ranking officers.

Weigh In or Get Out!

Civilians are sometimes surprised to learn that the military imposes fitness standards on all GIs, not just recruits. Everyone on active duty must pass physical qualification tests twice a year. To qualify, a GI must be able to do a certain number of push-ups, sit-ups, and run a mile or two within a fixed period of time. These standards vary from one branch to another, and there are different (lower) standards for women. The Marines, for example, require more of its personnel than does the Air Force. GIs of all ranks are encouraged to participate in organized calisthenics and group runs several times a week both before and after duty hours. It's fair to say that in combat units there is a "culture of fitness." Soldiers feel peer pressure to join an early morning run or hit the gym machines at lunch hour.

Those who fail their semiannual fitness test are placed on a special exercise regimen. If they continue to fail retesting, they can be discharged or be denied reenlistment. The same thing goes for "recommended" body weight. If soldiers exceed weight guidelines, they must diet or they may find themselves civilians again.

Conformity Is the Norm

As an institution, the military emphasizes conformity and discourages most displays of individualism. Attitude surveys in recent years have found that career officers and NCOs are socially and politically more conservative than their civilian counterparts. Someone has written that legendary World War Two commander George S. Patton would not have achieved such high rank in today's military since he made unconventional choices and refused to go by the Army's "book." Because many military tasks do require teamwork, strong individuals or "lone wolves" will often not fit into the military's way of doing things.

SELLING THE ARMED FORCES TODAY

The Pentagon is currently spending about $2.7 billion a year just on recruiters and advertising. Both the Army and Navy have about 4,300 full-time recruiters, signing recruits for both the active and reserve force. The Air Force uses 1,500 recruiters, and the smallest branch, the Marines, 1,600. The individual National Guard units in each of the fifty states conduct their own recruiting, but the Pentagon pays most of the bill. The sophistication of the military's recruiting operation today is comparable to that of a Fortune 500 corporation. Although the military's budget has grown 25 percent in the last four years, given our occupation of Iraq and current concerns with the threat of terrorism, there seems to be no serious political opposition to its steady growth in the years ahead.

No one who watches TV sports or youth-oriented programs can miss the steady drumbeat of ads directed at young people by the military. The goal is to make sure that everyone in the target audience of 17- to 21-year-olds is aware of the military as a job option. Recently, noted filmmaker Spike Lee was criticized by some antimilitarists for taking $2.5 million for a series of very attractive TV ads for the Navy. His spots depicted handsome young sailors working on or around ships at jobs that seemed both challenging and important. One advertising executive explained the philosophy behind this kind of advertising: "The purpose of these ads isn't to make you rush out and do something. [They're] intended to make that something known to you . . . and bring it within the range of acceptable [choices]."[8] The ads are also designed to catch the eye of another audience—the parents of potential recruits. Another ad exec explained, "Kids like to deny their parents' role, but our studies show that they can have a heavy influence in a matter like joining the military."

DEFINING THE TARGET AUDIENCE

The Pentagon and its advertising agencies conduct extensive polling among young people to determine what motivates them to enlist. Recent surveys have shown that college assistance, vocational-skills training, and loan repayment are the three strongest motivators for enlistment. A prospect's age, race, education level, and gender will all affect his or her propensity to enlist. Surveys show that about one in three young men have a favorable opinion about enlistment, compared with less than one in six for females. Black males are twice as likely as white males to think well of military service, while black females are three times as positive as white females.

ENTER THE INTERNET

In the last decade, the military has done an excellent job of using the World Wide Web to generate "leads." Its television commercials are designed to steer young prospects to their computers. "The advertising has been very successful. It drives people to 'goarmy.com.' That's powerful," explains Lt. General Dennis Cavin, commander of the Army's accessions command. Once on the site, Web surfers can go to the Army's very popular online game, "America's Army," and to the chat room (both discussed below).

"For every lead determined through [our] chat room to be a quality lead,"

Cavin continued, "eleven percent join the Army." Cavin also told the *Army Times* that they'll soon be able to track data about prospects from the video game, which over a million young people have played in the past year.

THE WORLD OF THE RECRUITER

The typical military recruiter today is a noncommissioned officer (NCO) sergeant (E/5 or above) who has already served about eight years in the military. In the Army, they must have served at least four years, but most will have put in eight. Because recruiting is a demanding job that requires strong interpersonal skills, most recruiters are "detailed" (chosen) by their commanders after considerable scrutiny of their service records and references. In the Army, about one-third of the recruiters are volunteers. Success as a recruiter is career enhancing and a strong argument for retention. As one senior NCO at the Army's Recruiting School explains, "You have proven that you can adapt and overcome in an area that is not your military specialty." All the branches have female recruiters, and the Army tries to keep its proportion of women recruiters close to their numbers in the active force—currently about 15 percent.

After undergoing an intensive multiple-week training course, recruiters are given the choice of being assigned to recruiting areas where they previously lived. Recruiters' performance is closely monitored during their first year in the field. The Army evaluates its trainees in the fifth and ninth month. They are judged on their ability to conduct canvassing by telephone and face-to-face prospecting, as well as their ability to make sales presentations to groups. Fewer than one in ten Army recruiters are found deficient; these trainees are reassigned to other Army duty.

Recruiters work within a complex personnel system wherein they must match up recruits with training and assignments for a couple of hundred different military jobs. The manpower needs of each branch change constantly depending on a number of factors, including the state of the civilian economy and whether an actual war is being fought somewhere.

THE TRAINING OF RECRUITERS

When the threat of the draft was removed in 1973, the recruiter's job became much more difficult. In the "old days" pressure from the draft meant that often recruiters were simply "order takers," processing volunteers who were trying to avoid being sent to Vietnam. All of the services had to modernize and revamp their approach to recruiting once the threat of conscription was removed. Consultants experienced in both personnel recruiting and sales were brought in to design programs for "selling the military." Soon, recruiter manuals were filled with sales jargon, like "buying motives," "features and benefits," "overcoming objections," "generating leads," and "closing the sale."[9]

One Army recruiter publication explains, "We are salesmen in every sense of the word. There are techniques that you must use to ensure that you don't find yourself an unsuccessful salesman."[10]

Any young person who is contacted by a military recruiter today should realize that he or she is dealing with a highly skilled salesperson who has been thoroughly trained to try to overcome any possible objection raised as to why someone shouldn't enlist. Like any good salesman, they are strategists who doggedly pursue prospects even if there's only a faint hope of making "a sale." They also emphasize the personal touch whenever possible. One recruiter told the author, "Today's recruiter must be a mentor, parent, counselor, and best friend. Lots of kids today don't have real families so recruiters can supply some of what's missing."

A VISIT TO ARMY RECRUITER SCHOOL

In November 2003, the author paid a visit to the Army's Recruitment and Retention School at Ft. Jackson, South Carolina. Housed in a modern, multistoried brick building, it could be on any college campus. During class breaks, the halls fill with attractive and fit-looking late-twentysomethings, many of whom are black and a few of whom are female. Because recruiting requires excellent people skills, the trainees seem outgoing and well spoken.

Recruiter trainees participate in an intensive seven-week course covering a broad range of subjects, from issues of dress and decorum to hours of role playing as students take turns standing in for prospects. Classes are devoted to telephone canvassing, techniques for "tabling" in shopping malls and other public areas, and the detailed regulations covering the preparation of an enlistment contract.

Each Army recruiter is issued a comprehensive *Recruiter Handbook* (USAREC Pam 350-2), which outlines the evaluation he or she will undergo during the first nine months of recruiter duty. Their learning curve is steep as they must master all the administrative and legal rules for qualifying a recruit for enlistment while simultaneously developing their sales skills. In addition, they are taught the elements of public speaking, telephone canvassing, and the art of negotiation, not so much for use with recruits as with parents, teachers, and counselors.

BRANDING THE PRODUCT

Each service branch tries to use advertising to establish a unique identity and set it apart from the other services. Until recently, the Army's ads conveyed an image of a diverse organization that offered many different kinds of skills training as well as college aid. With its new "Army of One" campaign, the Army has shifted to stressing its "warrior values."

In a memo distributed armywide on June 3, 2003, Army Chief of Staff General Eric Shinseki endorsed the "Warrior Ethos" concept. He defined it to mean, "Soldiers put the mission first, refuse to accept defeat, never quit, and never leave behind a fellow American." He stated that "a true warrior ethos must underpin the Army's enduring tradition and values. It must drive a personal commitment to excellence and . . . make our soldiers different from all others in the world."

One senior recruiting sergeant, who requested anonymity, told the author that he likes the America's Army game because it presents a realistic picture of Army life today. Instead of just focusing on what he called "Medal of Honor assaults on the enemy," it teaches that the Army has many different missions, including humanitarian and peacekeeping assignments.

Some recruiting companies and battalions have begun to set up tournaments that feature the America's Army game. The *Army Times* reported on one of these events in Kansas City: "Teams of twelve sit at computer terminals in separate rooms and wage battle with each other. Players take individual roles at the squad level and plan strategy before the game begins. The darkened rooms are draped with camouflage netting, stacked with sandbags and adorned with recruiting posters, banners and maps."[11]

Before the tournament begins, contestants are "sworn in" and awards are given out at the end to those who displayed the most teamwork and leadership. Recruiting Sgt. Erik Kuerst, who helped organize the event, told the *Army Times* that out of the six hundred contestants his battalion has hosted at tournaments, nine have signed enlistment contracts so far. "They ask questions: 'Is this how it is all the time?' 'What do you guys really do in the Army?' It opens up the conversation," Kuerst explained. While recruiting is not supposed to take place during the tourneys, recruiters obviously acquire lots of fresh leads.

THE CYBER RECRUITER: THE ELECTRONIC TOWN HALL

Another recent innovation is the Army's Internet chat rooms that have been created by the recruiting command at Ft. Knox, Kentucky. Staffed by experienced recruiters, the chat rooms are open each evening from 4–9 PM EST. Internet visitors are invited to express opinions as well as ask questions about Army service. An unlimited number of callers can simultaneously participate in a chat room. On a busy day, the Army's Web site (www.us.Army.mil) may receive 25,000 "hits." To experience the chat room, go to this site and use your toolbar to locate the "recruiter chat" section.

ARMED SERVICES VOCATIONAL APTITUDE BATTERY (ASVAB)

Since 1976, all the service branches have used the same aptitude test to assess their applicants.[12] The military offers this free three-hour test to high schools and community colleges. About 1.25 million high-school juniors and seniors take the test each year. Some schools require their students to take the test, while most leave it up to the student to decide. Many cash-strapped school administrators welcome the free ASVAB, saving them the fees charged by other tests. Each school is allowed to control how much test information is released to the recruiters. (Note that the *school*—not the parents—decides what to disclose.) Some schools release nothing about test results to recruiters, while others disclose everything. Under this option the recruiters receive a printout which contains personal information about the test-takers, including their scores, contact information, and data about students' post-graduation plans. Most schools fall between the two extremes. However, since anyone who enlists *must* have an ASVAB score, the recruiters can argue that disclosure is in the student's interest.

Each military branch makes different use of the test results to determine the eligibility of enlistees for assignment and training slots. The test is designed to rank a prospect's abilities in comparison to everyone else who takes the test. It consists of eight parts: mathematics knowledge; arithmetic reasoning; word knowledge; mechanical comprehension; electronics information; general science; auto and shop information; and paragraph comprehension. Recruits must score well above average on the first four parts in order to qualify for high-tech skills training.

Test results are divided into seven composite aptitude scores, three "academic" and four "occupational." The latter are divided into four categories: mechanical and crafts; business and clerical; electronics and electrical; and health, social, and technology. The military claims that the "occupational" scores help to predict one's trainability in a number of career fields, while the "academic" scores measure one's aptitude for higher education. One overall score, called the AFQT score, is also calculated.

The military states that the ASVAB test helps school counselors advise students about career choices, even if they are not considering military service. However, high-school counselors today are often responsible for so many students that they're unable to provide much individual counseling. My impression is that few schools make independent use of the ASVAB test results. It is primarily a tool for recruiters to identify likely prospects and to measure their skills.

The military works hard to have the ASVAB test given by as many high schools as possible. Currently about 14,000 high schools participate. One of the Army's recruiting manuals explains its importance: "Few sales organizations survive without a constant source of leads. Your ASVAB program is the seed from which your best leads will come. The amazing thing about the [ASVAB] is that you receive mentally prequalified leads . . . what would hundreds of prequalified leads be worth to you? Many recruiters have already discovered that mandatory ASVAB testing can convert a very difficult task into a pleasurable project."

The military uses four of the subtests to calculate one's overall AFQT score: word knowledge; paragraph comprehension; arithmetic reasoning; and numerical operations. AFQT scores are ranked as follows:

Category I: 93–99
Category II: 65–92
Category IIIA: 50–64 (50 is considered the minimum score for many jobs requiring skill training)
Category IIIB: 31–49
Category IV: 10–30 (only a few of these can be enlisted)
Category V: 1–9 (not eligible for enlistment)

At present, about 40 percent of the men and 42 percent of the women who take the test score in the top two mental categories. ASVAB scores are valid for two years from the time the test is taken. Sometimes a recruiter will encourage a prospect to retake the test if they think his or her score is abnormally low. Recently, the Pentagon contracted with the Princeton Review to develop a fifty-lesson online study guide, "March 2 Success," which helps prepare students to take the test. Lt. Col. Arnold Piper, head of the Army Recruiting Battalion, recently offered the following about the ASVAB, "It has increased our quality production as well as assisted (us) in efforts to penetrate high school."[13]

"THE NO CHILD LEFT UNRECRUITED" LAW: ACCESS TO STUDENT RECORDS

For years, military recruiters have chafed under the restrictions that administrators had placed on their access to schools. About 3,700 high schools, out of the 22,000 nationwide, barred recruiters from the premises. Many other schools place various restrictions on the frequency and duration of recruiter visits. In some states—such as New York, New Jersey, Vermont, and Rhode Island—the District of Columbia, Puerto Rico, and the US Virgin Islands, as many as 40 percent of the schools restricted access.[14]

After the 9/11 terror attacks, President Bush used the fear of terrorism and promilitary sentiment to get Congress to add a section to his omnibus "No Child Left Behind" education law that requires high schools to release personal data on their students as a condition for receiving federal funds. There is a little publicized and seldom used "opt out" provision that allows parents to request that their child's records not be released. The draconian law has had its desired effect: the *Army Times* reported that by the beginning of 2003, only six or seven schools in the whole country were still defying recruiters by not turning over confidential student records.[15]

While recruiters now have the right to demand that schools turn over students' cell-phone numbers and e-mail addresses, some schools still restrict their physical access. As one Army National Guard recruiter recently complained about the policies of Portland, Oregon, schools, "We military recruiters can show up only one day per month—only to be told we're not allowed to talk to students. We can only be in the counselor's office for a certain amount of time. If this is 'access' I would hate to see what limited access would be."[16]

HIGH SCHOOL JROTC

The Army, Air Force, Navy, and Marines sponsor hundreds of Junior Reserve Officer Training Corps (JROTC) programs in public and private high schools. Cadets are required to wear their uniforms to school on "drill days," when they are taught rudimentary military drills and customs. JROTC students are also instructed in first aid, navigation, calisthenics, and fitness drills.

Because 40 percent of the JROTC cadets who graduate from high school eventually join the military, these programs have been expanded in recent years. Currently, there are almost half a million cadets enrolled, half of which are minorities. The Army operates units in 1,555 high schools, while the Air Force is active in 945 schools. The Navy has the smallest program with about 600 units.[17]

ADVERTISING CAMPAIGNS

In the summer of 2003, Joint Services Recruiting experimented with a twelve-page, full-color advertising insert in several national magazines, including *Time, People,* and *Sports Illustrated.* It presents several different veterans at their regular jobs today; for example, as a professional quarterback, country singer, dentist, etc. The ad explains that they "saw military service as a valuable opportunity (and) took with them positive qualities . . . that are applicable to virtually all walk(s) of life." A Web site (www.todaysmilitary.com) and a toll-free number are provided for "Today's Military."

Carlin Nelson, a spokesperson from the Army's ad agency, Leo Burnett, told me that "all our advertising today drives potential recruits to our Web site, www.goarmy.com." Today, the Army places spots on MTV, Comedy Central, ESPN College Football, and similar programs. It also regularly advertises in *Rolling Stone, ESPN Magazine,* and *The Source*. Some of the ads offer a free gift, such as tube socks or an "Army of One" T-shirt, to anyone who requests it. When these gifts are mailed, the name and address of the recipient is forwarded to local Army recruiters for follow-up.

AIR SHOWS

The Air Force, Navy, and Army spend millions each year to underwrite the extensive touring of their daredevil air shows. The Air Force's Thunderbirds and the Navy's Blue Angels offer precision flying by jet fighters. Tens of thousands turn out to watch them perform synchronized stunts, flying just feet apart, upside down, at 500 mph. The Army's Golden Knights are parachutists who jump from helicopters and fixed-wing aircraft at great heights. Their spectacular jumps have been featured at recent World Series and Super Bowls. Recruiters make a point of attending these shows and sometimes organize "recommitment" ceremonies, where DEP recruits repeat their enlistment oaths to the cheers of the crowd. While some have questioned both the expense and potential safety hazards of these shows—two recent air-show crashes in Europe killed spectators—they continue to enjoy strong public and congressional support.

REFERRALS FROM RECENT RECRUITS, COUNSELORS, AND TEACHERS

Each service branch operates a program that sends new soldiers back to their home communities for up to a year to assist recruitment. The Army's program draws on corporals with two to three years of service, who are sent home to help recruiters to build rapport with their former classmates. Recruiters emphasize building good working relationships with guidance counselors and teachers in the high schools to which they are assigned. Years ago, recruiters would sometimes offend teachers by encouraging students to quit high school and enlist. Today, however, the Army operates a program called "Stay in Schools—Stay off Drugs," which encourages high-school students to finish school.

The relationship between recruiters and the public high schools varies widely across the country. John Aria, a high-school teacher in Toms River, New Jersey, says that recruiters are a frequent sight in his school. They regularly meet with the students in the counseling office and set up tables outside the cafeteria, where they pass out free T-shirts and "Army of One" posters, while talking with students on lunch break. On occasion, they have made classroom presentations. Aria also reported that a recent graduate of the school, who's now an Army corporal, accompanies recruiters on their visits, contacting old classmates.[18] Other high schools have more restrictive policies concerning access, requiring recruiters to schedule visits and then only allowing them to meet with students who have agreed in advance to meet.

Some states' education departments officially endorse recruiter access and the taking of the ASVAB test. New York State's policy, which "encourages close cooperation between the school and military recruiters," is typical. It also recommends using the ASVAB test, "to assist counselors and recruiters to accomplish the proper placement of students who're interested in joining the [military]."

One way that recruiters befriend counselors and teachers is by offering all-expenses-paid educator tours to military bases. The Army alone provides over a thousand such trips each year. A senior Army recruiter explained, "We look for someone who's never been in the military or who may be blocking access to students. We prefer to send someone who isn't that knowledgeable."[19]

A *Miami Herald* reporter accompanied twenty-eight Miami-area educators on a recent trip to the Marine Corps boot camp at Parris Island, South Carolina: "Flush with ammo, Donna Vallis, a high school counselor, wasn't much of a shot. Still, she expected her M-16 to be heavier and the Marines a lot meaner. 'I realized it's all about developing a brotherhood,' " Vallis told the *Herald*.[20]

COMMUNITY COLLEGES: A PRIME TARGET

Recruiters are urged to make a special effort at these two-year colleges. A recent *Recruiter Journal* offers the following advice: "Becoming knowledgeable [about] financial aid will give you a powerful recruiting tool because there is a higher student loan default rate among . . . vocational/technical training students. [Our] Loan Repayment Program can assist students in repaying their loans, thus lowering the college's student loan default rate. Administrators of these schools will welcome your assistance." The article also recommends that recruiters enroll in a class at the community college. "This will give you the advantage of being an alumnus," it explains. It also suggests that recruiters volunteer to tutor students and offer to give talks in classes that cover subjects in their career field.[21]

MOBILE RECRUITING VANS

In recent years, the Army has attempted to add some color and pizzazz to what some see as a khaki-drab employer. It now sends out a fleet of brightly colored vans, which crisscross the country. One or more recruiters are assigned to each van. Four cinema vans, which are essentially mini theaters on wheels, routinely stop at a school parking lot or park for a day. The van converts to a forty-seat movie theater that shows a variety of short, educational films. Programs offered include "Day of Infamy," a recap of WWII; "Understanding Flight"; "Seeing the Light," about cameras and vision; and "Black Holes: The Ultimate Abyss," which features Stephen Hawking and other physicists. Programs with Army themes are mixed in occasionally.

The recruiting command also sends out smaller Multiple Exhibit Vehicles, which can screen videos and provide an informal space for recruiters to connect with young people. For more combat-oriented youth, the Army offers three armored vans, which contain a simulation chamber in which visitors can pretend to fire the tank's gun or drive the vehicle. The third kind of exhibit van is the "Rockwall" van, which allows youngsters to learn about rock-wall climbing, with the assistance of an Army technician.

All of these vans ply the Interstates twelve months a year, visiting large cities, small towns, and everything in between. Local recruiters eagerly seek to schedule visits because the vans make it easy to mingle and chat with prospects in a relaxed and recreational setting.

WHERE THE BOYS ARE

As if all the above programs are not enough, all the service branches have signed endorsement deals with NASCAR race drivers. For instance, the Army sponsors a black-and-gold "Army of One" Pontiac Grand Prix in NASCAR races and has used NASCAR champ Tony Schumacher as an official spokesperson. The Army also sponsors the All American Bowl, in San Antonio, Texas, where the best high-school football players compete in an annual game. Recruiters commonly receive blocks of tickets for these events, which they distribute to recruiting prospects and their family members.

"THE ARMY BE THUGGIN' IT"

In a deal that would have "old brown shoe" soldiers shaking their heads, the Army recently signed up *The Source* magazine, the "hip-hop bible," to promote recruiting. A huge yellow Hummer, painted with patriotic themes, drives *Source* staffers to various black events around the country, such as NAACP gatherings, MTV's Spring Break, or BET's Spring Bling. Wherever large numbers of African American teens are gathering, that is where the Hummer will go. They can hang out in the Hummer, using the multimedia sound system or watching Army videos. *The Source* also sponsors basketball contests and rock-wall-climbing competitions. The winners receive Army-branded throwback jerseys and customized "dog tags."

As the director of Army accessions, Col. Thomas Nickerson explained to *Salon*.com online magazine, "You have to go where the target audience is. Our research tells us that hip-hop and urban culture is a powerful influence in the lives of young Americans. We try to develop a bond with that audience. We want them to say, 'Hey, the Army was here—the Army is cool!' "[22]

PRIVATIZATION: ARE RECRUITERS NEXT?

For the past year, the Army has been conducting a congressionally mandated experiment to see if civilian recruiting firms can do a job that has traditionally been the sole responsibility of the military. It has chosen two private recruiting firms and given each of them five recruiting stations to run for a five-year trial period. According to a senior Army recruiter, so far the civilian recruiters have "met mission," which is Army lingo for signing up their quota of recruits.

SELLING THE MILITARY: BENEFITS

Today's recruiters have many different ways of making contact with enlistment prospects. Once a dialogue has begun, what are the benefits that are offered? The primary benefits are outlined and evaluated below.

College Aid and Assistance

Military surveys consistently show this to be the single strongest inducement for many who are thinking of joining. Basically, there are two college assistance programs.

Montgomery GI Bill

This program requires a recruit to make a $1,200, nonrefundable contribution to a fund during the first year of service. A soldier who serves at least three years and receives an honorable discharge is currently eligible for up to $985 a month for up to thirty-six months for a maximum payout of $32,000. He or she must enroll for at least twelve credits per semester and must maintain passing grades to receive the stipend. The problem is that tuition and other costs at both public and private colleges and universities have skyrocketed in recent years. This means that at many schools, this monthly payment will not cover much more than the cost of tuition and books. If a veteran has dependents to support, he or she will likely have to work a full-time job in addition to attending school. This may explain why a VA study found that only 15 percent of those veterans who used some portion of their GI Bill ever graduated with a four-year college degree. Reservists currently can receive up to $285 per month.

The Army College Fund

If a soldier is willing to serve in the infantry, armor, or artillery, he or she may qualify for this more generous program, which pays about $1,400 a month for up to thirty-six months, up to a maximum of $50,000. Obviously, this will come closer to paying all college costs, at least at a public college or university. Again, a veteran must possess an honorable discharge and must carry a full load (twelve or more credits) in college to qualify.

Loan Repayment Programs

Because of the marked increase in college costs, many students accumulate substantial debt from college loans. Recruiters can offer to repay portions of federally backed college student loans. The Army, for example, will repay $1,500 or one-third of eligible student debt (whichever is greater) each year on a three-year enlistment. For example, if a soldier owes $30,000 in principal on loans, the Army will pay $10,000 directly to the creditor at the end of each of three years of honorable service. The soldier will receive a federal tax return, and he or she will be taxed on the amount of the repaid loan. Loan interest and any delinquent or late penalties will not be paid by the military. Also, the soldier is not allowed to participate in the GI Bill or Army College Fund.

Bonuses

All of the service branches pay cash bonuses as inducements for enlisting for selected military jobs. The Army and the Army Reserve pay bonuses between $1,500 and $20,000 to GIs who sign up for the less desirable and more dangerous positions, many of which are in the combat arms. You can determine the bonus qualifications by their names: "Hi-Grad," "Quick Ship," "Seasonal," "Priority MOS Enlistment," and "Airborne." To qualify for a bonus in the Regular Army, a GI must score fifty or higher on the AVSAB, sign for three or more years, meet all qualifications for the Military Occupation Specialty (MOS), and be nonprior service. Prior-service vets can qualify for signing bonuses of up to $20,000 if they reenlist to perform "critical" military jobs.

Skills Training

All of the service branches have a wide range of military jobs, each of which require some degree of training. Obviously, jobs like nursing or electronic repair provide training that can later be transferred to a civilian job. Infantrymen or artillery gunners, however, do not acquire skills that are transferable to the civilian job market.

According to a senior recruiting NCO at Ft. Jackson, the Army is the most likely of the four services to promise training for a specific job. Currently, the Army offers training for 212 different jobs in 32 different Career Management Fields (CMF). For example, for the Military Police CMF there are three different jobs: Military Policeman, Internment/Resettlement Specialist, and Criminal Investigation Special Agent. Some jobs in the combat arms, infantry, armor, and artillery remain closed to females. The Marines follow the same practice, while the Navy and Air Force have fewer jobs that are closed to women. The Navy, Air Force, and Marines also break their jobs down into "career fields" that reflect their respective missions: operating ships, flying airplanes, or conducting amphibious assaults.

WRITTEN PROMISES IN ENLISTMENT CONTRACTS: A GOOD IDEA

If a recruit qualifies, a recruiter can write a specific promise for job training into his or her contract. A senior recruiting NCO explains that the Army does this because it wants its recruits to feel satisfied and committed to their choice. Following the space where the specific promise of job training is typed in, the contract states, "In the event, through no fault of my own, that my enlistment program, school course, or training of my choice is cancelled or otherwise not available before I enlist . . . I will elect one of the following alternatives: 1) I will select another program, School Course, or training of my choice for which I am qualified and a vacancy exists (or) I will be 2) separated from the Delayed Entry Program."[23] A Ft. Jackson recruiting NCO stated that in his many years of experience 98 percent of enlistees will choose another training program rather than seek separation.

The Air Force, Navy, and Marines are more likely to enlist their recruits only in a "general career field" rather than for specific job training. The Navy often enlists recruits for "general assignment," meaning that they can be sent for training in any field at the Navy's sole discretion. Obviously, it is better for a recruit to have a promise of specific skills training entered in his contract than not. Then, if military cannot provide admission to a certain school or training program, the enlistee has some leverage in terms of selecting an alternative.

LEGAL WARNING

The current enlistment contract contains some language which is erroneous and appears designed to frighten enlistees. At section 3a, it states, "In the event that I willfully fail to report for active duty as specified in above [contract] I . . . will be in an Absent Without Leave Status (AWOL) and subject to apprehension and charged [sic] with Article 86 (deserter) [sic] of the Uniform Code of Military Justice."

As will be explained later, a person in the Delayed Entry Program (DEP) is part of the Individual Ready Reserve (IRR). Members of the IRR do not belong to any military unit, have no military rank or duties, and are not subject to the UCMJ. A DEP enrollee cannot be charged under military law until he or she returns to the Military Entrance Processing Station (MEPS) on DEP report day and is sworn in onto active duty. Legally speaking, for someone to be charged with desertion he or she must be on active duty and a jury must find that they intended to "remain permanently away" from duty.

There is also language in the contract which states that if "the Secretary of the Army determines that for military necessity or national interest members be available for immediate assignment/reassignment, any guarantees contained in this agreement may be terminated. [Then] I may be assigned or reassigned according to the needs of the Army."[24]

PROMISES OF ASSIGNMENT

Recruits can also have promises of specific duty assignment, such as duty stations like Hawaii, Germany, Korea, etc., assignment to a specific unit, e.g., 82nd or 101st Airborne Brigade or assignment to train with a "buddy," written into their contracts.

WORDS OF ADVICE IF YOU'RE CONSIDERING ENLISTMENT

When you visit the recruiter's office, it's best to have one of your parents or an adult friend accompany you. The recruiter should be happy to discuss military opportunities with both of you. If a dispute later arises over what was said or promised, it won't just be your word against the recruiter's. Also, you may be a little intimidated by someone who wears a uniform and talks with great authority. Your companion may be able to ask good questions that you didn't think of.

Don't Sign Anything on Your First Visit

Don't sign anything at the recruiting station until you and your companion are sure exactly what it means. It's best to take any documents and brochures home where you can read them over more carefully. Recruiters have been known to say that papers cannot be taken out of the office. However, once you have enlisted, you are entitled to a copy of your enlistment contract, so why shouldn't you be allowed to look over papers at home before you sign? You may also be asked to consent to your recruiter checking on your school, employer, and any police records.

Shop Around

You wouldn't buy the first car that you were shown on a dealer's lot, would you? Then why commit yourself after talking with only one recruiter? Make an effort to find out what each of the service branches can offer you. Sometimes a recruiter from one branch will tell you that you are not qualified for another branch. Why not find that out for yourself? Also, a recruiter may work harder to get you a training assignment if he knows you're considering offers from other service branches.

Don't Allow Yourself to Be Pressured

Don't let yourself be rushed or pressured by the recruiter. Sometimes a prospect is told that unless he enlists right away, he will miss out on a particular training program or assignment. Don't let such concerns stampede you into making a hasty commitment.

YOUR FIRST VISIT TO THE MEPS

Normally, your recruiter will make travel arrangements for your visits to the Military Entrance Processing Station (MEPS). If you don't live too far from a processing station, he will usually escort you on the morning of your appointment. If it is a long journey, say 100 miles or more, the recruiter may give you a bus or train ticket and arrange for you to stay overnight at a hotel near the MEPS. As a rule, recruiters like to "shepherd" their enlistees.

YOUR PHYSICAL EXAMINATION

You will arrive at the MEPS as dawn is breaking. First, you'll be shown a short video that will explain what will happen that day. Next, you'll be given a thorough physical examination that will take about two and a half hours. The recruiter will have already had you fill out a detailed medical history. The MEPS medical staff will check your condition against these forms, looking for possible problems. If you have suffered a health problem in the past, such as a sports injury, it is a good idea to bring a letter from your doctor stating that you are no longer affected by the condition.

If a health problem such as a vision or hearing defect is detected, the MEPS doctors will usually determine on the spot whether or not it affects your eligibility. In some cases, they may ask you to see a specialist before they will allow you to enlist. If you are found medically ineligible, your processing will be terminated.

Because today's military stresses fitness among all its members, your weight and height must fall within prescribed limits. If you are unusually muscular, the MEPS staff will measure your percentage of body fat because you may qualify for an extra weight allowance. If your weight falls just over or under the limits, you may be allowed to come back later for another weighing, assuming you are willing to lose (or gain) the required pounds.

Meeting with a "Guidance Counselor"

If your physical exam uncovers no problems, you will be sent for an interview with a MEPS guidance counselor, who is usually a former recruiter. If your contract contains written promises of training and assignment, the counselor will confirm this for you.

If you haven't already been given a written promise for training or assignment, then this brief session with the counselor will determine what you will train for and where you will serve. The counselor will ask for your preferences and then enter your ASVAB scores and other data into his online system. This system works somewhat like an airline reservation system. A training assignment might be available when the counselor turns on the computer in the morning, but it may disappear fifteen minutes later when a counselor at another MEPS computer "reserves" it for another enlistee.

IF YOU CHANGE YOUR MIND: VOIDING THE ENLISTMENT CONTRACT

All military recruits today sign a contact which places them in the Delayed Entry Program. This contains a promise that the recruit will report for active duty on a specific date, up to one year in the future. The military uses this type of contract for two reasons: it helps the armed forces plan their training activities and efficiently fit recruits into available "slots." Second, it helps reduce "sales resistance." Recruiters believe that it is easier to get young people to sign contracts if they don't have to report for duty right away. It's not much different from the "buy now, pay later" sales pitch.

An enlistee in the DEP is assigned to the Individual Ready Reserve, which is essentially administrative limbo. IRR members do not belong to any military unit, and have no rank nor military chain of command. IRR members cannot be involuntarily placed on active duty by a member of the recruiting command. Spokespersons for each service branch have stated that it is against military policy to try to force DEP enrollees onto active duty against their will.

However, it is common for recruiters to tell DEP enrollees that they must honor their contracts. Asked about this, a recruiter from Ft. Jackson was candid: "If a kid changes his mind, it's often just cold feet. It's usually fear of the unknown. I try to uncover what the real reasons are driving his decision. I find it useful to talk to both the parents and the recruit. Sometimes I tell them, 'You signed the contract and you're going to the Army.' Confrontation can be a useful tool."[25]

A DEP enrollee who has decided not to serve should write a letter to the commanding officer of the local recruiting command explaining that he or she has decided not to report for active duty as per the contract. The letter should request that a "certificate of separation" be issued, stating the reason: "refusal to enlist." State that your decision is irrevocable and ask that recruiters make no further contact with you. Send copies to local congressional offices (attention: "military caseworker"), school administrators, ministers, etc. After an interval, the DEP refuser will receive a certificate of separation in the mail.

RECRUITMENT OF OFFICERS

The military makes a big distinction between commissioned officers and enlisted personnel. Officers enjoy a special social status, as well as benefits and privileges that are not available to enlisted members. Officers function as both the middle-level managers and the top leaders for the entire military system. As such, they can exercise great power and authority over those serving below them. On the other hand, they are expected to meet higher standards of personal conduct than enlisted personnel. For example, one positive urinalysis for drug use will end an officer's career.

With a few exceptions, only US citizens with a four-year college degree are eligible to become commissioned officers. Officer candidates must meet the same standards of physical qualifications as enlisted personnel. Today, there are basically four ways to become an officer. They are listed below.

SERVICE ACADEMIES

The most prestigious way to receive an officer's commission is by graduating from one of the four service academies: West Point (Army), Annapolis (Navy), the Air Force, and the Coast Guard. These four-year colleges provide their cadets with an all-expenses-paid education, plus second lieutenant's bars (or the equivalent), when they graduate. The academies offer a regular college curriculum, although it is heavily weighted toward science, math, and technical subjects. Although much of the course material is similar to a regular college, a definite "military" atmosphere pervades each of the four institutions. Summers are spent undergoing rigorous military training at various military installations.

Academy graduates enjoy a special status within their respective service branches. Some military people believe that an informal network of academy grads (sometimes known as "ringknockers") boost each other with promotions and assignments. About 11 percent of all Army officers in 1994 were academy grads, yet 34 percent of all generals went to West Point!

The biggest obstacle for those who are interested in attending the academies is their restricted enrollment. In recent years, West Point admitted just one out of eleven applicants. For the Navy, one applicant was accepted out of every ten who applied.

Once admitted, some cadets find the high-pressure, competitive atmosphere a difficult adjustment. All of the academies stress athletic prowess. For instance, 80 percent of a recent graduating class at Annapolis had been varsity letter winners in high school.

At present, about one in four cadets at West Point fails to graduate. If you quit before your junior year, no military obligation is incurred. Theoretically, a cadet who resigns during or after his junior year can be ordered to active duty as an enlisted person. This is not done at present, but lawsuits to recoup college expenses have been filed.

If you wish to apply to a service academy, you should contact the school that you're interested in early in your junior year of high school. You will need to get a member of Congress to endorse your application. Each academy has liaison officers throughout the United States who can help you work through the complicated application process. The academies will provide you with their names and addresses when you write for application information.

Reserve Officer Training Corps (ROTC)

This is the military's single largest source of officers today. About 1,350 colleges and universities throughout the United States offer ROTC programs, which account for almost 40 percent of the military's new officers. Schools offer Army, Navy, or Air Force programs; some offer all three.

Each service operates a separate recruiting command for its ROTC program. The Army calls these recruiters "gold-mining teams," referring to the gold bars that the second lieutenants wear. These teams spend most of their time on college campuses trying to recruit freshmen and sophomores into the program. Although they employ some of the techniques described earlier, they try and adopt a style that blends in with the college environment. Recently commissioned second lieutenants are often sent back to their alma maters to spend a few months helping sign new cadets.

One problem for the military has been the low status of the ROTC duty among most career military people. Recently, there have been attempts to upgrade the "image" of ROTC duty to allay fears that these assignments may harm one's chances for promotion.

College students enlist for two-, three-, or four-year ROTC programs, depending on the service branch they choose. Legally, there are two separate parts to the ROTC program. During the first two years, ROTC candidates attend training and drills as volunteers, although they receive some college credit for the classroom work. During this period, cadets can quit the programs at will with no military obligation.

The second phase, which usually begins with the junior year, requires that cadets sign an enlistment contract that places them on Reserve status. These cadets begin receiving a monthly paycheck and other allowances. In addition, many receive partial or full academic scholarships for college expenses.

If a cadet fails to perform satisfactorily or quits during this phase, the military claims to have the authority to place him on active duty to serve out his obligation as an enlisted person. If you find yourself in this situation, you should contact Citizen Soldier (www.citizen-soldier.com) for referral to experienced lawyers who can represent you.

Sometimes college graduates are talked into joining the military as enlisted personnel. Recruiters sometimes argue that it is a good experience to "start at the bottom" and that enlisted personnel can attend Officers Candidate School (OCS). Actually, the competition for admission to OCS is quite intense.

Officers Candidate Schools

Each service branch operates special schools that train enlisted personnel, warrant officers with college degrees, and non-ROTC college graduates to become commissioned officers. As mentioned, competition for entrance is usually fierce, and only those with outstanding service records are normally admitted. The Marines offer commissions to a select number of enlisted people who have only two years of college, provided that they are between the ages of twenty-two and twenty-six.

Direct Appointment

Doctors, lawyers, dentists, engineers, priests, and ministers who are certified in their respective fields may be eligible for direct commissioning as officers. They immediately begin practicing their professions once on active duty with only a minimum amount of military training. About 13 percent of new officers receive their commissions this way.

2

Military Training: Basic Training

Christian G. Appy

> They tore you down. They tore everything civilian out of your entire existence—your speech, your thoughts, your sights, your memory—anything that was civilian they tore out and then they re-built you and made you over. But they didn't build you from there up. First they made you drop down to a piece of grit on the floor. Then they built you back up to being a Marine.
>
> —Marine veteran
> Gene Holiday

TEARING DOWN

A bus full of Marine recruits pulls into boot camp. It is well past midnight, but a team of drill instructors (DIs) stands ready to pounce. As the bus rolls to a stop, one of the DIs jumps in and screams: " 'YOU GOT THREE SECONDS TO GET OFF THIS BUS AND TWO OF 'EM ARE GONE.' "[1] The men scramble and shove their way off, ordered to stand on yellow footprints painted on the concrete parade deck. As the men line up, a second DI roars out of a nearby shed. He marches up to one of the recruits and comes so close their faces almost touch. The DI screams in the boy's ear: " 'You no good fucking civilian maggot. . . . You're worthless, do you understand? And I'm gonna kill you.' " Several other men are singled out for similar abuse. Then the drill instructor addresses the whole group: " 'There are eighty of you, eighty young warm bodies, eighty sweet little ladies, eighty sweetpeas, and I want you maggots to know today that you belong to me and you will belong to me until I have made you into Marines.' "[2]

The DI proclaims his ownership of the recruits, his civilian maggots. Screaming his taunts and insults, the sergeant asserts his absolute control of their lives. The most ominous threats ("I'm gonna kill you") are meant to inspire terror, but they also express a quite literal intention to destroy everything civilian in the recruits. Nothing in their former lives is deemed worthy of preservation. Every civilian identity is worthless. New recruits are the lowest form of life. They do not deserve to live. If they are ever to become Marines, they must acknowledge their total inadequacy. They must be torn down in order to be rebuilt, killed in order to be reborn.

Gustav Hasford, a combat journalist who served in Vietnam with the First Marine Division, writes about basic training in his novel *The Short-Timers* (the film *Full Metal Jacket* was based on this book). Hasford's drill instructor speaks these words to his new recruits: " '*If* you ladies leave my island, *if* you survive recruit training, you will be a weapon, you will be a minister of death, praying for war. And proud. Until that day you are pukes, you are scumbags, you are the lowest form of life on Earth. You are not even human. You people are nothing but a lot of little pieces of amphibian shit.' "[3]

After the initial hazing, according to Ron Kovic's account, the recruits are herded into a large building and lined up in front of long rows of empty boxes. " 'I want you to take your clothes off,' the sergeant shouted. 'I want you to take off everything that ever reminded you of being a civilian and put it in the box. . . . I want everything!' "[4] Naked now, the men are marched to a group of barbers. With fast, rough strokes, the barbers run electric razors over each man's head, shearing the hair down to the scalp in less than a minute. After the haircut the men are sent down long metal hallways, shoved along by drill instructors. The men get jammed up, the "young bodies tense and twisted together, grasping each other, holding on like children." They are run into a large shower room. A sergeant screams: " 'Wash all that scum off! I want you maggots to wash all that civilian scum off your bodies forever!' "[5]

Dripping and still naked, the men are moved to another room and are lined up in front of a row of boxes containing military uniforms. " 'Awright ladies! . . . We're going to begin today by learning how to dress. These are trousers . . . Not pants! Pants are for little girls! Trousers are for Marines!' " An overweight recruit in Kovic's training platoon cannot fit into the trousers he is issued. The drill sergeants circle around him, screaming and taunting and punching him in the stomach. When the recruit breaks down and begins to cry, one of the sergeants yells for everyone in the building to look at the crybaby. " 'Cry Cry Cry you little baby! That's what we want, we want you people to cry like little babies because that's all you maggots are. You are nothing!' "[6]

The first days of basic training were indeed designed to reduce recruits to a psychological condition equivalent to early childhood. As Robert Flaherty recalls, "It was like you were a little baby and you were starting all over again." The drill instructors acted as surrogate parents, seeking, in several intense weeks, to replace seventeen or eighteen years of psychological and physical development with wholly reconditioned minds and bodies. Every detail of life was prescribed, regulated, and enforced. Every moment was accounted for. There was a method and time for every action. Even using the bathroom was limited to short, specified times or required special permission. "Head calls," like all boot camp "privileges," were especially infrequent at the outset. Some men went for a full week before they were able to defecate in the time allotted.[7]

Moreover, the regimen was carried out in an environment of strict impersonality, a kind of collective isolation. Recruits were denied both privacy and intimacy. They could not be alone, nor could they engage their fellow recruits in unofficial activities or conversations. During the first week, conversation was forbidden altogether. Every form of language or behavior that expressed individuality or fraternal resistance to boot camp regulations was, when observed by the drill instructors, immediately and severely punished. Punishments almost always involved some physical ordeal or debasement: men were exercised until they dropped (sometimes locked in the DI's metal locker, "the sweat box"), forced to eat garbage or unauthorized possessions found in their area (often inducing vomiting), made to put their heads into the urinals they had not sufficiently cleaned, and so on. While the DIs called the recruits every insulting pejorative they could think of, the recruits could only address their sergeants in the third person. A recruit never said *I* to a sergeant. *I*—the individual—was not acknowledged to exist.

Robert Flaherty is about six-foot-three, a big, strong ex-Marine. His size and strength, however, did not protect him from the deep anxiety and fear induced by his drill instructors. "You get up in the morning at attention and you go to sleep at attention. You go to sleep from fright. Speak to the drill instructor in the third person only: 'Sir, Private Flaherty requests permission to speak to the drill instructor, sir.' Sir before, sir after. Look him straight in the face. Don't look any other way. Stand at attention at all times. Look straight ahead. You could get your head handed to you for looking another way."[8]

At the mess hall, recruits ate their meals in silence, looking straight ahead. Robert demonstrates the prescribed eating method: Keeping his head completely still, he uses his fork to probe the plate for food. Then he raises the fork straight up to a point about one foot in front of his face, brings it to his mouth, empties it, and returns it to the plate. "We called them 'square meals,' " he recalls, the term's extra meaning coming from the path of the fork from plate to mouth. If the drill instructor was on the other side of the room, men sometimes glanced at their food or at one of the other men, but it was a risky move. "If the drill instructor catches you sneaking a peak, he will just hop right up on the table and start walking through everybody's food. And you know what you do when he's walking through your food? You just keep eating your square meal. And the drill instructor will say: 'Motherfucker, you *better* not stab your sergeant with that fork.' And everybody at the table yells, 'NO, SIR!' It's that crazy. It's that intense."

In other words, much of boot camp was truly *basic* training. Recruits were told how to eat, how and when to speak, how to dress, when to go to the bathroom, how to walk, how to fold clothing and make beds, how to stand at attention and salute—how, in short, to perform the most elemental routine according to a rigid and standardized set of regulations. The drill instructors maintained this discipline with an iron hand. Though obedience was exacted by sheer intimidation, the physical stress of basic training also induced compliance.

Even well-trained athletes were taxed to the limit by the physical demands of Marine Corps boot camp. The day began between 4:00 and 5:00 in the morning, and between then and lights-out at 9:00 P.M. the recruits were continually subjected to torturous exercise. Aside from the regularly scheduled hours of physical training (PT), sergeants called for additional rounds of PT at any hour, for any reason. A speck of dust might send the entire platoon on a mile run or another hour of scrubbing down the barracks. A sloppy salute could bring fifty push-ups. "Man, the PT was constant. They PT'd you to death. At the drop of a hat the drill instructor would have you on the ground doing push-ups or sit-ups or squat thrusts. You wouldn't think you could sweat that much."[9]

Simple exhaustion was a key factor in explaining the willingness of recruits to follow orders. They soon learned that disobedience of any kind only brought more pain—more harassment, more cleaning, and more fatigue. If the standard forms of breaking down recruits to a level of unquestioning compliance were not effective, the DIs could always transfer inept or recalcitrant men to a special platoon. Drill instructors often reminded their men of the ordeal awaiting them if they were sent to a "Motivation Platoon" or, even worse, "Correctional Custody." (The Army version of the motivation platoon was called the "Special Processing Detachment," and the equivalent of correctional custody was the Army stockade.)

In these special platoons recruits underwent an excruciating round of forced marches, disciplinary labor, and even more constant verbal and physical abuse. Those recruits who proved themselves sufficiently motivated (that is, submissive to orders and able to perform the basic round of drills) were returned to their original platoons. Others had to repeat boot camp from the beginning with a new cycle of recruits. The rest were ultimately court-martialed and given dishonorable discharges.[10]

Given these circumstances, it is not surprising that most men followed orders and worked as hard as possible to avoid the wrath of their drill instructors. Gene Holiday speaks for many as he describes the series of responses that characterized his effort to adjust to boot camp. He moved from fear to self-doubt to absolute obedience. "I started out being real scared. And then I ended up feeling real worthless. I felt that I wasn't going to cut it and not because it was their fault for putting me through it, but because it was my own fault. And then I started to feel better by telling myself I'm just going to do everything these guys say. I'm going to do it so fast that if he says 'jump,' it's not even going to get out of his mouth and—BOOM—I'll be right there."[11]

Marine Corps basic training in the Vietnam years, conducted in only two places (Parris Island, South Carolina, and San Diego, California), was a highly standardized and predictable cycle. Accounts of the experience are so similar one can draw from them a fairly clear-cut model of its essential elements. The Army, the service that trained the most men for Vietnam, had a similar system but was less brutal, and veterans report a variety of training experiences. The Army operated about a dozen basic training camps throughout the country (for example, Fort Lewis, Washington; Fort Polk, Louisiana; Fort Dix, New Jersey; and Fort Jackson, South Carolina). While some Army veterans report training experiences that sound virtually identical to Marine basic, others indicate that the training was significantly less severe in both tone and substance. Nor does Army basic seem to have left such an indelible mark on its trainees. While former Marines almost always include boot camp anecdotes in their Vietnam stories, Army veterans often skip their training experiences unless asked about them specifically.

Until the early 1960s the Army used platoon sergeants and special instructors to train recruits. Drill sergeants were brought in to present men with a more dominant and ever-present authority. At least superficially, the drill sergeants were modeled on the Marine Corps drill instructors, even wearing the same forest ranger–style hats ("Smoky-the-Bear hats"). In practice, however, the Army drill sergeants were less omnipresent and less vicious. Even in the first days of boot camp, many organizational tasks were handled by squad leaders drawn from the ranks of the trainees. Although the drill sergeants subjected their men to demeaning verbal abuse, it was neither so constant nor so extreme as that of the Marine DIs. Though they called their men "shitbirds" and other epithets, they also addressed the recruits as "troops" and "men." Marine DIs would have found such language unthinkably polite.[12]

In Bo Hathaway's novel *A World of Hurt* (set in 1966), an Army lieutenant addressed a group of trainees:

> "I'm going to make soldiers out of you bunch of riffraff if I have to work you till you drop. And go ahead and write your congressmen. I think you'll find those congressmen on our side. They don't want a bunch of crybabies doing their fighting for them.
>
> "Most of you know by now there was one coward in the company who couldn't take it anymore. He decided he didn't have an obligation to defend his country. All he wanted was to get out of the Army and go back to his mommy. Last night this man put a couple of scratches on his wrist so we'd have to take pity on him and send him to the hospital. And let me tell you something, he's going to get his wish. He's getting out of the Army, all right—with a dishonorable discharge that will follow him the rest of his life.
>
> "I don't know if this fairy infected any of the rest of you, but if any of you punks out there don't want to become soldiers and men, just let me know, and we'll slap a dishonorable discharge on you, and you can run home, too. But just try to get a job."[13]

The substance of this statement is similar to that offered by Marine DIs: trainees are punks and riffraff, and anyone who is unwilling or unable to become a soldier is simply a crybaby, a coward, and a fairy. But there is a defensive quality in this speech that is ordinarily absent in accounts of Marine Corps training. If the lieutenant truly had absolute control, why should he even mention the existence of civilian authorities? This sense of constraint is made more explicit in Hathaway's novel by the response of a sergeant to a trainee who talked back: "If this was the old Army—if things were the way they should be—I'd beat the shit out of you."[14]

There is a similar tone in the lieutenant's warnings about dishonorable discharges ("just try to get a job"). He sounds like a man charged with controlling a group of men who will do anything to get out of their situation, a group that has to be reminded at every turn of the dire consequences of resistance or escape. In fact, suicide attempts were common among military recruits. At Fort Dix alone, there was an average of more than 200 suicide attempts per year during the Vietnam War. Actual suicides, though not uncommon, were far fewer; for example, at Fort Dix in 1968, six trainees killed themselves. The high number of what the Army called suicide gestures indicates that most men were not driven to kill themselves, but many were willing to take extreme risks to escape the military.[15]

Marine DIs revealed no doubts about their ability to keep their men in line. When a Marine trainee "botched" a suicide in *Sand in the Wind,* a novel by Vietnam veteran Robert Roth, the DI told his platoon that the man would "get court-martialed for the destruction of government property." Then he proceeded to instruct his men on the proper way to commit suicide. "The civilian turd did it the wrong way. I'm gonna show you the *Marine Corps way.*" He took a razor and moved the blade up and down his forearm. "*Remember,* up and down, not across—that way you get all the arteries."[16]

The Marine Corps relied primarily on verbal and physical abuse—behavioral conditioning—to indoctrinate its recruits. The Army put additional emphasis on ideological indoctrination. In practical terms this distinction simply meant that Army trainees had to sit through more films and lectures than did the Marines. For example, in an effort to swell the spirit of anticommunism, the Army ran films like *The Red Menace, The Anatomy of Aggression, Guardians at the Gate,* and *Night of the Dragon.* These films are packed with crude images of communist expansion—world maps inexorably covered by a tide of red ink and crowds of civilians apparently fleeing the advances of invading communists.[17]

Most Army trainees also heard a series of lectures by an Army chaplain on "character guidance." The central point of these lectures was to explain why soldiers ought to obey their commanders. Invoking God, honor, and prudence (that is, if you do not obey you will get into trouble), the chaplain followed a course outline called Character Guidance Discussion Topics provided in an Army field manual. "The freest soldier," the manual argues, "is the soldier who willingly submits to authority. When you obey a lawful command you need not fear, nor worry. You can devote all your energies to getting the job done." What is omitted from the discussion, as Peter Barnes points out, is any clear definition of what the trainees should consider an *un*lawful order and how they are to respond in such a situation. Though the Army modified its regulations, after the Nuremberg Trials, to hold individual soldiers responsible for their own actions, indoctrination stressed simpleminded obedience. There was no special training about the moral responsibilities and complexities encountered by soldiers fighting a counterguerrilla war among a civilian population.[18]

One of the most unusual and amusing accounts of Army basic training during the Vietnam War is Peter Tauber's *The Sunshine Soldiers* (1971). A reservist from New York, Tauber writes about his experience of basic training at Fort Bliss, Texas, in the spring of 1969. His detailed and imaginative journal presents a view of Army training at its most lax. Indeed, Tauber persuasively argues that most of the military authorities were more preoccupied with processing as many trainees as possible with the fewest hassles than they were with instilling military rigor or discipline. In Tauber's company, the trainees routinely ignored and openly defied their sergeants. They found dozens of ways to circumvent or undermine the routine. They slacked off, skipped drills, and opened a "clubhouse" in an abandoned barracks where they went to relax, smoke pot, and sleep. Even when drill sergeants were aware of the infractions, they did little, if anything, in response. So long as the trainees stayed on base, the authorities were content to tolerate repeated irregularities. (Some men even addressed their sergeants by their first names.)[19]

Lectures and films did not succeed in persuading the sunshine soldiers to toe the military line. Tauber describes his unit's response to a film designed to prevent trainees from using drugs:

> The Army's cinematic explanation of the drug scene seems to have replaced the traditional venereal-disease slides. No more full-color blowups of infected genitalia before lunch. No indeed. Sex is out, because drugs are farther out. *Trip to Where?*, a film about LSD, begins with a Russian roulette game which ends with a gun actually being fired at some poor acid head's head. . . . [Then] we settle down to a half hour of freaky music and light-show effects, which the movie tries to imply are horrific. The fatigue-clad audience begins to groove on the welcome vibrations; the soldier next to me whispers that he has been stoned since he took the oath a week ago, and has three day's supply left. On the screen an LSD freak-out party leads to an obvious sexual liaison between Good Joe and Clean Suzie, bringing lusty cheers from the audience. The announcer, who has remained silent for a half hour, breaks in to tell us that "you are beginning to see the dangers of LSD—now let's look at the medical facts." The main danger he has in mind, it seems, is Sex. Someone is always forgetting to pass the word to the Pentagon.[20]

Tauber concedes that his company was not typical. While some of the men in his unit went to Vietnam, about 50 percent were reservists (none of whom was sent to Vietnam). Tauber found the reservists considerably more irreverent and disobedient than the regular Army volunteers and draftees. The military may well have treated companies filled with reservists with greater leniency. Still, if Tauber's account does not reflect the majority experience of basic training for Vietnam-bound soldiers, it does help to define one end of the spectrum. It also reminds us that the military was not always successful in getting across its view of the world.

Army boot camp was hardly the all-encompassing, closed world of Marine boot camp. While Marines were completely isolated from civilian life throughout the basic training cycle, Army trainees were usually allowed occasional off-base passes after four or five weeks of boot camp. These leaves gave trainees a chance to gain some psychological as well as physical distance from the military. And for the increasing number of men who were seeking a way out of the military and who opposed the war, they provided a chance to make contact with a community of supporters. By the late 1960s, antiwar groups had established GI coffee houses near most training bases; here, trainees could gather informally to talk, meet civilians with antiwar views, and get concrete information on seeking exile abroad or filing for conscientious objector status. There were also, by 1969, more than forty antiwar, underground GI newspapers that circulated secretly among trainees off and on base (for example, *Shakedown* at Fort Dix, *Left Face* at Fort McClellan, *The Fatigue Press* at Fort Hood, *Last Harass* at Fort Gordon, and *Short Times* at Fort Jackson). In-service applications for conscientious objector status rose from 829 in 1967 to 4,381 in 1971. Primarily due to some key federal and Supreme Court decisions, the Pentagon began accepting many more of these claims, and the approval rate rose from 28 percent in 1967 to 77 percent by 1972. Desertions also mounted steadily—40,227 in 1967, 73,121 in 1969, and 90,000 in 1971. While 20,000 men deserted after serving full tours in Vietnam, a far greater number left the military during the training process. There were roughly 500,000 deserters during the Vietnam War.[21]

The level of resistance within the military by the late 1960s was extraordinary. Nonetheless, even antiwar draftees were frequently struck by the capacity of basic training to inculcate military values. However skeptical and resistant they may have been to military indoctrination, however much they may have loathed the mindless routines, and however opposed they were to the effort to instill obedience and aggression, most men who went through the process felt that it had changed them, in many cases far more than they had believed possible.

Take the case of Peter Milord. He was an upper-middle-class graduate of the University of Connecticut when he was drafted in 1969. At first he thought military training was having no impact on him: "In my mind I was being a cynical, satirical wit. . . . I was able to laugh and stone [smoke marijuana] my way through basic, staying above it." But gradually he found himself changing. He had always enjoyed sports and physical competition, and the military training drills began to tap those emotions. Along with his enjoyment he noticed himself becoming increasingly aggressive. Though at first he had simply mouthed, without feeling, the violent slogans ("Kill! Kill! Kill! To kill without mercy is the spirit of the bayonet!"), he began to suspect he was absorbing, through repetition, the real meaning of the words. "I didn't become a robot, but you can get so close to being one it's frightening." In Milord's case, the changes he felt in himself were decisive in setting him on the course of action he had seriously considered when he first received his draft notice. A few weeks after basic training he deserted to Canada.[22]

Another former Army trainee described basic training this way:

> When you first go in, everybody realizes [basic training is] a lot of horse shit. They show you all those movies about the good guys getting wiped out by the dirty commies—that they're going to come over here and rape your mom, and eat your apple pie, and that kind of thing. Everybody realizes it's horse shit, but by the end of training, there were actually guys who started talking about killing the dirty commies—it works. Other people didn't believe it, but they had been through so much smoke that they outwardly accepted it because it had been impressed on them so much. They realized that in order to survive they had to conform.[23]

Stan Bodner, an Army Vietnam veteran, described the effect of basic training in much stronger language:

> A soldier lives a very, very low life in the service—highly regimented, highly mechanical. He is ingrained with the spirit of the corps, but his own personal self is sacrificed. His personal identity is put on ice. I mean he forgets totally about himself, he becomes a sacrificial human being, a person who is totally acquiesced to a system, to a body-regiment. Unless you've been through eight weeks of boot camp you have no idea of what I'm talking about. Because what's taught in basic training is a whole unquestionable obedience.[24]

Thus, even while Army training was not usually as brutal or imprisoning as Marine boot camp, it was certainly capable of tearing down many of its trainees, stripping them of a personal identity, and making them feel like unquestioning members of a body-regiment. Also, many of the Army combat soldiers who fought in Vietnam went on to advanced training as paratroopers or Rangers, experiences comparable in intensity to Marine basic. Moreover, Army trainees who entered the military reluctantly may have found basic training more of an emotional jolt than Marine recruits who went to boot camp expecting the worst. After all, some men enlisted in the Marines precisely because they had heard it was "really bad," the toughest branch of the service.

Lt. Col. William E. Datel found extremely high levels of anxiety and stress among Army trainees throughout the 1960s. As chief of the Mental Hygiene Unit at Ford Ord, California (a major Army basic training center), Datel studied the stress levels of boot camp trainees for almost a decade. By the middle of basic training, Datel found, recruits became so intensely anxious and angry that their stress levels surpassed those of frontline soldiers. Producing and controlling that anger was, of course, not an unwanted by-product of basic training but one of its main goals.[25]

COMPLIANT AGGRESSION

Basic training was devoted to the tricky business of promoting two not always compatible traits: unswerving obedience and ruthless aggression. Recruits were trained to be both compliant and violent. Therefore, drill instructors tore down their recruits not only to generate the kind of fear that elicits obedience but also to inflame the sort of anger that might be channeled into aggressive soldiering. Uncontrolled aggression was not, however, the final object. Unfocused, undisciplined rage is not usually an advantage in a firefight. Instead, the military hoped to turn out soldiers who would be "cool under fire," men able to return fire quickly, calmly, and mechanically. Thus, basic training combined discipline and aggression, obedience and anger. The final goal was to instill in recruits a focused hostility aimed at a prescribed enemy.

Before drill instructors attempted to focus aggression on a specific enemy, they wanted simply to generate as much rage as possible, whatever its source or object. In part this was accomplished through the standard boot camp training drills in which men were pitted against one another in various physical competitions. In bayonet training, for example, recruits fought one another with pugil sticks (five-foot poles with heavy padding on each end). These were tough, often ferocious battles in which drill instructors encouraged recruits to perceive their opponent as an absolute enemy warranting no mercy.

Sometimes, especially in the Marine Corps, drill instructors went beyond the traditional boot camp regimen with their own unofficial methods of heightening aggression. For example, Robert Flaherty's drill instructor periodically called for an "air-raid." In the middle of the night the DI burst into the barracks screaming at everyone to get into the showers and take everything with them—their clothes, their footlockers, even their mattresses ("every goddamn thing"). The DI yelled "AIR-RAID," and everyone pushed and kicked to find a place on the floor of the packed shower room. Then the sergeant screamed "FLOOD," and everyone jumped up to get to the shower handles and turn them on—"hot, cold, indifferent." The sergeant encouraged the wildest behavior. "He wanted us to go absolutely berserk. Screaming, pounding, pushing—it was a raging free-for-all. They made you inhuman, my man, inhuman."[26]

Drill instructors were careful, however, to maintain control of the violence they provoked. They wanted to use the growing aggression of their recruits to help enforce the discipline and conformity of basic training. The goal was to make their units essentially self-regulating and self-disciplining, enforcing among themselves the demands initially made by the drill instructors alone. The technique was simple. Whenever a trainee failed to perform according to the DI's standards, everyone in the unit was punished. While they did their extra push-ups, the drill instructor repeatedly denounced the slacker who had caused their collective pain. In fact, DIs sometimes ordered particularly inept or intractable recruits to sit and watch while the other men did extra PT—an especially effective way of producing unitwide anger against those who could not or would not keep pace and maintain discipline. " 'I want you men to take a look at those cowards who have caused you to stay in this strain. You may think those men are your buddies, but they're cheaters and fuckoffs, and they're putting you in a world of hurt.' "[27]

Whatever initial sympathy a recruit might have for those unable or unwilling to conform was soon quelled by the additional suffering such lapses in discipline might bring to all. A single sloppy man could cause hours of extra scrubbing for everyone, so almost everyone scorned recruits who caused trouble. Some men bent or broke the rules without getting caught. That was a different matter. These men might be very popular indeed (especially in the Army), doubly respected for their ability to do what was required without becoming "ass-kissers." Those who caused problems for everyone, however, became outcasts and pariahs. Sometimes, especially in the Marine Corps, such men were beaten by the other recruits during midnight "blanket parties": "If somebody fucks you up—if somebody talks, or somebody gets caught doing something they're not supposed to do, and the whole platoon suffers for it—that night a bunch of guys will get together and throw a blanket over this guy's head when he's sleeping and kick his ass real good."[28] The blanket was used to muffle the screams.

Individual behavior of any kind was risky in basic training. Even when recruits decided to break rather than enforce the standards of basic training, they tended to do so collectively. At Fort Jackson in 1967, draftee John Picciano recalled occasional nights when someone took out a hidden bottle of scotch and passed it around the barracks. He dreaded those times because he felt pressured to drink when he did not want to.

> "Hey, we've got a bottle here. Have a drink," one of the guys would say.
> "No, thanks, I don't drink much."
> "You better drink. What's the matter with you, anyway?"

John believed that the military was making everyone a conformist and that "no one was allowed to be his own man even when the sergeants weren't around."[29] He also noticed a decided increase in the level of aggression. People were thinking and acting much more violently. "A perfectly regular guy could come into the Army, and before he knew it, he was doing things he'd never done before. Making fun of some poor fat guy after the sergeants had kicked him around. Talking about what it would be like to get a gang together and take the cafe waitress out in the alley."[30]

The verbal abuse hurled at recruits was crucial in fomenting these attitudes. Aside from the general terms of degradation DIs used to address their entire units ("scumbags," "hogs," "shitbirds"), individuals were commonly branded with their own particular derogatory name. Often these slurs were based on race, religion, class, region, or physical traits.

In *Sand in the Wind,* Robert Roth describes in detail the process by which the DIs labeled their men. Roth's fictional narrative, drawing on his own experience at Parris Island, is one of the most gripping and insightful accounts of Marine basic training in the enormous body of literature about Vietnam.

> Hacker [the DI] stopped in front of a dark recruit. He slowly moved closer until his mouth was within an inch of the recruit's nose, then shouted, "YOU A SPLIB OR A SPIC?"
>
> "Splib."
>
> "SPLIB, WHAT?"
>
> "Splib, sir."
>
> "COCKSUCKER, if you want to live, the first word out of your mouth will be *'sir.'* . . . ARE YOU A SPLIB OR A SPIC?" . . .
>
> "SIR, THE PRIVATE IS A SPLIB."
>
> "Remember that, you high-yellow come bubble."[31]

Another recruit was branded "Red-Neck" after a drill sergeant found out he was from a Mississippi farm. At one point a DI told him, "You're going back to Mississippi where you're needed . . . to slop the hogs, clean the cow pies out of the barn, move the outhouse around. Isn't that right red-neck? . . . I'm not gonna waste any more time trying to make a Marine out of white trash like you."[32]

Aware that most recruits were from the bottom rungs of the American social order (as were most drill instructors), the DIs used class and racial epithets to aggravate the pain many recruits associated with their civilian status. They called their men "bums," "losers," "morons," "riffraff," and "trash." The DIs sought to persuade their recruits that, so long as they remained civilians, they amounted to nothing more than a lumpen proletariat, a class of "low-lifes," "dead-beats," "punks," and "scum." As soldiers, however, society's losers were offered the prospect of professional standing. This particular version of social mobility was trenchantly voiced by a drill instructor in Roth's novel: " 'You ain't standing on no corner and you ain't sloppin' no hogs. You're professional men now, each and every one of you worthless cunts has a profession. YOU'RE PROFESSIONAL KILLERS *in the service of the United States government.*' "[33]

What about those recruits who were not poor or working class? How did drill instructors deal with the question of class among the minority of men from middle-class and privileged backgrounds? They, too, were singled out and subjected to ridicule. They were told that their civilian advantages were worthless in the military, that their class privileges were, in fact, a disability. Their comfort had made them even more soft and cowardly than the other recruits. They were "pussies," "faggots," and "candy-asses."

In *Sand in the Wind*, during one of the first formations, a sergeant said, "Any of you hogs that have been to college take one step forward." Of a platoon of eighty only five stepped forward. Only one had graduated from college, and he suffered particular abuse.

> "How many years did *you* waste, hog?" . . .
> "SIR, THE PRIVATE SPENT FOUR YEARS IN COLLEGE."
> "SPENT?" . . .
> "Sir, *the Private wasted four years in college.*" . . .
> "*I* DON'T *fucking believe it*! How could *anyone* with balls spend FOUR YEARS in college?"

Concluding the inquest, one of the sergeants said, " 'COME BUBBLE, your education has *just* started.' " From that point on, the recruit was called "College Fag."[34]

Paradoxically, one of the functions of these epithets was not to divide the men but to unify them. So long as everyone was insulted—the "college fags" along with the "morons," the "rednecks" and "wops" along with the "spics" and "bean-bags" (Chicanos)—everyone was, in theory, equal. The insults generated a sense of mutual degradation, a kind of solidarity of the despised. Ex-Marine Paul Atwood recalls his drill instructor saying, "There are no niggers in this platoon, there are no spics, there are no wops, there are no kikes, there are no poor white whatever. . . . You are all fucking maggots and maggots you will remain until you've earned the right to call yourself United States Marines."[35] Some recruits felt that the very abuse each man had to endure contributed to a sense of collective respect and helped to defuse potential conflicts among the men. "They figure if they put us through enough shit, we'll respect each other more."[36] But others noticed that despite talk about all Marines being equal, many drill instructors still differentiated their men with racist epithets.

No doubt the experience of basic training did, for many, create a sense of unit solidarity across lines of race, class, and region. That was the point. The goal, however, was not to eliminate racist thought entirely or to promote tolerance of individual, ethnic, or national differences. The goal was to mold a rigid and intolerant conformity to military discipline and to mobilize hostility against a foreign enemy. If the drill instructors' use of racist language served to defuse internal hostilities among the trainees, it also served to legitimize racist stereotypes when projected onto external groups such as the Vietnamese. If racist language seemed to lose its venom when used to homogenize American soldiers, it preserved its poison when used to demonize a foreign enemy.

This point is underlined by the way drill instructors used the language of gender and sexuality. One of the most common forms of harassment was to call recruits "ladies," "girls," "cunts," or "pussies." Any evidence of weakness or fatigue (or simply failure to conform) was typically attributed to a lack of manhood. Failure as a soldier constituted failure as a man and left the recruit with the status of a woman. Describing that status, Tim O'Brien writes, "[In basic training] women are dinks. Women are villains. They are creatures akin to Communists and yellow-skinned people and hippies."[37] And, he might have added, they are akin to homosexuals. Women and gays were referred to interchangeably as the epitome of all that is cowardly, passive, untrustworthy, unclean, and undisciplined. Moreover, homosexuality was more than a negative reference. Homosexual relations are forbidden by military law, and even the suspicion of a homosexual affair usually results in severe punishment. Bob Foley recalls the brutal treatment given an Army trainee at Fort Lewis, Washington, in 1968: "There was a kid that had been accused of being homosexual. So consequently he was followed around by a sergeant and called faggot and queer and everything you can call somebody. And he was kicked, and made to crawl on his hands and knees and police cigarette butts. And he was made to keep his eyes averted downward to the ground and was ridiculed in front of *everyone*. I saw that kid sitting in his bunk one afternoon and he was just rocking back and forth, banging his head against his pillow."[38]

The model of male sexuality offered as a military ideal in boot camp was directly linked to violence. Sexual talk permeated the distribution and handling of weapons. Recruits were instructed to call their weapons rifles, not guns. To emphasize the point, drill instructors might order their men to run around the barracks with their rifle in one hand, their penis in the other, chanting, "This is my rifle, this is my gun; one is for fighting, the other's for fun." The significance of this drill rests on the ironic linking of guns and penises. While the ostensible point is to distinguish between sex and violence, applying the language of weaponry to both does more to associate the two behaviors than to divide them. Rifles are for fighting and penis-"guns" are for fun, but the distinction is so slight (the drill mockingly implies) that most men need special training to understand the difference. Drill instructors repeatedly described war as a substitute for sex or as another form of sex. For example, the drill instructor in *The Short-Timers* ordered his recruits to give their rifles a proper female name (for example, "Charlene"). Then he made the following speech: "This is the only pussy you people are going to get. Your days of finger-banging ol' Mary Jane Rottencrotch through her pretty pink panties are over. You're married to *this* piece, this weapon of iron and wood, and you *will* be faithful."[39]

Thus, drill instructors used sexual, class, regional, and racial slurs not to render those categories irrelevant but to raise the level of aggression and to inculcate attitudes about each of these topics that conformed with dominant military ideology. DIs fostered a military sexual identity based on denunciations of women and homosexuality, demanded obedience to a military class system (trainees had to memorize the chain of command from the president on down), promoted dedication to the national interest (usually defined as militant nationalism), and sought to instill bitter animosity toward a foreign, nonwhite enemy. Directing men to these ends, military training served to legitimize bigotry and inequality founded on race, sex, nationality, and class.

In the first half of basic training, drill instructors fostered a general climate of aggression and anger. Much of it was focused internally. Trainees were encouraged to be angry at themselves, each other, and their drill instructors. As training progressed, however, drill sergeants increasingly sought to direct hostility outward. As American recruits were turned from "maggots" and "shitbirds"—worthless and subhuman—into "professional killers," "real men," "Marines," and "Soldiers," the foreign enemy became the central focus of animosity, the primary repository of all that was base and loathsome: "gooks."

BUILDING UP TO KILL

Midway through basic training you might find yourself near the end of a two-mile run. Just a few weeks ago, the same run brought you to the point of collapse, drenched in sweat and gasping for air; but today your legs feel strong, and you are breathing easily. Glancing around, you notice the other men are equally relaxed, bobbing along in the early morning light. For the first time you pay attention to the way the pine trees look against the sky. You hear birds singing and the echo of distant platoons calling cadence. You can't remember ever feeling so good, so full of energy. The thrill of your own new strength expands in recognition of the enormous collective power surging through the platoon. The others seem to feel it too. Running the final half-mile with no sergeant in sight, the group quickens its pace. Then, spontaneously, someone sings out an opening line of cadence, and everyone joins in, shouting the now familiar words with gusto:

> I wanna be an Airborne Ranger
> I wanna live a life of danger
> I wanna be a fighting man
> I wanna go to Vietnam
>
> I wanna jump out of the sky
> I wanna make the VC die.[40]

The once motley and uncoordinated collection of trainees has begun to think and act as organized units. Platoons that once were unable to keep a straight line or count off in sequence now march with precision, barking their cadences in crisp unison. At this point, the drill instructors began a subtle but crucial shift in their relationship to the men. Of course they still screamed and carried on, ranting, threatening, and punishing; but somehow the harassment lost some of its sting. Underneath, there seemed to be signs of genuine concern, perhaps even a grudging affection. The DIs actually seemed to want their men to succeed. Along with all the putdowns, they began offering some encouragement. Some of the drill instructors even stopped calling the men hogs and maggots. They had become "troopers" (Army) or "my herd" (Marines).

These changes were crucial to the second stage of training, the effort to produce strong, confident fighters. Having been broken down to nothing—their identities stripped, their compliance won, and their aggression heightened—recruits were gradually rebuilt into soldiers. The transition was gradual, but the key turning point, a moment of great significance, came when the trainees began weapons training. Peter Barnes describes the moment well in his book *Pawns.*

> This rebuilding process begins in earnest at about the fourth week, when the platoon moves to the rifle range. Here, for the first time, the recruit feels that he is

> being given something useful to do, that he is acquiring a skill that is of some interest and value. The anxiety and rage that develop during the first weeks of training now have an outlet. The recruit no longer merely absorbs punishment; he has an opportunity to perform. . . . He is tested on his proficiency with the rifle and he passes the test. Suddenly, he is no longer a worthless human being; he has a worthwhile skill for which he is rewarded by a lessening of harassment.[41]

On the rifle range, trainees were ordinarily taught by marksmanship instructors rather than their regular drill instructors. "The sergeants out on the range weren't hard like the drill instructors." They helped the men spot their rounds and adjust their sights. Even the hard drill instructors began to sound like potential allies—stubborn and tough but devoted to making everyone combat-ready. They began to talk about the importance of teamwork and unity, how in combat each man's life depended on everyone in the unit. A failure by one man could result in the death of all. The warning gained extra impact as the recruits began firing live ammunition. Suddenly the prospect of combat felt much more tangible. Of course, the DIs still regarded their men as incompetent, untrustworthy, and untested, and during training drills it was not uncommon for DIs to scream: "YOU'RE DEAD, BIRDBRAIN." "YOU'RE GONNA DIE." "YOU WON'T LAST ONE WEEK IN VIETNAM." Recruits began to listen to their DIs with new ears. After all, many of the sergeants were combat veterans, men who might very well possess lifesaving information.[42]

With these changes came an easing of restrictions. More conversation was allowed among the men. Recruits began to get to know one another, and the drill instructors encouraged them to take pride in their platoon. Harassment of individuals was less frequent and less brutal. Recruits were increasingly addressed as a group. Competitions within the training unit were gradually replaced by competitions against other units. Recruits were still encouraged to enforce conformity within their own units, to put pressure on slackers, but the focus was primarily on unit pride and solidarity. Most men embraced the change, some because they were developing a genuine sense of unity and purpose, others simply because it was such a relief from the torment of the first weeks. One Army trainee put it this way:

> The first four weeks, they work your ass off, they abuse you, they run you from 4:30 in the morning until ten at night. You are so tired, you're so afraid you are going to get abused, that you'll do anything. Then they start to lay off. They'll joke with you, they'll talk to you when you're having smoke breaks, and they tell you, "Now if you work hard there will be less smoke on everybody." And they encourage you to put smoke on the guy who is lagging behind in your unit. The thing is, "We are going to have the best platoon so we won't have to do as much work." Everybody falls in because they are so willing to get out from under this shit that they have been catching. By the end of training they're all gung-ho.[43]

Some men really enjoyed the second half of basic training. For Marine veteran Gene Holiday, the first weeks of basic were deeply traumatic. He felt scared and worthless. A few weeks later, however, his attitude completely changed: "After rifle range I just ate it up. I was having a hell of a lot of fun. I saw such improvement. When they weren't picking on you all the time and you got over that initial fear, it was nice seeing the improvement. Man, you're marching *nice,* you're looking *good,* you're working as a *team,* you really feel that unity, that camaraderie."[44]

As recruits began to feel more confident and less abused, they began to internalize the attitudes of the drill sergeants. Just as rifle training gave recruits an outlet for the intense anxiety and rage that came to a boil in the initial weeks, drill instructors also increasingly aimed their recruits' hostility at external enemies. The most obvious current enemy, of course, was the Viet Cong. Many DIs, however, also directed hostility at a variety of civilian targets. Recruits learned in their first minutes of basic training that civilians were scum and that to become soldiers they would have to eradicate their identities as civilians. As training proceeded, many began to share their instructors' hostility toward civilians. Drill instructors especially denounced "hippies," "draft-dodgers," and "demonstrators." These figures were portrayed as pampered cowards who were simply trying to escape the danger and difficulty of military service. On the other hand, such people were not to be taken lightly. They were "traitors" who posed a threat to the nation and the soldiers themselves. Recruits were encouraged to believe that all protesters supported the Viet

Cong and that the antiwar movement cheered when American troops got wiped out in Vietnam. Sometimes DIs embellished the civilian threat by introducing the specter of the hometown "Jody." A legendary figure in military culture, Jody is a civilian who steals girlfriends and wives while soldiers are away fighting wars. Promoting animosity toward draft evaders and Jodies (sometimes presented as the same figure) was a backhanded way to build support for the war in Vietnam. Somehow fighting in Vietnam would be a way to get back at those who had managed to escape the draft, those who had managed to escape the draft, those who had not shared the abuse of basic training, those who could sit home and criticize the war (and steal girlfriends).[45]

Being trained to suspect civilians has an even darker side in the context of the Vietnam War. The official American mission was to save South Vietnamese civilians from Viet Cong insurgents. However, most civilians either supported the Viet Cong, were themselves part of a local Viet Cong self-defense cadre, or were reluctant to act in opposition to the Viet Cong. How could civilians be saved when so many sided with the enemy? While this dilemma posed a fundamental contradiction to American policy, military training ignored it altogether. Trainees were often told that all Vietnamese were potential enemies, but they received no special training designed to reduce civilian casualties. Of course, given the American military effort to destroy the Viet Cong in heavily populated areas, perhaps no form of training could have done much to protect civilian lives. Yet, if anything, the training received promoted hostility toward noncombatants.

The foreign enemy was variously called Viet Cong,* VC, Victor Charlie,

* "Viet Cong" means "Vietnamese communists." The term was invented by the United States Information Service. It refers to the revolutionaries of *South* Vietnam and was intended to brand all of them communists. The "Viet Cong" called themselves the People's Liberation Armed Forces (PLAF) and called their political leadership the National Liberation Front (NLF). While the leadership of both groups was dominated by communists, the rank and file included many noncommunist members. Also, many Americans mistakenly used the term *Viet Cong* to refer to *all* anti-American forces, whether members of the North Vietnamese Army or South Vietnamese guerrillas. The North Vietnamese Army was referred to by the American command as the NVA. They called themselves the People's Army of Vietnam (PAVN). Sheehan, *Bright Shining Lie,* p. 189.

Charlie, Mr. Charles, Charlie Cong, the Cong, Communists, commies, dinks, slopes, zipperheads, zips, and gooks. The variety of names was telling. After all, the point was not to know the enemy but simply to despise him. At Fort Polk, Louisiana, one of the major training posts for Vietnam-bound infantrymen, billboards were put up around the camp to bolster morale. One billboard featured a painting of an American soldier using the butt of his rifle to knock down a man holding a rifle and wearing black "pajamas" (military slang for the traditional peasant garb that was worn by civilians and Viet Cong alike). Written under the picture in bold letters were the words BONG THE CONG. Another sign showed a man wearing black pajamas and a bamboo hat crouching down in a rice paddy. He is holding a large knife across his chest. This knife provides sufficient evidence that the man is a guerrilla, for above his head is printed, THE ENEMY, and below the picture, VIET CONG. At Fort Dix, one of the signs said, VIET CONG—BREAKFAST OF CHAMPIONS.[46]

Beyond these portrayals of the enemy, trainees learned little more about the Vietnamese revolutionaries and why they were fighting so hard against American forces. As one veteran recalls, "The only thing they told us about the Viet Cong was they were gooks. They were to be killed. Nobody sits around and gives you their historical and cultural background. They're the enemy. Kill, kill, kill. That's what we got in practice. Kill, kill, kill."[47]

RESPONSES BY CLASS

No single factor of a recruit's personality or family background provides a certain measure of how he would respond to military training, but class differences do indicate some rough commonalities of attitude. Middle-class trainees tended to feel socially isolated among the working-class majority. For some this was perceived as a great opportunity: "I loved that part of it. It was great to make friends with people who grew up with such different experiences and outlooks. I probably learned more about life, and about myself, from John [the son of a Pittsburgh steelworker] than I ever learned in college."[48]

Other men, however, felt alienated and lost:

> For a long time, I was lost in the shuffle. It was a shock. I never really got my bearings.
>
> The people in the Army were not intellectuals. Most of them were from working class backgrounds. A lot of them were Southerners. It was my first contact with blacks and they tended to stick together. . . . Blue-collar kids and city kids adjusted very quickly to the Army. Most of the middle-class kids like me didn't fit into what was going on. We hadn't had to do much on our own before. We grew up in a secure environment where a lot of things were taken for granted.[49]

For this man, boot camp brought a keen feeling of lost privilege. He was also convinced that working-class kids adjusted much more easily to military life. Some middle-class men were scornful of the other trainees, thinking them mindless robots. Tim O'Brien expresses this view in his account of basic training at Fort Lewis, Washington.

> The people were boors, a whole horde of boors—trainees and drill sergeants and officers, no difference in kind. In that jungle of robots there could be no hope of finding friendship; no one could understand the brutality of the place. . . . Laughing and talking of hometowns and drag races and twin-cammed engines—all this was for the others. I did not like them. . . . For the other trainees, it came too easy. They did more than adjust well; they thrived on basic training, thinking they were becoming men, joking at the bullyism, getting the drill sergeants to joke along with them. I held my own, not a whisper more. I hated my fellows. . . . I hated the trainees even more than the captors. I learned to march, but I learned alone. . . . I was superior. I made no apologies for believing it.

For O'Brien, the goal of basic training was to preserve himself from brutality and boorishness. He hoped to save some "remnants of conscience and consciousness," some individuality and privacy. But it was not simply the military as an institution that posed a threat to his sense of himself. Indeed, he reserved the greater share of disdain for his fellow trainees who, he believed, could not understand the brutality of the place.[50]

Peter Tauber was not so scathing about the other men in his unit. Like O'Brien, however, he wanted to withhold as much of himself as possible from the military, to do the minimum required and no more, aiming (as O'Brien put it) at a "tranquil mediocrity." Nevertheless, Tauber could not remain entirely distant from the challenges of military training. He began to compare his presence in boot camp to a life lived in material and social hardship. He wondered about his ability to survive without middle-class advantages. He asked himself, "Could I cut it in the world if I hadn't been born lucky? Could I pioneer, or could I even face a Harlem winter's morning? I may never know, so here is where I test myself."

So Tauber, despite his disdain for the military and his convictions against the war, worked hard to get himself in shape and to master the skills introduced during basic training. Though he poked fun at the mindless propaganda and found countless ways to avoid the most onerous aspects of basic training, he needed to prove to himself that he could do whatever the Army required. "It is fine to be a sloppy soldier," Tauber writes, "but another thing not to be *able* to be good when you want to." He discovered, however, that this was a spurious distinction. He could not have it both ways; he could not remain unaffected by the military and still seek to fulfill its requirements. By testing himself on the Army's terms, Tauber found himself changing. He noticed, for example, that he joined the others in ridiculing the few men who did not keep pace with Army drills.[51]

Accounts like these suggest that we approach with some skepticism the claim that working-class men adjusted or acquiesced to basic training more readily than did wealthier trainees. There is certainly little evidence to suggest that middle-class trainees were more likely to fail or resist the basic training regimen, and oral histories suggest that almost everyone found the first weeks of training extremely stressful, bewildering, and dislocating. In fact, the recruits who had the most profound trouble adjusting to basic training were neither middle class nor from stable, working-class families. Rather, from the poorest segment of trainees came the largest portion of military misfits, men who deserted, attempted suicide, were sent to special processing or motivation platoons, or were in some other way unable or unwilling to conform to military standards. These men were commonly high school dropouts from poverty-stricken and broken families. Describing this group, Peter Barnes writes, "In civilian life, most of them have been losers many times over. In the military, this pattern is repeated." According to Baskir and Strauss, the prototypical Army deserter of the Vietnam era "came from a low-income family, often with only one parent in the home. He had an IQ of 90, and dropped out of high school in the tenth grade."[52]

Although there is no clear indication of which social class tended to adjust most easily to basic training, it is probably true that working-class men were more likely to be enthusiastic about military life and more likely to find it a rewarding challenge that offered a genuine feeling of individual accomplishment and collective camaraderie. Mark Sampson, for example, found basic training gave him a fresh chance to succeed in an arena that struck him as more meaningful and egalitarian than school had ever been. He had found high school boring and worthless—"a big joke." In the middle of his senior year he was expelled for hitting one of his teachers. His mother, a factory worker, sent him to live with relatives in another town to finish high school (his father died when Mark was three). In the new high school the yearbook editors of 1966 put these words below Mark's photograph: "Comes new to us this year. Doesn't say much. Makes you wonder what he's thinking. Unexcited."

After high school Mark enlisted. "In basic [training] everybody blended in. No one gave a shit what you did before. No one cared what grades you made in high school or if you were a star athlete or if you belonged to the glee club. It was a whole new set of standards and it seemed like the drill instructors didn't play favorites as much as teachers do."[53]

For Mark, graduation from Marine Corps basic training was far more meaningful and moving than his high school graduation. During the ceremony tears filled his eyes. Afterward his drill instructor praised him, called him a Marine, and offered him a shot of whiskey. Many shared his sense of pride and achievement—men like Richard Deegan who had worried growing up that he would "never amount to anything," or Gene Holiday, whose high school guidance counselor told him he was not "college material." On graduation they stood in full dress uniform, listened to military bands, and heard speeches celebrating their progress and the important contribution they would make to their nation's security. For many, it was the first time in their lives they had received public acknowledgment and praise.

For most trainees, whatever their background, the first weeks of boot camp were a rude shock. Practically everyone would lie in their bunks at night asking themselves over and over, "What the hell am I doing here?" or "What have I gotten myself into?" Still, it is among working-class recruits that one tends to hear the most upbeat accounts of basic training. For example, Todd Dasher, a working-class volunteer from Long Island, went to Army basic training at Fort Jackson, South Carolina. "I graduated really high in my [basic training] class. Basic training was pretty easy I thought. I had a good time. It was the first time I'd ever been away from home, really. I was meeting all kinds of cross-matches of people—Spanish, black, white, American Indian. I thought it was just great."[54]

Few accounts of basic training are as enthusiastic as Todd's, but it is not unusual, especially among working-class men, to hear a similar discounting of the difficulty or brutality of boot camp. For men who grew up in hard-pressed or dangerous circumstances—be it a tough family life, economic hardship, or survival on city streets—boot camp might not seem such a radical break from civilian life. Frank Mathews, the Marine volunteer from Holt, Alabama, described boot camp as "just normal." "I had heard how bad [the Marines] mistreated their troops and I was prepared for the worst. But hell, my daddy had treated me worse than some of those drill sergeants. Boot camp was just normal. The sergeants were rough. I saw a lot of beatings and I took a few. But I got to where I could give out as much as I took and I felt like I toughened up into the Marine Corps attitude."[55]

Update: Army, Navy, and Marine Basic

Tod Ensign

ARMY BASIC TRAINING TODAY

As the excerpt from *Working Class War* emphasizes, Marine basic training has always been more demanding than that of the Army or other service branches. There are at least two reasons for this. First, the mission of the Marine Corps is to operate as highly mobile infantry, sometimes using amphibious tactics, to hold territory for brief periods. Second, the Corps prides itself on the hoary traditions of fierce warriors, as expressed by their mottos, "The Few, the Proud" and "Semper Fi" (always faithful).

During a visit to Army Basic Training at Ft. Jackson, South Carolina, in November 2003, training officers stressed that physical or mental harassment of recruits was no longer allowed. According to them, the abuse depicted in movies such as *Full Metal Jacket* is a thing of the past. However, it was obvious that the drill instructors still enjoy nearly total control over their recruits. They are allowed to order extra calisthenics for recruits who misbehave, and it's impossible to monitor what they say to recruits when they're alone with them. After all, one of the primary goals of basic is to indoctrinate recruits to comply with all orders immediately. They are taught that battlefield survival depends on such obedience.

PFC Jeremy Hinzman, of Rapid City, South Dakota, refused to deploy with his Airborne unit to Iraq in January 2004. When he underwent Basic at Ft. Benning, Georgia, in 2001, his unit marched to the chant, "We're trained to kill and kill we will." He also told a reporter that during bayonet training recruits were taught to scream, "Blood, blood, blood, Sergeant!" when asked, "What makes the green grass grow?"[1] A public affairs NCO at Ft. Jackson confirmed that recruits were taught the same response during bayonet training.

In order to rethink combat training for recruits who will deploy to war, Army Chief of Staff Peter Schoomaker created Task Force Soldier at Ft. Benning after the invasion of Iraq. This task force's report criticized current Army advertising, which gives recruits "non Warrior-like expectations [by] focusing on specialty skills and monetary rewards. New recruits must understand . . . that they will deploy to fight our nation's wars. The Army must develop a marketing . . . plan that sells the Warrior Ethos."[2]

Schoomaker spent most of his Army career leading Special Forces secret operations. He was brought out of retirement by Defense Secretary Rumsfeld to reorganize the Army so that it can fight asymmetrically against a decentralized terrorist network. This background sets him apart from most career officers, who were trained for land warfare using tanks and artillery against conventional military opponents like the Soviet Union or North Korea.[3]

The "Warrior Ethos" was promulgated after the first Persian Gulf War in 1991 in an effort to restore traditional martial values to the Army. In addition, all soldiers are expected to subscribe to seven core values: loyalty, duty, respect, selfless service, honor, integrity, and personal courage.

It appears that the Army essentially operates two kinds of basic training today. The basic training conducted at Ft. Benning, Georgia, is for every soldier who will serve in a combat unit, whether ordinary infantry, Airborne, Rangers, or Special Forces. This all-male training is reputed to be more arduous and demanding than the basic provided at most other Army bases. Ft. Jackson DIs told the author that the "ethics of killing" were only taught at Ft. Benning during the advanced phase of infantry training.

Training to Kill

> "Man is not a killer, but a group is."
>
> —Konrad Lorenz

The American military doesn't discuss it publicly, but it has carefully studied how to best train soldiers to kill other human beings. They began their research with the assumption that nearly all humans will instinctively resist killing other people. The challenge, from the command's point of view, is to mold and shape combat soldiers so that, when ordered, they will overcome this innate reluctance to kill.

On Killing, a revealing book by Dr. Dave Grossman, a military psychologist, explains that the military was disturbed to discover that during World War Two, only 15–20 percent of U.S. soldiers actually fired their weapons during battle. They set out to reform training so that many more GIs would actually fight the enemy. They honed their combat training to ensure that, with the proper conditioning, almost every combat soldier will kill when so ordered.

Grossman reports that during the Vietnam War, the number of GIs firing their weapons rose to between 90–95 percent. He attributes this to desensitization and conditioning techniques which foster a denial defense mechanism during infantry training.

"Every aspect of killing on the battlefield is rehearsed, visualized and conditioned," he writes. "The soldier has rehearsed the process so many times that when he does kill in combat, he is able, at one level, to deny to himself that he's actually killed another human being."[4]

Lifelike targets with human shapes now pop up on the shooting range, simulating as closely as possible battlefield reality, and GIs are taught to quick-fire without thinking.

Another analyst of military training, Ben Shalit, an Israeli military psychologist, has written, "The basic training camp was designed to undermine all past concepts and beliefs of the new recruit, to undermine his civilian values, to change his self-concept, subjugating him entirely to the military system."[5]

To this, Grossman adds, "Basic training is designed to teach that physical aggression is the 'essence of manhood' and that violence is an effective and desireable solution to the problems of the battlefield."[6]

None of this conditioning, however, comes without a price. As Grossman observes, "Societies must learn that their soldiers will have to spend the rest of their lives living with what they have done."[7]

As an economy measure, the Army tries to use the same base for both basic and advanced training. This means that someone assigned to artillery will train only at Ft. Sill, Oklahoma, while someone in armor will undergo training at Ft. Knox, Kentucky. Combat engineers and related jobs will train at Ft. Leonard Wood, Missouri, and GIs slated for administrative jobs will train at Ft. Jackson, South Carolina. This practice tends to isolate combat soldiers from other kinds of GIs. Female GIs undergo Basic only at Ft. Leonard Wood and Ft. Jackson.

President Clinton relaxed the "combat exclusion" rules, which had kept women out of many military jobs. Since then, large numbers of females began entering what had once been all-male bastions. Not surprisingly, this produced considerable friction. When the Army studied how gender integration was affecting training in 1995, many drill instructors complained that they were unprepared to train women, with almost half saying they'd received no training whatsoever.[8] Another military survey of 50,000 female GIs conducted the same year found that 56 percent reported experiencing at least one incident of sexual harassment, ranging from cat-calls to assault and rape, while on active duty.[9]

In 1996, the Army was confronted with a major scandal when female recruits at several training bases reported they'd been sexually harassed or assaulted by drill instructors. Conditions for female recruits were probably the worst at Aberdeen Proving Grounds, where twelve drill instructors and other training staff were eventually found guilty of sexual offenses. One drill sergeant testified that he and five other DIs operated an informal sex ring they called "The Game." This consisted of singling out new recruits as possible partners, pressuring them for sex, and then sharing the names of their conquests with the other DIs.[10]

At the same time, two drill instructors at Ft. Leonard Wood, Missouri, were convicted of multiple sexual offenses with recruits.[11] Eleven female recruits at an Army training base in Dormstadt, Germany, accused three drill instructors of various sexual crimes, including rape and sodomy.[12]

In response to this wave of negative publicity, the Army set up a confidential toll-free hot line which invited female GIs to report sexual harassment.

Over the next seven months, the line logged 8,305 calls, of which 1,354 were referred for criminal investigation. The Army turned off the line in June 1997, claiming that it had "done its job."[13]

Army Boot Camp: A Chronology

Men and women train together in the Army, Navy, and Air Force, while the Marines still segregate the sexes. All services house males and females in separate barracks.

Currently, the Army tries to keep a ratio of no less than one drill instructor for every twenty recruits. About 230–240 recruits are assigned to a Basic Combat Training Battalion for the nine-week course. On average, about one in every twenty recruits fails to complete training and is discharged, mostly because of unanticipated physical problems.

Drill sergeants are selected from career-minded NCOs who have already served six to eight years. About half volunteer and the rest are "detailed" by their commanders. DIs spend a minimum of two years "on the trail" and can extend for an additional year. Because of personnel shortages brought on by the occupation of Iraq, the Army has announced that drill sergeants will now be extended for an additional year of duty, giving many a four-year hitch.[14]

Reception Battalion

When raw recruits arrive at Ft. Jackson, they are sent to a reception battalion where they will spend between four and seven days. Here, they will undergo additional testing, including urinalysis to detect drug use. They fill out paperwork, get their uniforms and other supplies, and receive a general orientation to military life. During this period, recruits are tested to ensure that they meet minimal physical requirements. Male recruits must be able to do thirteen push-ups, seventeen sit-ups, and run a mile in eight and a half minutes. Females are required to do three push-ups, seventeen sit-ups, and complete a mile run in less than ten and a half minutes. Recruits who cannot meet these standards are transferred to the Fitness Training Unit, where they will work on these exercises until they can meet the standards. Recruiters encourage recruits to work on them while they're still in the DEP program prior to reporting to active duty.

Recruits are housed in modern brick "barracks," which the Army calls "star ships." Recently constructed, these air-conditioned dormitories are a far cry from the spartan wooden barracks used during the Vietnam era. Segregated by sex, recruits are housed in open-bay rooms and sleep in bunk beds.

Three Phases of Basic

First Three Weeks: "Red" Phase

The Fort Jackson Guide explains that basic combat training is divided into three phases "to keep soldiers motivated and focused." At the end of each phase, recruits are tested to ensure they meet minimum standards which are required for graduation.[15]

During the "red" phase, whose theme is "patriotism," recruits are introduced to military customs, drill and ceremony, physical training, and the wearing of the uniform. Soldiers are taught the manual of arms and rifle maintenance, plus first aid, radio and TV communications, and are introduced to chemical/biological/nuclear warfare. In the field, they take on the "Victory Tower" exercise, which requires rappelling with ropes and teaches confidence and teamwork.

Second Three Weeks: "White" Phase

The primary focus of this segment is to train recruits to qualify with the M-16 rifle. Recruits train at a state-of-the-art computerized firing range and must score a minimum number of targets to complete Basic. Virtually every recruit eventually qualifies, although some require much retesting. Recruits are taken on several road marches, beginning with three kilometers and ending with fifteen. At the end of this phase, recruits must complete a twenty-four-event "confidence course," which includes wall climbing and scaling a four-story "skyscraper" with ropes. Dexterity, endurance, and teamwork are required to complete the events successfully.

Final Three Weeks: "Blue" Phase

The final period, which the Army dubs the "warrior" phase, culminates with the three-day "Victory Forge" exercise. Recruits are expected to draw on the skills they've learned during Basic. They march with rifles and packs to a remote area, where they set up a defense perimeter and learn to use field equipment. They must demonstrate knowledge of combat skills, defensive tactics, fire and maneuver, land navigation, and radio communication.

One challenging part of this exercise is the night infiltration course, which is called "Omaha Beach" after the D-day landing site in World War Two. Recruits must crawl under barbed wire with their rifles as an M-60 machine gun is fired over their heads. When the author asked what would happen if a panicked recruit stood up, the response was that this had never happened in the range's twenty-year history. Less than two weeks later, the unlikely happened when Pvt. Joseph Jurewic, eighteen, of Altamont Springs, Florida, was struck and killed by machine-gun fire. The range was temporarily shut down, pending an investigation by the Army's Safety Center.[16] Its report found that the accident was caused by "human error." After implementing the center's recommendation that the machine gun be locked into a safe firing position and that two people be in charge of the gun, live-fire exercises were resumed in early March 2004.

The "Warrior Ethos"?

Some military instructors have recently questioned the Army's sincerity about preparing recruits for combat. In a letter to the editor of the *Army Times,* Sgt. First Class Jerry Decker recalled that when a group of Army drill instructors tried to get combatitives class (such as fighting with pugil sticks) approved, their commander turned them down. Decker alleges that training officials were more concerned about avoiding any injury to recruits than in teaching them how to survive in combat. "We will send these brand new soldiers off to Afghanistan or Iraq and hope they're never in a situation where a little bit of training could have saved their lives," he concluded.[17]

NAVY BASIC TRAINING TODAY

Navy Basic, like the Army's, has changed in recent years. All Navy recruits are now trained at the Naval Training Center in Great Lakes, Illinois, which lies just north of Chicago on Lake Michigan. This location means that the winter training is often bitterly cold and snowy.

The base handles about 45,000 recruits a year, with about 9 percent being discharged and sent home for various reasons. Most are discharged because a health problem emerged that was either previously unknown or concealed by the recruit. Because today's recruits are more mature and score higher on aptitude tests than their predecessors, the attrition rate is half of what it was three years ago.

The base graduated its first class of recruits in 1911, but in recent years many new buildings have been constructed. Of particular interest to recruits are the modern dormlike recruit barracks, which are called "ships" by the Navy. Recruits are still housed in large common areas, but amenities such as bathrooms and furniture are completely modern.

Females constitute about 18 percent of entering recruits today. Since 1993, the Navy has been completely gender integrated. Except for sleep and hygiene, both sexes perform all training activities together. However, since men outnumber women more than five to one, there are both integrated and all-male training units.

First-Week "P-Days" (Processing Days)

Every arriving recruit is sent to the Reception Center, Building 1405. There, they spend their first few days processing their records, getting haircuts, and receiving training gear. Each recruit receives a thorough physical exam, which includes a urine test to check for any recent drug use. Recruits are not allowed to keep money nor are they permitted to receive phone calls during boot camp. (They may make one call home to report their arrival.)

During this orientation period, recruits are given a brief introduction to

Navy life, including its core values: honor, courage, and commitment. Part of the process is "the moment of truth," when recruits are asked to reveal anything that might affect their eligibility to serve. Trainers stress that disclosure at this point will have no legal repercussions, although the revelation may bring about immediate discharge. Two common disclosures are hidden criminal convictions or illegal immigrant status; both will result in separation.[18] Recruits also receive their first drill instruction during this week then they are sent to a march exercise field called "the grinder."

Eight Weeks of Basic

After reception week, all recruits are assigned to a Recruit Division, each of which has about eighty-four trainees, who are commanded by three of four Recruit Division Commanders (RDC), Navy lingo for drill instructors. As with the other services, RDCs are forbidden from physically touching recruits. Abusive or obscene language is supposed to be off limits but some Navy recruits told the author that RDCs still use it when they're angry. RDCs have the authority to make recruits perform extra calisthenics as punishment for poor performance or misbehavior. Recruits reported that male recruits are more likely than females to be given individual training exercise (ITE). They also reported instances when ITE was imposed on a whole group of recruits because of misconduct by one recruit.

Daily Routine of a Recruit Division

Recruits are awakened at 5:00 AM. Following personal hygiene and breakfast, they participate in an hour of physical training, which includes stretching, calisthenics, and some running. Then they assemble for a "colors" ceremony, during which the American flag is raised in the morning (and later lowered at sunset).

Most of the day is spent in the classroom, where a wide range of subjects are taught in forty-minute segments. Course material ranges from Chain of Command to Damage Control to Survival at Sea. Where appropriate, classes are augmented with physical training where the actual equipment is used under simulated conditions.

Since most Navy personnel serve aboard ships, water-safety training is a priority. According to a swimming instructor, while most recruits eventually meet the minimum requirements for swimming, there are always a few who are discharged because of a deep-seated fear of water.

Weapons Training

Until 1998, Navy recruits marched, drilled, and trained with M-16 rifles just like recruits in the other branches. That year, however, the command decided to dispense with Navywide rifle training. This has reduced the cost of weapons training and has eliminated live-fire injuries, although some recruits have complained that it removes an essential part of the military experience. A new state-of-the-art weapons facility has since been opened on base where recruits are taught the rudiments of two weapons used aboard ship, the 12-gauge shotgun and the 9mm pistol.[19]

When asked how the Navy prepared recruits to take human life, Lt. Coxe responded, "We don't have to foster a 'kill or be killed' mentality like the Army or Marines. We're not front line like they are." The public affairs NCO, JO 1st Class James R. Stilipec, added, "We don't kill up close and personal, so we don't train for it."

Fighting Fires

Since fire is a special hazard aboard a ship, recruits are given intensive training in a Fire Fighting Training Unit spread over parts of five days. The first session teaches the fundamentals of fire damage control, including identifying the nature of a fire and handling pumps to counteract flooding. On the second day, recruits are taught to use breathing apparatus and distinguish the various types of fires. The third day is devoted to practicing with portable extinguishers and an introduction to chemical/biological/radiological weapons. On the fourth day, recruits work as shipboard fire teams and use the fire hose. On the last day, they put on full battle gear, including oxygen breathing apparatus (OBA).

Confronting Fear: The Confidence Course

The "Bluejacket's Manual" summarizes the philosophy behind this phase of basic: "In modern warfare, it is possible that the enemy may [use] unconventional weapons. In the Navy these are called CBR weapons, which stands for chemical, biological or radiological. . . . While these weapons are very different in some ways, many of the defensive measures employed against them are the same. In the event of a CBR attack, the [ship's] crew can do a great deal to minimize casualties and damage."[20]

The recruits are shown how to use the MCU-2p gas mask, which contains microfilters that will protect against almost any airborne pathogen or chemical agent. If a sailor wears a Chemical Protective Outergarment (CPO), an Oxygen Breathing Apparatus (OBA), and a gas mask, he or she can work around deadly gases for up to six hours. Each recruit practices putting on both the mask and CPO suit.

On test day, the recruits march across the base to the Confidence Chamber where they will experience exposure to poisonous gas, albeit briefly. First, recruits select a gas mask, sized small, medium, or large. Then they file into the gas chamber where they form columns of fifteen, five or six rows deep. While the recruits stand at attention with their masks on, an RDC places two CS tear gas pellets on a burner. Immediately, the room fills with noxious, but nonlethal, gas. After a few minutes, the recruits are required to take off their masks when so ordered by the RDC and then recite their names and division numbers. They then must calmly exit the chamber one by one, with some stopping by the sinks to spit or throw up.

CS gas is described as a "lachrymotor irritant" and is named for Messers. Corson and Stoughton who invented it in 1928. It is quite a bit more noxious than its name suggests. In fact, today its use in warfare is banned in over 100 countries, including the U.S. Its manufacturer warns against using it indoors and an Army manual on civil disturbances states that "persons reacting to CS are incapable of exercising organized actions."[21]

According to one RDC, Petty Officer Dan Kent, there are an average of five deaths at Great Lakes each year, mostly from undiagnosed medical ailments that flare up during PT.[22]

Battle Stations: The Mother of All Tests

Each recruit must successfully complete the all-night, multievent course called Battle Stations. A speech by one of the event's facilitators provides an overview: "Your classes have focused on the technical knowledge and the discipline and teamwork has steadily increased as you went along. Tonight is your call to arms! In a few short weeks, you will be on station. Tonight you must put yourself in the placc of sailors who are already on station and fight the enemy!"

Battle Stations is broken down into a series of exercises that require recruits to work as a team to solve various problems. Each event is loosely based on a significant incident in naval history to lend authenticity.

- USS *Holland:* in 1992 experienced a spill of hazardous material, which spread into berthing areas of the ship. The task is for recruits to form fire parties to locate any crew members who've been overcome by fumes.
- USS *Forrestal:* a bomb exploded on its flight deck in 1967, causing a fire that eventually killed 134 sailors and injured hundreds more. Recruits must work together to evacuate the ship while passing through a red-hot bulkhead. Teamwork is essential if they are to escape the burning ship.
- USS *Tripoli:* was clearing mines during the first Gulf War when it hit a mine that knocked out all power and began to flood the ship's ammo magazine. In this exercise, recruits are required to organize themselves to rapidly unload naval shells before they explode.
- USS *Oklahoma:* was hit during the Japanese attack on Pearl Harbor in 1941. The challenge here is to evacuate injured sailors using special stretchers.
- USS *Stark:* was hit by an Exocet missile in the Persian Gulf during the Iran-Iraq war. The explosion killed thirty-seven sailors and the ship came close to sinking. Recruits suit up in damage control equipment, OBA masks, flash-protection hoods, and gloves and form into six fire-fighting parties. They then must devise a plan to fight the fire, using fire hoses and other equipment.

If a recruit accumulates three "strikes" for making significant errors during the exercise, he or she is removed from Battle Stations and required to begin again, after a two-day rest. After a long night of these exercises, recruits take a short breather and then reassemble for their "Navy ball cap" ceremony. The exhausted sailors stand at attention as they are congratulated by their RDCs and commissioned officers. They watch several short patriotic videos. In one, a sailor says directly to the camera, "No one's going to come here and tell my kids what to do or take their freedom away." As the ceremony ends with the playing of Lee Greenwood's "God Bless the USA," some of the recruits have tears in their eyes. At this point they are given their "Navy ball" caps, which denote that they are now sailors.

MARINE CORPS BASIC TRAINING TODAY

The goal of Marine Corps training is still to turn recruits into elite combat fighters. In the preface to his *Into the Crucible,* James B. Woulfe writes that "there is nothing special about those who enlist in our Corps." Woulfe believes that it's Marine boot camp that makes the average person a battle-ready Marine.[23] The Corps encourages Marines to think of themselves as a special breed. From the beginning, Marines are taught that if they complete training they will join an elite group as "one of the few, the proud." *Semper Fidelis!* Always faithful and bound to one's brothers.[24] This is the Corps' highest ideal.

Turning the "Average" Person into a Marine

Marine recruit training has long been infamous for its toughness, which some would call brutality. The Corps considers its training methods appropriate given its primary mission. "Marines are expected to the *most* ready when the nation is the *least* ready," is how *Into the Crucible* describes it.[25] The Marines are trained as the landing party, which establishes the beachhead before other forces arrive. Typically, they are the first troops on the ground. Marine units rotate as "air contingency forces" (ACF). These units are ready to deploy anywhere in the world within sixteen hours of an alert. Once in a combat zone, they are equipped to fight without relief for up to forty-eight hours.

While the Corps was created in 1775 to assist the Navy, it didn't institute formal recruit training until 1911. Until the mid-1950s it wasn't unusual to assign the best of a group of recruits who'd just graduated boot camp to train the next group of recruits. While they may have excelled at being trained, this didn't mean they were adept at training others. Also, having just undergone a grueling experience may have made them more prone to sadistic practices than professional trainers would be.

The Corps suffered its worst training accident in 1956 while drill instructors, not recruits, were in charge. Six recruits drowned when they were ordered into a rain-swollen river. An investigation followed and reforms were instituted. As with the other branches, recruits still occasionally die, mostly because of undisclosed medical problems. In 1975, a recruit was beaten to death by fellow recruits during pugil-stick training. Pugil sticks are padded at one end to resemble rifles with bayonets. Today, the Army forbids such "combative" training, although it continues in the Marine Corps.

The Corps' response to these training problems was to create, in 1975, a drill-instructor training course, which lasts three months. They also improved the screening of drill instructors, seeking to weed out any with financial, marital, or other personal problems. In recent years, the average drill instructor has been twenty-nine years old, with about ten years of Marine service, and holds the rank of Staff Sergeant or Sergeant. Another book on Marine training observed, "The DI's are good but aren't the cream of the NCOs. The very best are shipped off to recruiting duty. . . . The DI is generally from the second tier—somewhere in the top 20–30% of the [Corps]. To make a twenty year career (and a pension) an enlisted Marine must either do recruiting duty or a tour as a DI."[26]

The DIs take recruits through eleven weeks of Basic. Because of its combat mission, every recruit must qualify on his or her rifle. Those who fail, after several attempts, are discharged. The physical training standards are also considerably more difficult than the other services. For example, twenty dead-hang pull-ups, one hundred crunches in two minutes, and a three-mile run in less than eighteen minutes are required of recruits.

In the Army, only those who are assigned to the infantry take advanced training, whereas in the Marines all graduates of Basic return for an additional two and a half weeks of Marine Combat Training. During this course, they spend fourteen continuous days in the field, learning to operate as part of a rifle squad, using a variety of infantry weapons.

During World War Two, the Marine Corps Women's Reserves served as support units. By 1975, women filled a number of Marine jobs, except ground combat, although they only constitute 5 percent of total force. Unlike the other branches, women Marines still train in gender-segregated brigades.

One of the key elements of Corps training is to get the recruit off balance and teach him or her to respond appropriately. In the past, DIs were notorious for using verbal abuse and cursing to achieve this effect. Now that foul language has become commonplace throughout American society, it no longer intimidates or has any shock value and has been discontinued. However, unlike the other branches, the Corps doesn't claim to have curtailed such language for reasons of "political correctness."

Another training technique is "incentive training" (IT) which consists of abruptly ordering recruits to perform extra PT. This is an immediate consequence when a recruit fails to obey a standing order. For example, recruits are told not to salute their officers if they are in a combat setting. If a recruit forgets and automatically salutes, punishment exercise is imposed to cause enough suffering to help reinforce the rule.

Recruits are regularly thrown off balance in an effort to teach them to control their emotions. Courage is described not as the absence of fear but as the ability to control that emotion. Even in a noncombat situation, great emotional control may be required of soldiers. For instance, a Marine could be overseeing food distribution in a hostile civilian setting and be assaulted by rock or bottle throwers. How the Marine reacts could determine whether the food distribution succeeds or dissolves into violence and chaos. In the modern world of the ubiquitous TV camera, that Marine's loss of control could be widely televised and even affect America's foreign relations. On the other hand, in combat, an immediate response is needed. There is no time to weigh a decision, as the first fifteen seconds of an attack can determine the outcome.

"Instant obedience to orders—that's what we're shooting for," Drill Sergeant Cortez Brown recently told a reporter. "You miss up, you mess up, but don't lose your military bearing. That's a sign of weakness."[27]

The Crucible: A Grueling Ordeal[28]

Before a recruit can become a Marine, the Crucible must be mastered. While it requires recruits to demonstrate physical dexterity and endurance, it teaches that although physical demands may be extreme, they're still secondary to the emotional challenges.

The Crucible exercise lasts two days and two nights for a total of fifty-four hours. During this period, recruits must pass twelve obstacles or warrior stations. Each warrior station is named for a Marine who won a Medal of Honor for exceptional bravery. At each station, a DI explains what the named Marine did to win his or her medal—often posthumously.

The DI picks a recruit leader for each warrior station and then explains the specific rules for passage. The DI's role changes at this point from being the omnipotent leader to a role model. Before entering the Crucible, recruits are told to stop addressing officers as "Sir" and instead address them by rank. This is to ensure that a Marine does not fear, but respects, an officer. Fear of a superior officer cannot compete with the fear of death, so Marines are trained to respond to orders from leadership that they trust.

Into the Crucible

At the first obstacle, recruits are told that they are in the basement of an abandoned building when enemy fire causes the building to collapse. There are no casualties, but the only escape route is through damaged ventilation ducts, represented by a web of rope. Each recruit must get his or her gear and rifle through the web without touching it within a specific time period. If the web is touched, the whole team starts over. Recruits must go through the web feet first, and each hole in the web can only be used once.

The recruit team leader confers with the other recruits, then informs the DI of their plan. Once through the obstacle, pass or fail, there is a debriefing when the recruits are asked what they did well, what needs work, and why. The DI offers lessons learned from the obstacle and relates it to the actions of the Medal of Honor winner for whom it is named.

Lessons of the warrior stations include:

- Rely on your brothers, trusting them to catch you if you fail, and to watch your back because you can't.
- Assist each member of the team for the benefit of the whole team.
- Recognize that individuals on the team have both strengths and weaknesses.
- Be committed to completing the task. This builds a spirit of determination and mastery of the arts of war. Sometimes a team completes an obstacle on the first attempt; other times it takes many tries before it accomplishes this.
- Fatigue affects decision making.[29]

Sometimes the recruits are deliberately put into a no-win situation. This is to teach them to be faithful to each other, no matter what the outcome, even if there is no way through. Another Crucible obstacle involves passing through a tire that represents a porthole on a sinking ship. How does the last team member get out when no one remains to lift him up to the porthole/tire? Some obstacles require more thinking and planning than others, but they all require teamwork.

The recruits must complete other courses as they do the twelve warrior stations. Between stations, recruits must hike hilly terrain carrying forty-pound packs, plus a load bearing vest, cartridge belt, ammo pouch, canteen, and rifle. They must complete the fifty-four-hour course with only two and a half Meals Ready to Eat (MREs) and a few hours' sleep.

For example, between stations 3 and 4 there is a bayonet assault course, where recruits fix bayonets and then crawl under wire, through culverts, and scale logs. This is immediately followed by a one-and-a-half-mile hike that features more barbed-wire obstacles and a sprinkler system that wets them thoroughly and ensures that they crawl through mud. They must also drag twenty-pound ammo cans and forty-pound crates through the mud. Without a rest, they proceed to the next course, which features hundreds of feet of barbed wire, water, and mud. To add to the difficulty, recruits are also required to drag a "casualty" with them. They are then given time to clean their weapons—their first priority—but not necessarily time to eat.

When recruits reach station 9 they have completed one-third of the course, with three hours to go. Having hiked fifteen miles, they are famished, soaked with sweat and mud with feet badly blistered. They sit in the cold, waiting to begin the night-infiltration course. This is followed by a three-mile hike to their bivouac area, where they must again clean their weapons before they're allowed to sleep.

The combat course is located between stations 11 and 12. This course is designed to simulate actual combat. Here, the recruits must crawl over logs while carrying a stretcher containing a ninety-pound "casualty." After climbing a twenty-foot-high rope, they hike three miles carrying all their gear. They are given the mission of reinforcing part of their platoon, so they move quickly into positions and fire at targets with live ammunition. Some recruits are designated as "casualties," and they scream in pain to add to the stress. These cases then must be evacuated to another location a mile away. This is followed by close combat in which two-person teams fight each other with pugil sticks. When someone is "killed," the surviving partner must then battle the opposing team alone. Each recruit is exhausted by having fought three different bouts.

After this, another hike brings the recruits to the reaction course, which requires them to again think about how to complete tasks. They must advance across a minefield and through an enemy barricade, hauling heavy equipment. Next, they cross a river using a damaged bridge, where there are still undetonated charges. After this they must set explosives in a booby-trapped area, where "enemy" patrols move into the area every twenty minutes. Finally, they cross another river using the rubble of a destroyed bridge. At each point, the recruits must actively work as a team—individual efforts would fail.

Completing the combat course, the recruits again hike, now in daylight, to their final station. After this, they arrive at the confidence course, which forces them to confront and manage fear. They are now thirty-seven hours into the Crucible, having already marched twenty-six miles. They are exhausted and hungry, not to mention filthy, aching, and emotionally stressed. They push on.

On the confidence course they climb a ladder with rungs spaced three to four feet apart, hauling heavy radio batteries to the top. There, they encounter vertical beams slanted outward, making it almost impossible to climb further without the help of teammates. At the top, they find a "casualty," whom they must take with them as they climb down a net. The last obstacle is a construction of crossed logs rising at a 45-degree angle. The recruits must go under one log and over the next to the top, dragging ammunition cans with them. This is followed by another reaction course with two more obstacles. Once finished, the recruits hike one and a half miles to another bivouac point, where they again clean their weapons. Here, medical personnel evaluate them to ensure they are healthy enough to continue. Those pulled from the group will start over later with another platoon.

When darkness falls, the men begin a one-and-a-half-mile resupply hike. They carry heavy ammunition back to their bivouac site, taking turns with the heavier loads. Then squads are allowed to sleep four hours, except the squad on guard duty, which will sleep only three. As a bedtime story, the DI tells them that a recruit in another platoon has been caught stealing food and is being charged under military law. He will be recommended for immediate discharge. Moral: a Marine does not steal.

After four hours' sleep, the recruits wake for their final test. The famous World War Two image of victorious Marines planting the flag on Mount Suribachi on Iwo Jima is a Marine icon, so the last obstacle takes it name. The recruits struggle up this hill, helping each other reach the top. After a rest, the company is called to attention, a prayer is read, and the battalion's top enlisted NCO addresses them, for the first time, as Marines. Their transformation is complete.

The Marine Corps, like the other services today, recognizes that in addition to combat training, soldiers must be taught to think creatively. A recent *Wall*

Street Journal article reports that in preparing for their return to Iraq, Marines are being taught to ask questions first and shoot second, at least in civilian areas. As Colonel Craig Tucker explained, "It's going to be a thinking man's war and the thinking man is going to be squad leader." Marines are being trained to distinguish friend from foe, how to fight in a civilian setting, and how to defuse politically charged situations.[30]

While military veterans sometimes complain that the military has softened boot camp to accommodate the "Y" Generation, no one is likely to say this about the Marines.

3

Voices from Iraq: Letters from GIs and Family Members

These poignant letters were drawn from a wide range of sources. In some cases they first appeared on the Web sites of grieving families who have lost their children to this war. These were then picked up by other Web sites and in some cases spread around the world. Others were written out of a strong desire to make a public protest against this illegal war. In two cases, Camilo Mejia and Peggy O'Rourke, the letters were written especially for this book.

While the letters express differing points of view about the war, all of them convey a deep sense of pain and loss. Reading the letters of young innocents like Rachel Bosveld or Holly McGeogh is particularly painful since they were clearly just starting to discover themselves as adults when they were killed. Their short notes brought to my mind the diary of Anne Frank.

If there is any justice in this world, George Bush and his clique must someday be called to account for all the Iraqi and American lives they've destroyed in this brutal and unnecessary war.

Three letters from **PFC Rachel K. Bosveld,** *of Oshkosh, WI. She was killed in a mortar attack, October 26, 2003. She was the first female soldier from Wisconsin to die. RIP.*

Mom, October 14, 2003

I'm doing fine. Yes, I did get into a sort of accident, if that's what you call it. We were hit by an IED or RPG which set our truck on fire because it struck the battery and fuel line. My neck and shoulder were pretty banged up for about two weeks. I lost my hearing in my left ear for a few weeks. I've been through my share of explosives. I'm sending pictures home to be developed of my truck (or what's left of it). I took a few of me with the truck, so you can all see that I'm O.K.

It's still pretty warm during the day, but it gets very chilly at night. Could you try and find one of my hooded sweatshirts to send to me?

Right now I'm soaking my feet. My feet take a beating in these boots. My feet are all cut up and sore . . . Feels soooooo good now, anyway. I guess I haven't been taking as good care of myself this month. We have a physical training test I'm getting ready for. This month and last we haven't gotten much time to do P.T. So I work, sleep, work, P.T., work—oh, and eat.

Well Mom, my 20 minute soak is up. Take care. I love you. Don't worry so much about me, Mom, my intuition has already saved a few lives around here, and my own as well.

Monday October 20, 2003

I'm doing great this week. Sure I've dodged lots of bullets and such, gotten little to no sleep and eaten nasty food, but I'm doing great.

I got to drive a tank! I got a tour, learned how to operate everything, load everything and I got to DRIVE IT! I was tooth from ear to ear!

I'm getting a Purple Heart for the accident, along with eight other people in my platoon . . .

Someone is always getting injured here. There have been no fatalities so far in my company, though, just a lot of injuries.

So, how are you? Eighteen days until my birthday! I can't wait! No one probably even knows when it is over here.

Well, bye for now, just wanted to let you know I'm OK and I miss you.

I love you,

Rachel

Dear Craig,

This is a story I only want to write once, so I'm sending it to you, in faith that you will share it with Mom and Dad and whomever else you wish.

A few days ago, the 12th of September around 0500 to be exact, I and five others were patrolling the area of our Iraqi Police station. It was a quiet evening, probably too quiet. My vehicle was the lead vehicle in our two-vehicle convoy. We were hit by an armor piercing RPG [rocket-propelled grenade]. It must have struck our fuel line because almost instantly our entire vehicle was in flames. There was fire and smoke everywhere. At first we thought we were hit by an IED [improvised explosive device]. It was loud, there was shouting, my teamleader's seat was on fire. I found my seatbelt but it was stuck. Damn it, I knew I shouldn't have worn it. I told myself several times that it would be the death of me. Not panicking, I continued to work at getting it loose.

The fire grew, my teamleader's beside me yelling something. He couldn't [get] his door [open] pleading for me to hurry. Where's my gunner? Pulling, pushing, yes, finally! Okay, the door. Open the door. Just my luck, now the door's stuck. First the seatbelt and now this. More shouting. Seems so far away, like a voice at the end of a tunnel. Got to get the door open or we're going to die. Where's my gunner?! I close my eyes and throw myself into the door. Still doesn't budge. This is it. This [is] how I'm going to die!
No! I open my eyes and throw myself once more. Oh thank God, it opened.

I'm stuck. My seatbelt's all wrapped up in my LBV [load-bearing vest]. Hurry, I gotta hurry. Once we're out, we stop to see if we're all OK. Everything's a blur. Now what? What was that? Someone's shooting at us. Go, go, go! No rifle, it's in the truck. Go, go. Back at the station we get another unit to escort us to a military medical facility. No one got shot but the gunner's bleeding. Gotta hurry, I'm okay, right.

I didn't really plan to write it that way. You should see the remains of our truck. Bagby, my gunner, had two shrapnel wounds. My team leader has one. I have none. Though I did pop my shoulder trying to get the door open. It's badly bruised and my neck's pretty stiff. I have had a constant headache since then. I throw up everything I eat. I'll be sore stiff and bruised for awhile. I lost all hearing in my left ear. Should come back in about seven days. Didn't pop my eardrums or anything. They put me on some meds that relax my muscles, so I sleep about 16 hours of the 24 hour day. I want you all to know that I'm okay.

Fortunately, two days prior to the attack, we got our armored vehicle back. Had we been in our soft shell, we'd be dead. Miracles do happen. That truck has a total of two weeks and two days of this war, but it saved our lives.

Whoever did it was there and saw us walk away from it. They won't win. After it happened, an informer went into the IP station and said there had been a planned attack because of Sept. 11th. He directed them to 3 other IEDs on the same road. We'd have been hit, no matter what that night.

I was able to get pictures of our truck. Everything was melted or destroyed. When they lifted it to put it on a flat bed to bring it back for inventory and investigation, you could see a perfectly shaped rectangle where the frame melted to the road. They found some melted remains of my M-4 [rifle] barrel, NODs [night observation devices] and something really strange. I had a personal bag with a notebook in it. Everything in the truck was ruined except for my notebook. With a letter to Dad, one for Mom and one to Craig and Family. Strange, huh? Unfortunately, when they found the notebook they threw it away, but it was still strange. Everything in the vehicle was melted or charred. Maybe it's a sign telling me how many great things I have.

Well, that's all for now. Oh, so that you aren't worrying (Mom) the Commander is giving us his vehicle to use whenever we go out on mission. I've been issued another M-4 and will soon be getting issued everything else I lost. Oh, and Mom, your package had great timing, my cd player and cds were burned. Thank you for all your love and support, Love PFC Rachel Bosveld

"I'm Back from Iraq: A quick update"
***Michael McKenzie** is a Gulf War Army veteran (1990–91), from Bloomfield, NJ.*

Hello Everyone, December 11, 2003

Well I'm back from my second trip to Iraq (the first was in Gulf War I or as I say "the 1st ground campaign of the current war"), but this time I made it to Baghdad. The week was something I find words cannot describe. It was both exhilarating and sad. I met wonderful people almost all of whom are experiencing great suffering. Many are brave people who are struggling to shape their future. In fact I met many nonviolent Iraqi patriots.

Saddam Hussein was a monster; of this there is no doubt. Most every Iraqi I asked said they were happy to be rid of him. Many thanked the U.S. for liberating them from the regime. But others feel that there is no difference between Saddam and U.S. occupation. For example, I visited a refugee camp in Baghdad, a tent village of sorts, of about 50 Palestinian families. Some said they see little difference. They could not own land or a car nor have access to quality education under and no citizenship under Saddam but he never bothered them. They find themselves in the same position today.

So while most are happy to be rid of Saddam and many thank the U.S., most all are unhappy with the current state of affairs and want immediate changes. Security is high on the list of priorities. Many Iraqis fear being harmed by criminals. They told me there was less crime under Saddam. Today there is not enough law and order. People are afraid to walk the streets at night and guns are everywhere. I'm not sure why, but an Iraqi actually showed me a gun he had hidden under his sweater. The fear of crime is equaled or surpassed by the fear of U.S. soldiers: our sons, daughters and friends or at least my friends and possibly my son.

Once again, while most Iraqis told me they are happy and grateful to be rid of Saddam they do not want occupation. They want the U.S. troops out of Baghdad streets and Iraqis to maintain security. Our troops are trained to be soldiers not police officers. They do not know how to treat the civilian population. They use overwhelming force when extreme force may be all that is necessary. They shoot before thinking and innocent people are hurt or die including children. Amazingly most of the people to whom I talked are not angry with the individual soldier. They are angry with our government. I was told that our leadership does not see an Iraqi life as equal to a U.S. soldier's life. Many people said that there are two victims, the soldier and the Iraqi. I was told to tell the American people that U.S. soldiers' and Iraqis' lives are equally important. One person stated that Iraqis hurt every time a U.S. soldier is harmed and they hurt when a soldier abuses one of them.

If one can rank these issues, second is restoration of the infrastructure. Most of the Iraqis to whom I spoke said the U.S. must deliver on it[s] promises. We (the U.S.) must fix what we have broken. Economic, political and social structures must be repaired. Hospitals do not [have] enough medical supplies. The electricity goes out 3 to 4 times a day, sometimes for hours at a time. To adapt people have pooled money to buy generators and agree to the number of lights that can be used per family when using generator power. Unemployment is extremely high and many times people are paid 2 to 3 months late. Iraqi business people are struggling to get back on their feet. Local contractors' access to reconstruction contracts is limited. People spend 6 to twelve hours in gas lines a mile or more long. Taxi drivers are missing a day of work just to fill up their cars. Off market (usually called black market) gas is sold less than 100 meters away. One Iraqi said to us, "We are the people of oil, how can this being happening?"

Third, an overwhelming majority of people to whom I spoke want the occupation to end quickly. These Iraqis want to run their country. Over and over I was told that while they are grateful for the liberation, they do not like occupation. Many are afraid of civil war, but others believe the Iraqi people will pull together and can handle their affairs right now. So the people will pull together and can handle their affairs right now. So the timetable may not be uniform, but the overwhelming consensus is that the U.S. needs to leave as soon as possible and they mean sooner than later. We can then return as civilian guest. The U.S. and Iraq should be friends.

Finally the troops we saw were very happy to see us. We gave them full support and told them we are working to bring them home. They are between a rock and a hard place.

What good is happening in Iraq? Well I stayed in a decent hotel with laundry service and had no problems taking a warm low water pressure shower. I ate good food in open restaurants. Commerce is happening on the streets. TVs, VCRs, washers and other goods are available. I bought a few items my last night on a street of shops and outdoor vendors. The same suitcase shops exist in Baghdad and New York. New cars are coming in from Jordan and Syria. There has been a boom on satellite dishes and access to the Internet. Human rights organizations and political parties are forming to include women organizations. Discussion and protest is alive. Democracy of some sort has sprouted. Self-determination is in the air.

But in my eyes the bad is too high a price to pay for the good. Due to the administration's poor planning and disrespect for the opinions of the Iraqis far too many U.S. troops and Iraqis are being injured (both physically and psychologically) and dying. If Bush thinks he is winning the peace I believe he is mistaken. I say again, soldiers are not police. They are trained to use overwhelming force. The kind of force used against opposing armies, not civilian populations. Our leadership has put our soldiers in a no win situation. The current state of affairs is creating new resistance fighters and the cycle of violence and suffering begins anew.

Of course there is a lot more that I will share over the next month through video and pictures so that you may see for yourself the stories shared with us. Thank you for your support. It is greatly appreciated. Take care and you will hear from me soon.

Open letter from ***Dale C. Jones.***

January 26, 2004

Like many of you I have a son in Iraq. A week ago I drove 580 miles to Fort Riley to see him for a couple of days before he shipped out. Less than a month before he had returned from a 2 year tour of duty in Europe which included being a scout radio man in Kosovo. As a veteran myself, I have never seen morale this bad since the Vietnam war. Every other car seemed to have a number of "bring them home" stickers and ribbons. Over

85% of the base is deployed. I just ordered 3 stickers for both my car and my sister's.

I spent '62 to '65 serving with the security forces in the Far East. I remember when they came to us in early 1963 and asked us to volunteer to join a "funny little war in a funny little country that would be over in six months." I had a top secret clearance and in the following years I worked on the biweekly reports going to the joint chiefs of staff and the president. I would see one thing in the reports and hear the President claim the opposite a few days later. We were being systematically lied to then and are being lied to again.

This administration claims to be backing the troops but my son tells me they have no ceramic plates for their bulletproof vest[s] which don't work worth a damn without them. Military families have had their support systems and financing cut, a registered vet has to wait six months for an appointment at the VA, and I nearly died because they waited 13 months to me a glucose tolerance test. When I showed up in the emergency room hours away from death, they asked me if I knew I had diabetes. This was after 13 months of telling them I had [had] it. The doctors at the VA are good, but they are under-funded and overworked. Guess it is more important to give tax breaks to George's buddies.

The sad thing is that I am now thinking maybe we will be lucky, maybe my son will just get wounded.

Dale C. Jones

New Year's Eve letter (2003) from ***Fernando Suarez del Solar,*** *father of Marine Jesus Suarez, killed in action in Iraq, March 27, 2003. RIP.*

Another year ends today, a year full of important events in the lives of the American people and especially many Latino families like mine. Exactly one year ago my entire family was gathered together, ready to enjoy a meal prepared by my wife and daughters. My son, Jesus, was so happy with his wife and their son Erick. Everyone sat around the table and we counted the

12 tollings of the bell and ate the traditional 12 grapes, hoping that 2003 would be full of joy, peace, love, and prosperity for all. We embraced and wished each other much happiness for 2003. I recall that my daughter Olivia told me, "Dad, you will have many opportunities this year," and Jesus told me, "Father, Thank you for educating me. I am a Marine now and I hope to do well so that you will be proud of me." I answered him that I had always been proud of him and that I hoped he would achieve his goals together with his wife and son. And so that terrible year began with much hope for the entire family and for the American people. February arrived with its rumors of war and with the stubbornness and inflexibility of Mr. Bush who insisted on attacking Iraq. The UN could not use its authority nor the rule of law to stop him and so the world waited with fear as Bush declared that the regime in Iraq possessed weapons of mass destruction. On the fifth of February, Jesus bid us farewell and headed towards his destiny in the faraway lands of Iraq. As he said goodbye we embraced alone outside in the driveway of our home. It was difficult for me to hold back my tears but he was optimistic and with great clarity he told me, "Father, do not fear, nothing will happen to me, we are well trained and well prepared. But if something does happen please take care of my son and educate him as you did me."

March nineteenth arrived and American troops began their offensive against Iraq. The war began without the support of the UN, without the support of the American people, without the support of the world community—a war started by Mr. Bush who lied to the American people and to the world community. Mr. Bush insisted that Iraq was a threat to the U.S. and the whole world and unfortunately many believed him and so the deaths began. On March 27 a young Mexican boy fell, full of hopes and dreams, deceived by the government, a good boy who had more important work ahead with a son to love, raise and educate. Jesus Alberto Suarez del Solar Navarro, the Aztec Warrior, died because of the negligence of the U.S. military command in Iraq. A U.S. cluster bomb had been dropped the night before but Delta Company was not advised and so the tragedy took place and two hours passed before helicopters could evacuate him. He did not die alone but rather he died with his friends, his brothers, and their love surrounding him. He died free of hate and in peace.

April 11 arrived—the day the Aztec Warrior was sowed, yes sowed because he is a seed of peace for future generations. We all wept because of his loss and his absence but his mother suffers the most, she who bore him, took care of him when he was ill, who taught him to respect and to love us. She is the one who has suffered the most.

And the rest of 2003 passed by and many more brave American youth have died and with them their dreams until we have almost reached 500 dead American troops and thousands and thousands of innocent Iraqis.

December 4 arrived, my grandson's birthday, and I found myself in the exact same place in Iraq where my Aztec Warrior fell. I placed a crucifix, said a prayer, and gathered the earth where his blood ran. I fulfilled my promise to my wife that I would find the sacred spot. During my time in Iraq I could see and witness that my son was right when he said that the children of Iraq were the ones who really needed our help. And I could witness the shortages of medicine as I visited the hospitals the lack of economic assistance provided by the Bush administration. In the schools I could see that the children were eager to learn but do not have what they needed since the Bush administration offers them nothing. I could feel it in the streets of Baghdad where shoeless children whose parents died in the war offered me a smile in exchange for a friendly word, a kiss in exchange for letters from American children. In short, I could see that the liberation of the Iraqi people has cost them a great deal and it has cost the U.S. as well.

December 14 arrived, the day the dictator and murderer Saddam Hussein was captured. And Mr. Bush tells us that now that we have him, peace has arrived for the Iraqi people. But in the ensuing days the deaths of young Americans increased and Mr. Bush continues to lie to us. At first he claimed that Saddam would be treated as a prisoner of war and tried under international law only to tell us days later that the Iraqi people must try and sentence him. What about international law? Why does Bush fear an international tribunal?

And so we arrive at the end of this terrible and unhappy year 2003 and what do we find? That everywhere, in every city and in every family, there is joy, optimism, and the usual New Year's Eve custom of conveying our best wishes. This is why I have taken the liberty to write this letter in order to tell you that in the coming year of 2004 we must be very focused in our actions, for this is the beginning of a Presidential election year in this great nation. And we must do everything in our power to make sure that Mr. Bush is not reelected and to ensure that he does not steal the election. I invite everyone to reflect on recent events that have cost so many lives, jobs, broken families, economic ruin, and do all we can to defeat Bush, a defeat that is in the best interest of the American people and world peace.

The hope of my entire family is that God will grant you the health and strength to continue this struggle.

Hold on to Your Humanity
An open letter to active-duty GIs from ***Stan Goff, former Sgt. U.S. Army (Ret).***

Dear American serviceperson in Iraq,

I am a retired veteran of the Army, and my own son is among you, a paratrooper like I was. The changes that are happening to every one of you, some more dramatic than others, are changes I know very well. So I'm going to say some things to you straight up.

In 1970, I was assigned to the 173rd Airborne Brigade, then based in northern Binh Dinh Province in what was then the Republic of Vietnam. When I went there, I had my head full of shit: shit from the news media, shit from movies, and shit from a lot of my know-nothing neighbors who would tell you plenty about Vietnam even though they'd never been there, or to war at all. The essence of all this shit was that we had to "stay the course in Vietnam," and that we were on some mission to save good Vietnamese from bad Vietnamese, and to keep the bad Vietnamese from hitting beachheads outside of Oakland.

When I started hearing about weapons of mass destruction that threatened the United States from Iraq, a shattered country that had endured almost a decade of trench war followed by an invasion and twelve years of sanctions, my first question was how in the hell can anyone believe that this suffering country presents a threat to the United States? But then I remember how many people had believed Vietnam threatened the United States. Including me.

When that bullshit story about weapons came apart like a two-dollar shirt, the politicians who cooked up this war told everyone, including you, that you would be greeted like great liberators. They told us that we were in Vietnam to make sure everyone there could vote.

What they didn't tell me was that before I got there in 1970, they had been burning villages, killing livestock, poisoning farmlands and forests, killing civilians for sport, and bombing whole villages, and the people who were grieving and raging over that weren't in a position to figure out the difference between me just in country and the people who had done those things to them.

What they didn't tell you is that over a million and a half Iraqis died between 1991 and 2003 from malnutrition, medical neglect, and bad sanitation. Over half a million of those who died were the weakest, the children, especially very young children.

My son who is over there now has a baby. We visit with our grandson every chance we get. He is eleven months old now. Lots of you have children, so you know how easy it is to really love them and love them so hard you just know your entire world would come to an end if anything happened to them. Iraqis feel that way about their babies, too.

So the lie that you would be welcomed as liberators was just that. A lie. And when you put this into perspective, you know that if you were an Iraqi, you probably wouldn't be crazy about American soldiers taking over your towns and cities either. This is the tough reality I faced in Vietnam. I knew that if I were Vietnamese, I would have been one of the Vietcong.

But there we were, ordered into someone else's country, playing the role of occupier when we didn't know the people, their language, or their culture, with our head full of bullshit our NCO's and officers had told us during training, and in preparation for deployment, and when we got there. There we were, facing people we were ordered to dominate, but any one of whom might be pumping mortars at us or firing AKs at us later that night.

So in our process of fighting to stay alive, and in their process for trying to expel an invader that violated their dignity, destroyed their property, and killed their innocents, we were faced off against each other by people who made these decisions in $5,000 suits, who laughed and slapped each other on the back in Washington DC with their fat fucking asses stuffed full of cordon blue.

That's you now. Just fewer trees.

We haven't figured out how to stop the pasty-faced, oil-hungry, backslappers in DC yet, and it looks like you all might be stuck there for a little longer. So I want to tell you the rest of the story.

I changed over there in Vietnam, and they were not nice changes either. I started getting pulled into something—something that craved blood. Just to make sure I wasn't regarded as a "fucking missionary" or a possible rat, I learned how to fit myself into that group that was untouchable, people too crazy to fuck with, people who desired the rush of omnipotence that comes with setting someone's house on fire just for the pure hell of it, or who could kill anyone, man, woman, or child, with hardly a second thought.

It's all an act, a cover-up for a deeper fear, and the reason I know that is that we had to dehumanize our victims before we did the things we did. They became dinks or gooks, just like Iraqis are now being transformed into ragheads or hajjis. We felt we had to kill them to survive, but something inside us told us that so long as they were human beings, with the same intrinsic value we had as human beings, we were not allowed to burn their homes and barns, kill their animals, and sometimes even kill them. So we used these words, these new names, to reduce them, to strip them of their essential humanity, and then we could do things like adjust artillery fire onto the cries of a baby.

Until that baby was silenced, though, and here's the important thing to understand, that baby never surrendered her humanity. I did. We did.

Then we finish our tour, and go back to our families, who can see that even though we function, we are empty and incapable of truly connecting to people any more, and maybe we can go for months or even years before we fill that void where we surrendered our humanity, with chemical anesthetics—drugs, alcohol, until we realize that the void can never be filled and we shoot ourselves, or head off into the street where we can disappear with the flotsam of society, or we hurt others and end up as another incarceration statistic or a mental patient.

You can [n]ever escape that you became a racist because you thought you needed that to survive, that you took things away from people that you can never give back, or that you killed a piece of yourself that you may never get back.

Some of us do. We get lucky and someone gives a fuck enough to emotionally resuscitate us and bring us back to life. Many do not.

So here is my message to you. You will do what you have to do to survive, while we do what we have to do to stop this thing. But don't surrender your humanity. Not to fit in. Not to prove yourself. Not to seek thrills. Not for some ticket-punching fucking lifer to make his career on.

The big bosses are trying to gain control of the world's energy supplies to twist future economic competitor's arms. That's what's going on, and you need to understand it, then do what you need to do to hold on to your humanity. They see you as an expendable commodity. They don't care about your nightmares, about the DU that you are breathing, or about how you[r] humanity is stripped away a piece at a time. They don't care. So you have to. And to preserve your own humanity, you must recognize it among the people whose nation you now occupy.

*Open letter from **Army nurse.***

January 2004

I am an Army Nurse Corps Captain stationed at Walter Reed Army Medical Center, in Washington D.C., and I feel compelled to share what I have seen with anyone who will listen. When OIF troops are evac'd out of Germany, the huge majority are brought here to WRAMC by the Air Force flight nurses and docs. I do not have access to any of the numbers of how many wounded and what types of injuries, etc., but I can honestly tell you that the OIF wounded occupy more than half or our two major intensive care unites (SICU and MICU) at any given time. At times, we get so full and are expecting more to arrive, that we have to hound the docs to transfer somebody out of our unit to a ward upstairs so we have some beds for these soldiers. Most of these wounded soldiers come in to our unit on a ventilator breathing for them, with severe wounds caused by IEDs [improvised roadside bombs] or AK-47 GSW [gunshot wounds]. Many, many soldiers have already lost arms, limbs, or eyes before they even get to us, and many have received dozens of units of blood before they left Germany. I am very proud that I am privileged to take care of these brave men and women, but it breaks my heart to realize that their incredible loss that they and their loved ones will have to deal with for the rest of their life seems to have not been for the good of our country. Rather, their pain and sorrow has merely allowed a few greedy souls to make a power grab for more wealth and control. One of my dear friends has tried to convince me that this is all part of God's plan, and the death and pain is for some greater purpose that our leaders are not telling us yet. I wish I could believe her. It would make my job and daily life much easier, but I cannot buy it. I apologize to the reader for my tangential thought processes, but this never-ending situation is getting to many military nurses.

As you might be aware, the press is being tightly controlled and what is being reported from a medical standpoint is only a fraction of the true reality. Yes, I do believe the daily number of killed that CNN and whoever report is accurate. What I am saying is that the walking wounded are being sorely ignored. Don't believe me? Walter Reed is an open base, not a tightly controlled fort. Just have a valid ID and consent to a vehicle search. Then park, and walk inside. You will see so many twenty somethings mostly male, missing arms, legs, and eyes. The blinders covering your eyes will be ripped away as you see the poor families making their daily walk from the Malogne house to the wards and units caring for their sons or husbands. It is so sad to see young wives and fiancées cry over their honey who was in Iraq less than one month before losing both legs and have several abdominal surgeries which leave his belly crisscrossed with staples, and now he is fighting for his life from the infection that the injuries have caused. And that is just one example of what I saw this week. I will spare you more wrenching true stories.

God help our men and women in uniform. Please do something to end this madness.

Open letter from ***Staff Sgt. Camilo Mejia.***

Camilo Mejia, 28, from Miami, Florida, fought in Iraq with Company C, 1-124 Infantry Regiment, 53rd Infantry Brigade, of the Florida National Guard, which was placed on active duty in January 2003. Mejia served in combat in the "Sunni Triangle" from April until October 2003. For reasons he explains below, he refused to return to Iraq after a 14 day leave in the U.S. With the support of Citizen Soldier and Louis Font, his civilian attorney, he surrendered to military control on March 15, 2004. In May 2004 he was tried by special court-martial for desertion at Ft. Stewart, GA, and following conviction was sentenced to a year in prison, a Bad Conduct Discharge, and reduction in rank to Private.

I can say from personal experience that commanders in Iraq often make soldiers carry out orders that have nothing to do with peacekeeping, or helping the people. A lot of times we did things knowing that it would cause social chaos, further destruction of a city that was already destroyed, and resentment toward American troops. All this was done with the clear purpose of instigating firefights so that infantry officers could get their combat experience, medals, CIBs, and all the glory they need to climb up the military ladder. I can say that for professional advancement, commanding officers have permanently altered soldiers' lives and killed innocent Iraqi civilians, and all from the safety and comfort of their command posts while yelling orders through a radio.

Invading Iraq, in my opinion, was an arbitrary decision. The reasons the Bush administration presented to the people of the United States, and the world, have all turned out to be lies, mere justifications to invade and occupy a sovereign nation. That, to me, makes the war illegal, arbitrary, and most importantly, immoral.

I cannot quietly accept and do everything I'm told just because I signed a military contract.

I was born in Managua, Nicaragua on August 28, 1975. My parents were separated when I, just months old, first came to the United States with my mother and older brother. Our first stay in this country wasn't very long, maybe six or seven months. We then moved to Costa Rica, my mother's native country, where we stayed close to five years before moving back to Nicaragua.

When I turned sixteen my mother decided to move back to her native country. I had lived almost all my adolescent years in Nicaragua where I had all my friends, many relatives, my school, my neighborhood, all the things that made that country my home. I remember the kids in my new school being particularly harsh on my Nicaraguan accent. They were rich and upper middle class children in a private Catholic school. I quickly became alienated from the world around me, and found solace only in literature and the Arts. In retrospect, my final years in Costa Rica were very hard, but they also marked the beginning of a new interest in the intellectual world.

When at age eighteen I left Costa Rica to come to the United States, I had not finished high school. I finished at night, and during the day I worked at a local fast food place. My days started at five thirty in the morning and ended at eleven at night. And even all that sacrifice did not guarantee a secure life.

My prospect[s] at that time seemed pretty grim, as I didn't want to continue working minimum-wage jobs without the promise of education, and I hated living from paycheck to paycheck without even having a social life. I wanted something that would bring some financial security, that would give the opportunity to pursue an education in the future, in other words, just what the Army was offering.

I joined the Army when I was nineteen years old. But my character and personality were still not done defining themselves. There was much room for me to start questioning, if not war itself, the reasons for war, and most importantly, the role I would play in it. The process of defining and redefining my moral principles and values was in high gear even in the Army. For instance, while being stationed in Fort Hood Texas, about a year before my release from active duty, I decided to adopt a vegetarian diet.

After my active duty Army tour was over I decided to continue my college education, and joining the Florida National Guard offered me the opportunity to go to college for free.

In January of 2003, the Department of Defense activated my unit, to prepare for a possible invasion of Iraq. From that moment, the Army gave us five days to prepare for deployment. During those five days we had to attend drill from early in the morning until late at night. The time allocated was barely enough to take care of all military official matters, such as vaccines, Powers of Attorney, medical and dental records, ID cards and tags, etc.

When we arrived at Fort Stewart, Georgia, we were subjected to what was supposed to be combat training that would better equip us to conduct our mission in the Middle East. Soon we learned that our training was merely intended to make our unit "deployable." There were lots of requirements to certify soldiers to go to war. A soldier, for instance, is not supposed to be deployed if he/she does not pass a physical exam. Another requirement was to qualify with individual weapons. Many soldiers did not qualify, but after many failed attempts at the range were judged qualified and deployable. Other requirements included NBC (Nuclear Biological Chemical) training, First Aid, passing the Army Physical Fitness Test (APFT), having the proper equipment, meeting the Army weight standards, etc. Everything we did at Stewart was aimed at fulfilling an official requirement. To meet the pass/fail quota, the cadres would initially fail a few soldiers and then give them a pass score. Not a single soldier ever had to go back to the range for testing. Every soldier passed every single task the very same day they were tested.

When the actual combat training beg[a]n, they sent our unit to the different ranges in order to get our pass[ing] scores. We were told we would attend every range, stay for a day or two, and return to our barracks for showers and hot meals before going to the next range. Soon after we got to the first range, we realized that we were going to stay there for a while. We went from range to range without ever going back to our barracks. The temperatures were in the thirties, yet we were rarely able to enjoy a cup of coffee or a bowl of hot soup. I once watched, disbelieving as our commander ordered a truck with hot soup and coffee to return to base. After only the first day of training, for which we received good review by an Observer Controller (OC), our Company Commander, a captain, in front of all the NCOs of our company, dismissed my Platoon Sergeant along with another platoon's Platoon Sergeant. Even if our commander had good reasons to fire these two NCOs, he could have done so in a way that did not humiliate them.

Later, during our stay at Ft. Stewart, I saw this same commander kick a soldier. This happened because the soldier, who was a truck driver, had not cleaned the back of the truck prior to arriving at our barracks. When he saw the trash laying on the ground, he began to yell at the soldier and then started kicking the trash; in doing so he kicked the soldier in the leg. While all of this happened, I stood behind my commander. I was curious to see if there would be any apology. There was none.

Later, enroute to the Middle East, I witnessed our commander hit another soldier. Our plane had made a fuel stop, and one of the soldiers had exited the plane without his headgear. Our Captain hit the soldier in the back of the head with his personal bag. The soldier, who had undergone surgery and still had an open head wound, turned to the captain and said he had a medical reason not to wear headgear. The Captain replied that he didn't know that, but again did not apologize.

Before we deployed, our battalion had to attend a parade in order to pose for unit pictures. During this parade, our battalion commander, Lieutenant Colonel Mirabile, told everyone that he was not going to return to Florida without a Combat Infantry Badge (CIB), a badge awarded only to infantrymen and special ops, and only after a unit has been under direct enemy fire. To many infantrymen, obtaining this badge is a great honor, but going out of one's way to engage in combat, just to get a badge, is something few service members would accept.

On May 30, my squad was ambushed for the first time in Ar Ramadi in the "Sunni Triangle." I had been talking with one of my team leaders about the intensity of the attacks on that day. Occupation resisters had attacked one of Saddam's coalition-occupied palaces, and there had been considerably more shooting than usual. It was one of those days that just didn't feel right. Apparently the attackers were still in the area and we wanted the mortars to light up the sky in order to find them. I got my squad ready and, though in a sandstorm, we departed to the palace. As soon as we arrived, there was a firefight outside the gate. The mortars men fired their flares and we escorted them back, along with the Executive Officer (XO), to our base, which was then called Eagle's Nest, on the east end of Ar Ramadi.

Once back at the Eagle's Nest the XO told me to get my squad ready to set up a Traffic Control Point (TCP) right by the palace that had been under attack. This mission, we thought, wasn't exactly the product of outstanding leadership. We understood the risk involved in going out in a small squad at a time when there had been several nasty night attacks without really knowing the surroundings. We set our TCP by a bridge that separated the two presidential palaces and stayed there for about three hours, which was a dangerously long time, again courtesy of our leadership. At about 0300 hrs we got on our two Humvees and drove back to the Eagle's Nest. About a quarter mile up on the highway, a whistle was heard as we rolled by a part of the road that was notorious for its bombed down buildings. Immediately after the whistle, an improvised bomb exploded in the middle of the road right in front of the lead Humvee. Following the blast, bullets began coming our way from the rooftops on both sides of the road (apparently the skeleton buildings had some fire left in them). We returned fire with our individual weapons and the machine-guns on top of the vehicles. Prior to this attack, I had briefed my squad, especially the drivers, if we were ambushed to simply "haul ass" through an attack. I told them to fire back and keep driving as fast as they could. This, I thought, was the Standard Operating Procedure (SOP) for an ambush.

As soon as we returned to base, we became euphorically happy about surviving an ambush, and that no one was hurt. I guess you could say we were pretty happy about not being dead after our first real combat experience, and we were very loud about it.

The commander, XO, and First Sergeant immediately asked to be briefed about the attack. I told them everything exactly as it happened. They asked me why we had fled instead of staying and fighting. I told them I thought it was Army SOP to keep driving during an ambush. They agreed and expressed their happiness that everyone was unharmed, but then said that we had just sent the wrong message to the attackers, that during an ambush, it was our mission to kill the enemy, not run from them.

They insisted that we should have stayed and fought, that they could have sent reinforcements which had usually taken 20 to 30 minutes to arrive in the past. They continued to say it had been an enemy victory, that we had shown them we were afraid. I left the meeting knowing I wasn't their most popular squad leader, but I had a clear conscience. We had lived through an ambush and managed to make it unscathed. There was no doubt in my mind that it had been a victory.

The next morning my acting platoon leader told me the commander had heard us celebrating our return from the ambush. The commander told him to please tell us that in the future, we should not celebrate our failures, that we were not here to run from the enemy but to kill them, and that celebrating our escape sends the wrong message to other soldiers. I understood then that our commanders were not acting out of inexperience. They knew exactly the risk involved in an ambush, but it was more important to them to send a message even when that meant doing the opposite of what we had been trained to do. It seemed to me that protecting the troops wasn't very high on our leaders' agenda. Medals, honor, and sending "the right message" were all worth the lives of a few soldiers. The war was more complicated than I ever imagined. Not only did we have to be careful with the enemy, but we also had to be careful with our own leadership.

What could be more impressive than an infantry officer with combat experience? What better evidence of the dangers of a mission than losing a few of their soldiers? Being an infantry officer, with twenty or thirty years in the service, with no combat experience or no CIB, is like being a firefighter for twenty or thirty years without ever fighting a single fire. They were going for the glory even if it meant losing a few lives, our lives.

Another incident that had an impact upon me took place in July. After a bomb on the road hit a friendly convoy and injured two soldiers, our commander decided to block the roads of Ar Ramadi. The official purpose was to prevent terrorists from entering the city, even though everyone knew that Ar Ramadi already had its own share. The time of departure, order of movement, routes to and from the positions the different platoons occupied, the number of soldiers of each platoon, the amount of time we spent at each position, remained the same for three straight nights. Then we got word that the mission had been extended to five nights. The battalion commander was also overheard saying that he wanted to "draw the enemy out." Everyone in the unit knew that we were violating everything we learned as infantrymen that would help us avoid an attack. We had given the enemy all the information they needed to plan and execute a deliberate attack, which was exactly what they did the fourth night.

As soon as we arrived at our position on the fourth night an explosion shattered one of their vehicles. A friend of mine lost part of his calf, another soldier lost three fingers, two others received shrapnel wounds. Right after the firefight, an unsuspecting vehicle approached the blocking position. After a few warning shots my peers opened fire on the occupants. One of the occupants took a superficial wound on his arm, the other was decapitated by fifty-caliber machine-gun fire. It was quickly determined that these men were innocent. The survivor was taken to the hospital, his friend to the morgue.

The mission continued, and that same night we were told we had to do the same thing the following night, using the same procedure. Many NCOs complained about following the same procedure after such an unfortunate incident, and after a heated discussion with our commander, the mission was modified.

The pro-war politicians at home kept saying that we did not need more troops in Iraq, but soldiers in Iraq, or at least those in my unit, had a completely different idea. Maybe this has to do with us being National Guard soldiers, who don't get replacements for our wounded or dead. This lack of troop replacements also extends to material supplies, because we never really got resupplied on ammo, vehicles, night vision equipment, weapons, etc. We even left the States without a basic clothing supply. The same thing with ammunition, we traveled with just a basic combat load and never got an official refit. In some instances we had to exchange magazines within the platoons prior to going out on missions. When Improvised Explosive Devices (IEDs) blew up our vehicles on the road, we didn't get new ones.

Lack of personnel drove my commanders to do some pretty despicable things. There was a Staff Sergeant who did not pass his physical at Stewart because his hearing was damaged. He had been in the artillery business fourteen of his twenty-one years in the military. This friend of mine was very hard of hearing. I remember having to lend him my notes after our daily squad leader meetings because he could not hear our platoon leader's briefing six feet away from us. This soldier didn't even dare to request to be sent home. He knew he was slowly losing his hearing and he knew [that] that would hinder his proficiency as a squad leader, so he began asking the Army doctors to help him get a hearing aid. In my opinion he should never have been deployed, especially as an infantryman, much less when his rank puts him in charge of troops' lives and tremendous fire-power. But since he thought it would be impossible to be sent home he settled for a hearing aid. Doctors first told him they could not help him because they were not specialists, and that to get anything done he would have to see our Captain who, in turn, told him that was something that had to be arranged with the doctors. Then we got another doctor, this time a reserve lieutenant colonel who was a civilian plastic surgeon. He told the sergeant to get out of his face and wait until the end of our deployment.

His wife wrote a letter to the commanding general of the Florida National Guard, asking him to demobilize her husband due to his bad hearing. She heard nothing until she got word that her husband's unit had been under a massive attack, and that a soldier had been critically wounded. The next day, an Army captain called the soldier's wife, and told her that due to her letter her husband had been sent to Germany. The captain forgot to mention the bomb incident. She also forgot to mention that it had taken two bombs for the Army to treat a soldier who should have never been deployed to a combat environment.

Commanders are preoccupied with insuring that their unit numbers [are] high, because if they fall below a certain level, they risk losing their commands. Perhaps it was the fear of going under combat strength that drove our captain to deny the emergency leave request presented by a Private First Class, who asked to visit his dying grandmother. But this didn't matter to our commander, who ignored Red Cross messages regarding his claim and called him a liar when he said his grandmother had raised him.

There is also the case of another specialist, who was driving a Humvee during one of our nastiest IED attacks. He took some shrapnel to his face and was evacuated for medical treatment. While at an Army clinical center, medical personnel told him he would be sent home. Supposedly that was the SOP for all soldiers whose injuries were serious enough to merit medical evacuation. But just before getting on a plane, they told him that he wasn't going anywhere. Apparently his commander had called, asking for him to be returned to duty (RTD) status.

Another famous case was that of Sgt. Mario Vega, who also was injured during a clearing mission of Highway Ten. He was riding in the back of a truck when an IED went off. The blast threw him to the rear of the truck, and his lower back hit a wooden bench. Mario also suffered lacerations to his eyes. He too was told he would be sent to the States to recover, and he too was later told his commander had denied his departure.

In May 2004, the Pentagon released an investigative report prepared by Major Gen. Antonio Taguba documenting the widespread torture of Iraqi prisoners by U.S. military personnel at Abu Ghraib prison between October and December 2003. He confirmed that such practices violated the Geneva Conventions for the treatment of military prisoners. Sgt. Mejia is reporting here that he witnessed the use of similar practices five months *earlier at an Army detention center at the al Assad airbase, next to Baghdad's International Airport.*

We took on the mission after brief training by 3rd ACR soldiers, whom we replaced at the site. The first thing we were taught was to separate the detainees into three groups; combatants, non-combatants, and the sick. Second, we were taught that detainees were to be kept blindfolded at all times. The detention space had been a concrete jet bunker, with an opening at one end and concertina wire strung all around it. The bunker had two other areas that we used occasionally. One, a small dark isolation room where we kept a man who wouldn't stop crying and another processing area, where we received new detainees.

Three mysterious interrogators, who didn't give us their real names, ordered us to keep certain detainees in sleep deprivation. This was done to break the detainees' resolve not to answer sensitive questions. Keeping detainees awake for periods of 24–48 hours required some pretty extreme measures. The easiest way to do this was to constantly yell at the detainees, making them stand up or sit down every few minutes and forcing them to wave their arms up and down. When these techniques failed, we would bang on the walls with a huge sledgehammer or load a 9mm pistol next to their ear. This usually did the job.

After the three mystery men conducted their interrogations, the detainees were placed in two categories—combatants and non combatants. The first group were sent on to "real" POW camps, while the non combatants were taken to a nearby town and released. One of the things that kept our camp from gaining POW camp status was that we weren't the kind of soldiers that should be running such a facility. We were infantrymen with no training in the handling of detainees. The way we treated these men was hard even for the soldiers, especially because we realized that many of these "combatants" were no more than shepherds.

One of our Sergeants shot a child who was carrying an AK-47 rifle. The two other children who were walking with him ran away while the wounded child began crawling for his life. A second shot stopped him, but he was still alive. When an Iraqi tried to take him to a civilian hospital, Army medics from our unit intercepted him and insisted on taking the injured boy to a military facility. There, he was denied medical attention because a different unit was supposed to treat our unit's wounded. After another medical unit refused to treat the child, he died.

Although I'm not a US citizen, the history that unites me to this country and its people is not derived from a passport or a certificate of naturalization. The love I feel for this nation and its people is what binds me to it, the same love in me that creates a sense of duty to protect my home creates in me the sense of duty to protect the United States, its people, and the principle by which the nation was founded: Freedom and Self-determination.

Sadly, I have to say that words like freedom and patriotism have lately become tools of manipulation to justify the war to the American people and the members of the armed forces. Patriotism is what soldiers are told to be fighting for in Iraq, even though the government hasn't proved its case of imminent danger to the US. I don't support the war, nor do I think we are fighting it to export freedom or make the country safer, yet I know deep inside that I have not been disloyal to America nor have I been disloyal to the Army, I have only been loyal to my conscience and my moral principles.

During my leave, people wanted to know about my experiences in war; answering them took me back to all of the horrors of combat, the firefights, the ambushes, the time I saw that young Iraqi being dragged by his shoulders through a pool of his own blood, the time that other man was decapitated by machine gun fire, the time my friend shot a child through the chest.

In the comfort of my home, away from the dangers of combat, I was left with my memories of war, and what's worse, I came face to face with my feelings. Many years from today, I won't be able to say I was part of an immoral war and did all the things that my own conscience warned me against because the Army forced me.

For instance, while in Ar Ramadi my platoon responded to a protest that had turned violent. The protesters had started throwing grenades at the Mayor's office and my squad was sent to a rooftop to occupy defensive positions. Our platoon leader relayed an order to shoot anyone who threw anything that looked like a grenade. A young Iraqi emerged from the crowd carrying something in his right hand. Just before he threw it, we all opened fire, killing him. The grenade exploded far away and I know that the man we killed had no ability to hurt us. This incident stayed on my mind for many weeks. The image of the young man, killed by a rain of fire, is still fresh in my memory. In this case, I had the benefit of bearing a collective guilt. My platoon leader later told us that three other Iraqis were also killed in the same incident, although I didn't see them die.

Since I became a conscientious objector I have become aware of the importance of promoting a peaceful society and government. But it was not until I saw with my own eyes what war can do to people, regardless of whether they are innocent or not, that a real change began to take place within me. My eyes have witnessed the suffering and desperation of the people of a country in ruins, who become further humiliated by an occupying Army, along with its raids, patrols, and curfew. It is the war that changed me forever.

A letter written by family members of the 3rd Infantry Division, 2nd Brigade Soldiers. They want their soldiers to come home. The letter includes excerpts from two letters their troops have sent home from Iraq.

To Whom It May Concern,

We are writing today about the 3rd Infantry Division. These soldiers have had redeployments held out to them and then snatched away from them repeatedly. If simply being there contributes to the defeat of morale, what must the denied hope of homecoming bring?

As you know, the United States Army has always frowned upon "negative publicity" and family members have always been told to keep quiet for the sake of not making the most "powerful Army in the world" look bad. A few months ago, when we had heard of them being delayed due to a "follow on mission" to Fallujah, a group of spouses, mothers, fathers, sisters, brothers, and friends began writing to members of Congress, and even the Commander in Chief in hopes that the situation might be reviewed. We contacted the news and print media and told our stories to the public. When the news media investigated our allegations that our troops didn't have enough ammunition, supplies and food, they were simply told by the commanding officer that it was being "taken care of" and the story was left at that. For weeks after, our husbands called home to tell us they were drinking un-sanitary water, their equipment was broken down and their morale was horribly low. I ask you, who should the family members believe? An Army commanding officer, who does not want the Army to sustain "negative publicity" or our husbands, brothers and sons who are actually there in the situation and experiencing it first hand?

The news media has been focused on members of the 3rd Infantry Division coming home to Ft. Stewart. As a matter of fact, another group of 250 soldiers returned last night. These men and women have been deployed for 4–6 months. The men and women of the 2nd Brigade have been overseas for 10 months now (some even longer than that). This is the THIRD time their redeployment has been changed or delayed, and for what reason???

We feel that the Americans' voices on this matter have been stifled, that the soldiers' voices on this matter have been altogether ignored. The following are quotes directly from the mouths of 3rd ID soldiers. The first is from a member of an armored division who has been deployed since September 2002, the other is a letter from an anonymous soldier from the 3rd ID/2nd BCT who felt he should remain anonymous for fear of reprimand from his commanding officers. These letters are from the men in Iraq, in their own words doubting their faith in this country:

I'm always the one who's positive, but I'll tell you it's hard sometimes. At times, I can't rationalize why we are still here and that is what makes me mad. Pretty much it confirms my belief that I am just part of a bar graph on a power point presentation to a "suit" in Washington. My life is a percentage of "well, we have X amount of soldiers in theater" . . . you really get the feeling that the government has abandon[ed] you, left you to rot, with no mission and no return date. But most days, I remember I'm here for my guys and it's my duty to make sure they're OK even if the higher-ups are messed up.

To Whom It May Concern:

When you hear about "heroes," you think of people whom you would envy. None of us asked to be called heroes, or anything else. For the past 9 months we have lived a hard life. We trained for nearly 6 months before the war started, were the first U.S. forces into Iraq on March 20th, and were responsible for the daring strike into Baghdad on April 7th and 8th that virtually ended the war.

We are the forgotten and betrayed soldiers of 2nd Brigade, 3rd Infantry Division, also known as the "Send Me" Brigade. Our Task Force motto is "Can Do," and we have been living true to those words—for a very long time.

We are also the unit that is sitting in the city of Al Fallujah, as we enter the month of July. Our men and women have completed every mission we have been given, even when that mission kept us from coming home on time. We have received the occasional newspaper, each one showing us that the rest of the armed forces are returning home . . . even as we are getting orders for our next mission. We also read the letters that our Commanding General writes in our local newspaper. Each time we read his words our desperation grows deeper, because we know that most of our countrymen are hearing his lies about our situation here.

Our morale is not high or even low. Our morale is non-existent. We have been told twice that we were going home, and twice we have received a stop movement to stay in Iraq. Where is the honor and integrity the Army preaches to soldiers in Basic Training? The closer you get to the front lines, the worse the soldiers get treated. Every single one of my men has diarrhea, because none of us on the front lines have had a single fresh vegetable in over a month. Meanwhile our commanding general and his cronies are enjoying Burger King at Baghdad International Airport (which we captured). The 3rd

Infantry Division soldiers feel betrayed, and forgotten. Many of our brothers in arms have paid the ultimate price to help liberate this country.

Every one of us has made sacrifices, and what is our reward? Being treated like farm animals. We have had more support from the press, who were embedded with us throughout the fight, than we have ever received from our chain of command.

Our troops, and our equipment are worn out. Many of our troops have been through some truly terrible experiences. They have been told by mental health professionals that they need to get out of this environment. They, however, either don't care about those of us out here on the front lines or they have been lied to by their subordinates and have passed those lies on to the rest of the world.

In closing, all I am really trying to ask for is your help. Please send this letter on to your representatives in Congress and to your local media, and ask them to get the 2nd Brigade, 3rd Infantry Division home. Our men and women deserve to be treated like the heroes they are, not like neighborhood mongrels. Our men and women deserve to see their loved ones again and deserve to come home. Thank you for your attention,

Sincerely,

The Soldiers of 2nd Brigade, 3rd ID.

Open letter from wives, mothers, brothers, sisters, sons, daughters, and family members of soldiers of the 3rd Infantry Division, 2nd Brigade.

In this day and age, with the American military being the largest and most sophisticated on earth, why must one division bear the brunt of a large part of the war on Iraq? Are we so short-handed that one division's morale must sink to rockbottom, then to disappear altogether? Why must the American people pay, not only with billions of dollars per month, but more importantly with the lives of men and women that may be too tired to fight effectively? This is illogical. This is wasteful. This impacts negatively on our efforts in Iraq and on our efforts at home.

The re-enlistment rate of returning soldiers has decreased dramatically since this effort began. Does this send a message to the government that the soldiers feel abandoned by their country?? That they have lost their faith in the government they've worked so hard to defend?? The soldiers and their families will have their say in the 2004 election and then will make their voices heard.

In closing, we would like to say that these men and women of the 3rd Infantry Division, 2nd Brigade have done their job and done it well. They are mentally, physically and emotionally exhausted. These men have had their promise of re-deployment ripped out from under them numerous times, and it's because of that, their morale is non-existent. We need to send these heroes home for a much needed and deserved break.

As the saying goes: "If not for the Home of the Brave, There would be no Land of the Free." What makes our nation so great is our ability and constitutional right to have a government for the people, by the people. These brave men and women and the people who love them have a choice, and our voices will be heard. If not now, in the 2004 elections.

Sincerely,

The wives, mothers, brothers, sisters, fathers, sons, daughters and family members of the soldiers of the 3rd Infantry Division, 2nd Brigade.

Colonel Michael G. Jones U.S. Army (Ret) September 13, 2003
Strategic Planning Office
Florida Department of Military Affairs

Dear Colonel Jones,

We, the relatives of the Florida National Guard soldiers want to express our position about the last postponement of the return of our soldiers back home. We want to inform you that we are united in the fight to return our soldiers.

This letter shall serve to remind you that these soldiers have now been away from our homes for eight months, away from their children, wives and parents, away from their universities and jobs, involved in a guerrilla war in an unknown country, not knowing the culture or the language of the place, menaced by mines, bombs and guns, risking their lives 24 hours a day, standing in their uniforms and carrying their equipment in temperatures of up to 130°F.

In less than 3 months, this small company has suffered countless attacks, leaving 4 soldiers crippled and another soldier in [a] coma, not to mention the injured soldiers at the Ar Ramadi.

The National Guard soldiers are civilians, not active members of the Army. They have never received the training for combat in the desert or to face urban guerrillas. We know that, since their arrival at Ar Ramadi, our young soldiers have been patrolling and searching the houses of presumed guerrilla forces. We know that they lack adequate equipment, that in many cases they have patrolled without bulletproof vests and without the necessary ammunition to face the guerrilla forces. Isn't this enough? How many months, how many abuses are we supposed to endure?

We will not mention each suffering and difficulty that our soldiers have endured. We just want to tell you that we know what they are going through and that we will not keep quiet in the face of this dishonor. We will not rest until our young soldiers come back to our homes.

We are determined to continue on this campaign to the end. If necessary, a group of mothers will go on an indefinite hunger strike. You will not only be responsible for the lives of our soldiers, but for [those] of their mothers. We shall not accept political apologies. Lack of governmental will by President Bush to work together with the United Nations and to restore the power to the Iraqis is the reason why the participation of an international force comprised by big nations is not possible. The coalition we are being told about does not really exist. It is our troops that carry the load of this war. It is our children who are being sacrificed due to an arrogant and unfair attitude.

For this and for other reasons, we demand the return of our soldiers now!! We shall not abandon our loved ones; we shall not abandon our troops. We shall continue demanding their return day-by-day, street-by-street, door-to-door. We will ask the world to join us. We will not abandon our fight until our soldiers are back in our homes.

Respectfully yours,
Maritza Castillo, Miladys Guerrero, Estela Guerrero, Maria Carrasquillo, Julio C. D'Augerot, Antonia Mendieta, Carlos A. Mejia, Teresa Lugo, Johanna Guevara, Anna Caballero, Mario Murillo, Patricia Luna, Ligia Sánchez, Patricia Cabadiana, Mirtha Bonilla, Claudia Gonzalez, Paola Gomez, Euri Velásquez, Ingrid Soriano, Ana Guerrero

"Freeing Iraq or Diverting America"
by Horace Coleman

Strolling and patrolling doesn't make a patriot.
Short of pennies, needing bennies, if they weren't paying would you be staying?
If you say it, you may
have to play it.

Ending up in a body bag, later under a flag, won't
make you sad folks brag. But you do more than a
Jody Grinder in some
sports bar keeping score.

Riding a Humvee in misery,
looking over your shoulder,
trying to get older while
those back home think *they're* bolder. The
armchair folk, not under
cold SandLand stars, fly
faded rags on their cars.

Heroes pull triggers
on Iraqi sand niggers.
CEOs stretch their checks

by a few more zeroes. *They*
never answered the call or had homecomings stalled.

The real (?) patriots (?) who
"Support our troops!" ignore the bureaucratic hoops and red tape loops you have to escape and evade.
I don't want to diss but what's up with this?
To get armor for your body, it's your *family* you lobby?

"We're #1!" and second to none—at jiving ourselves.
The WWE will set who free? John and Jane Public?
No law will make those patriots act. You do more.
They just snore and ignore;
root for the home team;
chase lotto dreams.

Life's a spectator sport
on someone else's court
(they shop—you drop).
Busy khaki elves dust fears
from the nation's shelves.

When you do get home,
they won't even send
a mojo bone.

The Grand REMF has a plan needing fresh flesh fertilizer,
more blood on more sand.

Troops duck RPGs, IEDs.
Please, it ain't no thing.
It's just you in the ring,
slouching to Bethlehem.

You know, putting on a reality show, as mall rats
and Washington brats,
flick the clicker quicker:

It's such an easy war,
let's have some more.
Twenty-four seven,
send 'em to heaven.

Take over, make over,
do over . . .

A Mother Speaks
by Peggy O'Rourke

As I sat on the couch in Nick's apartment waiting for the recruiter, my mind drifted to all the things leading up to this moment. It was Steve's fault, just had to be. Nick's uncle Steve, the only father figure he had ever known. Wonderful guy, big strong guy and a Vietnam war veteran as well as a former 82nd Airborne soldier. Nick had always hero worshipped him, wanted to be like him and envied his Army tattoos.

The recruiter arrived, Nick picked up his bags, gave his kisses and walked out the door. It was happening too fast. He was walking away and my heart felt nothing, it simply couldn't be real.

Nick went to basic training at Fort Benning, Georgia. Infantry training is long and hard and his was no exception. The letters I received were heart-wrenching, horrible letters. My stomach dropped each time I took a letter out of the mailbox, knowing I would be sobbing before I finished reading it. The conditions were awful there. He described it as being worse than a POW camp: overcrowded, no pillows, blankets or toilet paper, no basic essentials. They were treated worse than animals, he wrote.

Nick was allowed to come home for Christmas that year from basic training. It was a mixed blessing. I had to pry information out of him about his experiences and most of what he told me was bad. The beginning of basic was hideous, many young men attempted suicide, pretended to be gay and going AWOL. He was making some great buddies, yet the hardest thing was listening at night to these young men crying for home.

Nick told me everything the recruiter told them was a lie and he had been deceived from the beginning yet he was willing to go back and stick it out. My heart wanted desperately to find him a way out but we had nowhere to turn for advice.

Nick returned to basic training alone. I put him on a plane with my heart breaking and told him to keep being brave. It was one of the hardest things I have ever done. Even his war hero uncle Steve told him not to go back (He didn't want Nick to join in the first place, but would never tell him why).

Nick was doing his best and was proud to be succeeding and excelling at things he never thought he could do. I, who had never been on an airplane, proudly took my first plane ride down to Georgia to watch my soldier graduate.

Summer in North Carolina can be blisteringly hot. Nick's unit had weekly road marches consisting of 12 to 25 miles carrying 75 lb packs on their backs. Nick's feet were infected and raw. Everyday when he removed his socks, chunks of skin would peel off. I asked him over and over again why he didn't go to his command when he was too sick or hurt to continue. He always told me the same thing, you don't do that mom, you are told to "suck it up" and "drive on." If it doesn't kill you, he said, it only makes you stronger.

I was always horrified at the way the command took their soldiers for granted, no compassion, no mercy. Nick had told me many stories of soldiers who had died in basic training from causes such as heat stroke and live fire exercises as well as soldiers who died in routine training.

The 82nd Airborne performs their missions primarily in darkness so all paratroopers must become adept at parachuting from aircraft into the dark. This was a standard training mission, they would parachute out of C-130's into the black of night, seize and secure the enemy's territory, then march 12 miles back to base. All didn't quite go as planned for Nick though. When he hit the ground hard, he heard a crack, felt a blinding pain, and realized his foot was broken. I never did find out all the details of that night, but I don't think Nick said a word to his team leader, just continued on and completed the mission.

However on the long march back he could barely walk, still carrying his heavy pack he struggled in intense pain and his commanding officers told him to stop whining and "suck it up."

Nick's foot was broken. He was put on light duty and had a break from the rigorous daily training. Nick's foot healed in time for his first deployment in August. He was sent to the NTC (National Training Center) in the Mojave Desert for further training. This was an 18 day regiment of mock desert combat under difficult conditions.

Steve Kokales, Nick's uncle, had been a very vital part of his life. Who couldn't help but admire a man like him, a Vietnam vet, state champion weight lifter, Vikings football fanatic and all around wonderful, kind man? He had survived his time in the Army and Vietnam and rarely talked about his experience except to tell Nick: "Be careful, you can't trust the military, they will stab you in the back if you are not watching." Though he came home from Vietnam without injury, Steve was paralyzed in a motorcycle accident when Nick was 15.

The day Nick headed into combat, I received a phone call at work, it was the head of the Army's family readiness group. I heard her voice on the other end of the line, "I have official news to report," she said to me, "Boots are on the ground and our unit is on the move."

I found out later their original mission had been to parachute into the Baghdad Airport. Somehow the word leaked out and the mission was scrubbed—I could only thank God for that. It would've been horribly dangerous and Nick told me they had over one thousand body bags packed on the planes with them, as they had expected massive casualties.

I knew where his unit was almost every second. I watched the battles in Samawah and the 82nd's struggle to win the bridges over the Euphrates River. One early morning while watching CNN, my stunned eyes witnessed Nick in the middle of battle. He was crouching by a wall guarding someone's back as they crashed through a gate. Urban warfare, my worst fear, and Nick's worst fear. He was in the middle of it.

May came and went. The rumor now was home by the fourth of July. It was crushing for all involved to believe the soldiers were coming home by a certain date, then to have our hopes ripped away, time and time again. It was hell for the soldiers as well.

By July, Nick's unit was in Baghdad. Now the word was "maybe they would be home by September." Again we were crushed with despair. Nick's letters and phone calls were beginning to sound bleak. They didn't have enough clean water to drink, many were getting sick and collapsing with heat stroke, morale was down, food was horrible, the heat and bugs were indescribable.

One letter Nick sent me in July described a bit of the combat he went through, it chilled me to the bone:

"I was in two fire fights, one that kept us stuck in one spot for 5 days. One as we fought to get into Samawah and one taking the bridges. I had had RPG's and mortars landing all around me, some within feet. I have had bullets zipping by my head, shit blowing up next to me kicking up the sand just a foot away. Mortars and RPG's blasting so close to you, you can feel the concussion push you over, wondering how you didn't get hit.

"I have had an RPG rip by me so close I felt I could've caught it, but it blew up right behind me. If a bullet zings by you, it is within feet. If it POPS when it goes by, you're lucky to be alive cause that was inches. But you never hear the shot that kills you, the bullet is faster than the sound of the gun. There were a few times I thought I wasn't going to make it home. One of the worst was when a buddy got hit in the face and he went down hard, blood all over the place. We thought he was dead."

August arrived, the news was hideous, the military finally told the truth, our soldiers would be in Iraq for a year.

Desperation began to fill Nick's letters, he talked about the boredom and insanity of seeing no progress being made in the war. Now the hatred and danger that surrounded them was quietly oppressive, death lurked around every corner, you never knew when it would find you. Nick was tired, of the heat, of the relentless biting bugs, the stench and hopelessness. He had lost his spirit and hope for the future and was slipping into a darkness we couldn't pull him out of.

Then without much warning, Nick's dear uncle Steve died. I don't think Nick realized that he was saying goodbye to Steve on the day he left for Iraq. He knew Steve was sick but he'd always believed he was invicible, too good, too strong to die.

Nick was heartbroken that he didn't get to say a final farewell to his uncle—he missed the funeral by a day. But he was home and despite the sorrow of the time, I was filled with joy to hold my very thin and very tanned soldier in my arms.

Nick was different, there was no sparkle in his eyes, no expression in his voice, he seemed to be worn out and worn down. No smiles or corny jokes, just a somber, cynical, very serious young man. Nick seemed incapable of feeling joy, the Army had stolen something vital from him.

Nick's girlfriend was frantically opposed to him going back to war, the idea of caring for [their] precious baby alone was overwhelming. The young mother fell apart, she told Nick she loved him and she loved their baby with all her being, but she couldn't keep her and raise her alone. If he returned to Iraq, she threatened to give the baby up. With absolute faith in the compassion of his commanding officers at Fort Bragg, he went to them for help. Instead of help, he was reprimanded; he was slammed and berated, insulted and verbally battered. *They* would put the child in foster care; Nick *would* return to the Middle East.

I have never seen a man so miserable and lost in despair. He spent the time in his room or on the phone with his lady. It broke my heart to see the light disappear from his eyes. Nick was slipping into a depression so deep, he wasn't thinking clearly, and I felt utterly helpless to save him.

There is no comfort you can offer a soul-wounded soldier, no words to fix a heart so weary of battle it would rather lay down and die, and on the day Nick was to return to Iraq, he tried to take his life. My brave son, my courageous soldier, the Army had beaten him down until there was no fight left in him. He thought he would cheat the enemy of one more casualty and choose his own time to die.

As Peggy drove her son to the Minneapolis airport for his return flight to Iraq, he lapsed into semi-consciousness. She immediately took him to a hospital emergency room where he was treated for drug overdose. From there, he was transferred to the local VA hospital, where he was placed in a mental ward.

He didn't succeed, and now instead of a hero to his country, the Army considered him a criminal. Nick was removed in handcuffs from the psychiatric hospital and transferred down to Fort Bragg. The Army wanted him in Jail, the Army wanted to make an example of my son.

A nightmare was spiraling out of control before my stricken eyes. I couldn't believe how ruthless the military was, even after witnessing their total disregard for the well-being of their soldiers for two years. I couldn't comprehend their absolute heartlessness.

While Nick sat on base waiting for his court martial, enduring horrible insults from officers and others he had thought were his friends.

I was literally fighting for the life of my son, and feeling like I was taking on the world alone. I had found Tod Ensign of Citizen Soldier when I did an Internet search on AWOL soldiers. His name came up in an article about a conscientious objector he had helped—he was my last hope. A few days after I wrote to him, he called and I filled him in about Nick's desperate situation. Tod and lawyer Louis Font agreed to pay Fort Bragg a visit and stir things up by checking into Nick's case.

Hope can be an amazingly beautiful thing. From dark despair, I could suddenly see the sun beyond the storm. These two men who stood for justice were willing to take on the military for us. Nick was stuck in limbo, in a hostile environment, feeling despondent, hopeless and helplessly worried about the friends he had left behind in Iraq. As he waited, one by one he watched his buddies come back wounded from war, some visibly scarred, others carried their scars on the inside. What Nick didn't realize was that he too was one of the wounded who carried the scars of war inside his heart, but without the glory or the honor he had earned on the battlefield.

Once upon a time I had believed the military would take care [of] my son like family, but I was wrong. They turned on him with vicious cruelty and wanted to make an example out of him.

When things looked their bleakest, orders came through from the chain of command. There was to be no court martial after all, someone had approved a Chapter Ten discharge in lieu of prosecution. We had won, the Army was unwilling to take on an angry mom with two powerful voices standing beside her. Thanks to Tod and Louis, our fight was over.

Nick's battles are still uphill, he has his silent scars to deal with and the nightmares of war yet to conquer. He has untold stories of blood he has spilled and faces of death he has seen, horrors he may never share.

He is devoted to his country and has the greatest love, respect and loyalty for the soldiers who still serve (I do as well). He wants no other soldier to be treated as unjustly as he was, all deserve respect and human compassion regardless of their training to be warriors, they are still human beings first.

Interview with U.S. Army Lt. Colonel about his experiences in Iraq (February 2004).

No, to be honest, I am not enjoying being back [home.] I keep seeing the soldiers dying every time I turn on the news or pick up a paper. I can't get a sense of relief at being home when many of my fellow soldiers will not ever be coming home. It is hard to feel good about no longer being in Iraq. I just can't seem to put my feelings in any kind of perspective.

Imagine how terrible it is to be home and not be able to tear your mind away from the worst hellhole you could ever imagine. I pace the floor at night when I think about all the soldiers that are still there or imminently going over, I worry about the ones that are on call up or training to go take their turn at trying to stay alive.

I was in several other combat theaters and I have never seen something as bad as Iraq. I have well over 15 years in service and was in the first Gulf War. I thought I had seen everything that had to do with combat and police actions. I was wrong, and most of my fellow officers have said the same thing. None of us were really prepared for this, no matter what type of training or experience we have.

I saw an officer with almost 15 years lose it and just start screaming after he lost ten guys in two days. Some of the NCOs who should have been the most experienced at losing men are being devastated by the continued loss of troops.

The first thing I want to point out is that most of our troops are not trained for police action. They do not have any idea how to conduct peacekeeping operations or effectively act as a police force. They are trained to kill opposing forces, but not react peacefully to a civilian demonstration or day-to-day civil unrest.

The main line troops do not even know how to properly conduct peacekeeping exercises, and after many months of hostilities, they really don't care to learn. They see their buddies dying and getting severely wounded, and peaceful interaction goes right out of their minds. They are stuck in the middle of a massive civil unrest and factional strife, and the[re] is no way to expect battle hardened troops to be objective. That is not what they were trained for and the Army has very little actual hands on training opportunities with an occupied population.

It took us a few weeks to supposedly win the ground war, and then it was right into the role of peacekeeper and police force. I am going to make this very clear: We are not giving our troops the proper training to occupy Iraq over the long run. Even if there was relative stability it would be hard, and in the midst of continuing hostilities it is impossible. These men are trained in gun barrel diplomacy, not as police or aid workers.

Sometimes you have to weigh your duty to your government, and the duty to your fellow soldiers to protect them and keep them safe. I feel the duty to my fellow soldier out weighs any loyalty to my government. I do not see this as treason or betraying my command, especially in light of how badly the government has betrayed our troops at every level.

I feel it is my ultimate duty to do everything possible to make sure my men come home alive and unharmed.

You won't find a whole lot of support for the way Bush and the Pentagon are running this war, not in the military anyway. Someone has to come out and tell the truth so that the rest of the troops will not be afraid to be honest with themselves and the American public. There is such an undercurrent of fear among the troops about what might get you in trouble. There are soldiers worried that something they say in a letter or on the phone will get them court-martialed or thrown in the brig for treason.

I am doing this for all the soldiers who want to speak out but will not for reasons of fear and keeping a career intact. I know a few guys who got called into the O2 (intelligence operations for a military unit) after making harsh comments in e-mails home.

I swore an oath to defend this country, but I also swore to protect my men to the utmost of my ability. I am only doing this out of honor and loyalty to all the men who put their life on the line in my command and the command of others. I am sick of watching young men and women die needlessly. If there were a purpose behind it besides oil and the sick greed of our leaders, I would keep my mouth shut and drive on.

I don't see Iraq liberated and there are not any WMDs. I was there on some of the searches and I can tell you that we did not actually expect to find anything. Our leaders were telling us we would find them, but most of the officers knew that was bullshit.

I am sure that there will be many of my fellow soldiers who will hate me for speaking out like this. There are many of them that are still completely dedicated to the cause of the U.S.

I am in command at a higher level than the company command, so I saw first hand how badly prepared some of my unit commanders were. There was a level of chaos and confusion that almost brought the chain of command down around our ears. I really want to focus on some more recent stuff, but I will give some brief details on this one, because I think it caused many lives to be lost needlessly.

In the first few weeks, our supply chain was in shambles, whole columns were getting lost in the desert, there was a severe shortage of drinkable water, and unit level communication was completely unreliable. I could get my staff on the radio, but often we were out of contact with the more remotely located unit commanders for hours or days at a time.

That was a major problem when we were trying to scout the Iraqi positions. We did not hear from some units for days except by satellite phone communication and other non-standard communication methods. I heard one story of a guy who scrounged up some kids walkie-talkies and it was the only way the unit commander could keep in contact with his patrols. I also heard of one unit that found a pair of old field radios in an Iraqi vehicle and they had to use them for short-range communications.

Iraq is a powder keg right now and it is going to explode if things don't change. If it ever really turns into a classic urban guerilla war we are going to be in a very bloody, drawn out conflict. All you have to do is look at the situation that occurred in Lebanon in the last thirty years and you can get an idea of how bloody Iraq could become. The Israelis know all about jihad and urban warfare from the high toll the various Palestinian groups have extracted. Iraq is in a similar situation and some of our high level officials refuse to admit it.

If the deaths keep up at this rate we will lose over 2000 soldiers in the next year. I have heard some of the Pentagon insiders predict at least 1000 more deaths over the next year. The way they talk about it is just so casual it makes a combat commander cringe.

The fact that it is costing me the lives of my men and the brave coalition forces is not even coming into the picture. The disregard for the man in uniform who is out there on the frontline dying and shedding his blood is what we need to focus on.

The Army has started to take some steps to put better armor on Humvees. It is not going to happen soon enough to save the lives that will be lost before they give them better equipment. Not to mention the lives that have already been lost, and all the soldiers who have been, or will be injured. Let's talk about the thousands of our soldiers who have been permanently disabled either physically or mentally. They have evacuated thousands of troops with mental problems, and yet they claim that troop morale is high.

I'd say about 25% of my men actually wanted to be in Iraq and were happy to be in combat. Most of them were just there because it was their duty, and they had no choice in the matter.

I would not have this kind of problem if we were not losing good soldiers to such a stupid drive to completely rule Iraq. If this were about really liberating and freeing Iraq, we would have set up a different type of occupying force. We are trying to lock down a whole country while we keep telling the Iraqis that we are there to bring them freedom.

Some of the horrific injuries from the Humvees are actually causing major morale problems. I had a brand new vehicle and I was still worried that it was vulnerable to IED and rocket attack. The roadside bombs are tearing up the older hummers like they were made of cardboard. I have seen many that were torn open and the crew compartment was full of shrapnel holes. I have seen several that took an RPG or rocket hit and it was a bloody scene. I don't know if the casualty rate from the hummers has been as high as 80% but it has been well over 60%.

That is what reservists have really been complaining about. They have all the older vehicles and supplies. The vehicle situation was especially bad with the support units and some of the Reserve MP units. It gets even worse if you look at some of the National Guard units. The equipment in some of the units I saw was pathetic.

I never thought I would have to speak out so I didn't ever think about what the military would do to me.

My biggest reason for going public is to try to affect the death toll of our troops. I have seen my men die and it hasn't made Iraq any safer or more stable. The war takes away soldiers who can help defend our own shores and fight in a real defensive war should it become necessary.

It was probably the hardest decision I have made recently. I am not a traitor or ashamed of doing my duty. I want nothing more than to be the best leader I can be. I searched for some other solution and for a while I was going to keep my mouth shut. Sitting here the last week watching the soldiers die changed my mind like nothing else.

Excerpts from a letter to his mother and stepfather from ***Capt. Pierre E. Piché****, 29, of Starksboro, Vermont. Captain Piché was killed on November 15, 2003, when his helicopter crashed near Mosul. RIP.*

Wednesday, Aug. 6, 2003

I can say that I will be home by early February. . . . I am definitely looking forward to being out of the military. It was good for what it did for me, I don't regret it, but it is time to go. I see the future holding a lot more deployments. . . . I am proud to defend my country but I don't want to be defending it constantly for the next 10–15 years.

I am looking into both teaching and law enforcement when I get out. Either way, I still want to be doing a job that has a positive impact on the world. I am not some idealist who thinks I can change the world but I can still be doing some sort of good. I want to be able to believe in what I am doing. I prefer the teaching route because it has a more predictable schedule and I can blab about politics and history all day long (something I enjoy anyway). I had some good teachers growing up and I think it would be pretty cool if I could do what they did.

Excerpts from two e-mail messages to her family from ***SPC Holly J. McGeogh,*** *19, of Taylor, Michigan. SPC McGeogh was killed on January 31, 2004, near Kirkuk by an I.E.D., military parlance for an improvised explosive device. RIP.*

Monday, Jan. 5, 2004

Hi, you guys, what's going on on that side of the world? Things are O.K. over here. Today when my section rolled out of the gate we saw someone drop a can on the ground, and we thought it was an I.E.D. So I stopped right away and backed up. We got out and pulled security. Then we called Charlie Company out to take a look.

Well, it ended up not being an I.E.D. I felt a little embarrassed, but at the same time I knew that we had done the right thing. And I have full confidence in the people I work with that if they felt if anybody's life was in danger, they would do everything in their power not to let anything happen.

Anyway, that was the most exciting thing that happened today so far. Everything here is good and I'm doing good. . . . I am very thankful for having such a caring and loving family! I really can't wait to get home. I can't wait to see everyone, I really miss you all soooooo much! If it weren't for you guys, I would have never been able to make it through all this.

Little Grams and Pappa, Jan. 9, 2004

We're so close to coming home . . . The more people I talk to are all making me think that for sure we'll be home by April at the latest. I still can't believe that I'm only nineteen and had my combat patch when I was eighteen. That makes me feel very proud of my life. What's even cooler is that I will only be twenty years old when I get out. That's very young and I will already have accomplished so much in my life. Cool huh? I'm definitely going to sit back and relax and go to college. Then I'm coming back in as an officer. Well, I'm getting off here because my hands are getting cold. You guys take care. I love you and miss you guys a whole bunch. Love, Holly

Excerpts from letters to his mother from ***Specialist Robert A. Wise****, 21, of Tallahassee, Florida. Specialist Wise was killed on November 12, 2003, by a homemade bomb while on patrol in Baghdad. RIP.*

Monday, Feb. 24, 2003

So far I've been in a sandstorm (twice), I'm working on my third one as I speak (or write). I've also had the pleasure of experiencing a "sand-bomb." It's not what you think, but it is very interesting. When the wind is blowing really strong, it fills the tents, but when the wind stops, all the air rushes out of the tent and causes the sand to literally explode into the air and covers everything in a fine coat of dust. Yeah!

Every morning I wake up, and it's like a scene out of the movie "The Mummy." I get to shake the dirt out of everything, including my face and hair. One day I'll get a hold of a camera and I'll send you some cool pictures.

P.S.: You will be proud to know I have finished reading "The Hobbit" and "Halo." I've started on "The Lord of the Rings." That book is a workout both physically and mentally.

Wednesday, April 2

In case you were wondering, I stink. The kind of stink that you can only find in the desert. We call it "the scent of the Desert Rose." It's what you get when you haven't had a shower in over 20 days. Thank God for baby wipes. I had to get a filling replaced. I was chewing some gum and crack! I don't know how, but it broke and started to splinter in my mouth.

On to more positive news. Since I left Fort Stewart, I've read: "The Hobbit," "Halo," "The Lord of the Rings" ("The Fellowship of the Ring" and "The Two Towers"), "Aliens vs. Predator: War" and "Star Trek: The Eugenics Wars, Volume II." Nothin' like a little boredom to get ya in a readin' mood.

Well, I hope everything back at Fort Living Room is going well.

Thursday, May 8

Rumor has it that we'll be on a plane home June 22, so keep your fingers crossed. I'm really going to need your help setting up a budget when I get home and making sure I stick to it. I know the only way I'll complete my goals of paying off my car and getting all of that furniture for our house by the end of the year is by paying attention to what I spend my money on.

Well, I'm runnin' out of things to write about. I love you and I miss you. Tell everyone I said hi, and one day I'll get home.

P.S.: There's no place like home (click)
There's no place like home (click)
There's no place like home (click)
Damn, it didn't work again!

*Letters from **2d Lt. Seth Dvorin,** of Pennington, New Jersey, to family and friends. He was killed on February 3, 2004, while trying to dismantle a bomb near Iskandariyah. RIP.*

Mom and Dad, Sept. 17, 2003

Hello, from lovely Iraq. I'm doing pretty well. The worst part is how bad I miss all of you, especially Kelly. I have been very busy with my job and it has been pretty stressful, but I think I'm getting it under control.

I have special privileges most people do not have and that's a big plus. I even had a can of Coke today (ha, ha, lucky me). No one else at my base has had such luxury.

Good news is that I'm already more than half a month in, so just closer to me being home. Lucky for me I will miss my first Ft. Drum Winter. I bet it is already starting to get cold up there.

Mom and Dad, Oct. 10, 2003

It's odd but you never pay much attention to these things (change of seasons) when they happen at home. But when you're away you're not real sure about little things like that. I have been without a set of sunglasses, but my choices are to wear tinted lenses and not be able to see or wear my regular lenses and see. Since we are in a war zone I prefer to see. Thankfully, that's not been an issue thus far. Just a few more weeks and I officially take over my platoon, which I cannot wait for.

On the Fifteenth, I will lead a special team of Iraqis and Americans from my battalion to protect the exchange of new Iraqi money for this old stuff. I will have a special place in history even though no one but me really knows it. Kinda odd how the Jewish guy randomly ends up in charge of the money. Speaking of which, I went to Yom Kippur services yesterday in a palace that use to belong to Saddam. Now there's irony. I love and miss you both.

Mom and Dad, Nov. 2003

Hey, what's up at home—not too much here in Iraq. Me, personally I think I'm gonna have to call my travel agent and demand a refund. I've been getting integrated into my platoon and led my first patrol today. All went pretty well but it was very much a learning experience for me. I think things are going to be good once I get used to this job and the guys get used to me as their leader.

Dear Ellen, Dec. 25, 2003

Thank you for your letter. It's hard to explain just how much a letter from a complete stranger can mean. I must tell you, your letter made me cry. The part you wrote about your daughter makes me realize why I do this job. I have put her picture on my wall, which is something I've never done before. I hope to have a daughter one day and hope that she will be as beautiful as your little girl.

I miss my family but knowing that I am helping keep families like yours safe makes it easier.

Sincerely, Seth Dvorin

Sue Niederer, Seth's mother, also of Pennington, New Jersey, had badly wanted to meet the plane which was carrying Seth's remains when it landed at Dover AFB. She told the Army Times *that her request to visit was "totally discouraged" by military officials: "I wanted to see Seth come back to this country. I needed to know he had safely arrived. I didn't want him to be alone.*

I felt he'd know we were there. I wanted to at least meet his coffin and kiss his flag." (Niederer was unable to meet the plane carrying her son's body.)

Letters and e-mail from **Sgt. Michael DiRaimondo,** *22, of Simi Valley, California. He was killed on January 8, 2004, when his medical evacuation helicopter was shot down near Fallujah. RIP.*

Dear Mom and Dad, September 4, 2003

Well, I really don't know where to begin, so I'll just start with thank you. As a young boy growing up, I never knew how much I was learning from you; little did I know you were turning me into the young man I have become today. Never in a million years did you ever imagine me in some third world country fighting a war, but then again, neither did I.

For once in my life I think I'm finally starting to feel like I can make a decision about what I want to do without thinking about what other people will think.

Life is so precious. Living day by day in good health or just happiness is probably what makes me happy right now. I try not to think if what I do makes me happy. Just being alive, having a wonderful family, good friends, watching the sunrise morning after morning, that's what makes me feel good. I think people take their lives for granted. Some just haven't hit that part of their life where they stop and say, "I'm lucky to have the life I have." Recently, I figured out that if I live my life not everyday like it's my last, but that everyday is the best day of my life, I don't worry about the little things that would normally upset me or discomfort me.

Jan. 4, 2004

New Year's Day was very busy for me. It started at 5am and went on for hours. Mission after mission. I had eight patients that day. I lost one of them, but there was no helping him when we got to him. That was sad, but we all must move on. It's sad to think that I can see that and then just go to lunch like it never happened. I'll always remember that soldier, though.

Most guys don't like it because you see a lot of gory stuff. But I see it as training for the future. I've been thinking a lot about my future lately. Who's knows what's going to happen, right?

Excerpts from ***Tony DiRaimondo****'s eulogy at his son Michael's funeral:*

My last Mike story is a little more serious but has a happy ending. Michael had started taking EMT classes. He and his friends were snowboarding up at Mountain High when Mike saw a skier go off the trail into the woods. He knew he was in trouble. When he got to the man, he was seriously hurt. Mike sent his friends to get the paramedics while he stayed and administered first aid. When the paramedics got there and saw how well Mike treated the victim, they asked him to stay and continue helping them, saying he obviously knew what he was doing. Michael's purpose in life was starting to take shape.

To enhance his chances of becoming a Paramedic Firefighter, Michael joined the Army three weeks before September 11th, when the world was a safer place. He trained as a Combat Medic and was stationed at Ft. Carson, CO. He was so good at what he did that he was recruited to join the 571st Medical Company. He was going to become a Flight Medic. To put it in perspective, a Flight Medic is about ten levels above a Combat Medic and they are very selective about who joins their ranks. The mission of the 571st is Medevac. To go in and rescue people who are wounded in combat, to give aid and get them out, even when they are under enemy fire. When he successfully completed the training program he was the proudest soldier in the US Army.

The news media doesn't talk about it nearly enough anymore, but there is far more fighting going on in Iraq than the public is aware of. The 571st has several missions everyday. As many of you heard, Mike saved ten lives the day the Chinook helicopter was shot down on November 3d. He was nominated for the Air Medal for his actions that day and it was posthumously awarded to him. Every day he administered aid to people who were either shot or hit by a rocket-propelled grenade or some other awful thing. He made life and death decisions on the battlefield and he often did so under fire. He loved the work he did and the purpose of his life had now become crystal clear.

Michael died on one of those missions when an Iraqi fired a missile at their unarmed helicopter. We grieve for him but as sure as I stand here I know our son and brother would not want us to do that. He would want us to celebrate the good times, to laugh and be happy that he lived and not be sad that he died.

To borrow the words of Kris Kristofferson; "loving him was easier than anything I'll ever do again." I love you, son. Please be there to guide your mother, sisters and me in continuing your dream of helping others.

4

Women in the Military: The Military Culture of Harassment

The Dynamics of the Masculine Mystique

Linda Bird Francke

" 'Hey, tell me about the pussy,' " says a supply sergeant to an Army warrant officer in Nelson DeMille's best-selling 1992 novel, *The General's Daughter.* The warrant officer, who is about to arrest the supply sergeant for trafficking military supplies, gives the sergeant the answer he wants to hear. "Well, I got me a little slopehead 'bout as tall as a pint of piss, and I just pick her up by the ears and stick her on my dick, then slap her upside the head and spin her 'round my cock like the block on a shithouse door.' " The supply sergeant roars with laughter.[1]

Though fictional, DeMille's story of the gang rape of a female cadet at West Point and the investigation of her subsequent murder embodies many of the male attitudes ingrained in the military culture—the institutional promotion of male dominance, the aura of hypermasculinity, the collective male imperative to disparage women in general and specifically women in the military. "They squat to piss. Try doing that with sixty pounds of field gear," grumbles a DeMille colonel at the bar in the officers' club before ambling off to the men's room.[2]

Projecting the fictional colonel's attitudes onto all men in the military would, of course, be a stereotype as inaccurate as it would be sexist. Many individual men in the different services work well with women and respect both their contributions and authority. But individuals don't count in the military. The military culture is driven by a group dynamic centered around male perceptions and sensibilities, male psychology and power, male anxieties and the affirmation of masculinity. Harrassment is an inevitable by-product.

If the Freudian observation is true that the tenets of masculinity demand man's self-measure against other men, military service offers the quintessential paradigm. The services revolve around competition and graded contests, the results of which are publicly displayed on servicemen's chests. Servicemen who have proved their measure against a historically male enemy by earning combat ribbons and badges, prisoner-of-war medals and the Purple Heart are the models for military masculinity. Though a study of infantrymen in World War II found that only 15 percent ever fired their weapons in combat[3] and that fewer than 15 percent of the hundreds of thousands of military personnel who served in Vietnam are estimated to have been in a firefight[4] the minority of men set the model for the masses.

Short of experiencing combat, men in the most high-risk specialties define the masculine edge—the Navy SEALs, the 82nd Airborne, the Special Operations forces whose classified missions are shrouded in secrecy. "When you're around the 82nd Airborne or the Rangers, you can smell the macho, feel it, hear it," says Tod Ensign, director of Citizen Soldier, a civil liberties organization based in New York. "To be called 'STRAC' (Straight, Tough and Ready for Action) is a great compliment. That means you're ready to jump out this window, rappel down the side of the building and kill someone with a pencil."[5]

Military aviators are high on the masculine role-model scale. The entire Air Force exists to support the 3 percent who are pilots. In the Navy, fighter pilots fly off nuclear-powered aircraft carriers manned by crews of five thousand. So admired are fighter pilots that their recognition transcends enemy lines. When Germany's World War II Luftwaffe ace Adolf Galland died in 1996, his obituary merited four columns and a photograph in the *New York Times.*[6]

The aviator mystique grew around the early test pilots like Chuck Yeager, who, despite two broken ribs, flew what was little more than a primitive rocket straight up into the heavens in 1947 to become the first man to break the sound barrier. "*Manliness, manhood, manly courage* . . . there was something ancient, primordial, irresistible about the challenge of this stuff, no matter what a sophisticated and rational age one might think he lived in," writes Tom Wolfe about the pilots in *The Right Stuff*.[7]

The legend lingers in the almost erotic male worship between young men, competitive men, daring men. The love affair between the hero of the film *Top Gun*, played by Tom Cruise, and his girlfriend was secondary to the sexual tension between Cruise and a rival pilot vying for the Navy's top flying spot. The sexual payoff of the film was not between Cruise and his girlfriend, but in the clenched fist hug between the two men. Similarly, the payoff in *Independence Day* was the victory cigars shared between a Marine pilot and a computer scientist after they had destroyed an alien spaceship, not the embraces of their wives. "The military is a sexual fantasy built around images of masculinity," observed writer Nancy Chapkis at an international symposium on women and the military system in 1987. "Only other men can pose a sufficient threat and a sufficient challenge to serve as worthy objects of desire."[8]

Images of the ideal male play throughout the military culture, where men spend more time in the company of men than in any other institution save prison. Dress uniforms in the Marines are designed to set off the male body, to accentuate the slimness of the waist, the breadth of shoulder, the length of leg. Male vanity is understood in the military. "I can see why the Defense Department sent you," a retired general remarked matter-of-factly to a young Air Force officer at a 1992 hearing. "You're so handsome."

The image is especially important in the officer corps. During the Pacific campaign in World War II, Douglas MacArthur had his pants custom-pleated below the waist to make him look slimmer, and his hat heightened to six inches above the brim to make him look taller.[9] Army officers stand unflinching, and unprotected, in snow or rain. By policy, male (but not female) officers are not allowed to carry umbrellas. Even ears make the man. Among the disqualifying physical characteristics for candidates to West Point listed in the 1992 admissions catalogue were disfigured or uneven ears as well as "moderately severe acne or resultant scarring" and other "unsightly congenital markings."[10] "There used to be a medical regulation that ruled out ugliness," says Colonel Pierce Rushton Jr., West Point's director of admissions. "Extreme ugliness was a disqualifier."

Arrogance flows naturally from the institutional promotion of the alpha male. The symbolic power inherent in the uniform, in the weaponry and in the national license to resolve conflict by violence encourages military men to cast themselves as superior to their civilian counterparts. "It's very macho the way men see themselves as unique or special," says Tod Ensign. "One of the most important and guarded myths of the military is the necessity to maintain that hyped-up sense of maleness."

Psychiatric literature is steeped in the various passages young men feel they have to take to get away from their mothers and, by extension, all things feminine, to establish a masculine identity. Among militaristic cultures, the passage to manhood can reach epic proportions. In one legendary tribe in South America, young warriors went so far as to cut out their nipples to remove any resemblance to the female form.

The U.S. military practices its own exorcism of men's sexual duality or feminine "negative identity."[11] Thirteen years after women were integrated into the All-Volunteer Force, Marine Corps drill sergeants were still purging male recruits with a "torrent of misogynist and anti-individualist abuse," writes conservative icon George Gilder. "The good things are manly and collective; the despicable are feminine and individual."[12]

Though Gilder and his conservative ilk like sociologist Lionel Tiger are universally debunked by feminists as reactionary misogynists—author Susan Faludi scorns Gilder for "bemoaning the loss of traditional manhood in society"[13] in her 1991 best-seller, *Backlash*—Gilder's description of "the extirpation of feminine ties and sentiments" in the Marine Corps remains a contemporary catechism to many men in uniform.[14]

The methods were more subtle in the other services, but the underlying premise remained the same: the way to pump up masculinity was to tear down feminity. Army drill sergeants in the early 90s still humiliated lagging male recruits by calling them "sissies," "crybables" and "girls." "So are we having menstrual cramps this morning?" one drill sergeant at Fort Jackson, South Carolina, derided a male recruit struggling with push-ups.

The same techniques were applied to female recruits to drive out their "femaleness." "You wuss, you baby, you goddamn female," was the 1991 strategy shouted at a company of female recruits, also at Fort Jackson. So antithetical to the military culture is anything feminine that the reverse psychology backfired when practiced on female recruits at the former Naval Recruit Training Center in Orlando, Florida. "You boy!" a female company commander screamed at the occasional female straggler during the 5 A.M. formation run around the paved "Grinder." Against the backdrop of male recruit companies simultaneously jogging around the Grinder, the intended pejorative sounded more like a compliment.

The masculine forces driving the military culture made the enforcement of sexual harassment policies impossible. The systematic denigration of feminine attributes in the making of a military man required the very harassment the directives were supposed to eradicate. If the measure of a man was in his contrast to a woman, then she, by definition, had to display the feminine attributes for which she was derided.

Women could be "militarized," but not so much as to threaten masculine self-confidence. Women in the Army were trained to use weapons, but assigned to support units, not male combat units. Women recruits in the Marines received less training time than the men, as did female pilots in the Navy and Air Force; additional combat training was reserved for men.

The gender line never wavered. While male recruits' heads are ritually shaved in all the services to submerge their individual identities into the male collective, women are required to wear their hair "in an attractive, feminine style,"[15] not longer than their uniform collars, but not so short as to appear mannish. Male Marine recruits are instructed in the application of combat camouflage, female recruits in the application of cosmetics.

"Women Marine recruits receive instruction in hair care, techniques of make-up application, guidance on poise, and etiquette," read a Marine recruit training manual for women in the wake of the Gulf war.[16] The Corps even issued an official Marine lipstick to its female recruits in boot camp.

The Marine justification for the cosmetic feminizing of its female recruits underscored the separate roles for the sexes deemed necessary in the military culture. "This program is designed to give you self-confidence *and improve your ability to function as a Marine,*"[17] the section in the woman's manual on "Professional Development" concludes (emphasis added), thereby assigning female Marines the role of feminine standard-bearers by which male Marines could offset their masculinity.

Imperative in all the services was the buttressing of men's real or imagined sense of virility. A Marine platoon graduating from recruit training in 1989 proudly posed with their drill instructors for their formal photograph holding a blown-up picture of a naked woman and a hand-lettered sign reading "kill, rape, pillage, burn."[18] A poster of nude pinup girls plastered the interior wall of a Marine tank gunning down Iraqi tanks in Kuwait.[19] "Male sexual imagery has always been important in combat units," said Dr. David Marlowe, a social anthropologist and chief of combat psychiatry at the Army Institute of Research.[20]

The collective forces at work in the military culture demand women's marginalization. Accepting women as military peers is antithetical to the hypermasculine identity traditionally promoted by the institution and sought by many military men. Only by excluding women or denigrating them could men preserve their superiority.

The accumulating directives from the Defense Department on sexual harassment were supposed to change all that. Taking its lead from the Equal Employment Opportunity Commission, which in 1980 had expanded the definition of gender discrimination to include sexual harassment as a violation of Title VII of the Civil Rights Act of 1964,[21] the Defense Department had issued its first policy declaration that harassment was "unacceptable conduct" that would not be "condoned or tolerated in any way." [22]

By 1981, all the services had issued their first formal definitions of sexual harassment which included "unwelcome sexual advances [and] requests for sexual favors," and creating "an intimidating, hostile, or offensive working environment." [23] Sexual harassment awareness and prevention was added to existing programs on human relations. "For the first time, sexual harassment was treated as a different and separate form of discrimination, just like race, age, religion and national origin," says former Air Force Colonel Mickey Collins.

But nothing changed. By 1990, after DACOWITS had finally pressured the Defense Department into documenting the extent of sexual harassment in the services, it was epidemic. Two out of three women in the Defense Department study of 20,000 personnel reported experiencing at least one form of harassment in the past year, including pressure for sexual favors (15 percent) and actual or attempted rape (5 percent).[24] "The results are sobering," said Christopher Jehn, the assistant secretary of defense for force management and personnel.[25]

The Navy had not reached its goals first stated by the 1987 Navy Women's Study Group and, of necessity, repeated in 1990 to (1) "Eliminate sexual harassment practices in the Navy" and (2) "Create a professional environment predicated on mutual respect," [26] because it couldn't.

The architects of the All-Volunteer Force had concentrated on the effect women would have on men, not the effect men would have on women. The influential 1977 Binkin-Bach study advocating women as a personnel resource devotes only two paragraphs to what little was known about tokenism, whereas three pages are reserved for warnings about menstruation.[27] Similarly, the study expresses no major concerns about the as yet unexamined behavior of men in groups. "At the outset, it is important to point out that an understanding of the behavior and performance of *men* in groups, particularly under combat or sea-duty conditions, is far from complete . . . and precious little is known about the effects of combining men and women," the authors concede.[28]

Civilian academics and writers studying the group dynamic in the 80s cast a wide net, chronicling the behavior patterns and the perceived demands of "masculinity" in such varied male groups as sports teams, college fraternities and Little League. Virtually every characteristic pinpointed as unique to men in groups was rampant in the military culture. And every one of them fit the definition of sexual harassment.

Crude jokes and sexually demeaning talk about women, a group dynamic observed by Freud as directed *against* women by men in groups, but more sexual and clever when directed *toward* women, was the bonding mechanism among fraternity "brothers" studied on one college campus by Professor Peter Lyman, director of the Center for Scholarly Technology at the University of Southern California.[29] Reducing women to sex objects was considered essential to forging close fraternal bonds. "The group separated intimacy from sex, defining the male bond as intimate but not sexual and relationships with women as sexual but not intimate," observed Lyman.[30]

Talking "dirty" about girls and "faggots" was the group mechanism used by boys on ten Little League teams to prove their budding heterosexual identities.[31] Women, even among this subculture of preadolescent boys, were perceived as a threat to the integrity of the all-male group. "Girls can easily break the bonds of brotherhood among boys," noted Gary Alan Fine, a sociologist at the University of Minnesota.

In a prelude to the sexual exhibitionism of Navy pilots at the Tailhook convention in 1991, the preadolescent boys' aggressive pranks like "mooning" passing cars were always performed in the presence of the male group and, if successful, gave the boys group status.[32] Such male-to-male displays served to wean out the wimps in the male group and establish a leadership hierarchy based on daring. Just a few boys set the behavior standards for all, a group dynamic which would also play out a Tailhook.

The widespread display of pornography in male cultures from locker rooms to military bases was found by other researchers to further reinforce the separate and superior male position sought by men in groups. To many gender analysts in the 80s, pornography represented the greatest barrier to sexual equality by making sexism sexy. "Pornography institutionalizes male supremacy the way segregation institutionalizes white supremacy," writer John Stoltenberg told a 1984 conference on men and masculinity in Washington, D.C.[33]

In the extreme, the male group dynamic crossed the line into criminality. A study of twenty-six gang rapes reported between 1980 and 1990 revealed that men who raped in groups were already members of closely knit male collectives. None of the fifteen reported gang rapes by college athletes between 1989 and 1990 involved athletes in solo sports like swimming or tennis, but rather team sports like football, basketball and lacrosse.[34] The negative group dynamic was no less powerful in the military.

The forces which drove college athletes to rape as teams in 1990 paralleled the forces that had driven U.S. soldiers to rape as platoons in Vietnam. The civilian males were young, as were their military counterparts. Each group spent their time almost exclusively in all-male subcultures—sports teams trained, competed and traveled together; military units patrolled, ate and lived together twenty-four hours a day. The success of each group depended entirely on teamwork: in the case of sports teams, to win; in the case of military units in Vietnam, to survive. Under such intense pressure, the demands of the group often overrode personal morality, individual conscience and the law.

Among the college students and soldiers alike, men who wouldn't dream of raping a woman on their own raped in a group. "They only do it when there are guys around," Susan Brownmiller quotes a Vietnam veteran in her classic book *Against Our Will: Men, Women and Rape.*[35] In the gang mentality which would play out in the group molestation of women at Tailhook, the victims were incidental to the act. The men in Vietnam were raping for each other.

Even men who didn't take direct part in the sexual assaults were bound by the group dynamic. Some participated by taking photographs, as did soldiers involved in the violence surrounding the My Lai massacre in March 1968, during which over three hundred men, women and children in one village were killed between breakfast and 10:30 A.M.[36] Others practiced passive participation by remaining silent. In a forerunner to the stonewalling of investigators following Tailhook, a sergeant in Vietnam reacted to his squad of nine men raping a woman by going to another part of the village where he sat by himself, staring at the ground.[37]

Whether military or civilian, the grip of brotherhood overrode all. "There has never been a single case, in all the gang rapes we've seen, where one man tried to stop it," reported Gail Abarbanel, director of the Rape Treatment Center at Santa Monica Hospital in California. "It's more important to be part of the group than to be the person who does what's right."[38]

Women were little more than trophies in contests of male dominance. Navy fighter pilots at the Tailhook convention would sport T-shirts reading "Women Are Property," and affix squadron stickers to various parts of women's anatomy. In Vietnam, at least one woman's body was found spread-eagled with a brigade patch between her legs. Other women's bodies were found with their vaginal access blocked by entrenching tools, grease guns or grenades.[39] Sexually assaulting women was such a universally accepted by-product of military male behavior that it would be 1996 before rape was defined as a war crime by the International Criminal Tribunal in The Hague.[40]

In such a group-driven male culture, the sexual harassment directives from the Pentagon were doomed to sink like stones. The group dynamic which in the extreme drove the gang rapes by soldiers in Vietnam and athletic teams on college campuses stepped down only by degrees to the hanging of pornographic pictures of women in locker rooms and barracks and down again to the dirty talk and male initiation rites deemed so essential to bond fraternity brothers and even Little Leaguers. It was a bonding dynamic the military well understood.

While the civilian sector was just beginning to be educated on the dynamic of men in groups, the U.S. military had been exploiting it, unchallenged, for two hundred years. And rather than being seen as negative, the dynamic was positive.

The coarse, sexually demeaning language that bonded men in college fraternity houses multiplied out in the services to bond men in platoons, squadrons, companies, whole divisions and fleets of men. "We find ourselves cursing and swearing every two seconds," says Gloria Johnson, a Navy airman at school in Orlando in 1991. "That's all you really hear out here, instructors, everybody. You just get used to it. My first day at boot camp, our company commander said, 'If my language offends you, fuck it, you're just going to have to put up with it.' "

At the military academies, each service boasted its own repertoire of WUBA jokes, an official Navy acronym for "Working Uniform, Blue Alpha" issued for the first class of female midshipmen at the U.S. Naval Academy, but commonly understood as "Women Used By All." Freud would have delighted in the classic WUBA jokes unabashedly greeting women midshipmen at the Naval Academy as late as 1990.

"How are a WUBA and a bowling ball similar?" Answer: "You pick them up, put three fingers in them, and throw them in the gutter."

"What's the difference between a WUBA and a warthog?" Answer: "About 200 pounds, but the WUBA has more hair." [41]

The verbal denigration of women served a useful military purpose. In times of sharper gender divisions, vulgar language and profanity had been traditionally restricted to men. Its excessive use in the military culture served as both reminder and reinforcement of a separate male society with its own language and rules. And so, despite sexual harassment policies, the language continued.

Equally resistant to the sexual harassment policies were the sexually explicit and aggressive cadence calls which drill sergeants and company commanders had used to motivate their troops on training runs and twelve-mile road marches since the Civil War. The psychology of cadence calls was the timeless essence of male bonding.

In World War II, the cadences had been racist as well as sexual, the twin package of bonding criteria researchers would find in the 80s among all-white male fraternity groups and the members of the Little League. One vintage cadence call began: "LEFT! LEFT! Had a good job when I LEFT! / LEFT my wife with eight nigger babies, / Hay foot, straw foot . . . ," the latter referring to the technique drill sergeants used to help rural recruits identify which foot was which—hay tucked into the laces of the left boot, straw on the right.

Sexual aggression was pumped into the young men in 1944 as it would be fifty years later. The World War II regimental song of the 342nd Infantry began: "We're Colonel Heffner's raiders/And we're riders of the night;/ We're horny sonsabitches,/ We'd rather fuck than fight." The message was as collectively inspiring as it was loud. "Imagine three thousand men, 90 percent of us boys under twenty-one and a good many of us still virgins, marching along singing this," recalls Clement Wood, an Army private at the time. "I guess it made us feel tough and manly."

In the less innocent days of the Vietnam era, cadence calls became known in the Army and Marines as "jodies," a generic term defined admiringly by one drill sergeant as "a stud who's sleeping with everybody's girlfriend while they're working." But the basic message of male dominance was the same. "I wish all the ladies were piled on the shelf, and I was a baker—I'd eat 'em all myself," starts "Heybobareba," a classic jody still "called" in 1995 in the Marines.

To the men's great pleasure, jodies derided sentimentality as a hated sign of "feminine" softness and extolled "masculine" aggression. "There's a yellow bird with a yellow bill, sitting on a window sill. I lured it in with a piece of bread, and then I STAMPED its little head," was a West Point favorite in the 70s, accompanied by the synchronized stamping of cadet boots at the matching word.[42]

Midshipmen at the U.S. Naval Academy in Annapolis drilled to particularly graphic cadence calls. One classic extolled the sexual prowess of a downed, but hardly defeated, pilot. "Climbed all out with his dick in his hand/Said, 'Looky here, ladies, I'm a hell of a man.'/Went to his room and lined up a hundred . . . /Swore up and down he'd fuck everyone./Fucked ninety-eight till his balls turned blue/Then he backed off, jacked off, and fucked the other two."[43]

The young men loved the jodies. That servicewomen and female officer candidates did not made the calls even better. The women were kept in their inferior place while the men were maintained in their superior one. So the sexual harassment directives to clean up the jodies and to return to the more formal term of "cadence call" were spotty at best and met in at least one Army unit in the 90s with insurrection.

"The men shouted down the guy calling the politically correct cadence. It got ugly," says a drill sergeant who trained infantry soldiers at Fort Benning, Georgia, in 1992. "They wanted to hear how the man is masculine over the woman and that's what we sung to them and that's what maxed their PT tests. The response was tremendous whether I was running soldiers five miles or walking eighty people in a line down the street singing that or 250 soldiers in a company. The dirtier the better. It got results."

Equally ignored were the Pentagon directives to denude the military workplace of pornographic posters, *Playboy* centerfolds and other prominently displayed sexual erotica. Though the salacious depiction of women clearly fit the service and EEOC definitions of a "hostile work environment" shared by both sexes, men were not about to relinquish their sexual authority. "When I asked my boss to take down the pornography in our office because it was fueling male sexual discourse in the workplace and causing fractionalization, he told me I was too straitlaced," says former Air Force Captain Patricia Gavin, who subsequently filed a complaint about the harassment going on at the Fort Benjamin Harrison Defense Information School in Indiana in 1991. "You would have thought I'd asked for the Red Sea to part."

Go-go dancers and strippers continued to be prime entertainment at on-base service clubs, despite Pentagon directives to end the practice. Not only did the clubs depend on strippers and prostitutes to attract money-spending males, the strippers also reinforced the masculine collective. Unlike the ambiguous roles played by modern servicewomen, there was no end to the positive role played by exotic dancers and prostitutes.

The shared male delight in publicly exhibiting their collective libidos transcended rank, race and ethnic backgrounds, reaffirming the bonds among men. Strippers were also seen as safe. While other women might strike a romantic relationship with one of the men and thereby break the bonds of brotherhood, a paid commodity, especially of another race, was not a threat.

In the Philippines, servicemen at the now defunct Subic Bay Naval Station regularly sought the services of the "hospitality girls," as government officials called them, or "little brown fucking machines," as Navy sailors called them. For $10, servicemen could simultaneously enjoy lunch, a cold beer, and a blow job performed by a Filipino woman on her hands and knees under the table.[44]

Strippers were no less essential to the male collective in Korea. "When I left Korea in 1992, the whole unit threw a party," says an Army senior personnel specialist. "The commander danced with a stripper. The first sergeant danced with a stripper. I danced with a stripper. That was the top command level in the biggest aviation unit in the Army. There's no way you're going to change the military climate. It's a tradition."

The services had known everything there was to know about sexual harassment, and subsequently failed to control, since 1980. Members of DACOWITS were becoming increasingly convinced at the time that the hostile male atmosphere toward women and attendant sexual harassment were invisible, and unaddressed, factors in servicewomen's high attrition rate.[45] The advisory committee had heard too many stories on too many bases. "Where we experience it [harassment] is when we go out as individuals to visit a military installation and we meet with enlisted personnel," said Sally Richardson, the 1979 chair of DACOWITS. "We are very often seen as a channel for this kind of information."[46]

Congresswoman Marjorie Holt, the ranking minority member and only woman on the House military personnel subcommittee in 1979, was equally suspicious of the unexamined effects of sexual harassment on the morale and retention of servicewomen. As the number of women entering the services multiplied, so did the number of complaints swamping the Maryland Democrat's office from nearby Fort Meade, an Army base in Holt's congressional district.

What neither DACOWITS nor Holt knew was whether sexual harassment was as widespread in the services as their anecdotal evidence suggested or just concentrated in pockets. The services, which had documented everything negative about women from the lesser strength of their handgrips to their inability to do as many push-ups as men, had not expressed the slightest interest in tracking obstacles to their well-being. "Gender discrimination and sexual harassment were not issues in the 70s. Race was," says former Air Force Lt. Col. Mickey Collins, then an equal opportunity officer.

There were no records of harassment or assault in the 70s because virtually every sexual humiliation, great or small, was silenced or condoned by the male chain of command. When Diana Danis, executive director of the National Women Veterans' Conference in Denver, was raped four months after she joined the Army in 1973, her company commander had told her she would ruin the young sergeant's career if she pursued the "issue," and to forget the assault.[47]

Barbara Franco didn't even bother to report her second abduction and rape in August 1975. When she had reported being raped and stabbed in the arm by three men wearing dog tags during a weekend pass from Fort Lee, Virginia, her first sergeant had asked her, "What did you expect? You're not even wearing a bra," and ordered her out of his office.

Reassigned to Fort Hood, Texas, where the rape rate was so high that 6th Air Cavalry assault helicopters flew nightly patrols over the base, Franco had been raped again after the erroneous announcement at morning troop formation that enlisted women could not bring charges of rape against enlisted men because "rape was incidental to military service for women." So Franco didn't tell anyone after she was abducted by two men while walking to the motor pool, taken to a remote area of the base and "repeatedly sexually assaulted and tortured" until she escaped six hours later. Instead, she told a post–Gulf war congressional subcommittee, she tried to kill herself by taking an overdose of Valium.[48]

Women in all-female barracks were easy targets. Though the separate women's branches in the Navy, Army, Air Force and Coast Guard were being phased out in the 70s as women were integrated into the regular force, on most installations servicewomen were still housed separately from their units. "It gave the men one location, one prime area, to do whatever," says Sergeant First Class Vennie Hilton, who joined the Army in 1975. "We had rapes in Hawaii."

The violence was so intense at a "Wacshack" in Germany in 1979 that one

Army woman spent her own money to live off base in an apartment. "I came back from flying one day to find the building locked down and MPs in the hallways," says a combat aviation mechanic known as Dragon Lady. "It turned out two women had been murdered and left in the shower, one strangled, the other impaled on a broomstick. I never went back inside. We weren't even safe in our own building."

It had been no different in the continental United States. At Fort Devens, Massachusetts, in 1975, men from a field artillery company regularly climbed over the fence surrounding the female barracks and into the windows, sometimes accosting the women in their racks while they slept. One night the female barracks sergeant armed the women with baseball bats and positioned them by the windows. "I organized a full-staged combat incident and we bloodied the hell out of those assholes," says former Army Captain Tanya Domi, who used to carry a baseball bat for protection in the motor pool and a butcher knife in the field. "It was no way to live."

Women faced some degree of sexual humiliation every day. In the Navy, female recruits were ordered to dig trenches for their breasts before doing push-ups; their breasts were said to give them an advantage over men in lessening the distance they had to raise themselves on their arms. In the Army, women were forced to wear very short exercise shorts for physical training. Drill instructors calling the cadence for the "leg-spreader," a stomach muscle exercise which requires prone recruits to hold their legs off the ground and open and close them, often held the cadence while the women's legs were spread apart, then stood in front of them and stared. "We asked repeatedly for bigger shorts or the permission to buy them for ourselves. But they said, 'No. These are the only size. Wear them,' " recalls Sergeant First Class Ann Marie Fleming, one of five women among sixty men at an NCO primary leadership course in 1978.

The male chain of command had said no as well to the young women when they reported a male instructor for using his master key to come into the women's rooms. " 'If you want to graduate you will not submit this report,' " the commandant told the young women the day before graduation. The women had withdrawn their written statements.

Instead of protecting servicewomen, male chains of command often exploited them. In Maryland in the late 70s, one private first class listened incredulously as an Air Force colonel offered her as a prize to a group of student pilots. "He said, 'I'll give you an incentive. Anyone who passes their checkride the first time can have a weekend with Smith,' " she recalls. "I thought he was joking at first, but then I realized he meant it."

Recruiters took easy advantage of the Pentagon's long-standing policies against enlisting homosexuals. Barbara Alt was only eighteen in 1976 when she decided to join the armed forces—she didn't care which one—to get money for college. Because the Marines, as opposed to the Navy, could enlist her right away, she opted for the Corps. Her recruiter in Port Jefferson, Long Island, rehearsed the answers she should give at the regional military processing center in Fort Hamilton, New York, instructing her to say " 'No, I've never used drugs.' 'No, I'm not a homosexual.' I don't care if you are or not. Just tell them 'no,' " her recruiter told her.

The recruiter called in his sexual chip the night Alt was accepted into the Corps. "You know, I could get in serious trouble because I don't really know whether or not you're homosexual," he told Alt as they drove to the recruiting office, ostensibly to pick up some papers. On the bus to the processing center the next day, the young female recruits for all the different services discovered they had a bond. "Who'd you have to have sex with?" they asked each other, then pointed at their various recruiters. When Alt arrived in Parris Island for boot camp, she discovered from other female recruits that the homosexuality scam for heterosexual sex was nationwide.

Female officers, though far less likely to be sexually exploited by their male superiors than enlisted women, were not immune from "rank-rape." One such "rank-rape" in the Marines Corps effectively destroyed the health of a female officer who reported being assaulted by a senior officer. "If this goes beyond this office, you're dead," her commanding officer told her. "You can kiss your career goodbye." Frightened of starting a new life outside the Marine Corps, the young officer kept quiet. The men evidently didn't. The female officer became known among the brass as a safe lay, a good Marine who wouldn't rock the command boat. In the process, she also became a nighttime dependent on drugs. "They pound on the door every night, every night," the officer would whisper to me in 1992. "Sometimes I say, 'Fuck off . . . Sir.' "

The secret world of harassment and sexual abuse in the services intensified with the phasing out of the separate women's components. Until 1978 when the WAC (Women's Army Corps) was dissolved by Congress, women had had the protection of the "Petticoat Connection," the WAC term for its all female chains of command. "We had had WAC staff advisors who advocated for women, particularly enlisted women," says retired Army Sergeant Carol Ogg. "If they had problems within the male ranks, like sexual harassment, the WAC first sergeant would go to the man's sergeant and straighten it out." Losing the Petticoat Connection was a great loss for Army women who had nowhere to turn for help. "Nine times out of ten during integration, the woman was being harassed by the sergeant himself," says Ogg. "Who was going to advocate for that young woman?"

Marine women lost their protection as well after integration. "The Women Marine companies were safe havens," says General Gail Reals, the Marine's most senior woman until her retirement in 1990. "You had a place to live where you didn't have to be constantly on guard. You had a woman Marine company commander who would go to bat for you. With the opening of all the opportunities for women came a price."

It was just that suspected price that had driven Congresswoman Holt to press the services on their knowledge of harassment within their ranks during four consecutive days of congressional hearings on women in the military in November 1979. But the secret had been well kept.

The assistant secretary of defense for manpower, reserve affairs and logistics, Robert Pirie, assured Holt that though Defense Department statistics were "not as good" as he would like, the available data showed that harassment of women "does not constitute a major command problem." [49] The civilian leadership of the Air Force had fallen for the same smoke screen. The small number of "equal opportunity" complaints recorded by the Air Force in 1979—only 152—signaled good news for Antonia Chayes, undersecretary of the Air Force. "I do not think it [sexual harassment] is a very serious problem," Chayes told Holt.[50] The Army, too, denied any problem. Its data on harassment did not support "an area . . . which requires considerably more attention," William Clark, an acting undersecretary of the Army, assured Holt.[51]

The Coast Guard testimony was the most relevant. Unlike the Navy and Air Force, which were bound by the combat exclusion laws, the Coast Guard had dropped all gender-based restrictions on women in 1978. At the time of the 1979 hearings, Coast Guard women were serving as commanders of Coast Guard cutters, as pilots and crew in aviation units, as personnel assigned to isolated loran (radar) stations. But Rear Admiral William Stewart, personnel chief of the U.S. Coast Guard, acknowledged only a few cases of harassment. "I am satisfied from my personal monitoring of the situation that these are isolated instances, there is no pattern to them, and I think they are more a one-on-one type of situation than they are anything else," Stewart told Holt. "We are always concerned but we would be concerned about harassment of our males as well, ma'am."[52]

Within a month of the hearings, Holt's suspicions were confirmed. Blasted across the front pages of the *Baltimore Sun* in December 1979 were a series of articles on the harassment of Army women at nearby Fort Meade which mirrored the harassment complaints in Holt's in-box. In the same pattern the Army would follow in 1996 after accusations of rape and abuse surfaced publicly at the Army Ordnance Center and School in Aberdeen, Maryland, the Army ordered investigations into harassment at Fort Benning, Fort Dix, Fort Bragg and the Presidio in San Francisco.[53] Armed with the ammunition she needed, Holt called for another hearing on women in the military, the first to concentrate on sexual harassment.

On February 11, 1980, seven years after the architects of the All-Volunteer Force had folded women into its male ranks, the tip of the iceberg emerged in Room 2118 of the Rayburn House Office Building. By the end of the day, eleven years before the volcanic scandal of Tailhook and sixteen years before the unfolding of abuse at Aberdeen, both Congress and the services knew everything they needed to know—and would subsequently ignore—about sexual harassment.

The five enlisted women were young, all from the Army base at nearby Fort Meade. They served as ammunition specialists, military policemen and administrative personnel. Three were married.

One had joined the Army for training in law enforcement. Another had followed her brothers and father into the services "because they loved it so much." Another had planned to make the Army her career. But all five of the women were either getting out or had already left. The reason was sexual harassment.

To Private Sarah Tolaro, it was the "several very bad experiences" she'd had in the Army. Beyond the "general outlook on females in the services," beyond being talked to "extremely dirty and nasty," Tolaro most resented "being pushed into a corner by two NCO's and having them expose themselves to me and then laugh."[54]

To Lori Lodinsky, it was the accumulation of being "intimidated" into a relationship with her platoon leader the day she had arrived at Fort Meade, followed by an assault by her supervisor during a night training drive. "He told me to go real fast on the airfield and weave in and out of the lights to test my ability at high speeds in a police sedan," Lodinsky testified. "Then he started grabbing me, while I was going about 60 MPH, all over my body. I screamed. I knocked out a row of lights. . . . That was one of the incidents. There are many more."[55]

According to the women's testimony, virtually every safeguard the Army had established to meld personnel of disparate backgrounds existed only on paper. The Army's required "human relations" training which Specialist Jimi Hernandez had attended in Germany did not follow its syllabus on race relations, gender relations and religious and ethnic differences. Instead, she testified, the twenty men in her discussion group, in which she was the only woman, focused entirely on sex "as far as women do not belong in the service, etcetera."[56]

In keeping with the low number of official complaints registered by the services, none of the women had bothered to report the harassment they had witnessed or experienced, including the woman who had been forced into a sexual relationship by her platoon leader. "I was afraid to," said Lori Lodinsky, who subsequently accepted Chapter 5—the inability to cope with military life—to leave the Army. "He said if I was to tell anyone about this, I would be in serious trouble."[57]

Neither had Private Tolaro reported the men who had exposed themselves to her nor the drill sergeant who had told his male troops to hit on female recruits because "women specifically came in the Army for that reason." "Every time I have brought up anything that I felt was important to me, I have been told 'Do not make waves,' " Tolaro testified. ". . . I have discovered through my time in the service that if I take it any higher than me, I am going to come back with 'I'm sure you deserved it anyway,' so, you know, 'just drop it.' "[58]

There it was, every nuance of the harassment issue which would haunt the services and embarrass the Pentagon for over a decade, recorded in 1980. By any measure, both Congress and the services had enough of a snapshot to start tracking the problem, to collect data, to survey the captive military population to determine the extent and the ramification of sexual harassment and to take the same lead in accomplishing gender integration as the services had with racial integration. But they didn't.

Instead, the cultural roadblocks to the seriousness of the harassment issue in the Pentagon as well as the corridors of Congress were forecast by the subcommittee's response to the chilling testimony of Jacqueline Lose, another member of the Military Police, who had lasted only six months in the Army.

In the most graphic testimony of all, Lose described "several experiences" she'd had with male peers to the congressional subcommittee. "At one time I was held down in a room by one man, with two other men in the room present, telling me he was going to give me what I deserved and I didn't know what I deserved . . . ," she testified. "I had to look to the others for help, but nobody would give me any. I screamed and yelled, but nobody came."[59]

"Were they aware you were married?" asked Antonio Won Pat, the representative from Guam, voicing the commonly held perception of married women as inviolate male property and single women as fair sexual game.[60]

"Yes, they were aware," Lose replied.

"But you never succumbed, of course?" Won Pat pressed, as if a screaming woman pinned to the floor and being molested was still responsible for the outcome of the assault.

"I was held down on the floor and he sat on my chest and held my hands down with his knees while he was touching me and kissing me," Lose explained. "He eventually let me go. It was about forty-five minutes he held me down."

But the congressmen still didn't get it. "Did they try to sexually assault you or was it mainly a feeling maneuver?" asked Congressman Sonny Montgomery, as if anything short of penetration was acceptable male behavior.[61]

The impossibility of moving sexual harassment up the rung of congressional and service priorities played out time and again at the 1980 hearing. When one of the servicewomen testified of her discomfort every afternoon at 4 P.M. when her work supervisor left to watch the go-go dancers during happy hour at an on-base club, one congressman expressed outrage that the military shift ended so early; another suggested equalizing the situation by adding male go-go dancers. And to Tolaro's complaint of being talked to "extremely dirty and nasty," another subcommittee member reminisced almost nostalgically about the "barracks" culture which demanded speaking in "four-letter words."

The solutions to the harassment issue offered by the 1980 congressional subcommittee and by the senior women in the services who also testified would become a familiar mantra in congressional hearing rooms for decades to come. "It is a matter of educating people," concluded Congresswoman Holt. "If they realize the horrible situation, how terrible Mrs. Lose must feel when she has to remember that awful experience . . . then we can overcome it."[62]

The commitment of the chain of command and their congressional overseers to eradicating sexual harassment was the solution to Major General

Mary E. Clarke, the last director of the WAC and commander of Fort McClellan, Alabama. "The only way we're going to lick this problem . . . is for all of us to be very concerned about it. It is a leadership problem," said the highest-ranked woman in the Army.[63]

Opening combat jobs to women was the early and constant answer to Congresswoman Pat Schroeder. "Don't you think you all have a difficult role in being treated seriously unless women are allowed to voluntarily go into all slots?" Schroeder asked the senior women present.[64]

The male members of the House subcommittee remained incapable of seeing harassment as a professional problem, as a management problem, as a serious leadership problem affecting both men and women. Whereas racial harassment would have been seen as an institutional problem demanding swift leadership response, sexual harassment was reduced to a woman's issue and hardly worthy of male attention.

Congressman Montgomery was so determined to make harassment a non-issue that he produced nine other servicewomen representing all four services whom he insisted "had been selected totally at random" from computer lists by the subcommittee's staff.[65] Predictably, not one of Montgomery's witnesses admitted to being sexually harassed.

Where Holt's group objected to coarse and sexual language, Montgomery's group testified they "coped" with it. Where some women felt so intimidated and offended by the prurient behavior of servicemen in mess halls that at one point the Marine Corps had had to designate a separate chow line and eating area for women,[66] Montgomery's women paid no mind. Just as men had been mindlessly harassing women since time began, many women continued just as mindlessly to accept it. "The guys whistle, or, if you are going to eat in the chow hall, you will hear people making comments," a Montgomery airman said nonchalantly at the hearing's inconclusive end. "Most of the harassment is not directed at you per se, it's usually directed simply because you are female."[67]

And so harassment soldiered on. The hierarchical command structure would remain the paradigm for harassment it had always been. Forty-three percent of the enlisted women interviewed by Army auditors in 1982 reported that their superiors bartered sex for favoritism, an offer many young women either fell for or felt they couldn't refuse.[68] The 1990 Defense Department survey of sexual harassment came up with almost the same percentage. Forty-two percent of women experiencing some form of sexual coercion or harassment named their military superiors in the chain of command as the "perpetrators."[69]

Navy company commanders and Army drill sergeants would continue to wield the same power over young recruits they had always wielded. When a man identified himself as a drill sergeant to a recruit celebrating her first twelve hours of liberty after graduating from basic training at Fort Jackson, South Carolina, in 1990 and ordered her to produce the military ID she had left in her motel room, she didn't hesitate. She didn't even doubt his identity in the motel room while he raped and sodomized her. "He kept asking me questions and I kept answering, 'Yes, drill sergeant, no drill sergeant,' " she says. She gave the same explanation later to the Military Police who asked why she hadn't fought back. "He said he was a drill sergeant," she kept repeating.

Senior-subordinate abuse would remain entrenched. A twenty-two-year-old Navy seaman never told her alcoholism counselors at a Navy hospital in Florida about the commodore of her first duty station in 1991 who promised career favors if she would come to his office after hours in civilian clothes and sexually arouse him by talking dirty. "He's a damn captain in the Navy and I'm a measly seaman. What else could I do?" said the young woman at the time. "Every time I said, 'People are talking, this isn't a good idea,' he'd say, 'Don't worry about it, just don't worry about it.' "

The backlash began when the Navy captain was transferred to a new duty station. The seaman, the only woman in her squadron, was shunned by her male colleagues and written up for every infraction they could think of, including her increasing reliance on alcohol. "They didn't want me in the squadron anymore, they didn't want me in that building; they wanted me gone," she says. Because she feared even more retaliation, the seaman didn't dare tell the Navy therapists about her destructive relationship with the captain or her "punishment" by the men in her squadron—the very reasons she'd been sent into treatment. "I'm afraid," she says.

Harassment like the seaman's sexual exploitation was kept silenced by the military's reporting mechanism. The proper procedure was for servicewomen to lodge an "equal opportunity" complaint within their chains of command, the very structure that was often doing the abusing. The improbable equation required the complaint against someone in the chain of command to be evaluated, investigated, judged and adjudicated by that same chain of command. Save for jumping the chain of command and lodging the complaint with the inspector general, servicewomen had no other recourse. Whereas the thousands of civilians employed by the military, many of whom worked side by side with servicewomen, are entitled to bring harassment suits against the military under Title VII of the 1964 Civil Rights Act, their counterparts in uniform could not.[70] "The only person you have to be judge and jury is your commander," says Patricia Gavin, a former Air Force captain.

There was no incentive, however, for military supervisors to address or even to acknowledge harassment problems in their commands. In the highly competitive military structure, promotions and perks are awarded on the basis of problem-free leadership records. The mechanism to project seamless perfection depends on denial and deception, even at the company level.

"The officers in the company have people they have to answer to above them," says a former servicewoman. "And they are so worried about answering to those people that they don't want to even admit to themselves that there are any problems, much less try and solve them. They are too afraid somebody is going to find out about them and that puts their career on the line."

Even base commanders were kept in the comforting dark about harassment on their own turf. During Holt's 1980 hearing on sexual harassment, the commander of Fort Meade testified he had first heard about the harassment on his own base from reading the *Baltimore Sun*.[71] In the impetus to paint a rosy picture, harassment complaints were stonewalled at every level, starting at the bottom. "Between a young enlisted woman and the base commander you may have twenty layers of the chain of command that may have been telling her, it is all in your head," says Carolyn Becraft, director of the Women and the Military Project for the Women's Equity Action League in 1992.

Equal opportunity advisors whose job it was to be the vehicle for complaints often contributed to the silence. Save for the Air Force, which offered a permanent career track to equal opportunity advisors, the services treated equal opportunity as temporary, collateral duty. Already pressed by their other responsibilities, personnel assigned to equal opportunity often left the troublesome issues on the lowest rungs of their priority ladders. "They put the regulations in their back pockets, go out to the fleet and forget all about them," says a senior enlisted woman in the Navy.

Even when EO advisors took their roles seriously, they were institutionally handicapped. The advisors were enlisted, giving them little clout in the hierarchy of officers. Moreover, they had no authority to act on equal opportunity complaints, but could only advise their commanders on what action to take. The decision lay entirely in the hands of the commanders, who were more apt to bury the complaint to maintain the appearance of their trouble-free leadership. There was nothing an EO advisor could do without risking his or her career.

"We are taught to be loyal to our boss," says an Army platoon sergeant and EO advisor in 1992. "If we go around him, it's very dangerous. Even as an equal opportunity staff advisor, I can't think of a time I would not be loyal to my boss. I would document any complaint and let him know I was documenting it and how I feel about the situation. But I've been in personnel for seventeen years and I've been to bat for young soldiers who've been discriminated against, who've been assaulted. I know what the command problem is. Hopefully, he'll have a conversion overnight and come in and change his opinion."

The regulatory status of sexual harassment further complicated the reporting process. Harassment was not, and is not, included as a punishable offense under the Uniform Code of Military Justice. Though the UCMJ provides penalties of a bad conduct discharge and one year of imprisonment for dueling (Article 114) and three months of confinement and forfeiture of pay for abusing a public animal (Article 134), there are no such safeguards for abusing women. In the extreme, UCMJ penalties for rape carry the death penalty or life confinement and forced sodomy can put a man or woman away for twenty years, but the subtler forms of harassment are not codified.

To force sexual harassment charges under the UCMJ, servicewomen have to try to link their charges to such recognized offenses as "conduct unbecoming" (Article 133) if the harasser is an officer, or among enlisted, "maltreatment of subordinate" (Article 93), "Indecent, insulting or obscene language prejudicial to good order" (Article 134) or "extortion" (Article 127).[72]

The smoke screen made it impossible to track either the number of harassment incidents or their resolutions. Most complaints were resolved at the lowest level, and the punishment meted out, if any, reduced to the nonjudicial Article 15 for minor offenses. "Anecdotal evidence suggests that a slap on the wrist is much more common than severe punishment and that significant redress for victims is unusual," says Nancy Duff Campbell, co-president of the National Women's Law Center in Washington.

Most women didn't bother to report harassment at all. By reporting a problem in what was supposed to be a trouble-free command, she became the problem. She risked being written up by her superiors for the most minor infractions or losing seniority by being moved out of her company to a new company or being shunned by her peers as the Navy seaman had been and Navy Lieutenant Paula Coughlin would be after Tailhook. There were so many ways to backlash women that reporting harassment was just not worth it. In 1984, four years after the Navy established its sexual harassment programs and policies, only twenty-four sexual harassment cases were brought up for hearings, and of those, nine were dismissed as unsubstantiated.[73] In contrast, 31,488 sex discrimination complaints were lodged with the EEOC in 1984, 5,035 of which were for sexual harassment.[74]

The Pentagon's policies made it far easier for men to harass women than for women to defend themselves, especially during the presidency of Ronald Reagan. In 1981, soon after Reagan and his conservative entourage moved into the White House, the Defense Department tightened its policies against homosexuality to close any loophole from legal challenges in the courts. No longer did individual commanders have discretionary authority to retain or dismiss enlisted homosexuals. The new policy mandated the administrative discharge of "a person, regardless of sex, who engages in, desires to engage in, or intends to engage in homosexual acts."[75] By the time the policy was extended to cover officers in 1985, what can only be described as a decade of terror for women had begun.

Sexual blackmail became the order of the day. Service personnel who resented taking orders from women, who had received bad performance reports from women, who'd had their sexual advances turned down by women, could start the rumor mill rolling by dropping hints of lesbianism. Women's only recourse was to have voluntary or involuntary sex with their potential accusers. "Some women have allowed themselves to be raped by male officers, afraid that the alternative would be a charge of lesbianism," the late Randy Shilts writes in his 1993 book, *Conduct Unbecoming: Gays and Lesbians in the U.S. Military.*[76]

Lesbian-baiting became a military art form. At a joint Army and Air Force base in Kaiserslautern, Germany, in 1984, servicewomen gathering at local bars after work dreaded hearing the theme to the film *Ghostbusters* blasting out of the jukebox. The song signaled the arrival of the "Dyke-busters," a predator posse of servicemen sporting T-shirts bearing the word "dyke" with a slash through it who would press them for sex. If the women reported the "Dyke-busters" for sexual harassment, the odds were their superiors would tell them it was just a joke and to lighten up. But if the women refused to have sex with the men, they could be thrown out of the military. The men "reported those who didn't agree to the military investigative services as dykes," said Michelle Benecke, a former Army officer in Germany, Harvard Law School graduate, and advocate for servicewomen.[77]

That some women were homosexual goes without saying. An oft-cited study of 1,456 former service personnel in 1984 indicated that while the proportion of homosexual males seemed to be the same both inside and outside the services, homosexual women were more likely than heterosexual women to have had military service.[78] A former Army officer, herself a lesbian, estimated that as many as 20 to 25 percent of the women in the services in the 80s were lesbians. "Lesbians represented a significant population in the military," she says. "They were nontraditional women with high levels of confidence who would have been stigmatized in the private sector. They fit in better in the military."

The "witch-hunts" for lesbians, however, were way out of proportion. Entire bases were swept in the Army and Air Force, as was virtually every Navy ship in the new Women at Sea program. Twenty-nine of the sixty-one women aboard the USS *Norton Sound,* including all but one of the nine black female crew members, were investigated for lesbianism by the Naval Investigative Service. So were five of the thirteen female crew members aboard the USS *Grapple,* the salvage ship which would help raise the remains of TWA 800 off Long Island in the summer of 1996. "It has become the only accepted way, the only legal way to harass women in the Navy," USS *Grapple* petty officer Mary Beth Harrison explained to Connie Chung in 1991.[79]

No woman was immune, whether homosexual or heterosexual, married, single or a mother. The senior enlisted woman in one Army aviation brigade was called in by her sergeant major for taking the young female troops in the brigade to the NCO club. It didn't "look good," he warned her. People "were talking." But she held her ground. "Why deny these young women the same right to a mentor you had growing up in the military?" she challenged the sergeant major, who subsequently backed down. But the suspicion lingered. "Whenever they see more than one or two women together, they think we're either going to take over or we're lesbians," says the sergeant.

Ironically, the very qualities most admired in men—aggressiveness, strength, athleticism—made women suspect. Rosters for the women's softball teams were ready-made launch points for investigations by the Naval Investigative Service. So was the length of a woman's hair. "Sometimes they will call you, or accuse you of being a lesbian because your hair is short," said a crew member of the USS *Yellowstone.* "Well, we cut our hair short for the cruise because they won't let you have curling irons on the ship and [long hair] is too hard to take care of in the summer when it's hot."[80]

In 1988 the Marine Corps weighed in with the most far-reaching "lesbian" purge of all, this one at Parris Island Recruit Training Depot, the only Marine boot camp for women. Prompted by a spurned boyfriend after he kicked in the door to a motel room in 1986 and reported finding his former lover naked with another Marine woman, the investigation snowballed into accusations of homosexuality against seventy women at Parris Island, many of them drill instructors.[81] According to a report in the *Harvard Women's Law Journal,* almost one-half of the post's 246 women were questioned about alleged lesbian activity.[82]

One Marine sergeant was interrogated nonstop for seven hours, during which she was threatened with losing custody of her six-month-old daughter if she didn't cooperate. She finally signed a prepared statement admitting her "guilt" just to end the ordeal. Another sergeant under suspicion also capitulated after the Naval Investigative Service agents threatened to tell her critically ill mother of the lesbian allegations. Rather than defend herself at a hearing, she resigned from the Marine Corps.[83]

The women who did try to defend their careers met a wall of male ignorance. A charge of "indecent assault" against one of the accused stemmed from her putting her arm around the shoulders of a weeping colleague. Charges against another woman reported in *The Progressive,* a liberal Wisconsin magazine, were based on her habit of sending flowers to friends.

"Approximately, how many times have you sent flowers to a fellow Marine?" transcripts from the hearing read.

"About six times, sir," came the reply.

"Are you aware of any other Marines sending flowers?"

"No, sir, I'm not," replied the woman, who subsequently resigned from the Corps rather than face further inquisition.[84]

The lesbian purges reached the height of absurdity in the Navy in 1990 when the commander of the surface Atlantic fleet took it upon himself to ferret out lesbians by shifting the Navy's suspicious sights from female athletes to the Navy's best and brightest women. On July 24 the nearly two hundred ships and forty shore installations in Vice Admiral Joseph Donnell's domain received his personal instruction to deal "firmly" with "the stereotypical female homosexual in the Navy," whose characteristics he identified as "hard-working, career-oriented, willing to put in long hours on the job and among the command's top professionals."[85] In short order, a female chief electronics technician was brought up on lesbian charges aboard one Navy ship. So was the first woman to be selected as Sailor of the Year while serving aboard the USS *Yosemite.*[86]

The holy war against lesbians added unique stress to women already bucking male bias in the services. During her thirty-six-year career in the Marine Corps, retired General Gail Reals was locked out of her barracks while agents searched all the women's gear for proof of homosexuality. She was suspect because she played on a softball team which lost 75 percent of its members in a single purge, was pressured for sex by a married senior officer wielding the threat of lesbianism and questioned about her sexuality on several occasions.

The accumulating experiences had a direct and isolating effect on her life. "I gave up playing sports because I couldn't play and not be tarred by the same brush," says Reals, who had several security clearances to protect on her way from private to general. "I had to watch very carefully who I associated with. When I was able to have my own apartment, I certainly never had a roommate. It was a concern how you wore your hair, how you wore your watch, whatever. Everyone talks about the impact on homosexuals and lesbians, but the purges had a far broader impact."

Eighteen Marine women ended up being discharged in the purge at Parris Island, among them eleven drill instructors.[87] Two other women, both drill instructors, were demoted after testifying as character witnesses for the accused. Three other Marine women received criminal convictions for homosexuality and were sent to the brig. "They want women out and this is an easy way to do it," said former Marine Corporal Barbara Baum, who was busted to the rank of private, discharged from the corps and sentenced to a year in the Marine prison in Quantico, Virginia.[88]

No one knows how many other women voluntarily left the services out of fear of being ensnared in the lesbian drift nets. The unofficial total from the

Parris Island purge alone was sixty-five Marine women who either resigned or didn't reenlist.[89] Fully 10 percent of the Marines' only-female drill instructors were bullied out of the Corps in the Parris Island purge.

The ripple effect spread to other female athletes. At Camp Lejeune, North Carolina, a Marine corporal who had been named 1987 Marine Corps Sportswoman of the Year, a top athlete who had earned a place on the all-Marine female softball team in 1987 and the all-Marine volleyball teams in 1986 and 1987, reacted to the news that she, too, was under investigation by going into her garage, starting her car engine and sitting there until she died.[90]

Short of driving women to suicide, charges of lesbianism proved to be the single most effective weapon in driving women out of the services. In 1979 six times as many Army women as Army men were discharged for homosexuality.[91] The lopsided ratios were even greater in the Navy and Marines. Between 1982 and 1987 eight times as many Marine women as men were discharged for homosexuality.[92] In 1989 the discharge rate for women was ten times that for men.[93]

The tragedy of the lesbian witch-hunts is that they had so little to do with lesbians. In the hyperheterosexual military culture, men are far more threatened by male homosexuality than by female homosexuality. Lesbians wouldn't figure at all in the national furor over gays in the military following the 1992 election of Bill Clinton. The passionate debate about overturning the DOD ban against homosexuals would be led by men about men, without a nod to women. Sam Nunn, then chair of the Senate Armed Services Committee, would choose the cramped living quarters on board an all-male submarine as a photo op to illustrate the impossibility of mixing gay and straight men. Ignored would be the racks in berthing areas for women on Navy ships, stacked three deep and separated by only forty inches.

Male homosexuals in the military would turn out to be just as dismissive of female homosexuals. While women veterans would work tirelessly to overturn the military's discriminatory policies toward both servicemen and servicewomen, male advocates would take notice only of themselves. At a 1993 fund-raiser for the Campaign for Military Service in East Hampton, Long Island, not one lesbian veteran was on the invitation list. "The military is a man's world," campaign director Thomas Stoddard would tell me by way of explanation. "Besides, women can't afford a high-ticket event."

The harassment of women would continue in the military culture. The institutionalized gender discrimination that kept women out of core combat positions and specialized training would cast them as secondary players to men just as the regulations against homosexuality would continue to hold women sexual hostage. A 1997 study by the Servicemembers Legal Defense Network would find evidence of ongoing witch-hunts for lesbians and women's disproportionate discharge rate for homosexuality. While women made up 13 percent of the services in 1995, they made up 29 percent of the discharges. In the Army, women accounted for fully 41 percent of the discharges.[94]

The group dynamics at work in the military culture would make inevitable the collective abuse of women at Tailhook in 1991 just as they would the sexual misconduct uncovered throughout the services in 1996. The Navy men who gang-raped a female helicopter mechanic in a barracks in Coronado, California, in the 90s while other men watched were no different from the Army men who had molested Jacqueline Lose in the barracks in front of a male audience at Fort Meade, Maryland, in 1980; the soldiers in Vietnam who raped for each other in the 60s were no different from the men in the 90s who declared it a multi-service "contest" to "cover" the same woman and "brag about it." "It makes you more of a man in your peers' eyes," admitted an unidentified serviceman on ABC News' *20/20* in 1996.[95]

Update: Women in the Military

Tod Ensign

> If you want to create solidar(ity) among male killers, this is what you do: you kill the women in them.
>
> —George Gilder, *Men and Marriage (1986)*

The problems of sexual harassment and assault on military women discussed in *Ground Zero: Gender Wars in the Military* do not appear to have lessened since the book was published in 1997. In 2000, Congress created a Task Force on Military Domestic Violence to assess the scope of the problem and to recommend reforms. The twenty-four-member panel, divided between civilian and military members, made the following recommendations for the military in a 2003 report:

- Use its criminal justice system more frequently to punish harassers and abusers. Currently, too many cases are disposed of administratively with no jail time or criminal conviction.
- Establish intervention teams for domestic violence as now exist in some civilian communities. They should be authorized to investigate complaints of sexual abuse and harassment and to act as advocates for victims, helping them to develop safety plans, if necessary.
- Improve investigative resources, including forensics, for military-police units, so that they can more effectively handle complaints of sexual assault or abuse.
- Establish a confidential reporting system, so that vulnerable women aren't risking retaliation by reporting their boyfriends or spouses.

Shortly after the Task Force released its report, Deputy Defense Secretary Paul Wolfowitz (Rumsfeld's pitbull on Iraq) announced, "Commanders at every level have a duty to take appropriate steps to prevent domestic violence, protect victims and hold those who commit it responsible." [2] Subsequently, the Pentagon announced that it supported most of the panel's recommendations, although none of them have been implemented to date. Deborah Tucker, who served as a task force co-chair, told the *Denver Post,* "Philosophically, domestic violence has been viewed by the military as a [product] of family dysfunction, not through the lens of criminal behavior." [3]

Professor Catherine Lutz, a social anthropologist who has studied military family issues, offers another explanation for the military's reluctance to wage an all-out campaign against sexual assaults: "The military has an enormous investment in each of its soldiers, especially those in elite units like the Special Forces. This makes [commanders] very reluctant to take action knowing that the military would shrink quite a bit if they got rid of all the known abusers. There is a culture of hostility toward women in the military which is [reflected] in the rape of both females and some males, bashing of gays and lesbians, and brutal hazing rituals." [4] Lutz also reported on a sign in the Special Forces school which says, "Rule #1: There are no rules. Rule #2: Follow Rule #1."

A *Denver Post* investigative series found that in 2000 a total of 12,068 cases of spousal abuse were reported to the military's Family Advocacy Program. Of the 1,492 cases investigated by military police, only 26 led to court martial. The outcomes of 983 incidents were not reported.[5]

THE WAR AT HOME

In the summer of 2002, an epidemic of misogynistic violence swept Ft. Bragg, North Carolina. In the span of a few weeks, four soldiers killed their wives, with two of them then commiting suicide. In three cases, the murderers had served with either the Special Forces or the 82nd Airborne, both elite units.

Three of the killers had recently returned from fighting in Afghanistan. An investigation by mental-health professionals chosen by the Pentagon concluded that the killings resulted from preexisting marital problems worsened by long periods of separation. Although the Army announced that it would offer new mental-health programs for stressed GIs, it didn't accept the investigators' recommendation that mental-health workers be deployed at the brigade level in both Afghanistan and Iraq.[6]

In November 2003, the *Denver Post* published the aforementioned three-part investigative series on the military's continuing problems with sexual abuse and harassment of women. It concluded that leniency toward sexual offenders is "routine" in the armed forces, since sex offenders were twice as likely to be punished administratively (often a discharge) as they were to be court-martialed. This compares unfavorably with civilian society where four out of five rape suspects are prosecuted criminally.[7] The *Post* quotes a Colorado therapist who has counseled assault victims: "The military system is like [having] a 'get out of jail free' card."

AIR FORCE ACADEMY: AN EPIDEMIC OF SEXUAL ABUSE

Since admitting its first female cadet in 1976, the academy has had a persistent problem with sex abuse of women by macho future pilots. In the last decade, over sixty female cadets have lodged complaints of sexual abuse or rape. It appears that many additional crimes go unreported. Air Force officials recently acknowledged to the *New York Times* that the number of reported cases "represents only a small corner of a much larger tableau."[8]

"I probably knew 100 women when I was at the academy," Ruth, a cadet from Minnesota, told the *New York Times*. "I would say that 80 experienced a sexual assault and probably 40 of those were rapes." She left the academy in 2001, when she could no longer cope with the emotional trauma of an earlier rape.[9] One former cadet, whom the *New York Times* called "Marie," reported that when she accused a male cadet of sexually assaulting her in October 2002, the academy officials investigated *her* previous sexual activities at the school. She was given seven Class D demerits (one is enough for dismissal) and ordered to march for 265 hours in the school's public square. At this point, she quit the academy.[10]

JUSTICE DELAYED: JUSTICE DENIED?

In April 2003, Academy Commandant John Dallinger and three of his associates were sacked for their combined failure to properly respond to the complaints of female cadets. All 659 female cadets (15 percent of total academy enrollment) were asked to respond to an opinion survey. Of the 579 who responded, nearly 70 percent reported sexual harassment, while 22 percent said they'd been "pressured for sexual favors." A slightly smaller number (19 percent) said they were victims of rape or attempted rape. Significantly, four out of five had chosen not to report their assault.[11]

A civilian commission, headed by former U.S. Rep. Tillie Fowler, published a scathing report in September 2003 that denounced the Air Force leadership for its handling of sex abuse at the school. "Since at least 1993, the highest Air Force leadership has known of serious sexual misconduct at the academy," the report concludes. At a news conference to discuss the report, Chairman Fowler stated, "The sexual assault problems are real and continue to this day. We found a deep chasm in leadership during the most critical time in academy history."[12] Within days of this rebuke, the new commandment, Lt. Gen. John Rosa, issued a public mea culpa: "We realize that we had a culture and climate here that tolerates sexual assault and harassment. So, if you have such [an] environment . . . you have to change that."[13]

In its Agenda for Change, the Air Force has listed 165 items that can help reform the academy. Perhaps the most important change is to install a sexual-assault reporting system that has integrity and cannot be manipulated by commanders worried about the academy's image.[14] One former cadet, Andrea

Prasse, 23, of Milwaukee, Wisconsin, received a measure of delayed justice in December 2003, when the secretary of the Air Force ordered that she be allowed to graduate belatedly from the academy. She was expelled eight days before graduation because of trumped-up honor-code charges brought by the male cadet she'd originally accused of harassment. Prasse related that she hadn't even reported another sexual assault which occurred when she was a first-year cadet since she considered it part of a "culture of sexual intimidation" directed at female cadets.[15]

FEMALES AT RISK THROUGHOUT AIR FORCE

Alarmed by the large number of sexual assaults at the academy, the Air Force Pacific Command ordered a review of attacks from 2001–2003. Of the 105 GIs accused in 92 cases of rape, only 14 were court-martialed. Of these, only seven were convicted. More than forty others received non-criminal punishments such as reprimands or demotions.

Further afield, in Iraq, Kuwait, and Afghanistan, the Air Force Central Command counted at least 112 reports of sexual misconduct, including rapes, in the past eighteen months.[16] The intrepid *Denver Post* reporters found that at least 37 female service members have sought counseling from civilian rape crisis centers after returning home from Iraq and Kuwait. They also noted that the Senate Armed Services Committee has yet to hold hearings on the military treatment of handling of sexual assault cases, despite promises to do so.[17] Given the new and growing scandal of Iraqi prisoner abuse by U.S. troops, it seems unlikely that this problem will receive much attention, at least in the short term.

WOMEN IN CONGRESS ORGANIZE

On March 31, 2004, twelve female Congress members heard further testimony about the persistance of sexual abuse. Women's Caucus co-chair U.S. Rep. Louise Slaughter (D-NY) told the *Army Times* that she was tired of major sex scandals breaking every couple of years. She argues that they hurt and demoralize all women in uniform. According to one witness, Christine Hansen, director of the Miles Foundation, a sexual assault victims group, her organization has received 129 "credible" reports of sexual assaults in the Iraq war theater in the past 18 months.[18]

It may be that Linda Bird Francke's gloomy assessment remains valid today: "The denigration of women [is] an integral and, in some opinions, essential part of the military culture."

5

Minorities and Gays in the Military

Who Will Fight the Next War?

Martin Binkin

BLACKS AND THE ALL-VOLUNTEER FORCE

In 1968 presidential candidate Richard M. Nixon proposed to replace military conscription with an all-volunteer system. Although the proposal was met with wide public acceptance, some critics argued that a volunteer Army would be disproportionately black. They considered the proposal a scheme to use black youth to defend white America, a notion that Nixon, in a radio address given two weeks before the 1968 election, dismissed as "sheer fantasy."[1] This position was reinforced by the Gates commission in its report to the president in 1970. Reacting to concerns that "a disproportionate number of blacks will be in military service," the commission confidently predicted, "the composition of the armed forces will not be fundamentally changed by ending conscription." The commission's best projections were that blacks would constitute about 15 percent of enlisted men in all services combined and 19 percent in the Army. The commission left little room for doubt: "to be sure, these are estimates, but even extreme assumptions would not change the figures drastically."[2]

It soon became evident, however, that the proportion of blacks in the armed forces would grow beyond these predictions. From 1970 to 1973, during the phaseout of compulsory service, the proportion of blacks in the armed forces increased steadily, though modestly, from 9.8 percent to 12.4 percent; in the Army, the proportion increased from 12.1 percent to 16.3 percent. By the mid-1970s it was apparent that the volunteer force was much more attractive to blacks than to whites. The proportion of new Army recruits who were black, for example, grew from 14 percent in 1971 to 24 percent in 1976. The trend continued for the remainder of the decade; by 1979 blacks constituted 37 percent of all Army recruits and 32 percent of the total Army enlisted force. The growth in the other services was less dramatic. Despite a doubling of the proportion of black officers, to 5 percent of the total by 1980, the small numbers remained a subject of concern.

The influx of blacks during the 1970s can be attributed to a combination of factors. Most obvious were differences in the civilian employment prospects of white and black youth. The recession of the mid-1970s exacted a relatively greater toll on young black men: their rate of unemployment, already unacceptably high, grew 32 percent between 1973 and 1978, compared with 10 percent growth among white male cohorts. Deteriorating employment prospects are suggested even more vividly by the employment-population ratio, the number of workers as a percentage of the population. Between 1973 and 1978 the ratio for black men dropped by 13 percent; the ratio among white men increased slightly.

The extent to which the military had become a major employer for black youth was evident in their participation rates. During the 1970s nearly 700,000 black men entered the armed forces, 25 percent of all black men who turned eighteen years old. About 230,000, or one-third of the enlistees, had not completed high school.[3] The contrast appears even starker when one considers that blacks were less likely to qualify for enlistment. By conservative estimate two of every five black men in those age cohorts capable of meeting entry test standards had enlisted, compared with fewer than one of seven similarly situated white men.[4]

By the end of the 1970s, each of the military services had record-high proportions of blacks, with the Army and Marine Corps exceeding the percentage in the American population, the Air Force roughly in proportion, and the Navy slightly underrepresented. This trend, however, failed to concern the American public, according to a survey taken in the early 1980s. In fact, 70 percent of the respondents believed the mix was about right, while 12 percent said there were too many and 19 percent too few.[5] That depressed minorities, especially high school dropouts, were enlisting in disproportionate numbers was apparently viewed as a healthy sign that they could and would receive help. As Milton Friedman, the noted economist, had earlier observed, "it is a good thing and not a bad thing to offer better alternatives to the currently disadvantaged."[6]

In general, the black community appeared ambivalent about the situation. Some leaders were pleased that so many black youth were able to find employment.[7] But not everyone considered the trend so beneficial. Some black leaders complained of continued racial discrimination in the armed forces, as evidenced by the disproportionate share of disciplinary incidents and punitive actions suffered by racial minorities.[8] Others criticized imbalance, pointing out that blacks were mired in unskilled jobs in the lower ranks. Some decried the relatively small number of blacks in the officer corps, especially in light of the large numbers in the enlisted ranks.[9] Although there was some truth to each of the allegations, the armed forces could legitimately point to progress, especially compared to the dismal conditions outside the military. The comparison seemed to blunt the sting of the criticisms. On balance, the vestiges of racial discrimination that had haunted the armed forces in the aftermath of Vietnam seemed to have disappeared by the end of the 1970s. Those holding otherwise found themselves a distinct minority.

Meanwhile, some observers attempted to alert the public that while the military could provide a jobs program and be an engine for social reform in peacetime, its overarching purpose is to defend the nation. With memories of Vietnam still fresh, they expressed fears that a racially unbalanced military could endure black casualties that might exceed those of the early days of the Vietnam War. If that happened, racial discord could increase, with potentially damaging consequences for U.S. national security.[10]

These two viewpoints illustrate competing perspectives of a thorny issue. On one hand the *benefits* associated with military service should be available to all people regardless of race, color, creed, national origin, or socioeconomic status. On the other hand military service is a *burden* that should be borne by all members of society.

But in the 1980s, perceptions of benefits prevailed; concerns about the possible disproportionate burdens that would be borne by blacks in wartime were confined to a few scholars and social commentators. There was remarkably little public discussion of the racial composition of the armed forces.

The principal exception was a 1982 study that attempted to stimulate interest in the benefits-burden dilemma and promote an informed debate.[11] Some initial reactions to the study were critical or skeptical. In a review for the *Washington Post,* for example, Clifford L. Alexander, Jr., secretary of the Army during the peak years of growth in black participation (1977–81), dismissed the study as "romantic condescension."[12] Nicholas Von Hoffman argued that "history teaches us mercenary soldiers are generally highly reliable" and concluded that "wars should be fought by people who need the work."[13] Carl Rowan, a leading black social commentator, dismissed the prospect that disproportionate black casualties would be socially divisive.

> [The authors] must be joking. Blacks were the "grunts" in the Vietnam War, and they and other minorities and poor whites were the cannon fodder in every other conflict for the simple reason that they always have been powerless to alter this society one whit. . . . They are helpless going into the military, and if they die in combat their relatives will be impotent when it comes to raising a ruckus big enough to be called "socially divisive."[14]

Despite the early criticism and skepticism, a comprehensive discussion of the questions took place at a symposium conducted in 1982 by the Joint Center for Political Studies, a research organization focusing on black issues. Scholars, current and former public officials, and representatives of major civil rights organizations discussed the issues related to the growing participation of blacks in the armed forces. Although no attempt was made to reach a consensus, the group seemed resigned that little could be done or should be done to alter course. The general tenor of the meeting was summed up by Roger Wilkins: "In the end, the problem of equity and all the other problems that seem to worry people so—readiness, reliability, the reactions of the allies—must await a time when the focus shifts away from the military and toward the society that produced it and that it is supposed to protect."[15]

On the whole, the nation's black leadership remained silent, as did the coalition of liberal and conservative commentators that had expressed concern in the 1970s with the growing participation of blacks in the armed forces. Racial representation in the armed forces had become a non-issue. "What, if anything, the Pentagon, Congress or the White House should do about the high percentage of minorities in the military," one observer commented in 1983, "might be an important subject for debate—if there were a debate."[16]

Perhaps the public's apathy stemmed from a belief that, despite the Iranian hostage crisis and the Soviet occupation of Afghanistan, the United States would not soon get involved in a major conflict producing high casualties. By most perceptions in the early 1980s, the benefits of military service far outweighed the burdens.

The proportion of blacks in the military appeared to become even less relevant during the Reagan presidency as the armed forces found recruiting far easier, which resulted in fewer new black recruits and the prospect that a more racially balanced force was in the offing. Large increases in pay in 1980 and 1981, totaling 29 percent, improved the attractiveness of military service, especially since civilian wages in many comparable occupations were dropping in real terms.[17] The reintroduction of more liberal education benefits, similar to those in the Vietnam-era GI bill, also drew more recruits—the especially generous Army College Fund gave the Army a competitive edge. The services also appeared to have adopted better recruiting practices, deploying recruiters more efficiently and employing more imaginative advertising and recruiting techniques. Finally, the image of the armed forces improved, a development attributed by some to the pro-military attitude of the Reagan administration.

The net result was an increase in interest in military service among white youth, a growth in their participation rate, and an attendant decline in the number and the proportion of new black recruits. Compared with the 700,000 black men that had entered the armed forces during the 1970s, some 460,000, or 17 percent of those turning eighteen, entered during the 1980s.[18] In fiscal year 1990, blacks constituted 25 percent of Army recruits, down from a peak 37 percent in 1979.

The opportunities were especially diminished for high school dropouts because the services were able to attract record numbers of high school graduates. In the 1970s, for example, 230,000 black male dropouts entered the military services; only 25,000 were accepted during the 1980s. In fiscal year 1990, of a total of the 45,000 blacks who entered the armed forces, only 1,200 (less than 3 percent) had not completed high school.

Despite this substantial decrease, however, the overall racial composition of the Army was hardly affected, hovering near 30 percent black during the decade. The seeming anomaly is explained by the fact that even though whites entered the Army in growing numbers during the 1980s, they were less likely to remain beyond an initial enlistment. Blacks have traditionally exhibited a greater desire to remain in the military and have accounted for a larger proportion of reenlistments.

One consequence of these trends has been that black soldiers are now more concentrated in the middle and upper ranks. Their proportion in the lowest three grades (E-1 through E-3) dropped from almost 32 percent in 1981 to 24 percent in 1991, while the proportion in the highest three grades (E-7 through E-9) grew from less than 25 percent to more than 30 percent. Blacks in the middle three grades in these years remained at roughly 36 percent of the total.

The dramatic growth in the participation by blacks since the end of the military draft has been accompanied by modest improvements in their occupational opportunities. In the early 1970s, black soldiers were greatly underrepresented in technical positions and slightly overrepresented in combat billets. They now fill a nearly proportional share of technical jobs and are slightly underrepresented in combat skills. The most conspicuous change has occurred in health and administration; blacks now hold 45 percent of those jobs in the Army.

Whatever concerns might have existed about the potential burdens of military service all but evaporated in the late 1980s with the crumbling of communism and the disintegration of the Warsaw Pact, events that made even more remote the possibility of American involvement in a large-scale conflict. In fact, Pentagon plans to cut the size of the armed forces by 25 percent were met with questions about the racial implications of such a steep reduction. The nation's black leadership was once again ambivalent. Several leading commentators worried that blacks would bear the economic brunt of the impending reductions, while the Congressional Black Caucus, made up of twenty-four black members of Congress, urged the Pentagon to hasten the pace of the reductions, arguing that "military service should not be looked on as a jobs program."[19] Besides, they contended, their plan set aside "conversion" money to assist those separated from the armed forces. The Pentagon's reduction plan, however, was soon shelved by events in the Persian Gulf, which also served to refocus attention from the benefits of military service to its burdens.

The Persian Gulf Conflict

President George Bush's commitment in August 1990 to use military power if necessary to eject Saddam Hussein from Kuwait unleashed an almost immediate response from critics, both white and black, worried that the nation's socially unbalanced armed forces would soon be involved in a bloody and distant conflict. The prospect that large numbers of black youths might die commanded wide attention. Although representation of blacks in the armed forces had been growing since the end of the draft, the news media treated the trend as a recent phenomenon that had somehow sneaked up on an unsuspecting public.

Initially, charges of inequity were leveled in terms of social class. The armed forces, some scholars and journalists contended, consisted mainly of the lower socioeconomic classes in American society. These views were based in large measure on an assessment by Charles Moskos, the nation's preeminent military sociologist, who contended in 1988 that "whatever one's value judgment on the [all-volunteer force], the irreducible fact remains that without a citizen-soldier component, the most privileged elements of our youth population . . . will not be found in the enlisted ranks of the armed forces."[20] A report by the Democratic Leadership Council concluded that "we cannot ask the poor and underprivileged alone to defend us while our more fortunate sons and daughters take a free ride, forging ahead with their education and careers."[21] Ethical considerations aside, some argued that if the children of government officials, legislators, corporate leaders, journalists, and other prominent people were put at risk, policymakers' decisions to commit U.S. military forces might be taken more soberly. Moskos, for example, lamented that there were no "future George Bushes in the ranks in the gulf. . . . These are working-class youth, not the future leaders of the country. And they don't have much of a voice in the making of policy."[22]

These claims were dismissed in a 1991 Pentagon report as assertions "based on impressions and anecdotes rather than on systematic data." Synthesizing four independent studies of the socioeconomic composition of the armed forces, the report concluded that "the socioeconomic background of new recruits nearly mirrors that of youth in society."[23] These differences of opinion stemmed from critics' failure to account for the significant changes that had taken place in the services during the 1980s and from the absence of an accepted definition of social classes. What, after all, is the middle class? The Pentagon's report used educational attainment, marital status, employment status, home ownership, and occupation of the parents of the groups surveyed to construct a socioeconomic index score.

A Congressional Budget Office study, based on analysis of recruits' ZIP codes, came to a similar conclusion: "the socioeconomic characteristics of recruits' home areas are broadly similar to those of the general youth population, although recruits tend to come from areas with somewhat lower family incomes and education levels."[24] As more and more information surfaced debunking the notion that the military was filled with the poor and disadvantaged, social commentators turned their attention toward the racial imbalance in the armed forces—criticism more difficult to dismiss.

American involvement in the Persian Gulf was almost immediately cast in racial terms by a number of prominent black leaders. As had been predicted a decade earlier, the prospect of a great many black casualties was high on the list of concerns.[25] The likelihood, too, that a Persian Gulf conflict would be financed at the expense of social programs loomed large. And the apparent readiness of the United States to engage Arabs, or "people of color," to protect oil interests, while winking at similarly egregious acts by the white South African government, did not sit well with many blacks. The final straw, it appeared, was President Bush's decision to engage in a military ground action that could put many young blacks in harm's way while at the same time vetoing the Civil Rights Bill of 1990.

Among the most vocal black critics of the decision, Jesse L. Jackson warned, "if that war breaks out, our youth will burn first," and Coretta Scott King, branding the United States as the aggressor, "strongly deplore[d] and was deeply saddened by the White House decision to launch a war against Iraq." Eleanor Holmes Norton, delegate to Congress from the District of Columbia, condemned the war and dismissed the contention that black youth might have joined the armed forces for any but economic reasons.[26] Martin Luther King III urged blacks not to participate: "Every black soldier ought to say: 'You all do what you want to. I'm not going to fight. This is not my war.' "[27]

That black service personnel were mostly high school graduates from middle- or working-class families—the "flower of black youth"—was also a source of concern. Representatives of the African American community commented that great numbers of young black men had already been lost to drugs and crime; the community could not afford to lose more in a war. A leader of the National African-Americans against United States' Intervention in the Gulf, for example, protested that "the stabilizing forces in our community are being drawn out."[28]

This divisive rhetoric, coming as it did from some of the most influential black leaders, could have been responsible for shaping the antiwar attitudes of much of black America. A *Wall Street Journal*/NBC News poll conducted shortly after President Bush decided to send military forces to the Persian Gulf showed that 74 percent of white Americans approved the action but only 41 percent of black Americans did so.[29] In January 1991 as war loomed closer, black support dropped to 27 percent before rising to about 50 percent after the war began.[30]

President Bush's deliberations over whether to use military force or economic sanctions to drive Iraqi troops out of Kuwait took place amid widespread news coverage reflecting deep concerns among white and black Americans over the possibilities of heavy casualties. This prospect had to weigh heavily in the president's calculations, but there is no evidence that he recognized, much less was influenced by, the racial component of the issue.

The administration, it is worth noting, enjoyed a distinct advantage in having as its top military leader the first black ever to have held that position. As point man for the administration, General Colin Powell insulated it from some of the criticisms of the black community. Responding to concerns about the potential for disproportionate black casualties, Powell expressed his annoyance: "What you keep wanting me to say is that this is disproportionate or wrong. I don't think it's disproportionate or wrong. I think it's a choice the American people made when they said have a volunteer Army and allow those who want to serve to serve." Expressing pride that blacks volunteer for the armed forces in disproportionate numbers, Powell contended that they are drawn to military service for the same reasons that he was as a youth. "They come in for education. They come in for adventure. They come in to better themselves."[31]

Deployments and Casualties

As deployments commenced, many journalists closely monitored racial proportions, prompting the Pentagon to release a fact sheet in January 1991 showing that the racial and ethnic composition of deployed personnel, although overrepresentative of civilian racial and ethnic populations, was remarkably close to their participation in the military services.[32]

Of some 570,000 military personnel deployed between August 1990 and February 1991, 23.5 percent were black, compared with 20.5 percent of the total military population.[33] Most deployed personnel were Army troops, who closely mirrored the overall Army population. The Pentagon also indicated that 36 percent of deployed black personnel were in a combat status, compared with 42.7 percent of the total deployed forces.

As the possibility of a military confrontation loomed larger, concerns about casualties mounted. Experts offered predictions ranging from several hundred to 45,000.[34] There seemed little reason to believe that blacks would not suffer casualties at least in proportion to their numbers in Army combat specialties (27 percent) and possibly in proportion to their numbers in the theater of operations (23.5 percent). As matters turned out, of the 375 persons who died during the buildup (Desert Shield) and the campaign (Desert Storm), 63 (16.8 percent) were black.[35] The proportions were lower than expected because a difficult ground campaign never materialized. The Iraqi Army, apparently demoralized by a relentless allied bombing campaign, offered little resistance, and those units that did were readily defeated. Of the 375 American deaths, 148 were the result of combat activity, and 108 were attributed to accidents and illnesses that occurred before hostilities began.[36] Most casualties occurred among troops that were assigned to support rather than combat duties.

U.S. casualties would have been much higher and the proportion among blacks larger if the ground war had unfolded as most experts expected. Had the Iraqis resisted as resolutely as had been predicted, casualties among Army and Marine Corps combat troops would have been higher, certainly outnumbering those among support personnel, and most likely increasing the proportion borne by black personnel.[37]

Because the protest against military action by many influential black leaders appeared to resonate throughout much of the black community, heavy black casualties probably would have reinforced their criticisms, further eroding support for the administration's policy and further straining relations between white and black Americans at a time when, by many accounts, the gap between the races has been widening. As matters turned out, the small number of black casualties brought a sudden end to the controversy. With the end of the conflict, in fact, the prewar plan to reduce the size of the armed forces was reactivated and fears that blacks would become wartime casualties were displaced by concerns that they would become economic casualties.[38]

OPTIONS FOR CHANGE

If the clean and decisive Persian Gulf victory is accepted as a model for future military conflicts, there is a great temptation to ignore the seemingly intractable benefits-burdens dilemma. Realistically, however, any future conflict would likely be a tougher test for America's armed forces, probably producing a larger number of casualties and prompting the reemergence of the debate on racial equity. Any resulting racial discord could hamper the nation's ability to pursue what on all other grounds might be considered a just war. Are these prospects of sufficient concern to warrant considering interventionary policies to redress racial balance in the armed forces? If so, what options are available?

Back to Conscription?

Shortly after the U.S. military buildup on the Arabian peninsula began, some social commentators were calling for a reinstitution of the draft to redress socioeconomic or racial imbalances in the all-volunteer force.[39]

The advocates of a return to the draft, however, were short on details of how conscription would yield a socioeconomically or racially representative military force. They also failed to consider the disposition of the many young Americans who now volunteer for military service. Conscripts would make up the difference between the total need for new recruits and the total number of volunteers. The overall racial characteristics of recruits would depend on the composition of each group and their relative sizes. Also, the demographic profile of the career force is not a mirror image of the profile of new recruits, a fact that seemed to be lost on the advocates.

For a conscription system to affect the racial composition of the total recruit population, either the number of military volunteers must be severely curtailed or the total strength of the armed forces must be greatly increased. To illustrate, in fiscal year 1990 the Army recruited 80,000 volunteers, of which 20,000, or 25 percent, were black. Assuming that the number of volunteers was reduced by one-third and the shortage made up with conscripts, the percentage of black recruits would drop only to 20 percent—still well above their numbers in the overall population.[40] Even then, because the armed forces have successfully met their needs for volunteers for more than a decade, it must be assumed that a reduction in volunteers would have to be *induced* by adopting policies that would either discourage enlistments (perhaps by lowering military pay) or would accept fewer applicants (perhaps by tightening entry standards). Realistically, however, such measures would have to be justified on their own merits; a policy that denied youths an opportunity to serve *voluntarily* in order to force others to serve *involuntarily,* solely for the purpose of achieving racial balance, is not likely to be socially and politically acceptable.

Alternatively, a more representative racial balance could be achieved without denying volunteers the opportunity to serve by increasing the size of the force. The racial composition of the force, however, would not be highly sensitive to changes in strength. If the number of Army recruits were increased by 25 percent (80,000 to 100,000) to make room for 20,000 conscripts, blacks would then be expected to constitute 22 percent rather than 25 percent of Army recruits. Thus for an appreciable change to take place, total recruit requirements would have to be increased to a level at which the racial composition of conscripts would swamp the composition of volunteers. This option, too, is unrealistic in light of plans to contract rather than expand the armed forces.

Attaining racial balance among the recruit population, in any event, does not ensure attaining it in the overall military population. Once in the armed services, blacks are more likely than whites to remain beyond the first tour of duty. Of all male recruits who entered the Army between April 1981 and March 1982, 18 percent of the whites but 31 percent of the blacks were still in the Army as of July 1988.[41] The greater tendency of blacks to reenlist accounts for the fact that, while the proportion of Army recruits who were black was falling from 37 percent in 1979 to 20 percent in 1991, the proportion of blacks in the Army's enlisted ranks changed little, hovering between 30 and 33 percent. Little would be different under conscription, moreover, because blacks could be expected to be concentrated in the volunteer component of a mixed volunteer-conscript force, and volunteers typically remain in the service longer than draftees.

It is therefore difficult, under the circumstances, to imagine any realistic conscription plan that would yield a racially representative force. Besides, with the end of the cold war any conceivable rationale for a return to conscription has virtually disappeared, and it is unlikely that a military draft would be reinstated solely to meet a social purpose.

Redressing Racial Balance in the Volunteer Force

Attaining a more representative force under current volunteer conditions rather than conscription would also be no mean task. One eminent black scholar has recommended a direct approach: *"The Congress should establish a goal of proportionate participation in the military for minorities."*[42] But such extreme views are not widely embraced and, whatever euphemism is used, any approach that even hints at quotas is unlikely to gain support from legislators or policymakers. Left to market forces, then, the racial composition in the future, as in the past, will rest on the relative propensities of black and white youth for military service.

Preferences for military service are shaped by many factors, but most prominently by the availability of alternative employment opportunities.[43] It is therefore difficult to envision major changes in preference patterns, at least in the short run, given the existing imbalances in the educational attainment, job skills, and employment opportunities. Until these differences are narrowed, military service will continue to be more attractive to blacks than to whites, and there would not appear to be any basis for assuming that the racial composition of the all-volunteer force will change much.

Two developments in the early 1990s, however, suggest that the calculus of racial composition might change: the substantial reductions in the size of the military and signs of a declining propensity for military service among black youths.

Downsizing: Implications and Challenges

The Pentagon's plan to reduce the size of the armed forces by 25 percent between 1990 and 1995 has taken on racial overtones. Countering concerns expressed among some African American leaders, but mainly by the news media, that blacks would be squeezed out of a smaller military, the Pentagon's leading manpower official told Congress,

> we are convinced that our drawdown plans will not differentially affect minorities or women. We expect they will separate in numbers roughly proportional to their representation in the overall groups that are being separated. Perhaps most to the point, at the end of 1995 when the drawdown is completed, we expect the minority and gender representation figures to be virtually the same as they are today.[44]

The basis for the prediction is, however, unclear, especially in the face of the military services' traditional tendency to upgrade the quality of their work force as their requirement for recruits diminishes.[45] For example, as the Army's needs dropped from 80,000 recruits in 1990 to 70,000 in 1991, the proportion of "choice" recruits increased from 66.6 percent to 74.5 percent, and the proportion of black recruits fell from 25 to 20 percent.[46]

The services success in attracting these highly qualified volunteers has varied, depending mostly on supply and demand in the recruiting marketplace.[47] Since the remarkable easing of recruitment in the early 1980s, the armed forces have drawn an unprecedented proportion of these choice recruits. Compared with 1979, for example, when only 30 percent of all Army recruits scored at or above the 50th percentile, 75 percent in 1991 were in that category. But as the intake of these highly qualified recruits rose steeply in the early 1980s and again in the early 1990s, the proportion of black recruits fell, in part because of differences in the abilities of white and black youths to meet the choice recruit standard.

Blacks are less likely to have completed high school and far less likely to score among the top half of recruits on the standardized entry test. A nationwide administration of the entry test in 1980, for example, indicated that only 14 percent of black men can be expected to score in the top half of the population compared with 61 percent of white men. The mean score attained by blacks was 24.29 compared with 55.97 for whites, a difference of more than one standard deviation of the total population's score distribution.[48]

Are Blacks Losing Interest?

Although much of the recent drop in black recruitment can be attributed to changes in entry standards, black youths also seem less interested in military service than they were in the 1980s. The proportion with a "positive propensity" for military service, which has traditionally been much higher than for whites, has decreased since 1986 and, following a brief recovery, dropped from 53 percent in 1989 to 37 percent in 1992.[49] The number of black applicants also fell, from 120,000 in 1989, when they constituted 23 percent of all applicants, to about 66,000 in 1991, or less than 17 percent of the total.

It is premature to draw conclusions because the decreasing black interest has not been fully analyzed, but the decrease may have been prompted by the Persian Gulf conflict and the realization by youths and their parents that military service is more than just a peacetime job opportunity. This realization would have been strengthened by the general disaffection among the African American population for U.S. military involvement in the Gulf in the first place and the concerns about casualties expressed by many black leaders as the buildup progressed. Many young blacks also may have become discouraged and dropped out of the pool of prospective volunteers as enlistment prospects diminished sharply during the 1980s.[50]

In any event, if trends observed during the initial phases of the force reduction are any indication, the racial mix of the Army will become more representative of the population. A decreasing proportion of black recruits can be expected to continue if the services persist in emphasizing the importance of entry test scores and if the number of highly qualified blacks seeking to volunteer for military service shrinks.

The effect of personnel reductions on the composition of the career force is more difficult to predict. In the short run, much will depend on the specific plans, especially on how each category of personnel is affected. This has been a source of controversy as the various services have made different assessments of the trade-offs among the ways to trim the career force: accept fewer entrants into the career force by reducing reenlistment opportunities; induce those already in the career force to separate; or encourage those who are eligible to retire. Under any circumstance, the impact would likely be small for the Army because blacks make up such a large proportion of careerists, and particularly because the effects would be transitional.

Once the size of the Army stabilizes, the composition of the career force over the longer term would be influenced by the occupational characteristics of the smaller force. For instance, blacks have been overrepresented in health and clerical positions and underrepresented in technical occupations. If the combat-to-support ratio in the future force is smaller (perhaps because fewer forward-based forces would decrease logistics requirements) or if the forces require a greater concentration of technicians (because of more emphasis on technology), the percentage of blacks in the career force could be expected to decrease. The Army, however, does not anticipate major changes in its occupational structure. It has indicated that even though the enlisted force will decrease by 30 percent between 1991 and 1995, support positions will be cut 28 percent.[51]

By all indications, then, any change in the racial composition of the Army will be gradual and will probably not create undue concern, especially since overrepresentation was an issue raised by many black leaders during the Persian Gulf conflict.

Potential Challenges

In the event of a larger or more abrupt decrease in black participation in the armed services, however, legislators and interest groups could be expected to intervene to prevent any significant erosion of job opportunities for African American youth.

The most obvious means for protecting military job opportunities for blacks would be to provide affirmative action "guidance" or to set goals or objectives similar to those used by the services in the past to ensure equity on military promotion boards. This approach could prove difficult, however, because it would certainly evoke images of quotas—a code word with distasteful political overtones.

Besides, the Pentagon probably has little choice but to maintain what it has proudly called, since the advent of the all-volunteer force, a color-blind recruitment policy. To do otherwise now would fly in the face of the principle established during the early years of the all-volunteer force, when Army Secretary Clifford Alexander answered critics of the growing racial imbalance by contending that the number of blacks in the Army was "immaterial": "Who is going to play God and set a quota?"[52]

There are, however, other ways to "regulate" the racial balance of the armed forces. Entry standards are instrumental in determining the racial composition, and observers concerned with protecting black volunteers during the troop reductions could question whether the standards are valid predictors of performance and the entry test itself free of racial bias. Moreover, it would be fair to ask whether the services might be seeking volunteers with levels of education and test scores higher than are necessary.

The armed services have screened potential recruits with standardized tests since World War One. Used initially to identify the mentally unfit, in recent years the tests have been used to assess vocational aptitude. The services have placed great stock in them because research has shown that people with higher aptitude scores are more trainable—they complete skill training courses at a higher rate than low scorers, complete them sooner, get higher grades, and retain the information longer. Also, research has verified a close connection between entry aptitude and skill qualification test scores and rates of promotion.

At the same time, standardized tests have been heavily criticized as to how accurately they measure aptitude, achievement, or intelligence and whether they are truly divorced from the influences of education and environment. Such tests, it has been argued, also fail to measure idealism, stamina, persistence, and creativity, which to many observers are as important as cognitive skills. The primary charge, however, is that standardized tests do not measure the same dimensions of achievement across different groups.

In the early 1980s the Army itself questioned the validity of the tests. In response to a growing intolerance in Congress of the increase in low-scoring, mainly black, recruits, an ad hoc study group in the Army secretariat examined the validity of standardized tests and reported, "The Army cautiously states that results of the AFQT [Armed Forces Qualification Test] indicate, at best, trainability. The evidence we have gathered, however, suggests that the test has been so misrepresented over time, and the predictions derived from Mental Category results so overstated, that the future utility of the AFQT is in some doubt."[53]

The study group further argued that "linking Mental Category with job performance is not only inaccurate but against the best interests of manpower management in the Army—which requires finding the soldier who can do the job." To this end the group suggested that the Army convert from a norm-referenced system, which compares one candidate with others, to a criterion-referenced system, which compares a candidate with a describably constant standard of performance.[54] Prompted in part by this controversy, the Joint-Service Job Performance Measurement/Enlistment Standards (JPM) Project was established by the Pentagon in 1980 to develop "measures of performance in entry-level military jobs so that, for the first time, military enlistment standards could be linked to performance on the job."[55]

After more than a decade of research, a technical committee of the National Academy of Sciences concluded that "the JPM Project provided ample evidence that ASVAB scores are related to job proficiency," but found a "somewhat higher correlation between the entrance tests and the job knowledge performance measure than between the entrance tests and hands-on measures." This result, not unanticipated, was particularly evident among minorities. Compared with a difference of 0.85 standard deviation between whites and blacks on the entry test and 0.78 on the job knowledge test, both of which are paper-and-pencil, multiple-choice tests, the difference narrowed to 0.36 on the hands-on test, leading the researchers to conclude that "to the extent that we have confidence in the hands-on criterion as a good measure of performance on the job, these findings strongly suggest that scores on the ASVAB exaggerate the size of the differences that will ultimately be found in the job performance of the two groups."[56]

This suggests the possibility that the wide differences in predicted performance between blacks and whites implied by entry test scores are significantly narrowed as recruits gain on-the-job experience. The implications of these findings were skirted by the committee, which indicated that "this issue goes well beyond the JPM Project; it calls for the attention of the measurement profession as a whole."[57]

The Army, meanwhile, established its own elaborate research effort designed to develop new measures of job performance, validate existing selection measures, develop and validate new selection and classification measures, develop a scale to improve job classification decisions, and estimate the relative usefulness and validity of alternative selection and classification procedures. Among its many research objectives, the study was to "determine the extent of differential prediction across racial and gender groups for a systematic sample of individual differences, performance factors, and jobs." As of 1990, however, work on the jobs objective was described as "ongoing."[58]

It is also possible, if opportunities for blacks are substantially diminished, that the military's entry test will be scrutinized for racial bias. This question, too, had been raised in the Army's 1980 Lister report, which contended that certain words included in the test "will disproportionately reflect a cultural background typical of the majority male population of white test-takers."[59] The problem was not pursued, however, because blacks were passing the test and entering the Army in record numbers. In any case, there have been few charges of cultural bias in military testing, which is somewhat surprising since standardized tests in nonmilitary settings have been subjected to growing criticism.[60]

Nevertheless, studies conducted by the Air Force have indicated that the test meets appropriate federal standards and the equations for predicting training performance are essentially the same for whites and minorities and for men and women. In fact, where differences were observed, the predictions for the training school grades of minorities were too optimistic. In other words, the test predicted minority examinees would do better in training than they actually did.[61]

Finally, in a technical assessment of the test battery, the National Opinion Research Center found that responses were "free from major defects such as high levels of guessing or carelessness, inappropriate levels of difficulty, cultural test-question bias, and inconsistencies in test administration procedures." The investigators therefore concluded that the test results "provide a sound basis for the estimation of population attributes such as means, medians, and percentile points, for the youth population as a whole and for subpopulations defined by age, sex, and race/ethnicity."[62]

Considering such findings, the Pentagon's general counsel concluded in 1977 that the ASVAB met the Fifth Amendment due process standard, which requires that "no discriminatory purpose be present and requires proof only that the test predicts performance in a training course." Title VII of the Civil Rights Act of 1964, however, sets a stricter standard, requiring proof that a test predicts performance on the job. The Office of the General Counsel concluded that under its interpretation, Title VII "does not apply to members of the armed forces. If the Court disagrees and applies Title VII standards to the ASVAB test, we would not be able at this point to prove that the test is related to job performance."[63]

Admittedly, it is difficult to envision Pentagon decision makers or legislators debating the esoteric psychometric problems of standards validation and test bias. More conceivable, however, is the prospect that fiscally minded legislators or the Pentagon's civilian leaders could ask, how much quality is enough? Because the marginal costs—incentives, advertising expenses, number of recruiters, and the like—to attract and retain high-quality volunteers are higher, the services, especially the Army, might be put under greater pressure to defend their higher standards.

Clearly, every job in the armed forces does not need to be filled by people with above-average scores on the military entrance test, and it is reasonable to ask the services to specify the relation between test results and job performance. During the transition to an all-volunteer force, the Pentagon's civilian leadership acknowledged that too much quality could be counterproductive: "Overall, the learning capacity of new entries is adequate in meeting job requirements when the proportion of Mental Group IV personnel does not exceed about 22 percent. Conversely, when the overall proportion of Mental Group IV personnel falls below 15 percent, there is a tendency toward many people being under-challenged by their job assignments." [64]

The Army was more specific in a report to Congress in 1985, presenting a distribution of recruit test scores that "would be both cost effective and sufficient to support the Army's force structure and manpower requirements" (the actual 1991 mix is shown for comparison):[65]

Test score category	*"Cost-effective" mix (percent)*	*FY 1991 mix (percent)*
I-IIIA (GSMA)	59–63	74.5
IIIB	31–27	24.4
IV	10	1.0

It would thus appear that the Army is recruiting higher quality personnel than it recently considered cost effective, which suggests there is substantial leeway for adjusting entry standards without compromising military effectiveness.

A HOBSON'S CHOICE

It is easy to understand why the delicate issue of racial representation in the armed forces has gone largely unaddressed. Many observers, after all, deny the existence of a problem, contending that today's volunteers, black or white, are merely exercising their freedom of choice. Any suggestions that the volunteers might be economic conscripts or might be making uninformed decisions are dismissed as condescending. Besides, some would ask, is the alternative—unemployment—better? Other observers contend that the current distribution is about right and are confident that it would require a war bigger than anything foreseeable to impose truly disproportionate casualties on African Americans. Besides, as the Vietnam experience indicated, actions can and probably would be taken to hold casualty rates closer to the general population norms than to the composition of the force. To this group, the racial composition of the armed forces is not at issue.

Other Americans who, for a variety of reasons, harbor concerns about or are uncomfortable with fielding a racially unbalanced military force and would prefer a more representative force confront a Hobson's choice. Some are resigned to the fact that young African Americans are entering into a devil's bargain, made necessary by a society that has failed to provide them with the tools needed to compete in the nonmilitary marketplace. Their solution is social reform aimed at upgrading the status and skills of the underprivileged and redressing the disparities that make the armed forces the most attractive—and often the only—employment opportunity available to them. But the observers recognize that even the most successful programs would take years to undo what decades of social and educational neglect have created. In the meantime they would not limit the opportunities that blacks now enjoy in the armed forces. Some would even preserve the proportion at the current high levels.

Others, pointing to the inequities of a racially unbalanced military that became obvious during the Persian Gulf conflict, are unwilling to wait for social reforms. They would have the nation return to conscription or adopt policies that would yield a more representative force, neither of which, at this juncture, would appear to be socially or politically acceptable, much less accomplish the intended purpose.

The inescapable conclusion, then, is that the nation will field a racially unrepresentative force until it can resolve the many complex problems that contribute to the greater propensity among blacks for military service. It seems safe to speculate, however, that if the changes since the end of the Persian Gulf conflict become a trend, blacks' overrepresentation in the Army will diminish.

The pace of change will depend largely on how free the Army is to emphasize manpower quality as it shrinks. It would be wrongheaded to preclude the Army from pursuing that goal just to preserve a given racial composition. But it would be equally improper to permit it to do so without closely scrutinizing its standards and test instruments and the rationale underlying them.

If nothing else, the Persian Gulf experience has provided the nation with a better understanding of the racial composition of its armed forces and its implications. Perhaps the public's awareness that a higher percentage of African Americans than whites is in peril in time of war will foster awareness that a higher percentage is also in economic peril in time of peace.

An Overview of "Don't Ask, Don't Tell, Don't Pursue, Don't Harass"

Servicemembers Legal Defense Network (SLDN)

"Don't Ask, Don't Tell, Don't Pursue, Don't Harass" (DADTDPDH) is a ban on lesbians, gays and bisexuals serving in the military—similar to the policies banning service that have been in place for the past fifty years.[1] DADTDPDH is the only law in the land that authorizes the firing of an American for being gay.[2] There is no other federal, state, or local law like it. Indeed, DADTDPDH is the only law that punishes lesbians, gays and bisexuals for coming out. Many Americans view DADTDPDH as a benign gentlemen's agreement with discretion as the key to job security. That is simply not the case. An honest statement of one's sexual orientation to anyone, anywhere, anytime may lead to being fired.

A. THE HISTORY OF THE POLICY

DADTDPDH is the result of a failed effort by President Clinton to end the ban on gays in the military. Spurred in part by the brutal 1992 murder of Seaman Allen Shindler, then-candidate Clinton proposed ending the ban by issuing an Executive Order overriding the Department of Defense regulations that barred gays from serving. Congress, however, intervened and the ban was made law, theoretically preventing action by future Commanders in Chief.

This law was, however, significantly different from prior prohibitions on service in three respects. First, congressional and military leaders acknowledged, for the first time in 1993, that lesbians, gays and bisexuals serve our nation and do so honorably.[3] Second, the policy also states sexual orientation is no longer a bar to military service.[4] Third, President Clinton, Congress and military leaders agreed to end intrusive questions about service members' sexual orientation[5] and to stop the military's infamous investigations to ferret out suspected lesbian, gay and bisexual service members.[6] They agreed to take steps to prevent anti-gay harassment.[7] They agreed to treat lesbian, gay and bisexual service members even-handedly in the criminal justice system, instead of criminally prosecuting them in circumstances where they would not prosecute heterosexual service members.[8] They agreed to implement the law with due regard for the privacy and associations of service members.[9] The law became known in 1993 as "Don't Ask, Don't Tell, Don't Pursue" to signify the new limits to investigations and the intent to respect service members' privacy.

Small steps were made to keep some of these promises. Questioning on sexual orientation at induction stopped. Criminal prosecutions have decreased and witch-hunts have declined. President Clinton issued an Executive Order ending discrimination in the issuance of security clearances.[10] The Department of Defense issued guidelines on anti-gay harassment and limits on investigations.

Then, in 1999, PFC Barry Winchell was murdered by fellow soldiers at Fort Campbell, Kentucky. In the wake of this murder, the Department of Defense (DoD) issued new guidance on prohibiting anti-gay harassment. President Clinton issued an Executive Order providing for sentence enhancement under the Uniform Code of Military Justice (UCMJ) for hate crimes,[11] as well as a limited psychotherapist-patient privilege.[12] In February 2000, Pentagon officials added "Don't Harass" to the title of the policy. The Pentagon then did a survey on anti-gay harassment, finding it was widespread.[13] Thereafter the Pentagon formed a working group which issued a thirteen-point action plan to address anti-gay harassment which the services were then directed to implement.

These limited steps, spurred in large part by the murder of PFC Barry Winchell, have done little to fulfill the promises made when the policy was created. Intrusive questioning continues. Harassment continues in epidemic proportions. Little regard for service member privacy has been shown during the life of this law. Simply put, asking, pursuing, and harassing have continued since the law was passed.

B. THE DON'TS IN "DON'T ASK, DON'T TELL, DON'T PURSUE, DON'T HARASS"

Don't Ask

"Don't Ask" means that service members are not supposed to be asked about their sexual orientation.[14] Experience has shown, however, that some commanders, inquiry officers and investigators continue to ask service members about their sexual orientation, despite the rules to the contrary. Service members are not required to reveal their sexual orientation if they are asked about it. Lesbian, gay and bisexual service members who answer and reveal their orientation are likely to be discharged, even though it was against the policy for military officials to ask about their sexual orientation in the first place.

Don't Tell

Under "Don't Tell," lesbian, gay and bisexual service members facc discharge if they disclose their sexual orientation.[15] This provision was intended to target public declarations of sexual orientation. Lawmakers promised that service members would be left alone as long as they kept their orientation a "personal and private" matter. As the law has come to be implemented, however, there is no privacy for service members as promised in 1993, when "Don't Ask, Don't Tell, Don't Pursue, Don't Harass" became law. If a military commander finds out that a service member has confided their sexual orientation to anyone—even parents, a psychologist or chaplain[16] the service member will likely face discharge. One exception is security clearance interviews, where truthful statements about sexual orientation or activities are not supposed to be used as a basis for discharge.[17] "Don't Tell" also does not overturn the attorney-client privilege that exists under military law and that, in general, requires military defense attorneys to keep conversations with their clients confidential.

Don't Pursue

"Don't Pursue" was intended to stop the infamous witch hunts against lesbian, gay and bisexual service members. More than a dozen specific investigative limits as laid out in DoD instructions and directives comprise "Don't Pursue." It is the most complicated and least understood component of the policy. These investigative limits establish a minimum threshold to start an inquiry and restrict the scope of an inquiry even when one is properly initiated.

A service member may be investigated and administratively discharged if they:

1) make a statement that they are lesbian, gay or bisexual;
2) engage in physical contact with someone of the same sex for the purposes of sexual gratification; or
3) marry, or attempt to marry, someone of the same sex.[18]

Only a service member's commanding officer may initiate an inquiry into homosexual conduct.[19] In order to begin an inquiry, the commanding officer must receive credible information from a reliable source that a service member has violated the policy.[20] Actions that are associational behavior, such as having gay friends, going to a gay bar, attending gay pride events, and reading gay magazines or books, are never to be considered credible information of sexual orientation.[21] In addition, a service member's report to his/her command regarding harassment or assault based on perceived sexuality is never to be considered credible evidence.[22]

If a determination is made that credible information exists that a service member has violated the policy, a service member's commanding officer may initiate a "limited inquiry" into the allegation or statement. That inquiry is limited in two primary ways. First, the command may only investigate the factual circumstances directly relevant to the specific allegation(s).[23] Second, in statements cases, the command may only question the service member, his/her chain of command, and anyone that the service member suggests.[24] In most cases of homosexual statement, no investigation is necessary.[25] Cases involving private sexual acts between consenting adults should be dealt with administratively, and criminal investigators should not be involved.[26]

The command may not attempt to gather additional information not relevant to the specific act or allegation, and the command may not question anyone outside of those listed above without approval from the Secretary of that Service.[27] Such an investigation is considered a "substantial investigation."[28] In order to request authority to conduct a "substantial investigation," the service member's command must be able to clearly articulate an appropriate basis for an investigation.[29]

As with a "limited inquiry," only a service member's commanding officer has the authority to request permission to conduct a "substantial investigation."[30] By definition, a "substantial investigation" is anything that extends beyond questioning the service member, the service member's immediate chain of command, and anyone the service member suggests.[31]

Don't Harass

The "Don't Harass" component was added to attempt to address the rampant harassment because of perceived sexual orientation in the military. Officially, "[t]he Armed Forces do not tolerate harassment or violence against any service member, for any reason."[32] The Pentagon has also committed to implement a thirteen point Anti-Harassment Action Plan in 2002. As of 2003 this plan has not been fully implemented. There are many regulations and laws that prohibit harassment and can be applied to anti-gay harassment cases. However, these regulations are not well enforced and harassment remains a serious problem. Harassment can take different forms, ranging from a hostile climate rife with anti-gay comments, to direct verbal and physical abuse, to death threats.

C. THE THREE THINGS THAT WILL GET YOU DISCHARGED

Under "Don't Ask, Don't Tell, Don't Pursue, Don't Harass" service members may be discharged for homosexual conduct. The military defines homosexual conduct very broadly. Homosexual conduct includes (1) a statement that one is gay, (2) a homosexual act, attempted act or solicitation of an act, and (3) a marriage or attempted marriage to someone of the same gender.[33] Service members should review thoroughly the sections in this guide that cover these reasons for discharge. An abbreviated version follows.

1. Statements.

Statements are admissions, like "I am gay." There are many other statements that may form a basis for discharge under current regulations. Words that are not as direct as "I am gay" but convey the same sense, such as "I am not a gay man, but my boyfriend is," can lead to administrative discharge processing. Additionally, behavior, or words that a so-called "reasonable person" would believe were intended to mean that the person making the statement is gay, are now considered statements. According to Department of Defense hypotheticals, for example, carrying a gay pride banner that states, "Lesbians in the military say lift the ban" could be interpreted as a statement of sexual orientation.

"Don't Ask, Don't Tell, Don't Pursue, Don't Harass" presumes that service members who state they are gay engage in, intend to engage in, or have a propensity to engage in homosexual acts. Discharge is mandatory for service members who state their sexual orientation unless they rebut (disprove) this presumption, usually at an administrative discharge board. Rebutting the presumption has proven to be a nearly impossible task. Lesbian, gay and bisexual service members should not come out on the false hope that they can rebut the presumption and keep their careers.

2. Acts.

The military defines homosexual acts as more than having sex with someone of the same gender. Acts include any touching of a person of the same gender for purposes of sexual gratification, and any touching that a "reasonable person" would believe shows a propensity (likelihood) to engage in gay acts. Kissing, hugging, and hand-holding have all been viewed as homosexual acts under this policy.

Discharge is mandatory for homosexual acts. "Don't Ask, Don't Tell, Don't Pursue, Don't Harass" retains one long-standing exception for service members who can prove, among other criteria, that their homosexual acts were a departure from their customary behavior and will not occur again and that their retention is in the best interest of the service. Service members should be warned that, in practice, there is very little chance of being retained under this exception, which service members refer to as "Queen for a Day."

3. Marriage.

Though lesbians, gay men and bisexuals cannot be legally married at this time, the "Don't Ask, Don't Tell, Don't Pursue, Don't Harass" regulations prohibit marriage and "attempted marriage" anyway. Some commands have also initiated discharge proceedings based on evidence of same gender commitment ceremonies or civil unions. Domestic partnership registration may also trigger separation under the prohibition on "attempted marriage"; such registration could also be considered a "statement" of sexual orientation.

EVERYTHING YOU WANTED TO KNOW ABOUT "DON'T ASK, DON'T TELL, DON'T PURSUE, DON'T HARASS" BUT WERE AFRAID TO ASK

Acts

"Don't Ask, Don't Tell, Don't Pursue, Don't Harass" defines "homosexual acts" broadly. Acts can include kissing, hand-holding and other bodily contact between people of the same gender, not just sex.

A "homosexual act" means any bodily contact, actively undertaken or passively permitted, between members of the same gender for the purpose of satisfying sexual desires, and any bodily contact (for example, hand-holding or kissing, in most circumstances) that a reasonable person would understand to demonstrate a propensity or intent to engage in an act.[34]

The regulations treat attempts and solicitations the same as acts, putting members at risk of being discharged for attempted hugging or solicitation of a kiss.[35]

The regulations state that the "preferred method" of handling allegations of homosexual acts occurring in private between consenting adults is in the administrative system, through commanders' inquiries and administrative discharge boards.[36] This guidance is being followed in most commands.

Some commanders, however, have singled out gay service members for court-martial under the Uniform Code of Military Justice (UCMJ). Sodomy (oral or anal sex, whether heterosexual or homosexual) is a criminal offense under Article 125 of the UCMJ. Kissing, hugging and other forms of touching may be charged as crimes under the "general articles," Article 133 (officers) and Article 134 (enlisted or officers). Conviction under Article 125, 133 or 134 can result in up to five years in prison for each act, dishonorable discharge, reduction in pay grade and fines and forfeitures.[37]

While most service members do not face criminal prosecution for gay acts, the risk is very real.

Administrative Separation Boards and Boards of Inquiry

Most enlisted service members who are processed for discharge for homosexual conduct have the right to a hearing before an administrative separation board (also known as an administrative discharge board).[38] These boards allow service members to fight for retention, or to fight for a better discharge characterization than the command wants to give them.

In these hearings, service members can exercise the following rights:

- to have a military attorney represent them, and also to have civilian legal counsel arranged by them at no cost to the government;
- to bring their own witnesses;
- to introduce statements and other evidence;
- to ask the government to produce witnesses (though these requests are not always granted);
- to cross-examine witnesses called by the military; and
- to testify under oath or make an unsworn statement on their behalf.[39]

An administrative separation board usually has three officers[40] and/or senior enlisted members (in the case of enlisted personnel)[41] who hear evidence from the service member and from the military. The theoretically impartial board members are instructed to weigh evidence by the "preponderance of the evidence" standard.[42] The military must produce evidence that is of greater weight, or is more convincing, than the service member's evidence in order to persuade the board to decide in favor of the military. The slightest edge in the military's favor is enough for it to win. This is an easier standard for the military to meet than the standard used at court-martial, where the government must prove a service member's guilt "beyond a reasonable doubt."

Further, evidence that would not be allowed in a court-martial is allowed in administrative separation boards. The only restriction on evidence that may be introduced is "relevance."[43] Administrative separation boards may consider hearsay, rumors and circumstantial evidence if considered relevant.

Administrative separation boards are required to make findings of fact about whether or not service members have engaged in homosexual conduct (statements, acts or marriages). When board members find that homosexual conduct has occurred, with very few exceptions, they MUST recommend discharge and make a recommendation about the appropriate discharge characterization. The board can also make a finding, when appropriate, that a statement was NOT made for the purpose of seeking separation. The board can also recommend against recoupment.

After reviewing all of the evidence presented, the board then makes its recommendations and findings of fact to the separating authority. The separating authority can accept or modify the board's recommendations.[44]

Many experienced military-law attorneys believe that, as a practical matter, boards often do NOT weigh the evidence to the required standard. In their view, board members often make decisions based more on what they think the command wants than on the evidence (or lack of evidence) in a case.[45] Board members' anti-gay bias and the relaxed standards of evidence that allows rumors, hearsay, and illegally obtained information to be considered by the board can present major problems for service members accused in gay cases.

Command legal officers and other command representatives often tell service members that administrative boards will do them no good, will only prolong the separation process, will cause the command to pursue UCMJ proceedings, or will result in a worse discharge. These "scare tactics" are designed to coerce a service member into waiving their right to a hearing. It is done to save the command time and resources and is not usually done in the best interests of the service member.

Service members should never take such "advice" from the command that wants to discharge them. Instead, they should contact defense counsel (either military defense counsel, SLDN, or a civilian attorney well-versed in military law and procedure) for the information they need to make an informed decision.

Service members should strongly consider pursuing an administrative board if they have been wrongly accused, the evidence against them is weak, their accuser is not credible, the command is recommending a discharge characterization other than honorable, or the service member is concerned about their GI Bill benefits or recoupment.

Aggravating Circumstances

Aggravating circumstances are circumstances that permit the military to give a service member an Other Than Honorable (OTH) discharge characterization for homosexual acts.[46] Usually, service members discharged for homosexual conduct receive an Honorable or General (under honorable conditions) discharge characterization, depending on their overall service record.

An OTH based on aggravating circumstances can only be given if an administrative discharge board or a discharge authority (the officer authorized to order a discharge) makes a finding that, during the current term of service, the service member attempted, solicited or committed a homosexual act in the following circumstances:

a. By using force, coercion, or intimidation;
b. With a person under 16 years of age;
c. With a subordinate in circumstances that violate customary military superior-subordinate relationships;

d. Openly in public view;
e. For compensation;
f. Aboard a military vessel or aircraft; or
g. In another location subject to military control under aggravating circumstances noted in the finding that have an adverse impact on discipline, good order, or morale comparable to the impact of such activity aboard a vessel or aircraft.[47]

Asking

"Commanders or appointed inquiry officials shall not ask, and members shall not be required to reveal, their sexual orientation,"[48] according to the current regulations.

Despite the regulations, some officials continue to ask about sexual orientation. Some have asked service members directly, "Are you gay?" Others have used creative phrasing, such as, "Do you find other men attractive?"

Service members do not have to answer questions about their sexual orientation.[49] If service members reveal their sexual orientation, even in response to a direct question that violates the policy, they will likely face discharge.

Be aware that commanders are allowed to question service members about specific incidents of homosexual conduct, if they have received credible information about that conduct.[50] Homosexual conduct means: (1) a verbal or nonverbal statement by the service member that he or she is gay, (2) a homosexual act, or (3) marriage or attempted marriage to a person of the same gender.[51]

Service members have the right to say nothing, sign nothing and consult with an attorney if questioned about homosexual conduct.

Association with Known Homosexuals

Association with known homosexuals, in and of itself, is not a basis for investigation or discharge. The regulations state:

> [c]redible information does not exist when . . . [t]he only information known is an associational activity such as going to a gay bar, possessing or reading homo-

> sexual publications, associating with known homosexuals, or marching in a gay rights rally in civilian clothes. Such activity, in and of itself, does not provide evidence of homosexual conduct.[52]

Despite the regulations, service members should be cautious about associational activities. Co-workers and commanders are likely to become suspicious if they know service members have gay friends, read gay literature, or belong to gay organizations. This can lead to harassment and to intensified command scrutiny in an attempt to find a reason to investigate or discharge a service member.

Attorneys

A. Military Attorneys

Each service has military lawyers, officers in the Judge Advocate General Corps, detailed to assist members with legal defense. These attorneys have ethical obligations to be zealous advocates for their clients. Command attorneys, legal officers who advise commanders, may not keep information told to them confidential. Therefore, in discussing his or her case with a military attorney, a service member should not speak to any military attorney without asking two key questions: "Are you a defense attorney?" and "Is our conversation confidential?" If the answer to *both* questions is "YES" then it is OK to talk to that lawyer. If the answer to either question is "NO" then do NOT speak to them about a case.

Service members have the right to *consult* with a military attorney if they are questioned by a military investigator.[53] In nearly all gay cases, service members should ask to consult with an attorney before answering any questions. If a service member requests to consult with a defense attorney, investigators are supposed to stop the questioning and allow the service member to speak with one.[54] Some services or bases allow service members to consult with a military attorney at any time, even if they are not being questioned, but it is often difficult to see military defense counsel until there is an interrogation or a formal case.[55]

Typically, a service member may not be *represented* by a military attorney until after an investigation has been conducted and either criminal charges have been filed or the command has started discharge proceedings.[58] In the military, an attorney represents a service member when the attorney has been assigned to take the service member's case.

In nearly all circumstances, an attorney who represents a service member must keep conversations with that service member confidential, unless the service member gives them permission to do otherwise. When a service member consults with an attorney, the attorney is also supposed to keep this conversation confidential even if the attorney does not yet represent the service member and the attorney's only role is to advise him or her.

Service members should be warned that command staff judge advocates, command legal officers, prosecutors and "recorders" (attorneys or other officers who represent the government in administrative discharge boards) have no obligation to keep conversations with service members confidential. Anything service members say to these officials can and will be used against them.

B. Civilian Attorneys

Service members also have the right to a civilian attorney or legal worker (a non-attorney, such as a paralegal or military counselor, who is experienced with the military's administrative system), but must arrange for one on their own.[56] Civilian attorneys and legal workers can assist service members during an investigation, before charges or discharge paperwork are filed and before military attorneys are usually allowed to represent service members. Having a civilian attorney or legal worker does not prevent service members from requesting a military attorney.

Civilian attorneys and legal workers can do other things that military attorneys may not, such as help service members contact Congress or utilize the media if service members wish to do so. A civilian attorney or legal worker can work with the military attorney as soon as the military attorney is allowed to come to the service member's defense.

Civilian attorneys also have a duty of confidentiality. When a service member consults with a civilian attorney or is represented by an attorney, the attorney must keep his or her conversations with the service member confidential, unless the service member gives him or her permission to do otherwise.

Basis for Discharge

Under "Don't Ask, Don't Tell, Don't Pursue, Don't Harass" there are three grounds for discharge:

A basis for discharge exists if: (1) The member has engaged in a homosexual act; (2) The member has said that he or she is a homosexual or bisexual, or made some other statement that indicates a propensity or intent to engage in homosexual acts; or (3) The member has married or attempted to marry a person of the same sex.[57]

Bisexuality

Under "Don't Ask, Don't Tell, Don't Pursue, Don't Harass" a bisexual is "a person who engages in, attempts to engage in, has a propensity to engage in, or intends to engage in homosexual and heterosexual acts."[58] The law provides that a member who makes a statement that they are bisexual shall be separated from the armed forces.[59]

Despite what the law says, there is a tendency on the part of some commanders to disbelieve members who state they are bisexual. Often commanders believe that this statement is made only as a way to seek separation and conclude that the service member is someone who lacks the propensity to engage in homosexual conduct. While commanders are increasingly asking service members to offer "proof" of their sexual orientation before taking their statements as credible, this is even more pronounced in bisexual statement situations. This is particularly true if the service member is married or currently involved in an opposite gender relationship.

There is no requirement in any regulation, or in the law, for a service member to prove their sexual orientation. Because of the severe criminal consequences that can come from proof of homosexual acts, service members are strongly encouraged not to try to prove their orientation. The best advice for any service member thinking about making a statement or trying to prove their orientation is to contact a competent, experienced defense attorney.

Chaplains

Some services, particularly the Army, advise service members to speak with chaplains as a confidential resource, especially in situations where reporting anti-gay harassment is involved. Under military law, chaplains must keep conversations confidential when service members seek their spiritual guidance. Chaplains do not have to keep conversations confidential when a service member speaks with them for reasons other than spiritual guidance.

However, the Directives do not explicitly address issues of confidentiality in any fashion. The individual services do, however, have their own regulations concerning chaplains. For example, the regulation states that "[Chaplains] will not disclose confidential communications in private or in public." [60]

Service members should be careful speaking with chaplains. Some chaplains have turned in service members who revealed their sexual orientation. Others have instructed gay service members to turn themselves in. Some chaplains have carelessly talked about their conversations in enough detail that commanders could figure out the service members involved.

Service members confide in military chaplains at their own risk. Service members should speak with chaplains only about spiritual matters. Service members should specifically state that they seek spiritual guidance in an effort to increase the likelihood that their conversations will be protected by law.[61]

If a chaplain violates confidentiality and reveals the service member's sexual orientation to the command, the service member will likely face discharge.

Chaplains also routinely misinform service members about what the regulations say and about their legal rights. Do not expect chaplains to know the regulations or answers to legal questions; these are better addressed by a defense attorney or legal worker.

Civilian Police

As a general rule, service members should treat civilian police as they would military police and invoke their legal rights to say nothing, sign nothing and consult with an attorney if questioned about their private lives. If a service member is involved with civilian law enforcement authorities, it should be presumed that the military will be notified of any incidents. In most areas, civilian police routinely turn reports involving a military member over to the military.

Service members should avoid disclosing their sexual orientation to civilian police. If a service member's sexual orientation is noted in any reports, or is an issue in the civilian incident that required a police response, that information is often disclosed to the military and can be used by the military as a basis for beginning administrative or disciplinary proceedings.

A service member has the constitutional right to object to a search of one's off-base home without a search warrant.[62] There are many exceptions to this rule, however. A service member should state their objection to a warrantless search and call an attorney right away. Even if the police have a warrant the service member should state that he or she objects to the search. However, with or without a warrant, the service member should not interfere with a search.

Civilian police often bring a military police officer with them when they try to search a service member's off-base home. Even if a military police officer is present, a service member can object to a search.

A gay service member sometimes needs help from civilian or military police in situations that might raise questions about their sexual orientation or private life. For example, in a domestic dispute between a same sex couple where the police are called, questions will be asked about the relationship. With legal assistance, a service member may be able to obtain the help needed from the police without encountering problems with the military.

Problems may arise in emergencies where a service member faces an immediate threat of harm. If there is a real need to talk to police or other law enforcement officials and there is no time to seek legal help first, a member should stick to recounting the facts as they have occurred. A service member should avoid making any statement about their own orientation or private life, if at all possible. A service member should still speak with an attorney or legal worker as soon as possible.

For service members who have been UA or AWOL for eighty days or more, whatever the reason for leaving without authorization, the military usually declares them to be a deserter and issues a federal arrest warrant.[63] Civilian police have access to these warrants and will often arrest the service member.[64] Usually, this happens when a service member in a deserter status is stopped for a routine traffic violation. Service members arrested by civilian police for desertion should say nothing, sign nothing and ask for a defense attorney.

Civilian Protections Against Anti-Gay Discrimination in Employment

"Don't Ask, Don't Tell, Don't Pursue, Don't Harass" does not apply to civilians. Civilian federal employees enjoy much greater protection against discrimination based on sexual orientation.

President Clinton also issued an Executive Order in 1995 that is still in effect, which prohibits the government from denying security clearances to individuals based solely upon their sexual orientation. That order applies to both service members and federal civilian employees.

Civilians and Investigations

Generally, military investigators have no jurisdiction over civilians. While military investigators may attempt to question civilian friends and family members in an effort to obtain information against suspected gay troops, civilians have no obligation to answer questions or to let military investigators search their homes without a search warrant. Anything civilians tell military investigators, no matter how harmless it may seem, can be used against the service member.

Military investigators may bring civilian police officers with them when they try to question civilians. Even if a civilian police officer is present, civilians still have the right not to answer questions and to object to a search of their homes without a search warrant.[65]

COMING OUT

Coming out—openly acknowledging being lesbian, gay or bisexual—is usually a very personal, sometimes traumatic, experience. Ideally, being open about sexual orientation should be a non-issue in the military. The reality is that coming out to the military has many legal risks and it may have an impact on the service member's civilian life after discharge. Coming out should never be seen as an easy way to get out of the military or to avoid a service obligation.

Under the policy, coming out—usually by making a statement of homosexual or bisexual orientation—creates a "rebuttable presumption" that the service member engages in, intends to engage in, or has a propensity to engage in homosexual acts.

It does not matter to whom the service member comes out. If the military finds out, any statement acknowledging being lesbian, gay or bisexual can be used as a basis for discharge. If a service member wants to stay in the military, coming out to anyone could put their military career at risk. Even a private statement to family, a close friend, a doctor or a chaplain can result in the end of a career.

Therefore, service members should consult with a defense attorney before making a statement.

WHY DO PEOPLE MAKE COMING OUT STATEMENTS?

Integrity

Honor is a Core Value in the military. The policy's requirement that lesbian, gay or bisexual service members live in the closet, lying daily, evading, dissembling and hiding their sexual orientation from peers, superiors and subordinates, directly conflicts with the Services' basic values. Many service members see coming out as a matter of integrity, a way of demonstrating the Services' Core Value of being honest and honorable.

Harrassment

Another major reason for coming out is as a means of escaping anti-gay threats and harassment, or because service members find they are unable to serve in a homophobic military. The military, while recognizing that anti-gay harassment undermines unit cohesion and combat readiness, has consistently refused to take concrete action to end anti-gay harassment, hold harassers accountable, and address the widespread tolerance of anti-gay comments, slurs and "jokes."

Service members should be careful in how they report harassment so that they do not inadvertently "out" themselves. When reporting threats or harassment a service member should say: "I'm being harassed because they think I'm gay" or "I'm being threatened because I am perceived to be a lesbian." Do not say "I am being harassed because I am gay."

A service member who decides to come out to the military should *not* make a statement or write a letter on their own and give it to the command. Because there are legal risks involved, a service member is strongly encouraged to contact an experienced attorney or legal worker, who can help them make a careful, written statement that leaves no confusion about what was or was not said and that avoids the many pitfalls under this policy.

A service member who comes out to their command is likely to be questioned.

No matter what military officials may say, a service member should not provide information about any sexual activities or relationships and should not turn over photos, letters or other "proof" about their sexual orientation.

Civilians are under no obligation to answer questions from military investigators. Depending on the circumstances, military members may not have to answer questions about their co-workers and friends. Because this is a complicated area, military members are encouraged to consult with a defense attorney before making a statement so that they can be informed of the rules concerning permissible command inquiries.

"Coming Out" Has Some Risks

A Statement Does Not Always Equal Discharge

A common misperception among service members is that if they simply tell the military they are lesbian, gay or bisexual the military will discharge them almost immediately. Increasingly, this is not the case. The command may not believe the service member's statement or may not care that the service member is gay.

Commands May Inappropriately Investigate

Military commands may investigate service members' private lives following their statements of sexual orientation. The service member's command may search anything the service member has on base, including barracks room, locker, and car, without the service member's permission.

Benefits May Be at Risk

Service members risk losing several benefits, including the Montgomery GI Bill educational benefits, if they "come out." In order to receive benefits under the GI Bill, a service member must receive an Honorable discharge and have completed two or three years of a service commitment (depending on what the enlistment contract states). If a service member does not meet these requirements the service member will NOT receive the GI bill after discharge.[66]

Discharge Characterizations May Be Lowered

Every service member who leaves the military receives a discharge characterization. If discharged for "coming out" to the military, a service member may receive a discharge that is Honorable, General, or under some circumstances Other than Honorable. If the service member receives a less that Honorable discharge, the service member risks losing some VA benefits and may face added challenges in finding civilian employment. Some commands still try and improperly award lower discharge characterizations than a service member deserves just because he/she made a statement of sexual orientation.

Military May Ask for Money Back

If a service member has not served his/her entire commitment, the military may require the service member to repay scholarships, bonuses, or special pay they may have received. This is especially true in cases where service members "come out" to the military for the purpose of being discharged prior to the completion of their commitment.

False Statements Equal Criminal Offenses

If the military determines that your "coming out" statement is false or a lie, the military may retain the service member in the service and may also prosecute the service member criminally for providing a false official statement to the government.

What Will the Command Do When a Service Member Comes Out?

The command may react in one of many ways to a service member "coming out" to them. They may:

1) begin the process of discharge; or
2) issue a counseling statement to the service member; or
3) present the service member with a memorandum stating that an inquiry or investigation will be launched; or
4) tell the service member, formally or informally, that they do not believe the "coming out" statement and they will take no further action; or
5) say nothing at all and take no action on the statement; or
6) not talk with the service member at all until issuing a formal Notice of Administrative Separation.

Complaint-Making

Service members have the right to make legal complaints either through the military or outside military channels. Among others, they can use this right to complain about harassment or violations of "Don't Ask, Don't Tell, Don't Pursue, Don't Harass."

As a general rule, the military does not look kindly on people who make complaints. Service members who want to complain about improper treatment or violations of military regulations should have the assistance of an attorney in making their complaint. An attorney can help them decide the best complaint method for their situation, encourage the command or the service to treat the complaint seriously and help to protect against retaliation for making the complaint.

Normally, complaints cannot be used to attack discharge proceedings or disciplinary actions, though they can be useful in bringing the military's attention to problems in those proceedings. Sometimes commands take a second look at discharge or disciplinary proceedings if they realize that the proceedings are tied to improper or illegal actions.

Some of the more common complaint procedures are:

(1) "Writing Up." Any service member subject to the UCMJ can file charges against another service member for a violation of the UCMJ.[67] Service members can ask their commands to take disciplinary action against other members who violate the Uniform Code of Military Justice (UCMJ) or punitive regulations. Requests are normally made in writing.

Unfortunately, service members cannot demand that offenders be disciplined; it is up to the command to decide whether to take any action. Another practical reality is that a junior service member who attempts to place a senior service member "on report" can be retaliated against by the senior in ways that are hard to prove as retaliation—i.e., bad work assignments, assigned to guard duty or watch on weekends or leave periods, assignments to work details, etc.

(2) Article 138. UCMJ Article 138 permits service members to seek redress of a grievance against their commanding officer. Service members may seek this form of redress whenever they feel they have been wronged, whether or

not a law or regulation has been violated. These complaints usually begin with a letter to the commander asking for specific redress (an apology, a training session about the limits of the policy for all personnel, a dressing down for the offender, a transfer to get away from harassment, etc.). If the commander doesn't grant the request in a reasonable time, a formal complaint may be made to any commissioned officer, superior to the commanding officer, who shall forward the complaint to the officer exercising general court-martial convening authority over the commander. That officer must act on the complaint and report the matter to the Secretary of the Service.[68]

(3) Inspector General (IG). Service members may complain to the inspector general of their base, Service, or the Department of Defense about harassment or violations of regulations.[69] Once they are made, the handling of complaints is generally out of service members' hands. The inspector general's office does not itself have the power to correct problems, but its findings and recommendations are normally taken seriously by commands.

(4) Equal Opportunity (EO). Each branch of the service has equal opportunity offices or officers to handle complaints of race and gender discrimination and harassment. Complaints regarding anti-gay harassment are not part of EO representatives' mission. Service members are sometimes required to document EO complaints themselves. These offices also make recommendations to the command rather than taking action themselves.

(5) Congressional inquiries. Members of the military have the right to communicate with their members of Congress and to ask their help in resolving problems with the military.[70] Despite military rumors to the contrary, they do not need command permission to do so, and need not notify their commands. When presented with concrete evidence and asked for specific types of assistance, however, sympathetic members of Congress can urge the services or local commands to take concrete action about violations of the gay policy, such as witch hunts.

(6) Media / Press. The military hates bad press. Public attention brought by the press can often be an effective tool to make the military comply with its policies and hold violators accountable. Service members should not ap-

proach the media, or members of the press, on their own without talking to a defense attorney first to get appropriate legal counsel. While the press can be an influential tool, once the story is in the media stream, there is little the service member can do to control it. In addition, the service member may be ordered to not to communicate with the press after the initial complaint is made. In these cases, a defense attorney can represent the service member's interests to the press to protect the service member from getting into trouble for disobeying an order. Complaining to the press, and using its ability to influence the military, should only be done with legal counsel and only as part of a legal strategy to redress a wrong.

To be successful, complaints must normally be supported by documentary evidence, witness statements or other evidence. It is helpful, in most cases, to gather statements and other evidence before making a complaint, to avoid the possibility the offender or his or her friends may intimidate witnesses or destroy evidence. In addition, it helps to have legal assistance in evaluating the strength of the evidence and in preparing a complaint.

Service members who face retaliation for making complaints often have protection under the Military Whistleblower Protection Act.[71] Under the Act, service members who make certain types of complaints are entitled to prompt IG investigations of any adverse personnel action or threatened adverse personnel action taken to retaliate for their complaint.

If the retaliation results in formal adverse action, service members are also entitled to expedited proceedings before the Board for Correction of Military Records (BCMR) or Board for Correction of Naval Records (BCNR), depending on the service.

COMPUTERS

Many service members believe their computer correspondence and on-line discussions are secure. They are not. Government e-mails (.mil accounts) and government computer systems should not be used for personal matters unless authorized by the command and should NEVER be used by a service member for communicating information about sexual orientation or private sexual conduct (i.e., viewing pornography). Military members should never write personal letters or diaries on work computers, including authorized laptop computers used off base. Use of military computers for personal reasons risks violation of regulations and base policies on misuse of government equipment and may lead to detection by co-workers or investigators.

Statements of sexual orientation and information about gay activities obtained by military officials from computer drives, disks, e-mail or on-line services have been used to investigate and discharge service members.

Sometimes, military investigators go on-line to scan for gay military members or to catch suspected gay service members talking about their sexual orientation or activities. In the past, there have also been attempts to bait gay service members. Service members should never assume that someone is who they claim to be when they are on-line.

Investigators routinely search work computers and service members' government network accounts for security reasons. Investigators have retrieved suspected gay service members' e-mail. Investigators have also searched the personal computers and disks of suspected gay service members, using programs to retrieve deleted files. A service member should never consent to a search of their non-government personal computer without speaking with a defense attorney first. In general, the government needs a search warrant to search and/or seize information from a private computer that is not on base.

Corporal Klinger Provision

If a service member makes a statement, engages in homosexual acts or attempts to marry someone of the same gender solely to avoid military service, the military does not have to discharge him/her.[72] This clause was intended to prevent straight service members from claiming to be gay in order to miss a deployment or get out of the military. This clause has also been used by commanders seeking to keep gay service members in the military.

Credible Information

Credible information is the standard used to determine whether it is permissible to initiate an inquiry or investigation into homosexual conduct. Only a service member's commander[73] or the director, commander or principal deputy of a criminal investigative organization (CID, OSI, and NCIS)[74] may initiate an inquiry or investigation into homosexual conduct. He or she may initiate an inquiry or investigation only if there is credible information that a basis for discharge exists (a statement, act or marriage).[75] A criminal investigative organization should not initiate an investigation unless there is credible evidence of criminal activity.

In theory, credible information is not just any information. It has to be reliable. The policy states:

> [c]redible information exists where the information, considering its source and the surrounding circumstances, supports a reasonable belief that a [s]ervice member has engaged in homosexual conduct. It requires a determination based on articulable facts, not just a belief or suspicion.[76]

The regulations also explain when credible information does not exist:

> Credible information does not exist when . . . (1) the individual is suspected of engaging in homosexual conduct, but there is no credible information, as defined, to support that suspicion . . . ; (2) the only information is the opinions of others that a member is homosexual . . . ; (3) . . . the inquiry would be based on rumor, suspicion, or capricious claims concerning a member's sexual orientation; or (4) the only information known is an associational activity such as going to a gay bar, possessing or reading homosexual publications, associating with known homosexuals, or marching in a gay rights rally in civilian clothes.[77]

Again, these are examples, not a complete list.

In practice, many commanders and leaders of the investigative agencies are unaware of, or ignore, the requirement to have credible information before starting an inquiry or investigation.

CRIMINAL PROSECUTION

A service member cannot be criminally prosecuted simply for being lesbian, gay, bisexual or transgender. There must be some act that violates the UCMJ for the military to seek to criminally prosecute a service member. In general, "the preferred method of handling allegations of private consensual acts between adults of the same gender is through the administrative discharge system."[78]

Some commanders, however, file criminal charges against service members accused of homosexual acts. Others use the threat of criminal prosecution to coerce service members to accept lesser administrative discharges, either General (under Honorable Conditions), or Other Than Honorable (OTH) discharge in lieu of court-martial. The latter can result in loss of veterans and unemployment benefits and lead to substantial prejudice in obtaining civilian employment. While most service members do not face criminal prosecution for consensual, adult gay acts, there remains a legal risk.

Service members may be charged with violating Article 125 of the Uniform Code of Military Justice (UCMJ) for sodomy (oral or anal sex, whether heterosexual or homosexual) or the "general articles," Article 133 (officers) or Article 134 (enlisted or officers), for kissing, hand-holding or other forms of touching. Convictions under Article 125, 133 or 134 can, in some cases, result in up to five years of imprisonment for each act, a punitive discharge (Bad Conduct discharge or Dishonorable discharge), reduction in pay-grade and fines and forfeitures.[79]

Service members should be aware that commands often try to find ways to charge as many violations as possible out of each alleged incident.

Service members should be aware of other provisions under which suspected gay troops are at risk for possible prosecution. Service members are sometimes charged with fraud for collecting marital benefits while involved in opposite gender marriages.[80] Service members who have misrepresented their sexual orientation or activities during interrogations by military officials have been charged with making false official statements.[81] Some commanders have been quick to charge gay service members for fraternization in circumstances where straight service members would not be charged.[82] Some commanders have threatened charging service members with failure to obey orders (Article 92)[83] for making statements about sexual orientation after being ordered not to make such statements.

Regardless of their sexual orientation, HIV-positive service members have faced criminal prosecution for violating orders to notify health care workers or sexual partners of their HIV status, and for violating orders against unsafe sex (by not using condoms, for example). Some have also been charged with aggravated assault for having unprotected sex.

Service members who are questioned by military authorities face a Catch-22 situation. If they are ordered to reveal information about their sexual conduct and tell the truth, they may face criminal charges for their sexual conduct. If they lie about their sexual conduct when they are ordered to reveal it, they may face criminal charges for making false official statements.

Do invoke your Article 31 legal rights—say nothing, sign nothing and get legal help.

Delayed Entry Program (DEP)[84]

All service members enlist in the military and delay the date when they are to report for basic training. The UCMJ applies to "volunteers from the time of muster or acceptance into the armed forces."[85] An enlistee becomes a member of the armed forces, and subject to the UCMJ and military regulations, "upon taking the oath of enlistment."[86] Homosexual conduct, i.e., statements, acts or marriage, if brought to the attention of the military before the service member reports for basic training, most likely will cause the individual to be administratively released from their enlistment contract.

Members may be discharged from the delayed entry program—they are "attrited" with an uncharacterized discharge (DEP discharge).[87] The member does not receive a DD-214 because they have not been on active duty.[88] This type of separation can usually be approved by the commander of the local recruiting district where the member enlisted.

DISCHARGE CHARACTERIZATIONS

Upon discharge, military members receive a discharge characterization. An Entry Level Separation (ELS) with an uncharacterized discharge may be granted to a service member who has less than 180 days of active service and whose record warrants an Honorable or General discharge.[89] Administratively, only three types of discharges can be awarded: Honorable, General (Under Honorable Conditions), or Other Than Honorable (OTH). A Bad Conduct Discharge (BCD) or a Dishonorable Discharge (DD) can only be awarded by court-martial.

The standard for service members receiving a discharge under DADTDPDH is the same as for service members who come to the end of their term of service (ETS/EAOS) or, if officers, who resign their commission under routine circumstances. Service members should receive an Honorable or a General (under honorable conditions) discharge characterization based on their overall record.[90]

Some commanders recommend a lesser discharge characterization than the service member's service record merits, usually recommending a general (under honorable conditions) characterization when an honorable discharge is warranted. The service member must decide whether or not it is important to contest the command's recommendation. As a general rule, if a service member merits an honorable discharge, he or she should fight for one up-front—usually by requesting an administrative separation (ADSEP) board, or a Board of Inquiry (BOI) for officers.

Some commands have tried to persuade service members to accept a general discharge by saying it can be easily corrected later. This is not true. There is no "automatic" upgrade of a general discharge to an honorable after six months because of a homosexual discharge. Similarly, appealing to the Board for the Correction of Military or Naval Records (BCMR/BCNR) is not a guarantee of an upgrade. The standard for review at the BCMR/BCNR is to correct an "injustice or error."[91]

Administratively, there are usually only two ways to get an OTH discharge in DADTDPDH cases. In cases involving "aggravating circumstances," commanders and discharge boards can recommend an OTH discharge characterization.[92] Service members may also face an OTH discharge if they are "dual processed" for homosexual conduct and another reason for discharge, usually misconduct, which warrants an OTH. The misconduct may be based on a series of minor disciplinary problems that the command might otherwise have ignored, or on a single more serious offense.

Discharge characterizations determine eligibility for veterans' benefits and have an impact on civilian employment opportunities. An Honorable discharge entitles veterans to all veterans' benefits for which they are eligible,[93] and is mandatory for educational benefits under the Montgomery GI Bill programs.[94] A General discharge entitles veterans to almost all other benefits. A General discharge may raise some questions among some civilian employers about a veteran's performance in the military.

Service members with OTH discharges risk losing most, if not all, veterans' benefits; the Veterans Administration (VA) should make a case-by-case decision. They also face substantial prejudice in civilian employment and, in many states, an OTH discharge bars collection of unemployment compensation when they are discharged from the military.

DISCHARGE PAPERWORK (DD FORM 214)

Service members receive two copies of the DD-214 when they are discharged—a short form and a long form.[95] The long form includes the narrative reason for discharge, the discharge characterization, the three-letter or three-number discharge code corresponding to the reason for discharge, and a reenlistment code.

Under DADTDPDH there are three grounds for discharge—a homosexual (or bisexual) statement, homosexual act or homosexual marriage. Remember that under the policy each of these qualifies as conduct, even a statement or admission of a homosexual or bisexual orientation. If discharged under the service's homosexual conduct policy, the narrative reason for discharge will state "Homosexual Conduct–Admission/Statement," "Homosexual Conduct–Acts," or "Homosexual Conduct–Marriage," or words to that effect, depending on the basis for discharge.

The reenlistment code usually listed on the DD-214 when a service member is discharged for homosexual conduct will be an "RE-4." This means that the service member is ineligible to reenlist in any branch of the military or any component of a branch (i.e., active duty, reserves, or National Guard). The Air Force uses a different code than "RE-4" but the code used has the same meaning.[96]

Some civilian employers are aware of the long form and may ask for a copy during the hiring process. If applying for a government position, either municipal, state or federal, veterans should expect to be asked to provide a copy of their DD-214. Many state licensing authorities, such as nursing, medicine or bar examiners, may also ask for a copy when an applicant seeks a license to practice their profession. As a result, service members discharged under DADTDPDH often find that their DD-214 will "out" them to civilian employers (and anyone else who has access to their records).

6

Veterans and Toxic Exposures

Part 1: The Story of Depleted Uranium

Dan Fahey

No one told Raul Ramirez about depleted uranium until after he returned from the war. In late February 1991, Raul was a twenty-three-year-old Marine Corps rifleman and radio operator serving with Task Force Ripper, part of the 1st Marine Division, when the unit blasted through Iraqi tanks and infantry in southern Kuwait. "As soon as the war was over, we began to explore the massive graveyard of destroyed tanks and armored personnel carriers that littered the desert," recalls Raul.[1] "I had my picture taken on the top of a destroyed Iraqi T-72 tank, and climbed on many other destroyed vehicles. I even climbed into a destroyed armored personnel carrier and messed around with the numerous dials, buttons, and gears. I am very shocked to know now that many of those vehicles might have been contaminated with depleted uranium from ammunition shot by our own tanks and aircraft. It turns out I'm just one of the thousands of Marines, soldiers, sailors and airmen who the Pentagon says might have been 'unnecessarily exposed' to depleted uranium during and after the war."

In little more than a decade since Raul fought in Kuwait, ammunition made from depleted uranium (DU) has emerged from near total obscurity among combat troops and the public into the forefront of international discussion about war and its effects. At the center of the debate over DU munitions is concern about the health effects of exposure to DU dust and debris among veterans and people living near battle sites. Although many of the claims made about DU—by both military officials and anti-DU extremists—tend to be misleading or false, there is growing pressure to outlaw DU munitions at the same time that this new military technology is proliferating around the globe. Much of the debate over DU is dominated by politics rather than science, but there is little dispute that DU is a carcinogenic metal better deposited in radioactive waste dumps than dispersed on foreign battlefields.

Two related forces drive advances in military technology: the intent to inflict harm upon an enemy, and the desire to prevent him from harming you. Developments in offensive weaponry lead to advances in defensive technology that must be overcome by further improvements in offensive technology, and so on, in an endless search for the perfect war machine. Within this context, the use of depleted uranium (DU) metal in offensive and defensive weaponry may be seen as simply the incorporation of a new material into an eternal process of weapons development. What differentiates depleted uranium, however, are its chemical and radioactive properties, which contaminate battlefields and may harm friend and foe alike, long after the end of combat.

The story of depleted uranium munitions is inextricably linked to the development and use of nuclear weapons. The discovery of nuclear fission in 1938 spurred intensive mining and processing of natural uranium in the United States to create "enriched" uranium[2] for use in atomic bombs and, later, nuclear reactor fuel. The waste product of the uranium enrichment process is called "depleted" uranium because it contains less of the isotopes U235 and U234 (but marginally more U238) than natural uranium. After World War Two, increased production of enriched uranium created large stockpiles of DU in the United States, but the Atomic Energy Commission had no long-term plan for its safe disposal.

During the 1950s, as the Department of Defense (DoD) detonated hundreds of nuclear weapons and unnecessarily exposed tens of thousands of servicemen to radiation and radioactive fallout, the Atomic Energy Commission started giving DU to Army weapons developers. These developers experimented with high-density DU alloys in armor-piercing ammunition known as *kinetic energy penetrators.* This ammunition is simply a solid rod of extremely dense metal stabilized by tail fins; there is no explosive charge. The large energy of motion (kinetic energy) of the rod, traveling at speeds up to 1.8 kilometers per second, is sufficient to punch a hole in tank armor.[3] These penetrators generally have greater success in piercing heavily armored targets, such as the turrets on tanks, than traditional high-explosive tank rounds, whose effects may be deflected by modern armor. In addition, DU ammunition can achieve greater penetration of tank armor than tungsten alloy ammunition; tungsten alloy was used by the United States until the late 1970s and continues to be used by the armed forces of Australia, Canada, Germany, and other countries.

In the early 1970s, concerns about the high cost of tungsten alloy,[4] combined with improved performance of DU munitions,[5] prompted the U.S. Department of Defense to replace tungsten alloy with DU in kinetic energy penetrators. Depleted uranium also has an edge over tungsten alloy because its pyrophoricity produces burning fragments upon impact with a target, which can ignite flammable materials and cause secondary damage.[6] The energy of the impact combined with the burning of the round as it passes through armor creates a fine, respirable-size dust that contaminates an impact site and presents a hazard to combat troops and civilians. Seventeen years before the United States military used DU ammunition for the first time in combat, a military report noted: "in combat situations involving the widespread use of DU munitions, the potential for inhalation, ingestion, or implantation of DU compounds may be locally significant."[7]

By the late 1980s, the US military was using DU for ammunition shot by tanks, a Navy missile-defense gun, and the A-10 and AV-8B aircraft, which support ground troops and attack tanks. Starting in 1989, slabs of DU armor were placed on the front turrets of US tanks to provide additional protection; all Abrams tanks now have DU armor. DU is also used for balance weights in some aircraft and helicopters,[8] and about 0.1 g is used as a catalyst in certain antipersonnel mines.[9] The Department of Defense uses a DU casing in the bunker-busting B61-11 nuclear weapon to enable the nuclear warhead to penetrate the ground before detonating.[10] Although other missiles may contain DU counterweights,[11] the US military denies DU is used in operational cruise missiles.[12]

A U.S. Army report released six months before the 1991 Gulf War highlighted the potential health, environmental, and political effects of using DU ammunition in combat. The report stated that "aerosol DU exposures to soldiers on the battlefield could be significant with potential radiological and toxicological effects," including cancer and kidney damage.[13] The report also predicted, "Following combat, the condition of the battlefield and the long-term health risks to natives and combat veterans may become issues in the acceptability of the continued use of DU kinetic energy penetrators for military applications,"[14] thereby calling for additional "public relations efforts" due to "potential for adverse international reaction."[15] This and other pre–Gulf War reports and documents make clear that various military agencies knew the potential battlefield hazards of DU munitions, making the subsequent failure to provide warnings to US troops both inexplicable and unconscionable.

The Army trained Michael Stacy to load DU rounds into the main gun of an Abrams tank, but it didn't tell him that shooting DU rounds could contaminate battlefields with carcinogenic dust. Michael's tank was part of the 1st Infantry Division's invasion force, which blazed through southern Iraq during Operation Desert Storm's ground war. "We engaged Iraqi tanks, armored personnel carriers, trucks, bunkers—anything in our path," he states. "After everything was over, we went back through the areas we had shot up and climbed all over the vehicles we destroyed. We wanted to see the damage our tanks had done, and we were looking for souvenirs. I knew we were shooting DU rounds, but we were never told to stay away from destroyed vehicles. We didn't know any better, and were dipping [chewing tobacco], smoking, and eating without having washed our hands. Right after the war we saw lots of guys from other units climbing on the vehicles that we had shot with DU rounds."[16]

During the Gulf War, U.S. tanks and aircraft shot nearly 900,000 DU rounds (containing 315 tons of DU) during combat.[17] Although Abrams tanks shot thousands of large-caliber DU rounds, A-10 Warthog jets shot nearly 800,000 medium-caliber DU rounds, accounting for 83 percent (by weight) of the DU shot during the war. Since only 5 to 10 percent of the DU rounds shot during strafing runs by aircraft actually hit their target, it is likely that well over 80 percent (by weight) of the total DU rounds shot during the 1991 Gulf War did not hit a hard target and deposited relatively intact in or on the ground.[18] Over time, intact rounds and fragments will corrode, contaminating soil and possibly groundwater.[19]

In the years since the Gulf War, Pentagon spokesmen have repeatedly hyped the importance of armor-piercing DU munitions for the US arsenal, but tellingly, they have never released any estimate of the quantity of Iraqi tanks destroyed by DU rounds.[20] In fact, guided missiles and cluster bombs accounted for the destruction of around 3,200 Iraqi tanks.[21] A review of available evidence suggests DU rounds shot by tanks and aircraft destroyed about 500 Iraqi tanks.[22]

Even though only about one in seven Iraqi tanks was destroyed by DU rounds, troops on the battlefield were never told that some destroyed vehicles might be contaminated. Based on military documents released since the war, it is clear that during combat and as the shooting ended, stateside radioactive waste specialists sent warning messages to the US Central Command in Saudi Arabia; however, for reasons that have never been explained, this information was never shared with the troops on the battlefield. One message warned, "Any system struck by a DU penetrator can be assumed to be contaminated by DU. . . . Personnel should avoid entering contaminated systems. . . . Personnel exposed to DU contamination should wash exposed areas and discard clothing."[23]

People who do not wash exposed areas, discard their clothing, or wear respiratory protection when working on or in contaminated vehicles may ingest, inhale, or suffer wound contamination by DU dust. Normally, about 20 percent of a DU penetrator is aerosolized on impact with a tank,[24] creating about two pounds of extremely fine DU dust for each impact of an Abrams tank, or from a burst of medium-caliber rounds from an A-10 aircraft. About 90 percent of this DU dust falls to the ground within fifty meters of the target.[25] Some DU dust may travel farther downwind, but the risk to downwind populations is considerably less than to people in or near a vehicle when it is hit or who subsequently enter contaminated areas or equipment.[26]

Jerry Wheat developed a bone tumor in his left arm eight years after two DU rounds tore through his Bradley Fighting Vehicle, wounding him in the head, neck, and shoulder. His Bradley was hit by friendly fire from an Abrams tank during a battle between the 3rd Armored Division and an Iraqi armored unit. "After we were treated, I drove the Bradley back to camp," he recalls. "Everything was covered in dust. For the next week I slept in my sleeping bag, which was covered in dust and had been hit by shrapnel. I wore the same clothes for days and was never told about DU. I wasn't told I was exposed to DU until a year after the war, and I wasn't tested until 1993."[27]

Although Army regulations put in place just prior to the Gulf War required soldiers to be medically tested "when radioactive materials are used in such a manner that they could be inhaled, ingested, or absorbed into the body,"[28] no soldiers—not even Jerry Wheat and the more than one hundred other combat troops exposed to DU during friendly-fire incidents—were tested until one year after the war. What makes the failure to test any soldiers even more perplexing is the fact that in 1998 the Pentagon finally admitted "the failure to properly disseminate [DU warnings] to troops at all levels may have resulted in thousands of unnecessary exposures."[29] A cynic might think military officials failed to test troops exposed to DU in order to conceal their massive failure to provide basic safety warnings to frontline troops; a realist might also come to the same conclusion.

At the request of then-Representative Ron Wyden (D-OR), in 1992 the U.S. General Accounting Office undertook an investigation of US vehicles struck by DU rounds in friendly-fire incidents. The final report, aptly titled *Army Not Adequately Prepared to Deal with Depleted Uranium Contamination,* is a case study of gross negligence and bald-faced lies on the part of the Army Surgeon General's Office. In several instances, congressional investigators were the first to inform recovery and maintenance soldiers that they had spent hours or days working on contaminated equipment.[30] The congressional report bluntly criticized the Army for neglecting to inform servicemen and women about the battlefield hazards of DU, and for failing to monitor the health of veterans wounded by or otherwise exposed to DU on the battlefield.[31] The report recommended "the testing of all crew members inside vehicles penetrated by DU munitions," and the Army agreed to begin testing "all crew members" in July 1993.[32]

For reasons that have never been explained, someone within the Army Surgeon General's Office decided that not "all" surviving crew members would in fact be tested. Although a review of records developed in the weeks and months after the war makes clear that at least one hundred soldiers were inside American vehicles hit by DU rounds in friendly-fire incidents,[33] the Surgeon General's Office inexplicably told congressional investigators there were only thirty-five such veterans, twenty-two of whom may have been wounded by DU fragments.[34] Thirty-three out of these thirty-five veterans were enrolled in a study at the Baltimore, Maryland, VA Medical Center, known as the "DU Program."[35] Significantly, a 1993 VA memo noted: "The small size of the [enrolled] population . . . [makes it] highly unlikely that definitive conclusions concerning cancer induction will be obtained from the study."[36]

By 1999, a lymphatic cancer and a bone tumor had been detected among the few dozen veterans in the DU Program, but as noted by the VA in 1993, it is difficult to draw definitive conclusions from these findings because the study size is so small. Since 1993, the DU Program has examined approximately seventy different veterans, although only about thirty-four have participated in the study since 1999. VA doctors have found DU in the semen of several veterans and high levels of DU in the urine of veterans who retain DU fragments.[37] In 1999, study participant Jerry Wheat was diagnosed with a bone tumor; a second friendly-fire veteran newly added to the study had Hodgkin's lymphoma.[38] The cancer and bone tumor appear to be very significant, given that military studies have shown that DU causes cancer and tumors in rats,[39] and the Institute of Medicine has identified lymphatic cancer (along with lung cancer and bone cancer) as a possible health effect of DU exposure.[40] At about the same time VA doctors identified the cancer and bone tumor, U.S. A-10 aircraft were shooting DU rounds in Serbia, Kosovo, and Montenegro, and two years later these two events would collide on the stage of international politics.

It's hard to believe that a medical doctor who retired from the Navy with the rank of Captain would lie about the health of veterans, but that's just what Dr. Michael Kilpatrick did. In January 2001, Dr. Kilpatrick was director of the Pentagon's office for Gulf War illnesses when he traveled to Europe with several military doctors and scientists to quell an outbreak of European concern about the effects of the use of DU munitions in the Balkans.

In 1994–95, U.S. A-10 aircraft shot approximately 10,800 DU rounds in Bosnia,[41] releasing 3,260 kg of depleted uranium into the environment in and around Sarajevo.[42] In 1999, A-10s shot approximately 31,300 DU rounds,[43] containing 9,450 kg of DU, in over one hundred locations in Kosovo, Serbia, and Montenegro.[44] During both conflicts, DU ammunition was shot against a variety of targets, including armored vehicles, antiaircraft artillery, and barracks,[45] but as with the Gulf War, the Pentagon has never publicly released any estimate of what, if any, military equipment was destroyed by DU rounds. Extensive studies of soldiers and limited studies of local civilian populations have not found evidence of health problems related to DU,[46] although recent studies have found DU in air, soil, water, plants, and buildings.[47] Nonetheless, the development of leukemia and cancers among some European soldiers who served in the Balkans led in early 2001 to an international political debate about DU munitions.

Dr. Kilpatrick lied explicitly and precisely about the existence of cancer in U.S. veterans in order to downplay concerns about cancer in European veterans. In October 1999, Dr. Kilpatrick took part in a meeting with officials from an advisory committee to President Clinton, the Pentagon, and the VA where the case of a DU-exposed veteran with lymphoma was discussed,[48] but in January 2001 Dr. Kilpatrick told the ambassadors of the North Atlantic Council and the NATO press corps, "We have seen no cancers or leukemia in this group [participants in the DU Program], which has been followed since 1993."[49] A few months later, Army Colonel Frank O'Donnell echoed Kilpatrick's lie, convincingly telling dozens of scientists from NATO countries that no veterans in the DU Program had developed cancer.[50] More recently, another Army doctor has claimed that no veterans in the DU study have developed tumors.[51]

The truth about the health of veterans exposed to DU has been sacrificed on the altar of political expediency. Jerry Wheat comments, "These guys are not only lying about my tumor and the guy with lymphoma, but a bunch of the other vets [in the study] including me are having respiratory problems and other ailments that the VA and DoD always say are not related to DU. I'm not at all happy with the DU Program; the only reason I showed up last time was to see the guys I served with in the war."

During the buildup to the war in Iraq in 2003, Kilpatrick again emerged as the Pentagon's point man on DU, and again he twisted the truth in a misguided attempt to downplay public interest in DU munitions. A week before U.S. troops rolled into Iraq, Kilpatrick denied the existence of bone and lung cancer among veterans in the DU Program, but he inexplicably failed to mention the existence of Hodgkin's lymphoma and a bone tumor among the few veterans in the study—a notable omission not easily overlooked in the context of the controversy over DU. Kilpatrick also claimed the DU Program has examined ninety veterans on an annual basis since 1991 (VA says seventy have been examined, and an average of thirty-four have been examined on a biannual basis since 1993), and wrongly stated that "studies in the United States over fifteen years have not shown depleted uranium going from soil into groundwater."[52] (DU dumped in the ground next to a Concord, Massachusetts, manufacturing plant has resulted in severe contamination of an underground aquifer.[53])

Dr. Kilpatrick won't have the chance to lie about the health of Nolen Hutchings. Nolen was killed on March 23, 2003, near Nasiriyah, Iraq, when an A-10 aircraft strafed the armored assault vehicle he was riding in, killing him and wounding several of his fellow Marines from the 2nd Marine Expeditionary Brigade.[54] Nolen was one of four coalition soldiers killed by DU rounds in friendly-fire incidents; the other three were British troops.[55] Hundreds or perhaps thousands of others were likely wounded or otherwise exposed to DU during friendly-fire incidents, destruction of U.S. vehicles carrying DU rounds, or contact with contaminated equipment.[56] In February 2004, the UK Ministry of Defence acknowledged that "fewer than ten" veterans involved in friendly-fire incidents had tested positive for DU,[57] but as of May 2004, the DoD has not publicly released any figures about exposures among US troops.

Based on preliminary reports, it appears that U.S. and British forces shot approximately 118 to 136 metric tons of DU during combat in Iraq, or less than half the amount shot in 1991. As with previous conflicts, the A-10 aircraft appears to have shot more DU than all other weapons systems combined, but only about a third as much as in 1991.[58] In contrast to 1991, however, US forces shot DU in or near Iraqi towns and cities, including Baghdad, which could have deposited DU dust and debris where people live, work, play, draw water, and grow food.

Servicemen and women now on occupation duty in Iraq may be exposed to DU because there has been no comprehensive effort to identify locations where DU munitions were used. As of February 2004, the British military had identified eight Iraqi tanks in their sector of control (around Basra) shot by DU rounds,[59] and disclosed to the United Nations Environment Programme that its tanks shot about 200 DU rounds,[60] but the U.S. military has failed to publicly release information about the locations where its tank and aircraft shot hundreds of thousands of DU rounds. Until areas of DU expenditure are identified and cordoned off, the potential for soldiers to be exposed to DU persists, despite the fact that they now receive minimal training about the hazards of DU munitions. Civilian populations, relief and development workers, oil-industry employees, and other people who live in or frequent contaminated areas are also at risk of exposure to DU dust and debris.

Brett Page was security manager for a large relief organization about to go into Iraq when he searched for information on depleted uranium. A ten-year veteran of the Australian Army who had done relief work in Rwanda and the Democratic Republic of the Congo, Brett encountered difficulty obtaining information about DU through official channels. "No one I know of had any idea about DU prior to entering Iraq," he told the author. "I asked questions but no one could/would tell me where DU munitions were used. I fully briefed my staff to stay away from UXO [unexploded ordnance] and hard targets, which would have kept them away from the immediate threat. It's very disorganized here now [October 2003] and people are sensitive to many issues. DU just isn't high on the agenda here with everything else that's going on."

In the context of ongoing violence and insecurity in Iraq, DU seems like an insignificant threat. But based on past experience, it would be shortsighted for political and military leaders to ignore DU contamination and DU exposures. Indeed, the US government's reluctance to provide information about the use of DU munitions in Iraq, the Balkans, and possibly Afghanistan has helped fuel speculation about widespread and severe health effects caused by DU in those places; these claimed effects have further been cited by political groups to support opposition to the United States.[61] There are many people in the United States, Europe, and Southwest Asia who believe the U.S. military uses DU ammunition to intentionally cause cancer and birth defects among civilian populations in Iraq, the Balkans, and Afghanistan.

Pentagon spokesmen have summarily dismissed concerns about the health effects of DU among civilian populations.[62] Dr. Kilpatrick and other Pentagon spokesmen have dodged questions about the effects of DU on children, but in May 2003 a U.S. Army doctor in Baghdad stated that children playing with expended tank shells would have to eat and then practically suffocate on the DU dust before any health problems occurred.[63] The suggestion that children could eat DU without harm flies in the face of mainstream scientific opinion, and the British Royal Society and World Health Organization have both called attention to the possible adverse effects of DU on children.[64] A 2003 article in the *Journal of Environmental Radioactivity* stated, "children playing with soil may be identified as the critical population group [for DU exposure], with inhalation and/or ingestion of contaminated soil as the critical pathway."[65] Mothers and unborn children may also be at risk: U.S. military studies show that DU penetrates the placenta of pregnant rats and accumulates in the fetus, although at very low levels.[66]

Public pressure and improved weapons technology could lead the US and UK militaries to significantly reduce or phase out the use of DU ammunition within a decade,[67] but the proliferation of DU munitions makes it likely they will be used in conflicts around the world for the foreseeable future. The United States has sold DU rounds to Saudi Arabia, Kuwait, Egypt, Bahrain, Taiwan, and Turkey.[68] The United Kingdom has sold them to Oman; France has sold DU munitions to the United Arab Emirates.[69] Russia has been selling DU rounds since 1993,[70] and Pakistan started selling them in 2001,[71] but it is not clear to whom. U.S. troops found some DU ammunition in Afghanistan,[72] and Iraq was developing DU rounds prior to the 2003 war.[73] Other countries possessing DU include China, Israel, Thailand, and Ukraine; India is believed to have a development project under way.

It is easy to single out the Pentagon for criticism about the use of DU munitions, but if DU munitions haven't already been used in other conflicts, they probably will be soon, and eventually U.S. troops will face an enemy shooting at them with the very weapons originally developed in Indiana, Maryland, Massachusetts, New Jersey, and several other states.

Veterans exposed to DU on future battlefields also may have to endure stonewalling from the Pentagon and neglect from the VA upon their return home. Indeed, since 1991, the DoD has consistently presented false and misleading information about the extent of veterans' battlefield exposures and the health status of veterans in the VA's study. Either through incompetence, ignorance, or by design, the VA has facilitated these lies and acted more like the Pentagon's lapdog than the government agency whose mission is "To care for him who shall have borne the battle, and for his widow, and his orphan." The problems with past and current policies could be resolved through better congressional oversight and corrective action, but progress will likely be blunted by the Pentagon's power and desire to prevent a comprehensive assessment of the use and effects of DU munitions.

A handful of congressmen have forced the DoD and VA to address veterans' exposure to DU on the battlefield. In 1992, then-Representative (now Senator) Ron Wyden (D-OR) requested the General Accounting Office investigation that first described how Army negligence and incompetence might have resulted in "thousands of unnecessary exposures" among U.S. troops. The same year, Senator Donald Riegle (D-MI) helped to initiate a study of DU's health and environmental consequences by the U.S. Army Environmental Policy Institute (AEPI).[74] The final AEPI report, released in 1995, predictably downplayed the adverse effects of using DU munitions, but the report did articulate the financial considerations that influence Army and DoD decision making in this confused, but somehow quite clear paragraph in the introduction:

> The potential for health effects from exposure to DU is real; however, it must be viewed in perspective. It is unlikely that any of the DU exposure scenarios described in this report will significantly affect the health of most personnel. In several areas, neither the scientific community nor the Army have adequate medical or exposure information to defend this assertion. It would be fiscally prudent to develop a more comprehensive understanding of exposure potential and the concomitant medical implications. When DU is indicted as a causative agent for Desert Storm illness, the Army must have sufficient data to separate

> fiction from reality. Without forethought and data, the financial implications of long-term disability payments and health-care costs would be excessive.[75]

This and several other Army and DoD reports demonstrate the flaws of a process that allows the military to study itself.

Although the DoD began development of DU munitions in the late 1950s, it did not undertake any laboratory research on the health effects of DU until 1994. That was the year Representative Lane Evans (D-IL) inserted language into the DoD's budget requiring it to spend $1.7 million on research into "the possible health effects of battlefield exposure to depleted uranium, including exposure through ingestion, inhalation, or bodily injury."[76] The first studies were conducted by the Armed Forces Radiobiology Research Institute, which identified several possible health effects of DU, including cancer, central nervous system diseases, immune system disorders, damage to reproductive organs, and birth defects. Since 1994, the federal government has spent nearly $7 million on animal and cellular studies of DU, with current studies examining the transport of DU across the blood-brain barrier, and the potential for embedded DU fragments to cause cancer and changes in the immune system.[77]

As interest in Gulf War veterans' illnesses increased during the mid-1990s, various House and Senate committees held dozens of public hearings to listen to veterans' concerns and scrutinize DoD and VA officials, but hearing after hearing conspicuously ignored DU. While the reasons for this "oversight" may vary, the lack of public scrutiny is largely due to the fact that the Pentagon used its considerable political influence to convince key congressional committees—controlled by Republicans since 1994—to keep scrutiny of DU out of the hearing rooms. Only independent-minded Representative Christopher Shays (R-CT), chair of the Subcommittee on National Security of the House Government Reform and Oversight committee, examined DU as part of a June 26, 1997, hearing. DU has not been included in any of the dozens of hearings on Gulf War veterans' health held since that day.

The use of DU munitions during the 2003 U.S.-led invasion of Iraq prompted new congressional initiatives. In March 2003, Representative Jim

McDermott (D-WA) introduced the Depleted Uranium Munitions Study Act of 2003, which would require additional studies of the health effects of DU exposure, as well as cleanup of all DU manufacturing and testing sites in the United States.[78] This bill had attracted only thirty co-sponsors by the end of February 2004, and it is dying a slow death in committee, for two reasons. First, the Department of Defense resists the bill's call for expanded health studies and extensive environmental cleanup. Second, Congressman McDermott erred by promoting the unscientific and alarmist claims of extremists in the anti-DU movement, thereby ensuring the bill will remain nothing more than a symbolic gesture, and a wasted opportunity.

Representative Bob Filner (D-CA) and Senator Russell Feingold (D-WI)—the two congressmen who have done the most to help veterans exposed to DU—both initiated new investigations in 2003. Representative Filner initiated a General Accounting Office investigation of the problems with the VA's DU Program, as well as a review of DoD and VA policies to identify and provide medical care for veterans exposed to DU during Operation Iraqi Freedom.[79] This investigation, co-sponsored by Representative Ciro Rodriguez (D-TX), should be completed in late 2004.

In December 2003, Senator Feingold asked the Senate Committee on Veterans Affairs to launch an investigation and hold public hearings to examine the inadequacies of the VA's DU Program and the treatment of U.S. troops exposed to DU during Operation Iraqi Freedom.[80] In 1999, Senator Feingold had joined Representatives Lane Evans and Bob Filner in requesting a GAO investigation that determined US troops deployed to Kosovo were inadequately informed about the battlefield hazards of DU.[81] The 1999 report resulted in better training for servicemen and women about DU, but it remains to be seen what policy initiatives—if any—come out of the Veterans Affairs committee.

The fact that more congressmen have not stepped forward to help veterans exposed to DU can be attributed to several factors. First and foremost, the DoD has used its inordinate political power to limit congressional investigations of DU. The DoD has fended off repeated calls from congressional Democrats for hearings about the flawed military policies and practices that have resulted in hundreds—if not thousands—of veterans being unnecessarily exposed to DU. Congressional Republicans are generally more deferential to the Pentagon's wishes than Democrats, and since Republicans took control of Congress in 1994, the committees responsible for the health of veterans and current servicemembers have notably failed to exercise their oversight powers or hold military officials accountable for their mistakes related to DU. Protecting the health and welfare of veterans should not be a partisan issue, but on DU, Democrats have launched investigations and funded research, while Republicans—with the notable exception of Rep. Shays—have stonewalled investigations and thwarted hearings.

The nation's two largest veterans' organizations have sadly also limited progress. The Veterans of Foreign Wars and the American Legion have both passed resolutions supporting research on the health of veterans exposed to DU, but because both organizations rather unquestioningly support DoD policies, neither has been willing to make any substantive effort to get the VA to conduct a better study of veterans, and neither has pressured Congress to investigate DU.

The credibility of the DU issue has also been harmed in recent years by a small but vocal wing of the anti-DU movement. With the support of a handful of controversial scientists, these activists have made unsupported and exaggerated claims about DU's effects, and they have often embraced propaganda about DU spread by Saddam Hussein, Yasser Arafat, and others who use the DU issue as a political tool to criticize the United States and Israel. These activists' claims are easily disproved by the Pentagon's own propaganda, which carries considerably more clout with the major veterans' organizations and Republicans in Congress. Although a moderate and science-minded International Coalition to Ban Uranium Weapons was formed in late 2003 to seek a political solution to the DU issue,[82] the extremists continue to gain the most attention in the United States and abroad.

The end result of congressional inaction, VA indifference, DoD negligence, and activist ineffectiveness is that veterans who may develop lymphomas, bone tumors, or other conditions possibly related to their DU exposure will not be able to access VA health care or benefits. The VA does not recognize any cancers or other conditions as related to DU exposure, but there is some hope that Congress will act to require the VA to extend service-connected benefits for DU-related conditions to veterans who were involved in friendly-fire incidents or otherwise heavily exposed to DU. Interestingly, in February 2004, an appeals court in Edinburgh, Scotland, awarded a Scottish veteran of the 1991 Gulf War disability benefits for "breathlessness and aching joints" due to DU exposure.[83] This is believed to be the first such award of its kind among US or British veterans of the 1991 war.

There is no end in sight to the debate over DU munitions, but research on DU's health effects continues in the United States, thanks largely to the work of veterans. The willingness of Jerry Wheat, Michael Stacy, and dozens of other veterans to speak out about inadequate DU training, "unnecessary" DU exposures, as well as their health problems that might be caused by DU, has prompted congressional representatives to force a largely reluctant DoD and VA to research DU's effects. While the Veterans of Foreign Wars and American Legion have stood idly by, the National Gulf War Resource Center (formed in 1995) has become the leading advocate for Gulf War veterans, and a consistent leader in the effort to expand the VA's study of veterans and fund new DU research.

Chris Kornkven was a co-founder of the National Gulf War Resource Center who spearheaded efforts during the late 1990s to help veterans exposed to DU. Between March and May 1991, he estimates he closely examined more than thirty destroyed Iraqi tanks while serving with the 304th Combat Support Company. "I didn't find out about DU until 1993 when I read an article in a newspaper," he states. "I was shocked that something this hazardous would be used, and no warning whatsoever had been given. The military command certainly should be ashamed of itself for fielding a weapon such as this without providing training and proper medical care for exposed troops. After the war in Iraq, we might have lots of exposed troops and the only thing we can be sure of is that the Pentagon and VA will lie about how many veterans might have been exposed and the role of DU in any health problems veterans might develop. And then there are the civilians . . . we need more research and we need to give health care to veterans whose health has been affected by DU, but we also need accountability at the Pentagon and VA for the negligence that resulted in unnecessary exposures and health effects."[84]

Accountability at the Pentagon and VA is hard to come by. During the last fifty years, veterans have fought both the Pentagon and the VA to obtain health care and benefits for health problems resulting from exposure to atomic testing, Agent Orange, LSD, experimental vaccines, fallout from destroyed chemical weapons depots, and a long list of other toxins. The DoD and VA tolerate, and even appear to reward, negligence and incompetence that would end careers and result in massive health and safety lawsuits in the civilian world.

In a very real sense, the solution to the controversy over DU lies in holding military officials to account for their recklessness in allowing "thousands of unnecessary exposures" to soldiers and civilians, and for their habitual lying about the extent of these exposures and the health of veterans in the VA's study. The VA prefers not to ask questions about DU, but ignorance is no defense for a woefully inadequate study of veterans that ignores lies told by Pentagon doctors about veterans' health. Nonetheless, emerging scientific opinion indicates DU may potentially cause a range of serious health problems, particularly among combat veterans. So the ultimate resolution of the DU debate may come about when government policies are influenced more by science and common sense than by politics and economics.

Part 2: Gulf War Illnesses

Charles Sheehan-Miles

Parades of smiling, happy returning soldiers. Yellow ribbons. A swift victory, with almost no casualties, followed by a warm welcome home that was a wonderful contrast to the reception received by Vietnam veterans a generation before.

These were the impressions of the public in the wake of the 1991 Gulf War. Nice impressions, happy impressions, and almost all wrong.

The Gulf War began while I was in basic training at Fort Knox, Kentucky. On a clear and beautiful August morning I was standing guard duty at the motor pool with another soldier I'd befriended, coincidentally a native of Syria, raised in Pittsburgh. He arrived with interesting news—overnight, Iraq had invaded Kuwait and toppled the emirate's government. Recognizing that the United States had taken no action when Iraq had killed thirty-seven American sailors when it struck the USS *Stark,* and we'd prevented action by the UN in the early 1980s when Iraq used chemical weapons on its neighbors and its own people, my reaction was a shrug. There would be no US response.

Clearly I was wrong, and the next days would show on a very personal level just how wrong I was. By the end of the week, my entire basic training class had been reassigned to First Brigade of the 24th Infantry Division at Fort Stewart, Georgia, which was already mobilizing for war. On August 10, on my father's (a Vietnam veteran) birthday, he watched me board a C-130 bound for Fort Stewart instead of taking me on my first leave from the military. It was sobering and frightening, but, for a nineteen-year-old soldier who had just joined the military, also exhilarating.

In the end, a huge force assembled in Saudi Arabia—several air and ground divisions from the United States, plus Seventh Corps (five divisions), which deployed from Germany, no longer needed there after the collapse of the Cold

War. Seven hundred ninety-five thousand U.S. servicemen and women would be deployed to the Kuwait theater of operations by the time the cease-fire was called in April 1991.

Actual combat operations were conducted against Iraq beginning on January 17, 1991, with a six-week aerial bombardment, followed by a brief and incredibly violent ground invasion of Kuwait and Iraq. By the end of February 1991, most of the Iraqi military had been destroyed, and large portions of Iraq and all of Kuwait were in the hands of the US military.

My part in that war was a small one—a tank crewman in an armored task force, we entered Iraq on February 24, 1991, and left three weeks later. By Saint Patrick's Day I was home, feeling a hundred years older. I'd killed in the war, and it had changed me in ways I couldn't fathom. It would be years before I dealt with that, and in some ways it will always continue to be with me.

For America, the Gulf War seemed to be over by March of 1991. In a spring and early summer of parades and self-congratulatory pats on the back, the president declared the "Vietnam Syndrome" dead.

For the soldiers it wasn't so easy. For one thing, thousands (including myself) were traumatized by the incredible violence of the ground war. Two hundred ninety-three of my fellow service members, twelve in my division, died in the war,[1] and for their families, the war would never end. Nor for the POWs, the thousands of injured, and especially for those who came home ill and tried to get help from a government that inexplicably turned its back on them.

By late 1992, however, it was clear something else was happening. Thousands of returning soldiers had reported strange illnesses to VA or military hospitals—low-grade fever, joint pain, memory loss, and worse. Theories began to float around in the media (remember, this was before the public advent of the Internet) that a "mystery illness" was plaguing Gulf War veterans, and pundits on the left and right jumped into the debate, despite the absence of any evidence, to declare the soldiers malingerers. By the end of 1993, Mona Charen and Michael Fumento, both conservative columnists with ties to the chemical industry, were making money denying that Gulf War veterans were really ill, and shortly they had the backing of the military brass in their position.

The media furor resulted in kneejerk government reactions. The Pentagon tasked the Defense Science Board, chaired by Nobel laureate Joshua Lederberg, with the job of investigating the illnesses. The board, denied access to information about the war, conducted its investigation with a remarkable lack of data and concluded there were no problems. As it turned out, Dr. Lederberg had been a director of the Maryland-based American Type Culture Collection, an organization now the subject of a class-action lawsuit brought by Gulf War veterans against companies that sold the ingredienets of chemical and biological weapons to Iraq, while Lederberg served on its board.[2] Lederberg's ATCC had shipped massive quantities of deadly bacteria, including anthrax, botulinum toxin, and more exotic varieties to, of all places, the Iraqi Atomic Energy Agency, with the full cooperation of the Departments of Commerce and Defense.

Clearly Lederberg should have disclosed the conflict of interest, which was later uncovered by the media. In any event, by 1996 he disavowed the findings of his own panel, blaming the Pentagon for withholding critical information regarding chemical weapons that were destroyed by coalition troops, raining toxic fallout on over a hundred thousand soldiers. Lederberg called for the investigation to be reopened.[3]

Additional "blue-ribbon" panels were created at National Institutes of Health to investigate the illnesses, and all seemed to come to the same conclusion: they could not find any single cause for illnesses among Gulf War veterans. In fact, they couldn't even agree on a case definition. Veterans continued to have problems getting help when visiting VA hospitals, in some cases simply being turned away, and in others being shunted off to psychiatrists with a diagnosis of post-traumatic stress or somataform disorder.

It was very clear by the beginning of 1994 that if Gulf War veterans were going to get any effective help, they were going to have to fight for it. Independently, across the country, grassroots efforts were shaping up as veterans and family members sought assistance and information from each other. In

Oklahoma, the Desert Storm Justice Foundation began recruiting members, and in Texas the Operations Desert Shield/Storm Association changed its focus from supporting the troops to tracking down what went wrong when they came home. Other organizations formed in California, Arkansas, and Colorado.

The Gulf War Veterans of Georgia, headed by 3rd Armored Division veteran Paul Sullivan, got off the ground in late 1993 and began focusing its efforts on Freedom of Information Act requests to the Pentagon, seeking information on chemical exposures in Iraq. Soon, they released a bombshell—despite adamant Pentagon denials that any soldier had been injured by chemical weapons, the group uncovered a Purple Heart awarded to a Private First Class Fisher who had been injured by mustard gas. While one soldier did not explain all of the illnesses, it put the lie to consistent denials from the Pentagon that Iraq had any chemical weapons in the theater of operations.

In Washington, Senator Donald Riegle's Banking Committee had begun its own investigation. It was an odd venue for an investigation into Gulf War veterans' illnesses, especially in light of the fact that the Armed Services and Veterans' Affairs Committees had been silent. The Banking Committee, however, had a key area which gave them jurisdiction: U.S. exports of chemical and biological weapons components. During a hearing in front of the committee, Undersecretary of Defense Edwin Dorn incredibly testified that Iraq's chemical weapons were all deployed "at locations a great distance from the Kuwait Theatre of Operations."[4] This despite the fact that Riegle had uncovered multiple instances of chemical detections, thousands of alarms sounding after the beginning of the air war in January 1991, and incidents at al-Jubayl and King Khalid Military City, which strongly indicated that chemicals were detected. The Pentagon's answer: every single one of the thousands of chemical alarms was a false alarm.

Veterans continued to organize. In Atlanta and later in Boston, I started an Internet mailing list (the GWVM) of Gulf War veterans to distribute news and trade ideas. Jackie Olsen, of Long Island, New York, whose two sons had served in the Gulf, did the same. Soon, the various mailing lists had linked up with the thousands of local dial-up bulletin board services and networks.

Grassroots groups around the country linked up via these lists and through the Gulf War Veterans Resource Pages, one of the first nonprofit Web sites, started by then–VA social worker Grant Szabo in the spring of 1994.

The administration responded to the organizing efforts of the veterans by announcing the formation of a Presidential Advisory Committee on Gulf War Veterans Illnesses, composed of various health experts, which was to review the situation and advise the president.

Ultimately, the Presidential Advisory Committee criticized the Pentagon severely for its handling of the investigation, but its findings were inconclusive: first, that veterans were, in fact, sick; second, that nothing in particular seemed to have made them that way; and third, that stress needed to be explored more as a causative agent. Interestingly, nearly half of the panelists called for the conclusions on chemical weapons to be reversed, and one member, Rolando Rios, a lawyer and Vietnam veteran, asked that his name be removed from the final report if the conclusions were not changed.[5]

The question remains: what went wrong? What were Gulf War veterans exposed to that made them sick, and why did they have so much trouble getting help from their own government? Amid repeated Pentagon statements that they couldn't find "any single cause" for Gulf War illnesses, what was the public, and more importantly, Congress, to believe?

The more appropriate question is, what *weren't* Gulf War veterans exposed to? The battlefield was a toxic mix of pesticides, experimental medications, fallout from chemical weapons facilities and a variety of other problems, not to mention endemic diseases. A brief review shows that in some form or another, all of these issues contributed to the problem. The Pentagon statement that they couldn't find any "single" cause of Gulf War veterans' illnesses was technically correct—as long as they continued to search for a single factor, they would fail.

One of the first suggested causes for problems among Gulf War veterans was an endemic parasitic infection caused by the bite of the sand flea: leishmaniasis. Prompted by the fact that the disease has a long latency period and can't be detected easily, the American Red Cross barred donations of blood by Gulf War veterans early in 1991. With symptoms including rashes, memory loss, and low-grade fever, this seemed a likely candidate for contributing to Gulf War illnesses. Complicated by the fact that few American doctors have seen the illness, identification of leishmaniasis as an infection was problematic, and, when left untreated, it is often fatal.[6] Yet studies conducted by the Department of Veterans Affairs found few cases (a total of twelve viscerotropic and nineteen cutaneous cases),[7] and in the end this was ruled out as a cause of widespread illness among veterans. Early reports indicate this may be a much wider problem among veterans of the current Iraq War, many of whom have spent extended periods in urban areas in Iraq.[8]

In addition to leishmaniasis, a number of endemic diseases exist in the region, including brucellosis, Q fever, sandfly fever, West Nile virus, Crimean-Congo hemorrhagic fever and dengue; but in all these cases, virtually no instances of infection were found among Gulf War veterans.[9] All of this leaves us with the question: what did make the veterans sick? Or, as Mr. Fumento suggests, were tens of thousands of veterans engaged in a vast conspiracy to create an imaginary illness and bilk the government out of hard-earned taxpayer dollars? The hard scientific answers to these questions would be years in the making.

Another key area of questions arose around the use of experimental drugs in the Gulf War. Historically, the military has inoculated soldiers for a variety of diseases before overseas deployments as a necessary precaution. In the Spanish-American War, the United States suffered thousands more casualties due to disease that due to enemy fire, a tragedy that the military remembered well in later conflicts.[10] Before leaving Fort Stewart in August of 1990, we lined up to receive dozens of shots, for a variety of common and not-so-common diseases we might be exposed to in Saudi Arabia and Iraq.

In December of 1990, a few weeks before the beginning of combat operations, the Food and Drug Administration issued a waiver to the Department of Defense authorizing the administration of certain experimental drugs to soldiers without their informed consent. As a practical matter, this was clearly a move intended to provide the best possible protection to the troops. A legal challenge to this proposed use of an unapproved drug failed, and the Pentagon went ahead with its plan.

Unfortunately, it failed to keep the most basic records of whom the vaccines were administered to, one of the key requirements of the FDA waiver. The consequence of this failure was all too clear, and was underlined by the Presidential Advisory Committee; because the Pentagon did not record the exposure data, there is simply no way to scientifically determine whether the vaccines had an impact.

Three drugs were used under this waiver: pyridostigmine bromide, botulinum toxoid vaccine, and anthrax vaccine. Pyridostigmine bromide (PB) was given as a nerve-agent pretreatment drug, issued in small blister packets to as many as 250,000 troops. Normally approved only for the treatment of a severe neurological disorder, myasthenia gravis, limited animal studies indicated the drug might reduce the impact of exposure to soman, a key nerve agent known to be in Iraq's arsenal. Unfortunately, it turns out that it may actually heighten the effects of sarin, another deadly agent in the prewar Iraqi arsenal. Further, the drug had only been tested in very limited human experiments—experiments that excluded all women, smokers, and individuals with heart problems, and even in those trials significant side effects were found. The health impact on healthy or pregnant women is unknown. Unfortunately, even in light of clear evidence that the drug may have played a role in the illnesses of veterans, in February of 2003 the FDA again authorized the issuance of this drug to soldiers deploying to fight in the Iraq war. At this time it is unknown whether any ill effects have been registered.

Approximately 8,000 U.S. troops received the botulinum toxoid vaccine. Once again, the Department of Defense failed to keep any records of who received the vaccine. No research has been done to date to determine what effects this may have had.

The anthrax vaccine was administered to roughly 150,000 troops during 1990 and 1991, and once again, the Pentagon failed to keep any records of whom the vaccine was given to. While many veterans believe the vaccine may have played a role in their illnesses, to date no studies have been completed to prove or disprove this theory. One key issue with the anthrax vaccine is that it is only tested and approved for cutaneous anthrax—skin exposure. Whether or not it is useful at all for inhalation exposure is unknown.

The vaccine itself came from a Michigan Department of Health plant, which was later privatized and sold to BioPort, a company that has since been mired in controversy as the sole producer of the vaccine. Despite the Pentagon production contract and a healthy infusion of cash, the company was never, throughout the 1990s, able to meet FDA quality and safety requirements. Despite the questions surrounding the vaccine and its manufacturer, in 1997 the Clinton administration announced it would begin a mandatory anthrax vaccination program for all 2.4 million active-duty, reserve, and national guard troops.

Another key question about the Gulf War was the devastation brought about by the demolition of more than 700 Kuwaiti oil wells during the ground war. For weeks during and immediately after the war, tens of thousands of troops camped in sight of the wells and struggled to live in an environment where noon was turned to midnight. Oil and soot permeated the troops' clothing, food, and water, and the atmosphere. Yet, the first Defense Department team seeking to measure exposure levels arrived in the country in May 1991, after virtually all of the ground forces who fought during Desert Storm had returned home and many of the fires had been extinguished. Only then did they begin to take atmospheric samples, from May until December 1991. From those measurements, the Pentagon established an "average" exposure and determined that this average was below the safe limits of exposure.

Virtually no research has been conducted in this area, nor has the large body of published data on exposure to oil-fire smoke been correlated with Gulf War veterans and their illnesses. This lack of genuine investigation is clearly frustrating to Gulf War veterans and demonstrates just how seriously the Clinton administration took this issue.

One of the early hypotheses put forward by veterans was exposure to Iraq's vast chemical weapons arsenal. Let us not forget, for months preceding the beginning of active combat with Iraq, we trained with protective gear for chemical weapons, and heard over and over that Iraq not only had them but had repeatedly used them both against the Iranians and their own people. It was fully expected that Iraq would use chemicals in any engagement with American troops.

Thus, it didn't come as any surprise when, less than twenty-four hours after the US bombardment of Iraq began on January 17, 1991, the M8 chemical weapons alarm just upwind of my own unit's assembly area went off with its characteristic siren, and we all scrambled to get in our chemical suits and seal up our tanks. However when we tested for chemicals the results came back negative.

What I didn't know at the time was that alarms were ringing all across Saudi Arabia, tens of thousands of them, all beginning just after the air war started. Interestingly, the Pentagon testified in front of Congress in 1993 and 1994 that *every single one of those alarms was false.*

As if that weren't enough, Undersecretary of Defense Edwin Dorn testified that not only were all the alarms false, but Iraq hadn't even deployed chemical weapons anywhere in the combat theater—despite prewar intelligence indicating they would, despite chemical alarms that went off. He made this claim despite the United Nations' finding thousands of chemical warheads in southern Iraq, and despite the revelation three more years later that U.S. troops destroyed massive chemical weapons dumps after the cease-fire.

Especially in light of the hysteria surrounding Iraqi chemical weapons a decade later, preceding the second Iraq War, these claims are nothing short of astounding. The Pentagon stuck with this line, however, until the public release of key documents flat out put the lie to their statements.

In March 1995, on CBS TV's *60 Minutes* ran a story devastating the Pentagon line. First, in an interview with Deputy Secretary of Defense John Deutch (later director of Central Intelligence), Ed Bradley confronted Deutch with the NBC (Nuclear Chemical and Biological) Officer's Desk Log from Central Command, which clearly indicated a series of detections of chemical weapons across the theater of operations, which had been serious enough to report all the way up to General H. Norman Schwarzkopf's Central Command headquarters. The logs, of course, were incomplete, and according to a response to a Freedom of Information Act request submitted by the National Gulf War Resource Center in 1995, most of the records were destroyed following the war. However, the evidence available was damning. Finally, the news piece made one of the first public mentions of a word that would soon become familiar to hundreds of thousands of Gulf War veterans: *Khamisiyah*.

On March 14, 1991, at a weapons depot in Khamisiyah in southern Iraq, soldiers of the 82nd Airborne division detonated several thousand tons of munitions containing sarin, cyclosarin, and mustard gas. Sarin is one of the deadliest substances on earth, and a drop the size of the head of a pin is enough to kill. Eventually, following the disclosure of the event, the Pentagon admitted reluctantly that as many as a few hundred veterans may have been exposed to low levels of these chemical agents following the detonation. Computer modeling later forced a dramatic revision upward, first to twenty thousand, then to over one hundred thousand. Finally, in 1997, the Pentagon sent letters to over one hundred thousand Gulf War veterans detailing the incident, explaining that they may have been exposed to low levels of exposures from these weapons, and helpfully letting them know that the levels were too low to do any harm.

Of course, the statement that the chemicals couldn't harm them was completely devoid of any scientific basis. It wasn't until 2001, ten years after the first war, that the Pentagon provided the social security numbers of those veterans to the Department of Veterans Affairs. The VA's Data Management Office compared that list with its list of Gulf War veterans drawing disability, and made a startling discovery: veterans downwind of the Khamisiyah plume were 37 percent more likely to be disabled in 2001 than veterans who were not downwind.

In 1997 a team of researchers from the University of Texas Southwestern Medical Center began publishing a series of articles reporting on their studies of ill Gulf War veterans, with results dramatically different than those of the Pentagon. The UT Southwestern team, led by Dr. Robert Haley, identified three primary syndromes, each with a different cluster of symptoms. Importantly, for the first time, a clear, scientific method had determined clear physical damage to the affected veterans. Further, the affected group (as opposed to the controls in the study) showed a clear pattern of exposures, primarily to a combination of low-level chemical agents, pyridostigmine bromide tablets, and chemical insect repellents. This confirmed the findings of earlier research showing that this combination of toxins caused brain injury in lab animals.[11]

Today, a number of key findings are available. First, veterans who were downwind from the Khamisiyah plume, or stationed at al-Jubayl, Saudi Arabia, during the Gulf War, are statistically more likely to be disabled than their counterparts—as much as 37 percent more likely. The Department of Veterans Affairs study, including a survey followed by detailed review of medical records, show that the children of male Gulf War veterans are more than twice as likely to have birth defects as their undeployed counterparts. Finally, VA epidemiologists have reported that the incidence of amyotrophic lateral sclerosis, better known as Lou Gehrig's disease, is about twice as high among Gulf War veterans as the general population. In short, after more than a decade of denials by the Pentagon, and a decade of cries of "malingerer" from conservative columnists, the science has borne out exactly what we were saying in the early 1990s—Gulf War veterans came home sick.

The question today is, what do we do with this knowledge? Of course, it is critical to find appropriate treatment and compensation options for those who served in 1991, but another issue arises from the ongoing Iraq war. While we know that the exposures will be different this time around, there is already substantial evidence that problems are arising among the next generation of veterans. To begin with, despite criticism from every scientific body to review this issue, and the requirements of a 1998 law on force health protection, the Pentagon failed once again to conduct predeployment physicals of troops as they were leaving for Iraq.[12] In other words, if unexplained illnesses arise out of the second Iraq war, today's troops will suffer the same bumbling investigations that we did in the 1990s. If you don't have the data, how can you answer scientific questions?

The new Iraq war has already been deadlier than the first, with 765 killed and over *eighteen thousand* medically evacuated from the combat zone as of mid-May 2004. As it was in 1991, post-traumatic stress will be a problem (the rate of suicides of soldiers deployed to Iraq is already stratospheric and climbing), as will other health issues. Further, the injuries in this war are unusually devastating. Early reports have indicated that gunshot wounds are far fewer than normal, but injuries from improvised explosives are far higher than expected. In short, the number of injuries involving the loss of one or more limbs and severe head trauma is extremely high. Will the Pentagon and the VA be equipped to deal with these problems? Not if currently available data tells us anything.

A lot of lessons from the first Gulf War are lying there waiting to be learned by both the Pentagon and Department of Veterans Affairs, provided they are willing to learn them. First, it is absolutely clear that the Pentagon cannot be trusted to investigate itself. A decade of obstruction by the Pentagon prevented over a hundred thousand Gulf War veterans from receiving timely medical care, and the obstruction continues today. Future medical surveillance of combat veterans should fall under the auspices of the Department of Health and Human Services, with plenty of outside and independent participation and oversight. It is critical that veterans themselves be intimately involved in the process.

Further, the Pentagon has available plenty of simple steps that would make health monitoring, follow-up and research much more effective. To begin with, as a minimum, the Pentagon must begin complying with the 1998 Force Health Protection Act, which requires them to conduct predeployment and postdeployment health monitoring of soldiers deploying to a combat zone. Tracking exposure data is critical, and just as important, that information must be made available to the VA and independent researchers. Bear in mind that it was half a decade after the end of the first war before the extent of exposure from the Khamisiyah demolition became public knowledge, causing the chair of the defense science board and members of the Presidential Advisory Committee to backtrack on their original conclusions. Had they had the data in the first place, scientists and policy makers would have known years earlier the direction to take in their research.

As the old saying goes, an ounce of prevention is worth a pound of cure. Much of the distrust of the Pentagon arises from its own actions. One result of the botched mishandling of the anthrax vaccine is that among the troops there is a high level of distrust of medications provided by the command structure. During the 2003 deployment to Liberia, more than half of the Marines deployed contracted malaria, with a quarter of them requiring hospitalization. The culprit: many of them did not take the preventive drug larium, because of both the distrust engendered by the anthrax vaccine, as well as suspicions that larium, which can cause psychotic breaks, may have been a contributing factor in the murders of several Fort Bragg spouses the previous year after family members returned home from combat in Afghanistan.[13]

The Pentagon has a long way to go to regain the trust of the troops. That trust was further broken in 2003 with the failure to discover a single weapon of mass destruction in Iraq, though hundreds of U.S. troops died in a war based on the assumption they were there. Though recruiting is still on target within the military, the signs indicate there may soon be an exodus of experienced noncommissioned officers, particularly in the reserves, which have been dramatically overextended in recent years.

What about those who are still sick? Though research has now pinned down some of the key causes of the illnesses, and over one hundred thousand veterans are receiving financial compensation for their disabilities, most simply want to be able to return to work and have a normal life. What are the prospects for an actual cure to their illnesses?

Unfortunately, those prospects are dim. Understanding the cause of nerve and brain damage does not readily lend itself to a cure, especially for those suffering from severe degenerative illnesses like ALS and Parkinson's. The real tragedy may be that now that we have answers, it may be too late to do anything for this generation of veterans.

The motto of the Vietnam Veterans of America is "Never again shall one generation of veterans abandon another." They've held true to that by being out front in helping organizations like the National Gulf War Resource Center advocate on behalf of Gulf War veterans. Our society, and especially those of us who served in the first Gulf War, now owe the same care to those who are only now returning home from another battlefield in the Middle East.

7

Military Justice: An Oxymoron?

Tod Ensign and Louis Font

> The need for special regulations [for] military discipline and the consequent need . . . for an exclusive system of military justice is too obvious to require extensive discussion.
>
> —U.S. Supreme Court (1983 decision)[1]

The American military has always used its own legal system to punish soldiers who break its rules. Originally, military officers dished out harsh punishment right on the battlefield. Slowly, this system of "drumhead justice" was changed, with military courts and lawyers taking over some of the commanders' powers. It's fair to say, however, that even today, the primary purpose of the military's justice system is to enforce discipline and to ensure the commander's authority over his troops.

The military command places a strong emphasis on top-down control as a principal means of enforcing its authority. There are various ways to motivate people to do their jobs, but historically the military has preferred the authoritarian approach. An excerpt from the *Army Officer's Guide* demonstrates this: "One difference between a fine military unit and a [bad one] is the degree of obedience to the will of the leader. He [sic] has strong powers to exact obedience. The leader must detect transgressions, determine the cause and apply sound corrective action. If [the leader] habitually overlooks transgressions or lightly passes them by, he or she is lost. When the big test comes, the unit will fail to take the hill and soldiers will die who should have lived."[2]

After World War Two, the US military underwent a major overhaul. One reform occurred with the adoption by Congress of the Uniform Code of Military Justice (UCMJ) as the basic legal code for all the service branches. The UCMJ, along with the *Manual for Courts-Martial,* defines criminal conduct and outlines the procedures that the military courts are to follow.

Out of the 166 sections of the UCMJ, 57 deal with specific crimes. Some of the statutes concerning rape, robbery, assault, etc., are the same as those found in state and federal criminal codes. But the military has also kept a number of offenses on the books, such as adultery, possession of marijuana for personal use, drunkenness, and homosexual acts between consenting adults, that are no longer treated as crimes by most civilian prosecutors. Despite occasional policy reviews, such as the Cox Commission (see below), the military hasn't significantly altered its legal system to reflect societal changes over the past half century.

The military also has a category of crimes, such as disrespect, AWOL, desertion, disobeying an order, and fraternization (between officers and enlisted), which have no counterpart in civilian society, Finally, the UCMJ has two catchall articles whose vague language ("conduct unbecoming an officer" and "bringing discredit to the military service") can be stretched to include a multitude of sins.

Since its adoption in 1951, many critics, including military lawyers, have complained that the UCMJ leaves too much power in the hands of the commanders. For instance, the commander as "convening authority" decides which, if any, criminal charges shall be brought against a GI. He then picks the prosecutor and all members of the jury. A jury convicts by a vote of two-thirds; that is, up to a third of the jury members can vote for acquittal, yet the verdict announced in open court is guilty. After trial, the convening authority must review and approve any guilty verdict as well as the sentence. Each juror knows that his commander will have to approve his future promotions and assignments. The UCMJ was changed so that commanders are prohibited from considering how a juror voted in making any personnel decision. However, it would be very difficult to prove that any such discrimination occurred. A training manual the Army has used to teach ROTC officers about the military justice system states that the UCMJ "left the commander essentially in control of the court-martial machinery."

In 1951 Congress outlawed unlawful "command influence" over the military judicial system. The UCMJ provides that

> No person subject to the code may attempt to coerce or, by any unauthorized means, influence the action of a court-martial or any other military tribunal or any member thereof, in reaching the findings or sentence in any case or the action of any convening, approving, or reviewing authority with respect to such authority's judicial acts.[3]

The UCMJ also provides that the convening authority shall not "censure, reprimand, or admonish any . . . counsel . . . with regard to any exercise of his functions."[4] Unfortunately, it remains a common practice for commanders to transfer military lawyers who work too diligently for defendants to the prosecutor's office.

One of this chapter's authors, Louis Font, has twenty-seven years' experience in military trial defense work. He notes that while there have been many dramatic changes in the U.S. military over those years he believes that its justice system has changed the least. In fact, he argues that the highest-ranking commander still rigs the most controversial cases.

One Supreme Court justice, William O. Douglas, a noted civil libertarian, wrote in an opinion that "There are dangers lurking in military trials which were sought to be avoided by the Bill of Rights and Article III of our Constitution. Free countries of the world have tried to restrict military [courts] to the narrowest jurisdiction deemed absolutely essential to maintaining discipline among . . . troops."[5]

During the Vietnam War, the Supreme Court issued decisions that limited courts-martial to only those cases where there was a clear "service connection." In recent times, however, the pendulum has swung the other way. In 1987, the Supreme Court reversed its earlier rulings. Now, military courts are allowed to try soldiers for alleged crimes that took place off base and when they were off duty.[6]

There are various ways that a GI can be punished for what his superiors believe to be misconduct. GIs are prosecuted for things that most civilians today consider not to be crimes or nobody's business. Summarized below are the various components of the military disciplinary system, beginning with the least punitive measures, such as restriction to barracks, and moving up the scale to courts-martial, sentences that may bring long prison terms or even the death penalty.

In the military, a minor offense can be treated as warranting counseling, or can be elevated into a criminal charge. For example, failing to come to a formation on time can be treated by the command as a minor infraction, or can, with little, if any, additional effort be transformed into a refusal to follow an order which may carry a maximum punishment of years in prison.

INFORMAL MECHANISMS

Counseling and Instruction

Military commanders, including enlisted NCOs, have the right to counsel or instruct a GI about almost anything. An unkempt uniform or a GI's failure to promptly pay his debts will be considered appropriate subjects for counseling by many commanders. Although this counseling is generally informal, it carries the implied threat that more action will follow if the GI doesn't heed the "advice."

Admonitions and Reprimands

Sometimes a commander will decide to warn a GI about his conduct. This places him on notice that he must change his behavior. Often such warnings are oral and no record is made. "Letters of concern," however, are written and can be placed in the "temporary" section of your personnel file. These letters can have a negative impact on decisions about promotions or assignments. Normally, a GI has thirty days within which to rebut the allegations in such letters.

ADMINISTRATIVE PUNISHMENTS

Although these measures may appear trivial when compared to a court-martial, they can set in motion a chain of events that can end your military career. In co-author Font's experience, these administrative actions can be very damaging, yet most GIs don't realize that they should fight them until it's too late.

Withholding Privileges

Officers can withhold permission to do things as a form of punishment. For instance, a commander can refuse to issue a weekend pass that a GI needs to go home or can deny him entry to the Enlisted Club. A commander is supposed to withhold only privileges that are reasonably related to the offense committed. For example, he shouldn't suspend someone's right to drive on post unless the misconduct concerned driving.

Reduction in Rank

If a GI's rank is E/4 or below, a field-grade officer (Major and above) has the authority to take away a stripe if he decides that he or she is "inefficient" in their job. He also can reduce a soldier convicted of a civilian offense, such as disorderly conduct or shoplifting, one grade in rank. The accused must be given written notice of the reasons for the proposed reduction, and he or she has the right to offer rebuttal evidence. A soldier who's punished can appeal the decision to a superior officer. As a general rule, however, officers stick together on matters of discipline and do not like to second-guess one another.

Noncommissioned officers (NCOs) (E/5 and above) must be provided with a hearing before an administrative board before they can be reduced in rank. Just one nonjudicial punishment (see discussion of Article 15 below) is enough for a commander to "take a stripe" from an NCO. This can have the effect of stripping a GI of his status as an NCO.

Bars to Reenlistment

If someone's commander decides that he or she is a "substandard performer," a bar to reenlistment can be placed in your permanent military file. This bar prevents reenlistment. Common reasons for imposing it include repeated tardiness, short periods of being absent without leave, several nonjudicial punishments (Article 15s), or antisocial conduct, such as repeated conflicts with co-workers. A soldier must be given a written statement spelling out the reasons for the recommendation. As with the reduction in rank, a soldier can (and should) file a statement rebutting the allegations. Both the commander's statement and that of the accused are then sent to the next higher commander for decision.

If a bar to reenlistment is imposed, it is supposed to be reviewed every six months to determine whether it should remain in effect. If a soldier changes units, his or her new commander can rescind the bar at his discretion. Promotion boards, which review GI records to determine eligibility for promotion, can also issue bars to reenlistment.

Reclassification of Military Occupational Specialty (MOS)

Commanders sometimes remove someone from his designated job because of misconduct. Typical cases would be where a medical corpsman has become a drug addict or a finance clerk has been caught embezzling. This sanction is serious in the military, because if a person isn't working in his assigned job, he may not be eligible for further training, promotion, or even retention.

A case in which this authority may have been abused occurred at the Marine Corps' training facility at Parris Island, South Carolina. Some years ago a female drill instructor (DI) had testified as a defense witness at the court-martial of a fellow DI for homosexual conduct. Apparently, her testimony upset someone, because after the trial ended, she was removed from her job as a DI. The drill instructor's job is an important step on a Marine's career path; therefore, this action placed a cloud over the witness's future in the Marines. An ACLU appeal of the involuntary removal of this soldier from her job was unsuccessful. Needless to say, any unjust attempt to remove a soldier from his or her assigned MOS should be opposed. It is advisable to submit a written rebuttal to all allegations.

Separation from Service (Discharge)

The military can discharge its service members in one of three ways. First, during the first six months of enlistment, each service branch has blanket authority to discharge any trainee whom it decides is not performing satisfactorily. Those discharged during this period usually receive "uncharacterized" discharges, meaning the person hasn't served long enough to justify either an honorable or other-than-honorable discharge. About 10 percent of all trainees (depending on service branch) are separated in this fashion even before they complete basic training.

Second, a military commander can initiate administrative discharge action against a service member at any time during his career. Some of the more common reasons for doing so include:

- Misconduct—repeated acts of relatively minor infractions
- Unsuitability—the inability to learn, a personality disorder, etc.
- For the good of the service—usually requested by a GI facing court-martial charges
- Criminal conviction by a civilian court

- Fraudulent enlistment
- Personal abuse (alcohol or other drugs)
- Homosexuality (doesn't require homosexual acts)
- Conscientious objector (usually on application of GI)

An adverse involuntary discharge often is based on a factual determination (for "alcohol dependence"), which may be inaccurate. The accused should attempt to rebut the determination with evidence to the contrary.

The rules and procedures governing administrative discharges are very complicated and vary from one service branch to another. For further information on this subject, you should consult with an attorney or skilled military counselor about how to handle a particular case.

Normally, a commander will present a soldier with a written notice informing him or her of his intention to discharge them. This notice should spell out the reasons for the discharge. If the allegations are vague the soldier should ask for more detail. This notice should also specify the type of discharge that the command is seeking: honorable, general, or other than honorable. Finally, the notice should summarize your right to a hearing or to submit a written rebuttal.

If the command is recommending you for an honorable or general discharge, you may not be entitled to appear personally before an administrative board. Generally, only GIs who have served a minimum number of years (six or more is common) have the right to demand a personal hearing, unless an other-than-honorable discharge is sought by the command. If you are not eligible to appear personally, you should still prepare a detailed written rebuttal. If you can, get supportive letters from your superiors and other GIs to buttress your case. Technically, the recommendations of the elimination board are only advisory, but the commander who appointed it will normally approve them.

Over the years, both Ensign and Font have heard a number of GIs report being told that their "bad" discharge would be automatically upgraded to an Honorable discharge six months or a year after they've left the service. Perhaps unscrupulous supervisors tell GIs this to dissuade them from fighting involuntary discharge. There is no such thing as an "automatic upgrade" in the military!

Finally, the two worst discharges, Bad Conduct and Dishonorable, can only be imposed as part of a court-martial sentence. In general, both of these will bar all veterans' benefits. The military is fond of saying that a Dishonorable is the equivalent of a federal felony conviction. Although it doesn't carry that level of stigma, it is still not the kind of record you want to have in your permanent file.

NONJUDICIAL PUNISHMENT (ARTICLE 15)

This system of punishment is unique to the military. It is called "Article 15" in the Army and Air Force, while the Navy and Marines use "Captain's Mast" and "Office Hours," respectively. The primary purpose of nonjudicial punishment is to provide commanders with a way to deal with minor infractions quickly and simply. This is the most commonly used disciplinary measure in the military: about 100,000 GIs have been disciplined in this manner annually in recent years.

A GI has the choice of "accepting" or "rejecting" an Article 15 when it's offered by his commander, unless he is stationed aboard a ship; then he must accept. Acceptance is *not* a guilty plea; it is an agreement to dispose of the alleged offense using the Article 15 procedure, rather than taking the case to court-martial. It follows from this that an Article 15 could only be based on an offense that is spelled out in the UCMJ (and thus can be tried at a court-martial). Serious offenses, however, for which someone can be sentenced for a year or more or a dishonorable discharge, will usually be referred for trial by court-martial.

If a GI "accepts" an Article 15, his commander (or another officer designated for the job) will conduct an informal hearing into the charges. These hearings have sometimes been called "kangaroo courts," since they provide defendants with very limited rights. For instance, no verbatim record of the proceeding is made, and lawyers cannot formally participate. A GI can, however, choose a representative (or even a lawyer) to speak on his behalf, although this is seldom done. The accused can offer written evidence and also call those witnesses who are "reasonably available" in an effort to prove his innocence. However, the hearing officer is not required to call reluctant witnesses or those who are not physically nearby to testify. No formal rules of evidence are applied, so either side can bring in virtually any kind of evidence. Finally, guilt or innocence is decided by the same person who brought the charges in the first place.

Article 15 proceedings are often held in a commander's office with all participants, except the commander, standing. The commander typically will hear from subordinate commanders, give the accused a brief turn, and then impose punishment.

The overwhelming majority of Article 15 hearings end with imposition of punishment. The rank of the hearing officer determines how much punishment he can impose. Captains (lieutenants in the Navy) can give any or all of the following as a punishment:

- Up to seven days of correctional custody (jail)
- Forfeiture of up to seven days' pay
- Up to fourteen days of extra duty
- Reduction of one pay grade (rank)
- Restriction to certain areas for up to fourteen days
- Up to three days' diet of bread and water (if serving aboard a ship)

Higher-ranking officers can impose greater punishment, such as thirty days' correctional custody, sixty days of restriction, or loss of all rank. If an officer feels that the sentence he can impose is not severe enough for the offense, he can refer the case to a higher-ranking officer for disposition.

An offender can appeal his punishment under Article 15. Except for reduction or forfeiture of pay, the punishment cannot be carried out until the appeal has been decided. The appeal can be written or oral. It goes to the commander of the officer who conducted the Article 15 hearing. This officer can then reduce or suspend any portion of the punishment, as he sees fit. Note, however, that when the Article 15 is given for a crime such as car theft (which is not a "minor" offense), you can later be tried at court-martial for the *same* offense. (The military doesn't consider this double jeopardy.)

Drug Testing and Article 15

In 1982, the Pentagon embarked on a vast campaign to make the US military "drug free." As part of this effort, every GI on active duty and every reservist and guardsman is required to submit periodic urine samples. Laboratories test these samples for residues (metabolites) of various illegal drugs (marijuana, cocaine, PCP, LSD), which can be detected in minuscule amounts days and even weeks after the exposure to the drug.

The service branches offer "self-referral" drug counseling that a drug user may want to consider. If a GI voluntarily acknowledges drug use and is accepted into the program, he will not be prosecuted. This option should be discussed with a military lawyer in advance.

Any GI who registers "positive" on a urine test will be investigated about drug use. Military investigators are particularly interested in learning the identities of drug sellers and of other users. A detainee may be promised leniency in exchange for "cooperation," but most commands follow a policy of punishing anyone who fails their urine test.

The urine-test program has greatly simplified the job of military investigators in drug cases. Military courts now routinely allow juries to convict service members of drug use or drug possession when the prosecution's only principal evidence is the lab report showing a certain level of drug residue in urine. Military courts have ruled that compulsory testing is constitutional. They have also ruled that testing doesn't violate one's right not to incriminate oneself. Courts have placed some restrictions on the use of blanket testing where civilian workers are involved. However, where GIs are concerned, military law applies.

Since millions of GIs and reservists have been tested by now, tens of thousands of them have been caught in the drug prosecutor's net. In 1982, 45,051 Article 15s were given for drug use, while 6,202 GIs were court-martialed for the same offense. By 1987, word had spread and these totals dropped to 24,854 Article 15s and 2,740 courts-martial. Lab-test results played a central role in most of these proceedings, and a substantial number of those who were punished were discharged against their wishes. Those who are not prosecuted are required to participate in drug-rehabilitation counseling and are closely watched for signs of further drug use.

There has been a good deal of scientific controversy about the accuracy of lab tests on which most military prosecutions are based. Most of the testing is done by commercial labs, which are paid based on the volume of specimens processed.

The military's highest court ruled in November 1988 that the government must pay the costs of an expert witness called by a defendant to challenge the validity of a urinalysis test. This may help defendants in cases where there is legitimate scientific issue about the interpretation of a urine sample.

The military uses the Article 15 nonjudicial punishments much more frequently than courts-martial to dispose of drug cases. From this, one may conclude that the military treats drug cases with leniency. However, this is not the case. Consider the statistics for just the Navy for one year, fiscal 1984. That year, it reported 27,581 confirmed positive urine tests. Of these, 17,417 sailors were given nonjudicial punishment, while 1,710 were court-martialed. However, 6,596 were involuntarily discharged. Apparently, a significant number of those who "accepted" Article 15 punishment were later tossed out of the military. Herein lies a sticky problem for anyone who is offered nonjudicial punishment due to a positive drug test.

It appears that many commanders have a preference for using the Article 15 procedure to dispose of drug cases. It appears that some commanders tell GIs that accepting nonjudicial punishment will resolve their problem and also avoid the harsh punishment that can result from a court-martial. However, once they were punished under Article 15, they were immediately processed for an administrative discharge for "misconduct-abuse of drugs."

If a GI has served less than six years active duty, he is usually not entitled to a formal hearing by an administrative separation board, unless he is facing less-than-honorable discharge. These restrictions change from time to time, according to the branch of service.

Years ago, a single nonjudicial punishment would not have been enough to support a discharge action. However, drugs are a very sensitive subject in today's military, and a drug-related Article 15 is enough to set discharge wheels in motion. To make matters worse, discharge papers bearing the words "drug abuse" may also create problems with future civilian employers.

This situation means that anyone should think long and hard about "accepting" an Article 15 for drug use. Since a special or general court-martial provides a better forum in which to present a defense, it may be best to "go for broke." However, the stakes are much higher if you lose.

Deciding Between Article 15 and a Court-Martial

You should make the decision only after you have consulted with an experienced attorney and weighed all the factors involved. As mentioned if the charge is drug use, the best choice may be to stand trial by court-martial. However, in many situations the wisest choice is to dispose of the matter via an Article 15. Also, unlike a court-martial conviction, Article 15 punishment is not considered a criminal conviction.

A soldier always has the right to discuss an Article 15 with a military lawyer. If the threat of discharge is also present you should consult a civilian attorney as well. If you are innocent and feel that you can collect enough witnesses and evidence to make a convincing case, then a court-martial provides the best forum in which to argue your innocence. Refusing an Article 15 doesn't always mean that a court-martial will follow, especially if the commander fears a strong defense. No commander or prosecutor likes to see cases that are sent to court-martial end in acquittal.

A GI has at least forty-eight hours (seventy-two hours in the Army) to decide if he will "accept" an Article 15 or not. He has an absolute right to consult with a military lawyer; however, the amount of assistance they will provide varies widely.

A Word About Military Lawyers

Military lawyers are licensed to practice by the state to whose bar they were initially admitted. For many, the Judge Advocate General (JAG) Corps is their first legal job. They are generally referred to as JAG lawyers. Advertisements that are used to recruit law students promise that as military lawyers they will be trying cases in the courtroom while their civilian counterparts are still consigned to the law library. For clients, however, this may not be such a good deal. It normally takes trial lawyers years to become proficient litigators.

Another problem is that graduates of prestigious law schools and top students at less competitive schools can earn upwards of $100,000 in private law firms, right out of law school. Law students who are public-service minded are more likely to go to work for a nonprofit, public-interest group, or Legal Aid, than they are to join the military.

Although some JAG lawyers are conscientious and dedicated despite the pressures and restrictions under which they work, the military's legal corps has its share of marginal performers. Also, if a JAG lawyer decides to make a career out of the military, he or she learns very quickly that antagonizing or challenging his commanders is not the path to promotion and good assignments. Look at it this way: military lawyers all work together in the same building, with prosecutors right across the hall from the defense lawyers. Being fellow officers, it's not surprising that they socialize and treat one another as friends and associates, rather than as adversaries. Their first loyalty is to the military not to their clients.

Under the regulations, a defendant has the right to request any military lawyer on active duty to represent him, provided he or she is "reasonably available." In the average case, the choice will usually be limited to the JAG lawyers who are stationed at the military installation where the trial will take place. It's a good idea to request a specific lawyer who has a good reputation but the command may deny the request.

The workload of the JAG corps is often so heavy that even the most diligent military lawyers will not have the time it takes to fully prepare a case for a trial. The workload is heavy because the military employs relatively few lawyers, given the scope of their responsibilities. For instance, the Navy only has 800 JAG lawyers to service 593,000 sailors, and nearly 180,000 Marines have only 450 lawyers to represent them. In addition to conducting criminal trials, these lawyers must advise military families and retirees on civil-law matters and handle a variety of other cases, including environment and international legal claims.

JAG lawyers don't normally have access to the kind of investigative resources that can win a case by uncovering evidence or locating key witnesses. For this reason military defense lawyer will often try to persuade defendants to swap a guilty plea in exchange for what he or she says is a light sentence, even if the facts strongly suggest that you are innocent. One option is to retain a civilian attorney who will be immune to command pressures. Unfortunately, his or her fees must be paid by you. Usually, the civilian lawyer acts as the "lead" counsel, with the military lawyer assisting him. Some civilian lawyers believe that military prosecutors and defense lawyers are more scrupulous about respecting a defendant's rights when he or she is represented by an outside attorney.

Be careful whom you select as your civilian attorney. If you can, ask co-workers and local attorneys for recommendations. When you meet with an attorney, ask probing questions about his court-martial experience. Some of the lawyers who set up practices near military bases are former JAG lawyers who may be psychologically unable to fight the command aggressively on your behalf. This is particularly true if the civilian lawyer is an active military reservist. It is very difficult to mount a successful appeal of a conviction based on incompetence of counsel—especially one chosen by the defendant.

Congress has tried to insulate JAG lawyers from command pressure by assigning them to a separate command. Army defense lawyers, for example, serve in the Trial Defense Service, which is based in Washington, D.C.

COURTS-MARTIAL

A Word of Caution

Army lawyers are required to turn in their client if they believe that he intends to commit a future crime that is likely to cause death, substantial body harm, or will significantly endanger national security or military readiness. If the command suspects you of being involved in the commission of a crime, you will be visited or called in for questioning by either military or civilian police officers. Sometimes, your commanding officer will summon you for questioning as well. The guiding principle here is simple: tell them *nothing*. Investigators are allowed to use virtually any ploy to get someone to talk once he has consented to an interview. One ploy is for the investigator to tell a suspect that they may have to identify him or her to the inquiring media unless he or she is "cooperating."

Everyone has seen television shows and movies where suspects "take the Fifth" when questioned to protect themselves against self-incrimination. Yet all too often, intelligent people give prosecutors invaluable information because they think that they can talk their way out of trouble. Any prosecutor knows of cases that resulted in convictions only because the defendant volunteered information. Usually a suspect's effort to cooperate with prosecutors will only dig them into a deeper hole.

Please don't think that there is anything unpatriotic or cowardly about choosing to remain silent. The Bill of Rights of our Constitution guarantees that no citizen can be forced to give testimony against him or herself. This is an important hallmark of a free society and helps prevent the use of torture to extort confessions. The Fifth Amendment to the Constitution and Article 31 of the UCMJ both protect GIs against involuntary self-incrimination. Article 31 reads in part: "No one subject to [the UCMJ] may compel any person to incriminate himself or to answer any question . . . which may tend to incriminate him."

Sometimes an investigator will try to bait suspects who refuse to answer questions. He'll state that innocent people are only too happy to give their version of the events. Technically, if you are a suspect, Article 31 requires the military police to inform you of your right to remain silent, that any statement you make can be used against you, and that you have a right to consult a lawyer.

This is not to suggest that there aren't times when it's desirable to cooperate with investigators. On the contrary, sometimes it will be the best choice. However, such cooperation should always be arranged under the auspices of a defense attorney.

Sometimes a commander or military investigators will ask a suspect to speak to a military doctor or a psychologist about matters under investigation. Caution is necessary since the usual doctor-patient privilege of confidentiality that civilians enjoy doesn't always apply in the military. In some branches of the service, doctors are supposed to report to higher authorities what their patients tell them about their "crimes."

Assuming that you have been accused of a criminal offense or you have decided to face trial rather than accept a nonjudicial punishment, there are three kinds of court-martial that you should know about: summary, special, and general. Their distinctive features are outlined below.

Summary Court-Martial

The simplest and most informal proceeding of the three, it operates like an Article 15 hearing in that one officer (sometimes, but not always, a lawyer) acts as a judge, prosecutor, defense counsel, jury, and court reporter. The Supreme Court ruled years ago that the military doesn't have to provide defendants with lawyers at summary courts. Also, a defendant will not normally be allowed to use a lawyer that he has hired on his own.

Although a summary court does not offer much in the way of due-process protections, it can only do limited damage in terms of sentence. Maximum penalties are thirty days of confinement, forty-five days of hard labor, sixty days of restriction, forfeiture of two-thirds' pay for one month, or reduction to the lowest rank.

As with an Article 15, a GI must consent to be tried by this court. If he doesn't, he will be taking his chances at the next level—a special court. This may be a big roll of the dice, however, since a special court can impose much stiffer sentences, as explained below. You should consult with a competent, experienced lawyer before deciding whether to be tried by a summary or special court.

Special Court-Martial

This court can consist of trial before a judge alone, before a judge with a sitting jury of three or more members, or before a panel of at least three members if a military judge is not available because of physical conditions or military exigencies. The trial is conducted usually by a military judge who is a trained lawyer, and you must be represented by an assigned military defense counsel. If you are an enlisted person, you have the right to have at least one-third of the jurors drawn from the enlisted ranks.[7]

It is practically a truism in military justice circles that an enlisted defendant should never exercise his or her right to have the court-martial jury composed of at least one-third enlisted. Many military lawyers believe that because the enlisted personnel chosen by the commander are often career noncommissioned officers and often of high rank, this significant right should not be exercised. On the contrary, co-author Louis Font usually advises enlisted clients to exercise their right to have enlisted members on the panel. The experience of the enlisted members is invaluable and he believes it is best to have enlisted members on the court.

A special court can give a maximum sentence of one year in prison, hard labor without confinement for up to three months, forfeiture of pay (up to two-thirds' pay per month for as long as a year), reduction to the lowest enlisted rank, or a bad conduct discharge. Congress recently changed the maximum punishment from six months to a year.[8] If the judge is not a lawyer then he cannot impose a bad conduct discharge. A verbatim record of trial is required if the sentence includes a bad conduct discharge, confinement for more than six months, or forfeiture of pay for more than six months. If any of the prerequisites for a complete record of the proceedings are not met, the defendant receives only a summarized record that may be only a few pages long. This makes it much more difficult to argue legal points on appeal.

As you might expect, the convening authority for a special court must be of higher rank (brigade or regimental commander, commander of a ship, etc.) than one who can call a summary court. General court-martial, being the most important court, requires convening by the commander of a military installation, headquarters, or corps.

General Court-Martial

This court is reserved for trying what the military regards as serious offenses. In the military, however, this does not just mean serious crimes like robbery, rape, or murder. The Table of Maximum Punishments allows heavy sentences for such offenses as "unauthorized use of a military pass" (three years maximum), "unlawfully altering a public record" (three years), or "writing a worthless check for more than $100" (five years). In civilian courts, except for murder cases and other crimes involving a weapon, a first-time offender is usually placed on probation. Military juries, by contrast, often impose near-maximum prison sentences for what civilians would regard as minor crimes.

One highly publicized general court-martial during the Vietnam War concerned an Army doctor, Howard Levy, who was charged with disobeying orders to teach medical procedures to Green Berets. Dr. Levy refused because he believed that the Berets withheld medicine from Vietnamese prisoners as a means of torture. Levy was convicted of several offenses, including "conduct unbecoming an officer," and sentenced to several years in prison. He appealed to the US Supreme Court, arguing that "conduct unbecoming" was unconstitutionally vague, since a GI couldn't know in advance what conduct was forbidden. Chief Justice William Rehnquist rejected this in a majority opinion that concluded that the military's criminal code may contain provisions that might not be permitted for civilians.[9]

Under Article 32, a pretrial investigation must be conducted before a general court-martial can be convened. This proceeding most closely resembles a preliminary hearing in a civilian felony case. The prosecution must present enough evidence to convince the hearing officer that the accused should be tried for his alleged crimes. Lawyers for the defendant are allowed to cross-examine the prosecution's witnesses and to inspect other evidence.

The defendant's lawyers must be prepared to fight vigorously at this hearing. An aggressive defense effort at this stage can sometimes persuade the command to reduce or even drop the charges. The defense should make every effort to tape record the proceedings and transcribe the proceedings verbatim. The military command often only makes a summarized record, which consists of the summarized notes of the Article 32 investigating officer. Without a verbatim record, the record of the proceedings is practically worthless for use at trial.

Military commanders can lock up any defendant before trial if they think it is necessary to ensure his appearance at court-martial. The military has no bail system, and it is very difficult to get pretrial confinement orders changed once they are imposed. Locking a defendant up until trial makes it difficult for him to fully assist his lawyers in preparing for trial. This can also be very demoralizing, especially if the person knows that he is innocent. If he is acquitted, then all the time he spent in jail is wasted.

A general court-martial most resembles a civilian felony trial. Two or more lawyers present the case before a military judge, with a verbatim transcript being taken. For the most part, rules of evidence are similar to those used in federal district courts. A jury of five or more members (depending on the number of jurors selected by the convening authority) decides guilt or innocence. In 2001 Congress passed Article 25a of the UCMJ, which provides that in death-penalty cases the number of jurors must be at least twelve.[10] A unanimous verdict is not required, except where the death penalty is imposed.

A shocking aspect of military justice concerns the power of subpoena. Only the prosecution has the power to compel witnesses to attend the trial. The defense is required to submit a list of witnesses asking the prosecution to issue a subpoena to each witness requested by the defense.[11] The list submitted by the defense must specify the expected testimony of each defense witness and usually must justify why each witness is necessary to the defense. Often, especially in controversial cases, the prosecution will refuse to subpoena defense witnesses that would prove detrimental to the prosecution. To obtain a subpoena the defendant must then petition the military judge. Often the military judge will enter into a colloquy with the defense and prosecution in which the defense is required to reveal its case, theories, and rationales for witnesses in open court, with the result often being the denial of witnesses and the prosecutor's learning everything about the defense case. Co-author Louis Font believes that the denial of subpoena power to the defense in military cases is a joke, especially in controversial trials, and a travesty of justice. The defendant should have the same power to subpoena witnesses as does a defendant in federal district court.

An unusual feature of the military system is the extensive use of pretrial agreements that fix the maximum amount of punishment in exchange for a guilty plea. Defense attorneys often negotiate such agreements with the prosecution because of the great likelihood that a military jury will both convict a defendant and impose a heavy sentence. The Navy's chief appellate lawyer told a national seminar on military law that 97 percent of all courts-martial end in convictions, and only 3 percent of those convicted received any relief on appeal.

If a pretrial agreement is in effect, the military judge's or the jury's role is limited to setting the appropriate sentence through a sentencing hearing. Pretrial agreements often specify that the defendant will be sentenced before the judge alone. If the defendant agrees, then the judge is not informed of the terms of the pre-trial agreement until after he or she imposes sentence.

If a defendant pleads innocent, a sentencing hearing is also held after a verdict of guilty. In a sentencing hearing, both sides offer evidence about the defendant's character, work history, reputation, etc. Character witnesses are typically people who have commanded or worked with the defendant.

During the hearing on sentencing, a military defendant has the right to make an "unsworn" statement. This can be a spontaneous statement, or it can be read from a prepared text. The prosecution can offer evidence to rebut such a statement, but the prosecution is not allowed to cross-examine a defendant concerning the unsworn statement.

If the defendant has elected to be tried by judge alone, then the judge also sentences; otherwise the decision on guilt or innocence and the decision on sentencing are made by the jury. After deliberation, the judge or jury, as the case may be, announces the sentence in open court. In a pretrial agreement case, if the announced punishment exceeds that specified in the pretrial agreement, the defendant receives the lesser sentence. If the court imposes a lighter sentence than the agreement, the defendant gets the benefit of the leniency.

Military lawyers often tell clients, in an effort to persuade them to plead guilty, that the agreement on sentence is merely an "insurance policy" and that the chances are good the defendant will be able to get a lesser sentence than the pretrial agreement. However, in our opinion, it is very rare for a defendant to do better at trial than the sentence agreed to in the pretrial agreement.

In most cases the command insists that the accused, in exchange for a pretrial deal, agree to be tried by a judge alone. The military judge knows what a reasonable sentence under the circumstances is, and usually imposes a sentence that will be higher than the agreement. If the sentence comes higher than the agreement, then the trial participants look good—the convening authority seems fair, the judge looks tough, and the defense counsel can tell his client how lucky he is that he followed his advice and took a deal that has now spared him some prison time.

Another problem with the military justice system is that it does not allow any defendant to be tried by a "jury of his peers." By law and regulation, each member of the jury should outrank the defendant. The jurors are hand picked by the convening authority on the basis of their age, education, experience, training, rank, and judicial temperament.[12] The services usually don't allow military doctors, nurses, and chaplains to serve on juries even though such jurors could bring common sense to a number of issues, including the trial of conscientious objectors or persons who have gone AWOL or have deserted for medical reasons.[13] Instead, the convening authority usually stacks the jury against the accused by appointing hard-nosed commanders and subordinates whose judicial temperament is prosecution-oriented.

Black and Hispanic defendants' chances of being tried by a jury that includes black or Hispanic military members may have been improved by a decision of the Court of Military Appeals in 1989 that prosecutors cannot remove jurors solely because of their race or ethnic origin.[14] Upon motion by the defense, the prosecutor is required to provide reasonable, plausible reasons for a peremptory challenge of a non-Caucasion court member.[15] However, the convening authority can still keep minority members off the jury by simply not calling them in the first place.

In the late 1970s, the Government Accounting Office (GAO), an investigative branch of Congress, conducted a two-year investigation into the functioning of military juries. The GAO's investigators examined trial records from hundreds of courts-martial and interviewed many military lawyers and judges. In its report to Congress, the GAO recommended that the same officer who convenes a court-martial no longer select court-martial jurors. Instead, they proposed that jurors be drawn anonymously from a broad cross section of military personnel on a given base.

During this same time period, the Army conducted a survey about military juries among its personnel at Fort Riley, Kansas. Sixty-eight percent of those who responded favored the random selection of jurors. Nonetheless, all of the service branches opposed the reforms proposed by the GAO, and to this day, commanders can still handpick jury members for trials that they have ordered.

The end result of the military judicial system described here is an eye-popping conviction rate. In fiscal year 2002, the Army held 788 general courts-martial, and only 31 persons were acquitted, for a conviction rate of over 96 percent. Of special courts-martial empowered to adjudge a Bad Conduct discharge, 592 persons were tried in the Army, and only 18 were acquitted, for a conviction rate of almost 97 percent. In the Navy, 499 general courts were held in 2002, and only 18 persons were acquitted. The Navy held 2,188 BCD special courts in the same year, and only 44 persons were acquitted, for a conviction rate of 97.9 percent. Of 2,098 Navy summary courts, there were only 20 acquittals. Air Force defendants did not fare any better. In 2002 the Air Force held 564 general courts with only 30 acquittals. The Air Force held 384 BCD specials and there were only 19 acquittals. These Air Force statistics show conviction rates of 94.9 percent and 95 percent, respectively.[16]

After the Court-Martial

If a defendant is found guilty and is sentenced to at least one year in prison or given a punitive discharge, the Staff Judge Advocate (SJA) will conduct a formal review and submit a summary of the case, with his recommendations, to the convening authority. He can approve or disapprove any or all of the findings, but he cannot overturn a not-guilty verdict. In most cases, the SJA will rubber-stamp the decisions of the court-martial. If the convening authority approves the conviction and the sentence of a general court-martial the case is automatically reviewed by the Judge Advocate General in Washington, D.C. The JAG is empowered to modify or vacate the finding of guilt or alter any portion of the sentence. Technically, convictions by summary and special courts-martial can be appealed to the JAG, but the defendant must initiate such a review, and it is seldom done.

Confinement After Conviction

The military has no system of appellate bail, so in most cases the defendant will serve his sentence while his appeal is being considered. The convening authority has the authority to allow a convicted person to remain free until his appeal is decided, but this does not happen very often. In many cases, the defendant will have already completed his sentence before his case has received its final review.

Courts of Criminal Appeals

Each branch of service has at least one court of criminal appeals, formerly known as Courts of Military Review. Each of these courts sits in panels of three judges, who are high-ranking career officers. The courts of review were originally created during World War One, following a public outcry when thirteen black soldiers were summarily executed in Texas one day after they were convicted of participating in a race riot.

These courts automatically review any conviction that results in a sentence of one year or more, a Bad Conduct or Dishonorable discharge, or the dismissal of an officer. The Judge Advocate General also may refer other cases to the courts of criminal appeals if he believes that they contain an error of law. The defendant is assigned an appellate lawyer who prepares his petition for review by the appropriate court of criminal appeals.

The military's highest court is the U.S. Court of Appeals for the Armed Forces (CAAF), formerly known as the Court of Military Appeals (COMA), which hears appeals from all five service branches. Its five judges are all civilians, although most have military legal backgrounds. They are appointed by the president and have fifteen-year terms. With a few exceptions, CAAF decides what decisions it will review. Like the U.S. Supreme Court, it grants review to only a small fraction of the cases that request it. Although CAAF has the authority to issue extraordinary writs to protect constitutional rights or to prevent irreparable harm, the court rarely is willing to grant them. CAAF was the ultimate authority on review of court-martial decisions until 1984, when Congress changed the law to allow some service members to appeal certain cases to the U.S. Supreme Court.

ATTEMPTS TO REFORM THE UCMJ

Over the years there have been several attempts at reform. Critics have long pointed out significant flaws in the military justice system that have never been rectified and should be changed for the sake of fairness and discipline.[17] Chief among the reforms sought has been an effort to limit sharply the role of commanders in military justice.

Upon the fiftieth anniversary of the UCMJ in 2001, the Cox Commission issued its recommendations for reform of the military justice system. This commission comprised a few individuals, acting on their own and without government funding, and was headed by Chief Judge Cox of the Court of Appeals for the Armed Forces. The commission held a public hearing in Washington, D.C., and the commission was assisted by the National Institute of Military Justice, a nonprofit organization.

The commission's recommendations are noteworthy for emphasizing the need to balance the scales of justice, and for pointing out that the UCMJ has not kept pace with evolving law or with the reforms of military justice that have taken place in other countries.[18] The commission recommended that the pretrial role of the convening authority be modified in both selecting court-martial jurors and making other pretrial legal decisions that are best left to a military judge. It recommended that commanders "must not be permitted to select the members of courts-martial" and that instead the members should be chosen at random from a list of "eligible service members prepared by the convening authority." It also recommended an increase in the independence, availability, and responsibilities of military judges; the implementation of additional safeguards in death-penalty cases; and the repeal of various sexual-conduct offenses in the UCMJ, and recodification of sexual offenses in a comprehensive criminal sexual-conduct article. Significantly, the commission pointed out the need for public discussion of changes to the *Manual for Courts-Martial* and the Uniform Code of Military Justice.

Much to its credit, the Cox Commission questioned the trial instructions used in conscientious-objector cases, and the wisdom of the Feres doctrine, which bars members of the military from suing the United States for negligence that harms soldiers. Unfortunately, the commission failed to endorse the need for the prosecution of commanders who obstruct justice and engage in unlawful command influence and control.

A CALL FOR CIVILIAN OVERSIGHT AND ACTION

The military justice system will never change if it continues to function without public scrutiny. Few people living near a military base have ever seen a military trial. Call the staff judge advocate's office and find out when the next trial is scheduled to be heard. Go and watch. Military trials are public trials, but usually the only persons in the courtroom are military personnel.

As a civilian, you may be astounded by what you see. Military trials sometimes start at 7 in the morning and may go on until midnight. Often military trials are characterized by a hurry-up-and-get-it-over-with attitude. Three minute recesses and twenty minute lunch breaks are not uncommon. You may see a military judge walk off the bench and step into the well of the courtroom and speak with trial participants or witnesses—all of which are matters that are not supposed to take place but can be all too common in military trials.[19]

The public often attend civilian trials to watch the drama of the proceedings. Retirees, college students, or others who have time, sometimes spend many hours watching trials. There is no reason why military trials should not be scrutinized by the public in the same fashion. The significant differences between civilian and military trials will be readily apparent to even the most casual observer.

There is also a dire need for civilian criminal-defense lawyers to represent military defendants. The art of cross-examination and the principles of advocacy are readily transferable from the civilian to the military realm. There is no reason why an experienced, competent, and dedicated civilian attorney should not take military cases. The civilian attorney must be vigilant to watch out for unlawful command influence and control, and if it exists, to expose it and litigate the issue.

8

Policing America: A New Role for the Military?

Tod Ensign

A strong sentiment against military involvement in domestic law enforcement can be traced all the way back to America's founding. Recent acts of terrorism, from the September 11 attacks to the anthrax mailings, have caused some public officials to advocate the removal of all restrictions on the US military performing domestic police functions. Shortly after 9/11, Senator John Warner (R-VA), the Chairman of the Senate Armed Services Committee, stated that traditional opposition to criminal law enforcement by the armed forces may be outdated. Paul Wolfowitz, deputy secretary of defense, later publicly agreed with him.

In July 2002, the White House released its National Strategy for Homeland Security which recommended a "thorough review of the laws permitting the military to act [domestically]." Later, General Ralph E. Eberhart, the head of the newly created Northern Command, who commands all military forces within the United States, commented, "We should always be reviewing . . . Posse Comitatus and other laws which we think tie our hands in protecting the American people."[1] The Posse Comitatus law was adopted after the Civil War to keep federal troops from performing civilian police duties.

While acknowledging that new terrorist threats have arisen, this chapter argues that giving our armed forces greater control over civilian law enforcement will not defeat terrorism and could permanently impair our freedoms and liberty. One of the driving forces for American independence was disgust at the intrusion of the British military into daily life. The Declaration of Independence condemned the British rulers for keeping a large standing Army in the colonies without the consent of the colonial legislature. It also criticized the fact that this military was "independent of, and superior to, civil power."

America's Constitution sets three controlling principles for her military: first, the militias of the separate states will be the first line of defense for the new country; second, any standing Army will be kept small; and last, civilian control of the military is a bedrock principle. Because the first two principles have been completely eroded in the twentieth century, the third principle of civilian dominance is more important than ever. One of the more radical Founding Fathers, now better known as a premium brand of beer, declared: "A standing Army is always dangerous to the liberties of the People. Soldiers are apt to consider themselves [apart] from other citizens. They always have arms in hand and their rules and discipline are severe."[2]

The Constitution assumes the need for a standing Army by promising each state a "republican form of government" and to protect them "against invasion and domestic violence."[3] Until the Civil War broke out in 1861, the federal military remained small, under forty thousand troops, in relation to the state militias. As secession by the Confederacy appeared inevitable, Congress began to exercise its Constitutional power to "call forth the Militias(s), execute the laws of the union, suppress insurrections and repel invasions."[4]

The framers struck a delicate balance by authorizing a federal military while hoping that civilian control could keep it from evolving into a tyrannical force: "The President shall be the Commander in Chief of the Army and Navy and of the (state) militias when call(ed) into service."[5] In addition, the first five Constitutional amendments were adopted to protect citizens directly or indirectly from abuses associated with the British military.[6]

The Federalist Papers consist of illuminating essays that discuss various issues debated by the Constitution framers. In one, Alexander Hamilton argued that although the Constitution authorizes a standing Army, state militias should keep it on the sidelines. He also contrasted what he called "civilian values (of) liberty, democracy, equality and peace" with "military values of obedience, hierarchy, force and war." James Madison explains in another essay that the Second Amendment right to bear arms was designed to ensure that a well-armed citizenry could fight back if a standing Army became tyrannical.[7]

During America's first fifty years, there was little friction between the standing Army and citizens, primarily because state militias were commonly called upon to deal with insurrections or enforce federal laws. However, as the poisonous stain of slavery spread, this began to change. Federal military officers followed a practice of appointing citizen posses to conduct various operations. When these posses began to apprehend runaway slaves and return them to their owners they became controversial, at least in the North.

SLAVERY ENDS: JIM CROW TAKES ITS PLACE

After the Confederacy's defeat in the Civil War, thousands of northern troops occupied much of the South, but only for a brief period. As troops were withdrawn, southern whites formed vigilante groups, like the Ku Klux Klan which terrorized black Americans who dared to own property, vote, or hold office. In some areas, the violence was truly horrific. Over a thousand black citizens were murdered by white mobs in just one three-month period in Louisiana in 1868.[8]

When federal troops responded to some of these attacks, they earned the undying enmity of southern whites. Many northern officers also found this garrison duty distasteful. One historian writes, "Commanding General Sherman, like his officers, was concerned about the future of the professional soldier. He has convinced that acting as constables or bailiffs was beneath a soldier's vocation."[9]

During the 1876 presidential election, President Grant ordered federal troops, supported by posses, to oversee balloting in South Carolina and

Louisiana. When a deadlock over twenty electoral votes prevented the election of a president, the issue was thrown into the House of Representatives. There, a deal was struck between northern industrialists and southern planters to name Rutherford B. Hayes as president. The northerners won the right to use federal troops as needed to suppress "labor disturbances," while the southerners were promised that all federal troops would be withdrawn from their states.[10]

Within weeks of taking office, Hayes delivered, ordering that half of the occupation troops be withdrawn immediately, with the balance returned to their barracks. That summer, he called out 2,000 federal troops to assist over 40,000 state militiamen who had been deployed against a strike by railroad workers, which had shut down every rail center in the eastern and midwestern United States. Less than a month after the federal troops entered the fray, the strike was broken and the workers returned to work without winning any of their demands.[11]

THE POSSE COMITATUS LAW IS ADOPTED

Posse Comitatus is defined in *Black's Law Dictionary* as "the power or force of the county. The entire population of a county [over] age fifteen, which a sheriff may summon to . . . aid him in keeping the peace, in pursuing and arresting felons, etc."

In response to this use of federal troops on the employer's side and bitter memories in the South, an unlikely alliance of northern and southern Congressmen passed a statute making it a criminal offense to use "any part of the Army as a posse comitatus or otherwise to execute the laws."[12] In 1975, a federal appeals court succinctly summarized the modern purpose of the statute: "It is the nature of their primary mission that military personnel must be trained to operate under circumstances where the protection of constitutional freedoms cannot receive the consideration needed."

Since its adoption 125 years ago, a number of exceptions to the Posse Comitatus law have evolved. Despite the fact the no one has ever been criminally charged for violating the law, it continues to stand for the general principle that the armed forces, except in national emergencies, should not be involved in the enforcement of domestic criminal laws. Although two other laws (the Ku Klux Klan and Civil Rights Acts) adopted in the same period did authorize the president to use troops to protect the civil rights of Americans, white racism was so strong that nearly a century would pass before an American president dared to use this power.

Despite the Posse Comitatus law, a number of presidents continued to use federal troops in labor disputes, claiming that their use in "emergencies" was to ensure "public order," not to "execute" or enforce criminal laws. Two prounion historians summed up some of this violent history as follows: "Federal or state (militia) troops were sent against miners in the bloody strikes at Coeur d'Alene, Idaho in 1892 and 1899, where they were held for months without charges. [Martial law was also imposed for two years during this strike.—Ed.] Thousands of strikers and family members were herded from their homes at Cripple Creek and Telluride, Colorado and loaded into freight cars (like) cattle and deported by the military."[13]

AN EARLY EXAMPLE OF "PRIVATIZATION" OF MILITARY

Partly due to these restraints on the use of troops, the Pinkerton Detective Agency grew to employ more than 30,000 "private" policemen, who intervened on behalf of employers during many of these labor disputes. This private "Army" outnumbered the federal military at the time.

In more recent times, Republican presidents have used federal troops as strikebreakers. Most notable was Nixon's calling out 30,000 soldiers in a futile attempt to have them deliver the mail during a 1970 strike by postal workers. As his first presidential act in 1981, Ronald Reagan permanently fired 12,000 striking air-traffic controllers and operated the nation's airports with military controllers and "replacement" workers.

Another modern development has been efforts by presidents to slow the growth of military budgets by privatizing as many military tasks as possible. In recent years, military mess halls, laundries, maintenance, and even guard posts have been taken over by private contractors who use low-wage workers.

OTHER EXCEPTIONS TO THE POSSE COMITATUS LAW

• Federal troops can be sent to assist local police agencies when they are overwhelmed by serious public disturbances. One of the most infamous uses of federal troops was when General Douglas MacArthur led his troops in a rout of impoverished "Bonus Marchers" who had descended on Washington, D.C., demanding to be paid a promised veteran's bonus.

• National Guard units (formerly state militias) while they're under the command of state governors. The validity of this exemption seems questionable since virtually all of the Guard's costs, including salaries, equipment, and training, are paid for by federal funds.

• The Coast Guard is not considered a military branch, unless mobilized during wartime. The Navy places personnel aboard Coast Guard ships to assist in identifying, pursuing, and seizing ships suspected of drug smuggling.

• Aerial photography and visual surveillance by military aircraft.

NEW ROLE FOR THE NATIONAL GUARD

Dwight Eisenhower was the first president since the Civil War to order a state National Guard "federalized," so that it could be used to protect citizens from racist violence. He broke with precedent in 1957 by sending Guard members to protect black students who had enrolled in Little Rock, Arkansas's all-white public schools. Although he was known to privately oppose the Supreme Court's ruling that ended public segregation, Eisenhower nevertheless felt he had no choice but to use troops to ensure compliance with federal court orders. As later became common practice in the South, he "federalized" Arkansas's National Guard units, thus removing them from the control of a governor who wanted to use them to *enforce* segregation laws.

As urban rebellions and riots broke out in many American cities in the 1960s, Presidents Johnson and Nixon sent both federal troops and "federalized" National Guard units in to quell rioting and restore order. In general, the White House maintained close control over these missions by using high-ranking military officers who reported directly to the White House. Posse Comitatus problems were skirted by using local police officers to actually arrest and incarcerate the looters and rioters. One persistent problem was poorly trained and undisciplined National Guard troops, who shot and killed many innocent bystanders. The most infamous such incidents occurred at Kent State University in Ohio and Jackson State College in Mississippi, where local guardsmen shot and killed unarmed student antiwar protesters.

MILITARY VS. POLICE OPERATIONS

Some argue that a basic philosophical difference between police and military training explains why this type of killing occurs when military troops replace civilian police. Lawrence Korb, a former assistant secretary of defense, stated, "To put it bluntly, the military is trained to vaporize—not Mirandize."[14] A NYU law professor who's also studied the differences has written: "Armies are well organized and trained for killing a more or less well defined enemy; not (to provide) service and law enforcement among a civilian population . . . in situations (where) they have to make fine-grained legal and social distinctions about what action is required."[15]

Military professionals have also expressed doubts about the recent trend of assigning troops to jobs that are essentially law enforcement. Large numbers of US troops have been deployed for peacekeeping duty in Haiti, Bosnia, and Kosovo. Commanders worry that such duties may dull the "combat edge" of their soldiers. For example, GIs are taught "rules of engagement," requiring the use of force that will "decisively counter the hostile act or hostile intent and to ensure the continued safety of US forces." They are also instructed to continue firing "until hostile force no longer presents an imminent threat."[16]

These are the opposite of rules that are taught civilian police officers. They are trained to fire their weapon only as a "last resort," after all other options, including retreat, have been exhausted. The restraint expected of police officers as they comply with various legal rules governing searches, arrests, and interrogations of suspects could be fatal in a combat situation. As one Marine colonel told *Newsweek*, "Combat-trained Marines shouldn't be diminishing hard-learned skills by squeezing off warning shots."[17]

MISSION CREEP: FROM CHASING SPIES TO DOMESTIC SPYING

The Army established its first intelligence corps during World War One. Its initial job was to collect information on the strengths and weaknesses of the German military. However, new missions were added as the corps grew. As one historian described the process. "Army intelligence had become a vast force at home for the first time in history. It [shifted] from counter-espionage to counter-dissent."[18]

Following the Bolshevik revolution in 1917, a new hysteria about the growth of revolutionary movements swept Washington. This spurred the renamed Military Intelligence Division (MID) to accelerate spying on thousands of innocuous organizations and citizens. "War Plan White" was developed to coordinate a domestic war against radicalism.[19] The name was probably inspired by the "Whites" who had invaded the Soviet Union and fought a bloody civil war against the Bolsheviks, vainly hoping to overthrow their "Red" revolution. Plan White was put into effect on two occasions: first during the Depression-era fiasco with the Bonus Army marchers and again during Detroit's race riot of 1943.

The MID continued to search for disloyalty and subversion, carried along in the wake of the anti-Bolshevik hysteria that consumed the White House in 1919–20. "No Army agency had ever stepped so directly into political activity or collaborated so closely with civilian antiradical groups. MID operated with so substantive civilian oversight," wrote another historian of the period.[20]

On another front, the Attorney General was conducting his eponymous "Palmer Raids," which generated hundreds of arrests, detentions, and deportations of suspected radicals. In 1920, he chose an ambitious young lawyer to head his Radical Division. Over the next fifty years, J. Edgar Hoover worked tirelessly to ensure that his beloved FBI controlled as much of the "bureaucratic turf" focused on subversion and the Communist threat as possible.[21] This megalomania probably led him to oppose some of the military's more ambitious Red-hunting schemes.

RACISM MIXED WITH FEAR: A DEADLY COMBINATION

It is critical to discuss a dark chapter when the American military was used to intern 120,000 Japanese Americans, over half of them U.S. citizens, for the duration of World War Two. Following Japan's surprise attack on Pearl Harbor, Hawaii, on December 7, 1941, the commander of the Western Division Command in San Francisco recommended that all persons of Japanese ancestry be interned. General John De Witt argued that the defense of the West Coast depended upon such forcible evacuations. Before long, California's governor and attorney general, along with Los Angeles's mayor, endorsed De Witt's plan, deferring no doubt to his military expertise. (In one of history's ironies, Earl Warren, California's attorney general, later wrote, as chief justice of the US Supreme Court, the historic *Brown vs. Board of Education* decision, which outlawed racial segregation.)

One historian of the internment program has speculated that General De Witt's logic was determined by his "military mindset." Working from a worst-case scenario common to the military, he likely thought, "if Japan actually invaded California, how can we best stop some of our local Japanese from aiding them?"[22] Racism also played a part in General De Witt's thinking. In testimony before a House committee considering internment, he stated. "A Jap's a Jap. . . . There's no way to determine their loyalty. It makes no difference whether he is an American. Theoretically, he's still Japanese and you can't change him."[23] One civil liberty attorney charges that while the Bush administration officially speaks against ethnic profiling of Muslims and those of Arab descent, it has "sent a very different message through its law enforcement policies." Otherwise, why would virtually all of the noncitizen residents detained by the Justice Department since 9/11 be a member of one or the other groups?

In 1950, Congress adopted a law that created a contingency plan for rounding up citizens who were suspected of being potential subversives. By the mid-1950s, the names of over 26,000 Americans had been collected on a secret list. The law was finally repealed in 1971.[24]

As we've seen from the current occupation of Iraq, elected officials are very reluctant to criticize military commanders once fighting has commenced. At the time, Earl Warren was planning to run as California's governor and was rumored to aspire to the presidency. For whatever reason, he reversed his initial opposition to internment when he wrote, "I've concluded that the Japanese situation . . . may well be the Achilles heel of the entire civilian defense effort."[25]

Once President Roosevelt signed Executive Order 9066, authorizing internment, General De Witt divided the West Coast states into "military areas," from which all persons of Japanese ancestry were banned. Army units forcibly removed 120,000 Japanese residents, of whom 70,000 were citizens, from their homes. They were sent to twenty rustic camps in rural parts of the western states, where most remained until the war ended.[26] J. Edgar Hoover came up with an Orwellian term for these citizens: "Japanese non-aliens."

Lawyers brought three different appeals to the Supreme Court challenging the constitutionality of the internment program. Each time, they were turned away by a close vote. In one case, normally liberal Justice William Douglas wrote, "We cannot sit in judgment on the military requirements of the hour."[27] In one famous dissent, Justice Frank Murphy nailed the fundamental flaw at the heart of the internment program—"military necessity": "Not one person of Japanese ancestry was accused or convicted of sabotage after Pearl Harbor while (they were) still free." He concluded, "I dissent, therefore, from this legalization of racism."[28]

Forty years later, the Commission of Wartime Relocation and Internment of Citizens, a blue-ribbon panel, issued a report condemning the unlawful incarceration of Japanese residents and citizens.[29] Its recommendation that the federal government make a formal apology and pay reparations to each internee or their survivors was accepted.

DÉJÀ VU ALL OVER AGAIN?

One could easily argue that the federal government's treatment of at least 2,000 resident Arab and/or Muslim noncitizens after September 11 is not much different from our earlier treatment of the Japanese. Even though there are currently an estimated *eight million* illegal immigrants living in the United States, virtually all those detained or arrested after September 11 have been Muslims and/or Arabs. In hundreds of these cases, they were detained, interrogated, confined, and then forcibly deported to their original homelands, leaving wives and children, who are often citizens, behind.[30] Only a handful were ever prosecuted for a terrorist-related crime.

Recently, the Supreme Court let stand a lower-court ruling that allowed the Bush administration to keep the identities of these detainees secret.[31] The Justice Department's inspector general did publish a report strongly criticizing these detentions.[32] One can only wonder if, forty years from now, another commission will be convened to assess the irreparable harm done to thousands of Muslim residents who were torn from their families and careers solely because of their religious affiliation or country of origin.

THE CIVIL RIGHTS AND ANTI-VIETNAM WAR MOVEMENTS: THREATS TO NATIONAL SECURITY?

When the American military was reorganized following World War Two, a furious bureaucratic battle was waged over a proposal to fold the Marine Corps into the Army. When the Marines survived as an autonomous entity, albeit as a branch of the Navy, Harry Truman wisecracked, "The Marine Corps is a landing party that got out of control."

Something similar happened with the Army's military intelligence corps in the 1950s. In 1957, military agents were sent to Little Rock, Arkansas, to help identify groups and individuals who were working to defy court orders to integrate the schools. Since 3,000 National Guard and federal troops were at some risk from attack by white vigilantes while enforcing court orders, this surveillance seemed appropriate. However, within a few years, a small network of military spies in mufti had ballooned into fifteen hundred plainclothes agents operating from 304 field and resident offices nationwide. They created files on thousands of Americans who were "guilty" only of advocating for civil rights or organizing against the escalating Vietnam War.[33]

In its final report, *Military Surveillance of Civilian Politics,* the Senate Judiciary Committee drew two important conclusions: "Army surveillance of civilians engaging in political activities in the 1960s was massive and unrestrained. The chief subjects were protest groups and demonstrators whose activities the Army attempted to relate to its civil disturbance mission." The committee complained that it took the Army's civilian leaders two full years to bring the spying under control after it was first disclosed. Their report expressed a related concern: "We have only the assurance of the Army and Executive Branch that domestic intelligence files have been destroyed. No independent inspection has been permitted. We've (been) assured that surveillance will not resume, but we cannot evaluate the worth of that assurance."[34]

At another point, the committee disagreed with the Supreme Court decision in *Tatum vs. Laird*: "The simple allegation that one's First Amendment rights have been abridged should be sufficient to invoke the courts' jurisdiction. . . . the Court should have found that the military surveillance is a violation of the First Amendment. We conclude that military surveillance was both unauthorized and in violation of the First Amendment."

According to *Army Surveillance in America,* once the antiwar movement began to challenge the military on several fronts, spying on civilians mushroomed. The protesters challenged the legality and morality of the war in Vietnam, the draft systems, as well as campus-based defense research and ROTC training. Military agents' involvement in the conduct of background investigations for security clearances often brought them into close contact with local and campus police units.[35]

A FEW GOOD MEN

As the history of the My Lai massacre shows, sometimes it takes only one honest soldier to bring out the truth about some dark military secret. In this case, Christopher Pyle was a young ROTC officer, who trained, along with hundreds of other soldiers, to spy on civilians for the military at Ft. Holabird, Maryland. He felt that such spying was illegal and began to write about his experiences. When he was published in a small Washington magazine, the media and then Congress began to pick up on the issue.[36]

Following a public outcry, the Army promised Congress that it would cease secret spying, but it continued to collect unverified information for its computerized data bases, which it continued to exchange with the FBI, local police units, and campus security agencies.[37] A number of states and large cities, such as New York, also created their own "red squads" to spy on alleged subversives and dissidents. One historian argues that the Army's spying touched a sensitive nerve because "military investigations of civilian protests was precisely the kind of abuse by standing armies that the Eighteenth Century anti-militarists had feared."[38]

Although the Nixon White House issued statements condemning the military's spy program, it covertly sanctioned similar programs that were run by the FBI. One example was the COINTELPRO operation, which was originally created in 1956 to investigate the Communist Party. In the early 1960s, it shifted its attention to the Socialist Workers Party and then broadened its focus to the Civil Rights and antiwar movements. FBI Director Hoover was an enthusiastic advocate, calling for "harassment and disruption" of black organizations and leaders, even when their activities were completely lawful. In one COINTELPRO memo he expressed his hope that the program could "prevent the rise of a black messiah who would unify and electrify the black nationalist movement."[39]

For its own dark reasons, the Nixon White House created its own clandestine spy operation, dubbed the "Huston Plan." One of its "black bag" jobs was the botched Watergate break-in, which eventually led to Nixon's impeachment and resignation.

A number of antiwar activists, joined by conservative-libertarian Senator Sam Ervin (D-NC), filed a lawsuit (*Tatum vs. Laird*) that asked the Supreme Court to declare that military spying abridged their rights to free speech and association. A closely divided Court rejected their claim, ruling that such surveillance served legitimate "national security" needs and that the claimants had failed to show how they'd been injured by the spying.[40]

A number of other federal and state agencies also regularly spied on civilians. One was the CIA's mail-monitoring program, which surreptitiously opened 215,000 pieces of mail over a twenty-year period, beginning in 1953. Over a million-and-a-half names and addresses were taken from these letters and entered in the CIA's computerized database.[41]

As mentioned, one favorable result of congressional alarm over the pervasive spying on civilians was its repeal of the detention provisions of the Internal Security Act. In 1952, Congress had also authorized the creation of six detention centers, in Arizona, California, Florida, Oklahoma, and Pennsylvania, where "detainees" were to be sent in case a "national emergency" was declared. When Congress adopted the Non-Detention Act it declared that, "No citizen shall be imprisoned or otherwise detained by the (government) except pursuant to an act of Congress."[42] In December 2003 the Second Circuit Court of Appeals relied, in part, on this law in ordering the release of Jose Padilla, an

American citizen whom the Bush administration had been indefinitely detaining without filing charges.[43] Padilla's confinement without charges is currently under review by the Supreme Court.

NO LEGISLATION BARRING SURVEILLANCE

Both the Ervin and Church Senate Committees documented and publicized a large amount of information about the Pentagon's and FBI's programs of covert surveillance. Unfortunately, legislative proposals by the Church Committee, which would have outlawed such spying, failed to win passage.

Instead, FBI Director Edward Levi issued administrative guidelines that restricted surveillance to persons who were reasonably suspected of engaging in criminal activities. Over time, pressure grew to relax these restrictions, as Attorney General William French did in 1983. He allowed spying where a "reasonable indication" of criminal conduct—not probable cause, as required by the Fourth and Fifth Amendments—existed. Then, after 9/11, Attorney General John Ashcroft issued even more permissive guidelines. FBI agents are now allowed to initiate a full investigation whenever "facts or circumstances reasonably indicate that a federal crime has been, is being, or will be com-smitted."[44]

INCIDENT AT WOUNDED KNEE: POSSE COMITATUS IN THE COURTS

The 1960s were a time of political ferment when social movements came to life in part because of the dynamism of the Civil Rights and anti–Vietnam war movements. The American Indian Movement (AIM) began organizing Native Americans to fight for social justice. They alienated the old-boy network of tribal elders and the Federal Bureau of Indian Affairs by challenging their control of tribal affairs.[45]

One bitter struggle evolved at the Sioux reservation at Wounded Knee, South Dakota. AIM activists occupying a trading post had refused federal agents' demands that they withdraw. U.S. military advisors were at the scene to advise and assist the federal agents. After a shootout in which two FBI agents and one AIM member were killed, a number of AIM leaders were convicted of various crimes and sent to prison. In the aftermath, several AIM supporters attempted to sue the federal government, contending that the military's aid to local police had violated the Posse Comitatus Act (PCA). Three different federal courts applied different tests to determine if the military had violated the PCA.

In the first ruling, the court held that there had to be "direct active use" of military personnel for there to be a Posse Comitatus violation.[46] It found that providing military equipment and supplies didn't qualify as "active" use of the military. In a criminal case, the court asked whether the military's conduct "pervaded the activities" of the civilian police officers.[47] Although the court didn't find a violation of PCA, it ruled that the evidence cast doubt on whether the authorities were "lawfully engaged in the performance of their official duties." Therefore it dismissed an indictment for obstructing law-enforcement officers. A third ruling proposed that the test for PCA violation should be whether "military personnel subjected citizens to (conduct) which was regulatory, proscriptive, or compulsory in nature."[48] While neither of the civil plaintiffs succeeded in winning damages based on Posse Comitatus violations, these rulings demonstrate that the doctrine potentially can still be used where military units "execute" domestic law.

The confrontation at Wounded Knee was also an early case study in how the military implemented its Operation Garden Plot scenario. The American Indian Movement takeover of the trading post had "triggered" the Army's contingency plan for domestic disturbance. According to *Army Surveillance in America,* "Emergency Plan White—now codenamed "Garden Plot"—brought in the Army. Three Army colonels disguised as civilians and reconnaissance planes assisted. . . . [Ignoring] the Posse Comitatus Act, the Justice Department used the Army to conduct intelligence for civilian law enforcement."[49]

THREE HUNDRED BILLION UP IN SMOKE: CHASING THE DRAGON

One depressing trend in politics today is the tendency of elected officials to use war terminology when discussing various social problems such as poverty, hunger, AIDS, or drug use. Let's talk about the "war on drugs." The use of the term "war" is intended to be polarizing. In wars, the "good" side battles the forces of "evil." Eliminating drugs becomes white against black, with no shades of gray. A British press baron in the nineteenth century explained it as follows: "War not only supplies the news, it creates the demand for it."

Today declarations of "war" are still useful in garnering media attention. The Murdoch / Fox brand of tabloid journalism, which grows ever more popular, loves a simplistic, "good guy, bad guy" war story. "War" provides the red meat of sensational headlines, lurid plot twists, dazzling photographs of suitcases crammed with C-notes, and drug "perps" who are indistinguishable from the cops who drag them into court. Therefore, it's no accident that a media-savvy candidate like Ronald Reagan would pick the "war on drugs" as a theme for his presidential campaign. It fit perfectly with his overall theme—that America was in military and moral decline.

Reagan was actually borrowing a page from the playbook of Richard Nixon, who'd launched the first "war on drugs" back in 1971. One hilarious photo from that dubious battle shows Nixon pinning an honorary DEA agent's badge on Elvis Presley, a raging drug addict.

The fact that a large percentage of illegal drugs consumed by Americans aren't imported, but rather are produced domestically, didn't seem to register with Reagan's drug warriors. Marijuana, amphetamines, LSD, ecstasy, etc., were produced on farms and in drug labs spread across America. Later, when the ballyhooed campaign to stop the importing of drugs flopped, the military turned its National Guard helicopters and herbicide spray planes loose on marijuana crops, especially on the West Coast.

Emotions ran high when Congress debated Reagan's proposal to amend the Posse Comitatus law to allow the military to play drug cop. One proponent, US Rep. Charles Bennett (D-FL), enlisted the memory of his son, who'd died of an overdose, in the cause. Another congressman, Stewart McKinney (R-CT), described his daughter as drug addicted and begged for military help: "Interdict the slimiest, lousiest enemy . . . those who profit off killing our kids. . . . is it not the job of the military to protect this country and its future, for God's sake?"[50]

Within a year of Reagan's election, Congress had approved his request to allow the military to participate fully in civilian law-enforcement efforts against drug smuggling. However, soldiers were still barred from search, seizure, arrest, and similar activities.[51] In the quest for a quick fix, a basic fact was ignored: thousands of state and local police, as well as the Border Patrol, Customs, and the Drug Enforcement Administration agents, had miserably failed to staunch the flow of drugs.

To the surprise of some, image-conscious First Lady Nancy Reagan threw herself into the antidrug crusade. She made regular visits to drug treatment centers, sometimes with luminaries like Princess Diana in tow.[52]

Alas, the "silver bullet" of military intervention possessed no magic. "Only an incurable optimist would argue that America's thirty year war on drugs has been a success," wrote one observer. "Despite $300 billion (spent) by federal, state, and local governments . . . drugs remain cheap and easily available throughout the U.S."[53]

As much as anything, it was the explosive growth of international travel and the conversion to cargo containers that doomed any effort to stop imported drugs. The Customs Agency estimates that today it can inspect less than 3 percent of the nine million cargo containers that land in the United States each year.[54] A similar problem exists with people who arrive in the United States by airplane, private auto, or boat. Only a tiny fraction of the forty-two million airlines passengers who are expected to enter the United States in 2004 can be searched for drugs.[55] For every "drug mule" who's apprehended, a hundred or a thousand more slip through.

The extreme poverty and geography of drug-producing countries such as Pakistan, Afghanistan, Burma, Laos, Colombia or Peru makes it virtually impossible to stop drugs at the point of production. A recent White House study reported that Afghanistan had 152,000 acres of opium poppies used to make heroin and morphine under cultivation in 2003. This compares with 4,210 acres of poppies just two years earlier when the Taliban still ruled.[56] A UN study estimates that the country now accounts for three-fourths of the world's opium production.

A classic book, *The Politics of Heroin,* describes how the CIA paid the Afghani mujahedin warlords to fight the Soviet military occupation in the 1980s while ignoring their export of large quantities of heroin to the West.[57] One Al Qaeda expert recently suggested that even if western countries were able to freeze the terrorists' bank accounts and stop foreign donations, the profits from heroin sales are sufficient to bankroll Osama bin Laden and his network in the future.[58]

THE PENTAGON TRIES TO WIN ONE FOR THE GIPPER

Despite the misgivings of career military officers, the Pentagon's formidable public-relations machinery began to spew forth optimistic assessments of this new mission. Win or lose, they knew that under Reagan their budgets would continue to grow. In fact, they nearly *doubled* during his eight years in office. In the first years, Reagan's budgeters paid for the military's interdiction efforts by diverting more than $700 million from drug-treatment and education programs.[59] It took public officials years to realize that reducing *demand* for drugs was a better approach than trying to restrict their *availability.*

During the 1980s, lurid media accounts about the "crack-cocaine epidemic" and apocalyptic warnings by Reagan's "drug czar" William Bennett kept Congress clamoring for a greater military role. One voice against the hysteria was Defense Secretary Caspar Weinberger. He feared that using troops in the drug wars would undermine their military readiness, and it wasn't cost-effective. He spoke against further amending the Posse Comitatus law, warning that it would violate the "historic separation between military and civilian spheres of activity. . . . we strongly oppose the extension of civilian police powers to our military forces."[60]

Sometimes a public issue, like drug use and crack cocaine, becomes so highly charged that Congress simply demands something be done. This seems to be what happened when it broadened the law to allow the Pentagon to invade other countries where illicit drugs are produced. Bolivia was the first target of American drug warriors, who were sent in 1986 to destroy its coca fields as part of Operation Blast Furnace. The military conducted many other such forays in the following years. Domestically, the Pentagon established three joint task forces, which were assigned different parts of the United States to patrol in coordination with other police agencies. Joint Task Force Six became the most important since it had responsibility for the Mexican and Canadian borders.

Early in the Pentagon's drug campaign, it commissioned the Rand Corporation to study the pros and cons of drug interdiction by the armed forces. Its comprehensive report, published in 1988, which concluded that even with a major commitment of resources the military could only slightly reduce drug smuggling, was virtually ignored.[61]

SOLDIERS AND COPS: TWO DIFFERENT BREEDS

Working as part of Task Force Six, a Marine antismuggling patrol in south Texas killed a young American goatherd, Esequiel Hernandez, in 1991. The Marine Corps defended the shooters, claiming that they were following military rules of engagement. The Corps refused to assist the local grand jury probing the killing and transferred the Marines out of state. Following this episode, there was discussion in the Pentagon about how to protect GIs from civilian prosecutors when they followed military rules of engagement.[62]

Hernandez's killing touched off intense public controversy over the proper role of the armed forces in local police work. Three years later, the military had still not sent GIs back to patrol the border areas of Texas. Eventually, the federal government paid the boy's family $1.9 million to settle their civil lawsuit.

MILITARIZING AMERICA'S POLICE

As part of the antidrug crusade, Congress passed the Military Cooperation with Civilian Law Enforcement Agencies Act in 1981. This authorized the military to train local police agencies in military tactics and to supply them with surplus weapons and other military gear.[63] This opened the floodgates to the training of hundreds of police departments by "special ops" units like the Army's Green Berets and Rangers, as well as the Navy's SEALS. They drilled civilian police units in the strategy and tactics of standard urban-warfare doctrine, called Advanced Military Operations on Urbanized Terrain (AMOUT). Before long virtually every American city could deploy a paramilitary unit (PPU) or SWAT (Special Weapons and Tactics) team. A majority of these teams had been trained by active-duty specialists.[64]

The net effect of this training is that civilian police units, especially in larger urban areas, have adopted aggressive military-style tactics and use more lethal weapons. This has caused an increased number of civilian injuries and deaths, which in turn means more civil lawsuits. It has been estimated that these special-weapons units now conduct about 40,000 drug raids each year.[65]

OPERATION GARDEN PLOT: BLUEPRINT FOR MILITARY TAKEOVER?

This clandestine program has its origins in the urban riots that swept American cities in the 1960s. "Garden Plot" is military code for an elaborate plan for military intervention in concert with civilian police in periods of civil unrest. The plan's formal title is DOD Civil Disturbance Plan 55-2, "Operation Garden Plot." It was first disclosed publicly during Senate Subcommittee on Constitutional Rights hearings in 1971. The hearings focused on details of the Army's vast surveillance of civilians, which was discussed earlier.

The primary consumer of this domestic intelligence was the Directorate of Military Support, which operated from a "domestic war room" in the basement of the Pentagon. Staffed by 150 people using data-processing machines, closed-circuit TVs, teletype networks, and elaborate situation maps, the operation used the latest technology.[66]

Operation Garden Plot is a detailed plan to integrate active-duty, National Guard, and local police units when responding to major civil disturbances. Both active and reserve units are trained to "resolve urban conflicts," using planning packets which provide contingency plans for joint military-civilian operations for every city in the United States. A special course for senior officers was created at Ft. Stewart, Georgia, to train them to maneuver in politically sensitive operations.[67]

Periodically, the Army has updated and revised the manuals that provide guidance for domestic operations. *Domestic Support Operations,* dated July 1, 1993, summarizes its mission: "Today, the U.S. calls upon its Army to perform various functions . . . for example, controlling civil disturbances. (We) provid(e) operational and non-operational support to law enforcement . . . and can be a formidable force-multiplier for civil authorities."[68] *Military Assistance for Civil Disturbances,* a DOD directive, states that the Army, as lead agency, "shall provide guidance to other DOD components through . . . the Plan (Garden Plot)."

Since 1994, many Army and Marine combat units have undergone special "Urban Warrior" training at the Army's Special Operations Command at Ft. Bragg, North Carolina. Training objectives include improving "domestic national security" by conducting operations in "an urban environment against a backdrop of civil unrest (to) restore order." On the training center's Web site, Col. Mark Thiffault wrote with more foresight than he may have realized, "Potential foes view cities as a way to limit the technological advantage of our military. They know that cities, narrow streets, confusing layout and large numbers of civilian non-combatants place limits on our techno-superiority and especially our use of firepower."[69] Hello, Baghdad!

In 1998, the Marine Corps published a 350-page manual, *Military Operations on Urbanized Terrain*. Some military analysts have urged all the service branches to adopt this as the bible for urban-war fighting.[70] It describes in detail offensive and defensive operations in cities. It also provides a comprehensive overview of logistics, organization, combat weapons, and tactics. It describes urban areas as "incredibly complicated and fluid environments," which may be "significant sources of future conflict." However, the manual reveals a parochial and rural mindset when it states, "Cities are historically where radical ideas ferment, dissenters find allies, a mixture of people cause ethnic friction, and discontented groups receive media attention." It notes that unlike conventional warfare "urban intervention must often be planned and executed in a matter of hours or days, to take advantage of the turmoil surrounding a developing crisis."[71]

Although Operation Garden Plot remains current military doctrine and is unclassified, details are releasable only to military personnel. When rioting broke out in Los Angeles in 1992 after the acquittal of the police who had assaulted Rodney King, President Clinton quickly signed an executive order creating the Joint Task Force—Los Angeles. This provided the legal basis for sending thousands of reserve and active-duty GIs into the streets of Los Angeles to restore order. When a California National Guard commander later wrote about the riot experience, he described the "DOD Civil Disturbance (Garden Plot) plan," dated February 15, 1991, as the standard "source."[72] Should civil disturbances erupt within America's cities in the future, it seems certain that active-duty GIs will be immediately deployed according to the Operation Garden Plot game plan.

THE STRYKER VEHICLE: FUTURE URBAN WARRIOR?

Defense Secretary Donald Rumsfeld has advocated a transformation of the American military into a highly mobile and flexible military force. He wants to shift the emphasis away from slow-moving, heavily armored units to lightly armed units that can be deployed in a matter of days to any place on the globe.

Rumsfeld has endorsed the development of the Stryker vehicle and recently arranged for three hundred of them to be battlefield tested in Iraq. A lightly armed tank, which weighs two-thirds less than the main battle tank, it is described in Army materials as designed "to resolve urban unrest, infiltrate and clear buildings and fight at close range."

The Stryker can only operate where there are rudimentary roads, since it is equipped with tires, not tracks. Because of its speed—up to 65 mph—and ability to carry up to eleven soliders, it enjoys an advantage over both tanks and the Bradley vehicle. It carries only a .50-caliber machine gun and grenade launcher, and its light armor cannot repel rockets or bombs. Since rocket-propelled grenades (RPGs) are a constant hazard in Iraq, the Strykers in Iraq have been fitted with special "slat armor" to help deflect them. However, since this plating adds 5,000 pounds in weight, the Strykers now must be deployed by ship, not C-130 cargo jets. This, in turn, works against one of the vehicle's selling points: that it can be deployed anywhere in the world within 96 hours.[73] If the Strykers prove themselves useful in Iraq, it is likely that they will become standard issue for National Guard and reserve units throughout urban America.

THE WACO TRAGEDY: MILITARY OVERKILL

The marriage of military and conventional police tactics that was encouraged by Reagan's antidrug crusade caused a major catastrophe near Waco, Texas. The Branch Davidians, a cultish offshoot of the Seventh Day Adventists, had withdrawn to a fortified compound in which several hundred adherents lived. The Bureau of Alcohol, Tobacco and Firearms (ATF) had targeted the cult in the mistaken belief that its members were manufacturing drugs and stockpiling weapons. The ATF badly botched its initial raid, causing a firefight, in which four ATF agents and six Branch Davidians were killed.

A prolonged seven-week siege followed, during which time the ATF and Texas law-enforcement agencies received advice and training from both the

Joint Task Force Six and the Army's ultrasecret Delta Force. The JTF-6 provided weapons and equipment, while the Delta Force reportedly helped plan the second attack.

One bestselling account of the tragedy charges that the ATF and local law-enforcement officials hyped allegations about drug manufacture at the compound as a way to secure as much federal military help as possible.[74] Unfounded allegations about sexual abuse of the children living at the compound were leaked to the media and soon spread throughout the nation. This apparently convinced newly appointed Attorney General Janet Reno to give her approval for a second assault.[75]

When ATF agents and local police attacked the compound, they used M-60 tanks and Bradley Fighting Vehicles, from which they fired CS gas canisters. (This weapon had been banned by international treaty six months earlier, but Reno later claimed ignorance of this fact.) As the tanks punched holes in the buildings' walls, they caused oil lamps to ignite. The complex nearly burned to the ground by the time the fire trucks arrived.

The Waco tragedy demonstrates what can happen when military weapons and tactics are employed in a situation where negotiation—not firepower—should have been employed. The nation was shocked by a military assault that killed seventy-six civilians, including twenty-seven children. Some far-right groups later accused the Pentagon of a power grab to supplant local law enforcement and to nullify the Posse Comitatus Act. However, a congressional investigation, chaired by a politically conservative lawmaker, disagreed: "We found no evidence that any (soldier) at Waco violated the Posse Comitatus Act. Available evidence indicates that the U.S. Special Forces Command (was) present but . . . they acted only as observers and technicians."[76] The parent agency of the ATF, the Treasury Department, performed another postmortem, which found "The law enforcement officials botched virtually every aspect of their plan to capture the (cult leader) and then . . . misled Congress about their mistakes."[77]

THE WAR ON TERROR: PART ONE

It is better to be feared than loved.

—Machiavelli, *The Prince*

Using the threat of terrorism as justification for preemptive strikes and reprisal raids abroad first appeared in a secret National Security Decision Directive 138, signed by President Ronald Reagan in April 1984. He signed this policy document in response to the bombing of the Marine barracks in Beirut, Lebanon, which had killed 241 Marines a few months earlier.[78]

The first known Al Qaeda attack on American troops was the bombing of a hotel in Yemen in December 1992. The target was US troops on a humanitarian mission, but they escaped injury.[79] Just two months later, Al Qaeda achieved worldwide notoriety by setting off a massive car bomb in the basement of the World Trade Center. Six civilians were killed and hundreds injured as both mammoth towers had to be evacuated. Few realized at the time that Al Qaeda had hoped to collapse one tower into the other, causing thousands of casualties.

Almost a decade before September 11, federal authorities began to understand that America was facing a serious threat from a well-organized terrorist group. As part of this recognition, President Clinton signed an executive order declaring that "the proliferation of nuclear, biological, and chemical weapons and the means of delivering them" constituted a national emergency. When a huge bomb brought down the federal office building in Oklahoma City, killing 168 civilians and injuring hundreds more, federal terrorist experts feared that it might be the work of Al Qaeda. According to Stephen Jones, Tim McVeigh's lawyer, immediately after the bombing the FBI Counter-Terrorism Center put out a directive that "all CIA stations search . . . for possible leads among foreign terrorist groups."[80] Jones also claims that co-defendant Terry Nichols made at least six trips to the Philippines prior to the bombing, where he could have met with Al Qaeda operatives.[81] Finally, he alleges that Yakov Yerushalmi, an Israeli explosives expert, visited the bomb site and wrote a report that attributed the "bomb's design to Arab sources."[82] Even if there was no link between the bombing and Al Qaeda, the explosion took place on the second anniversary of the Waco assault, and Tim McVeigh later told interrogators that he considered Oklahoma City revenge for all the innocents killed at Waco.

The killing of nineteen American service members in the Khobar Towers bombing in Dhahran, Saudi Arabia, the following year erased any doubt that America's foreign military bases were being systematically targeted. The refusal of the Saudi government to fully cooperate with American investigators was one measure of the fear that Osama bin Laden and Al Qaeda engendered in the Muslim world. Two months later, Osama bin Laden issued a worldwide call to Muslims to join a jihad (in Arabic, "struggle," in the religious sense) in his "Declaration of War Against the Americans Occupying the Land of the Two Holy Mosques."[83]

Congress passed the Defense Against Weapons of Mass Destruction Act in 1996 because of the escalating terror campaign. This act provides the bureaucratic structure and funding so that federal, state, and local emergency workers can be trained to respond properly to threats of weapons of mass destruction (WMD). The law also assesses federal capabilities and shortcomings in responding to various WMD threats. It names the Army Soldier Biological-Chemical Command as "lead agency" for training civilian "first responders."[84]

In an effort to restrict terrorist access and fundraising in the United States, Congress also adopted in 1996 the Antiterrorist and Effective Death Penalty Act. This law gives the secretary of state authority to designate groups as "terrorist organizations." It then becomes a crime to give money or other material support to any such group, even if the gift is for social or humanitarian programs. All members of the designated groups are barred from entering the United States, and any noncitizen found here is deportable. Finally, banks must freeze and report any assets belonging to such organizations.[85] Civil-liberties lawyer David Cole has written that prosecutors like to use these "material support" statutes because "they don't require proof that an individual intended to further terrorist activity. (This) is a classic instance of guilt by association." [86]

Although by 1998 the United States was spending at least $50 billion annually to combat terrorism, Al Qaeda was able to pull off two more spectacular bombings, this time of American embassies in Kenya and Tanzania, killing 301 civilians, including twelve Americans, and injuring hundreds more. Urged to retaliate, President Clinton approved the hopefully named Operation Infinite Reach. This involved five US warships, stationed in the Arabian and Red Seas, firing eighty Tomahawk cruise missiles, mostly into suspected Al Qaeda camps in remote parts of Afghanistan. A secondary target was the Al-Shifa (in Arabic, "cure" or "healing") pharmaceutical plant in the Sudan, which the Pentagon suspected of producing VX gas. After US missiles demolished the factory, Human Rights Watch condemned the attack both for killing innocent civilians and for destroying medical supplies badly needed by as many as 2.4 million Sudanese.[87]

THE WAR ON TERROR: PART TWO

> Americans feel (very) vulnerable today. President Clinton once observed that at such moments (they) prefer a message that is "strong and wrong" to one that is "weak and right."
>
> —James Traub, *New York Times*

After the devastating attacks of September 11th, most Americans harbored a strong desire to strike back against the shadowy Al Qaeda network. The spectacular success of the terrorist skyjackers made it clear that our previous efforts to punish or deter them had failed miserably. In a highly charged atmosphere in which fear and anger seemed nearly balanced, President Bush quickly won broad bipartisan support for his plan to invade Afghanistan and oust those who had given sanctuary to Al Qaeda. Within weeks, thousands of American troops, many of them special-ops fighters, were streaming into

Afghanistan. No match for such a powerful foe, many of the Taliban's irregular troops, along with at least command elements of Al Qaeda, melted away into their remote mountain redoubts and trickled across the country's porous borders into exile.

In the aftershocks of 9/11, Americans welcomed the presence of thousands of National Guard troops patrolling our airports, highway bridges, and even the subways of New York. The sight of reservists in their camouflage fatigues, M-16 rifles at the ready, provided an illusion that we were at least for the moment, safe from terrorist violence.

Soon, George Bush was able to announce that the Taliban had been ousted, replaced by a regime that was friendly to America. But the principal objective of our invasion of Afghanistan—the destruction of the Al Qaeda terrorist network—has not been accomplished. Combat assaults across difficult terrain and bombardment from artillery and jet aircraft will produce many casualties, mostly noncombatant, but it has little effect against small bands of disciplined fighters. America should have learned this from its defeat in Vietnam.

Investigative reporter Sy Hersh recently reported in the *New Yorker* that American troops' victory over the Taliban has been exaggerated. He cites considerable evidence that it remains strong outside Kabul and two other cities.[88]

In fact, some experts on terrorism have argued that by sending large numbers of troops to occupy Iraq, the U.S. military has become diverted from its main goal, which should be the destruction of a highly organized but decentralized network of terrorists. Also, our unilateral invasion of Iraq has driven our closest allies away and has made international police coordination that much more difficult. The fact that subsequent bombings in Bali, Indonesia; Rabat, Morocco; Riyadh, Saudi Arabia; and Madrid, Spain have killed hundreds of innocent civilians confirm that Bush's military campaigns haven't defeated those who resort to terror in the name of Islam.

MILITARY TRIBUNALS: OLD WINE IN NEW BOTTLES

President Bush signed an executive order on November 13, 2001, declaring an "extraordinary emergency" and authorizing the military to detain and put on trial any noncitizen who assists domestic or foreign activities that Bush determines to involve international terrorism or the harboring of terrorists. He empowered special tribunals, staffed entirely by military members, to meet in secret, hear evidence of terrorist offense, and impose any sentence, including death.[89] In his order, Bush retains sweeping power over these tribunals: to name the defendants; appoint the judges, prosecutors, and defense counsels; write rules for the tribunals; review sentences upon conviction; and decide any other appeals. Finally, all of these activities are to be conducted in secret.[90]

There was strong criticism of these initial tribunal rules, and in March 2002, the Pentagon released revised rules, which reflected some concessions to the critics. Defendants will now enjoy the presumption of innocence, they will have the right to remain silent, and they must be found guilty beyond a reasonable doubt. They will also be provided with government defense lawyers and can retain counsel of their choosing, provided these attorneys can meet government standards for a security clearance. Despite these modifications, some critics such as Yale law professor Ronald Dworkin still find the tribunal rules "indefensible." Dworkin objects that Bush or the presiding officer of the tribunal can still close all, or any part, of the proceedings to the public if they determine that a threat to national security exists. Also, there is still no way to appeal rulings of the tribunals to federal courts.[91]

THE NUREMBERG AND TOKYO TRIBUNALS: A PRECEDENT?

At the end of World War Two, the Allied powers convened military tribunals to try high-ranking German and Japanese military officers and other officials for "war crimes" and "crimes against humanity." Virtually all of the defendants were found guilty, and a number of them were put to death. There are several differences, however, between these tribunals and those proposed by President Bush. First, the Allies prosecuted only the highest-ranking officials—middle-level or low-ranking soldiers were not tried, even if evidence of their guilt was abundant. Second, these tribunals came at the end of a declared war, and the military defendants had all been military combatants. Third, all defendants were confined in accordance with international legal rules, and all had access to defense lawyers from the outset.

MILITARY DETAINEES: LEGAL LIMBO

In the course of their whirlwind occupation of Afghanistan, U.S. troops captured hundreds of suspected Taliban fighters. In some cases, the detainees were suspected of being part of the Al Qaeda network. After intensive interrogation, which probably included torture by our Afghani confederates, nearly 700 detainees, along with a few captured elsewhere, were flown to the US military prison at Guantánamo Bay, Cuba. Since confining them in Cuba, the Bush administration has claimed that it can hold the detainees indefinitely without trial and deny them access to lawyers.

In December 2003, the US Supreme Court agreed to decide whether Guantánamo detainees can file constitutional claims in US courts. A lower appellate court had ruled they couldn't because the foreign base was outside the reach of federal courts.[92] Then in January 2004, the Supreme Court dropped the other shoe by agreeing to decide whether Bush could deny a civilian trial to Yaser Hamdi, an American citizen charged with terrorism.[93] Since Yaser Hamdi had been "captured in a (foreign) zone of active combat," the Bush administration took the position that it could confine Mr. Hamdi indefinitely without trial. Both cases were argued before the Supreme Court in April 2004.

Bush's order establishing the military tribunals appears to be modeled on one used by President Roosevelt during World War Two to try eight German saboteurs who were caught in the United States. According to one analyst, Louis Fisher, the government chose to create a secret tribunal in that case because it wasn't certain if it had enough evidence to convict the saboteurs of serious offenses. They were easily rounded up before they could commit any sabotage, after one of them disclosed the plot to the FBI. Fisher also speculates that since J. Edgar Hoover enjoyed the praise erroneously given his G-men for catching the saboteurs, he wanted to conceal that no sleuthing had been involved.[94]

In the case of the German saboteurs, the Supreme Court upheld their convictions and approved the execution of six of them. It found that if a defendant is an "unlawful combatant," he can be tried by a military commission, citizen or not.[95] As with the German cases, Bush may prefer secret proceedings to hide the weak evidence in many of these cases.

In August 2003, the mainstream American Bar Association adopted a resolution calling on the Bush administration to ensure that all tribunal defendants have full access to civilian lawyers. It criticized Bush's monitoring of attorney-client communication, withholding of exculpatory evidence, and barring lawyers from consulting with each other to develop a defense. Another bar group, the National Association of Criminal Defense Lawyers, has urged its members not to represent accused terrorists unless the Pentagon's restrictions on attorneys are lifted.[96]

As the Supreme Court began accepting appeals that will allow it to scrutinize the administration's handling of detainees, new changes have been announced by the White House. First, it announced at the end of 2003 the creation of a Military Commission Review Panel, whose job will be to review the proceedings of the military commissions. "The panel may consider written and oral arguments by the defense, the prosecution, and country of which the accused is a citizen," said a senior defense official. "If the review panel finds a material error of law (it) can return the case for further proceedings, including the dismissal of charges." Panel members, who will hold the temporary rank of major general, include Griffin Bell, Attorney General under Jimmy

Carter; William Coleman, a former Secretary of Transportation; Frank Williams, Chief Justice of the Rhode Island Supreme Court; and Edward Biester, local judge in Bucks County, Pennsylvania.[97]

A few days later, the Bush White House announced that it would release some of the 650 detainees being held at Guatánamo Bay. Apparently, they had been classified into three threat categories: dangerous, medium, and likely harmless. The military is negotiating with the parent countries of detainees in the bottom categories. They may be sent home if their government agrees to prosecute them or at least monitor their future activities.

One legal critic has pointed out that Bush's practice of arbitrarily detaining noncitizens directly conflicts with a recent Supreme Court decision which held that, "the Due Process Clause applies to all persons within the United States, including aliens, whether their presence here is unlawful, temporary or permanent."[98]

THE FUTURE

The degree to which the armed forces continue to encroach on civilian police functions in the future will be determined by several factors. One certainty is that a high level of fear and hysteria will follow any additional terrorist attacks, especially within the United States. As Justice William Brennan wrote in 1988, "There's a good deal to be embarrassed about when one (considers) the shabby treatment civil liberties have received . . . during times of war and perceived threats to national security. . . . After each crisis ended the U.S. has remorsefully realized that the abrogation of civil liberties was unnecessary. But it (was) unable to prevent itself from repeating the same error when the next crisis came along."

Clearly we cannot rely upon the Posse Comitatus Act to provide us with much protection. As military historian Joan Jensen has noted, "It has played little or no role in the development of (war time) surveillance policies. Policy makers (also) didn't apply it in the formulation of peacetime surveillance. No one has ever been prosecuted under it and it was not considered to be a limitation by either high officers or regional commanders."[99]

As always, it will be up to an informed citizenry to struggle to keep the armed forces in their barracks during the next crisis. Democratic countries like Brazil, Uruguay, Chile, and Argentina provide horrific examples of what can happen when the military displaces civilian police functions.

9

Filling the Ranks: Volunteers or the Draft?

Tod Ensign

George W. Bush's decision to unilaterally invade Iraq in March 2003 has placed severe strain on the American military. About 60,000 of the 140,000 US troops deployed to the war zone at the end of 2003 were activated Guard or Reserve troops. Their proportion of GIs in Iraq rose to 40 percent by May 2004. *USA Today* reported in January 2004 on a survey of 5,000 National Guardmembers, which found that 22 percent of them were unlikely to reenlist, up from a 12.5 percent attrition rate in recent years.

The Army currently has four of its ten combat divisions deployed to Iraq. These four will rotate home in 2004 for at least six months' rest and retraining. With three other divisions scheduled to take their place in Iraq and another being sent to Afghanistan, 80 percent of the Army will either be on active-combat status or recuperating in 2004. This personnel crunch has led some in Congress to use the dreaded D-word ("draft"). They argue that without the goad of conscription, the military may soon find itself short of GIs in a number of critical skill areas.

For its part, the Bush White House, led by Defense Secretary Donald Rumsfeld, has adamantly opposed any discussion of a return to the draft. Rumsfeld insists that today's volunteer GIs are smarter and more dedicated than conscripts would be. He told reporters in September 2003, "The all-volunteer force is a booming success . . . with a remarkable sense of mission."

At the end of 2003, the Army National Guard reported that it had fallen 10 percent short of its recruiting goal for the year. If recruiting and reenlistment rates decline during 2004–05 the Pentagon will have to seriously consider a return to some sort of draft, if only as a way to compel young people to volunteer.

The creation of the all-volunteer force (AVF) in 1973 ended forty-three years of conscription. America's first peacetime draft was approved as World War Two loomed on the horizon, in order to build a massive American military force. This led to twelve million GIs in uniform, with over ten million brought in by the draft. Conscription was first used in the Civil War, and America has used draftees in every war since, except for the Spanish-American War in 1898.

The emergence of the Soviet military bloc and the Cold War after World War Two led to a decision to demobilize only a portion of the enormous military machine. With the exception of a one-year hiatus, in 1947, America's armed forces continued to rely on the goad of conscription to fill its ranks, until our bitter defeat in Vietnam brought the draft to an end in 1973.

Thousands of books have been written describing the long and bloody descent of the U.S. military into a protracted war in Indochina. It is enough to say that the eventual collapse of our military there led directly to the decision to end conscription and to rely instead on an all-volunteer force. As one alarmed military analyst summarized the situation in 1971, "Our Army that remains in Vietnam is in a state approaching collapse, with individual units avoiding or having refused combat, murdering their officers . . . drug ridden and dispirited, where not mutinous."[1]

One measure of the anger felt by combat troops about the unending and futile war in Vietnam was a dramatic increase in "fraggings," whereby GIs attacked their superiors, sometimes with fragmentation grenades, when they believed they were needlessly endangered. In 1970 alone, the Army reported 209 such incidents, and it's likely that some assaults went unreported. Combat refusals, a military euphemism for disobeying orders to fight, also became more common as soldiers became increasingly antiwar.[2]

In the United States, West Germany, and on Okinawa, antiwar activists opened coffeehouses near military bases and actively recruited GIs as participants. These projects became off-base havens where service members could receive legal and political support as well as antiwar literature. Coffeehouses worked hard to involve active-duty GIs in every aspect of their work. One popular activity was writing, producing, and distributing antiwar newspapers. Over the course of the Vietnam War, over 145 different GI publications came into being. Some were tabloid newspapers which used sophisticated graphics and incorporated elements of the countercultural style popular among most youth at that time. Others were simple, mimeographed sheets that reported on antiwar activities of GIs at a particular base. They usually had colorful names, for example, "Up Against the Bulkhead," "Fatigue Press," "A Four Year Bummer," or "The Ultimate Weapon."[3]

On the domestic front, the Selective Service System, once a respected symbol of national unity, which had the thankless task of administering the draft, had become a prime target for the antiwar movement. Its crusty leader, retired General Lewis Hershey, was morphed into a hated symbol of the cabal of warmakers. Some of the system's 6,400 local draft boards experienced repeated protests and sit-ins. Sometimes protesters destroyed draft records by pouring blood on them or setting them afire. The Tet Offensive in early 1968, when Vietnamese independence fighters briefly seized control of over 200 cities and towns, demonstrated that America was not winning the war. Following this epochal event, the number of refusals to take physical exams or report for induction grew steadily. By 1970, Selective Service had sent the names of 210,000 draft violators to the Justice Department for further action. Partly because of antiwar sympathies among federal prosecutors, fewer than 2 percent of violators were ever convicted.[4]

As further evidence of eroding support for the war, 121,000 draft registrants sought exemption as conscientious objectors in 1971, only slightly less than the total number drafted, 153,000, that year.[5] In some cities, such as Oakland, California, and Madison, Wisconsin, the constant protests prevented the draft boards from functioning normally. Such protests, however, tended to be concentrated in urban centers and college towns. The great majority of local boards were able to conduct business as usual, shipping off their quotas of young inductees each month. Following the rapid escalation of U.S. involvement in Vietnam in 1965, this rate quickly grew to 40,000 or more draftees each month.[6]

At the height of US involvement in 1968, two million young American males were reaching draft age each year. With over half a million troops deployed in Vietnam, the military needed slightly more than 700,000 to fill its ranks, once those with college, work, or physical exemptions were removed from the pool. As one historian has observed, "President [Nixon] decided to end the draft, not because it was failing, but because its political cost had become too high."[7]

SAYING GOODBYE TO CONSCRIPTION

By the time of the presidential elections in 1968, political leaders from both parties realized how badly our military intervention in Vietnam was damaging the coherence and social fabric of American society. They were eager to restore the average American's faith in the integrity and mission of America's military. For the past quarter century, tens of thousands of U.S. troops had been deployed at hundreds of military bases around the world. These leaders likely feared that our deteriorating position in Vietnam might lead to questions about the wisdom of our military commitments in Korea, Japan, the Middle East, and even in Western Europe. Was it far-fetched to imagine that the contagion of antiwar sentiment might spread from Indochina to U.S. strategic commitments in other parts of the globe?

It seems reasonable to conclude that the draft was scrapped primarily because our leaders wanted to remove a prime irritant from the body politic. They also believed that bipartisan support for keeping tens of thousands of

American troops permanently stationed abroad could be better preserved if the risks of such deployments were borne by a smaller sector of society. Losses to volunteer enlisted people are easier to tolerate than to those who have been drafted. If signing an enlistment contract is seen as an act of free will, then it follows that death or injury is just one of the risks assumed by those who volunteer. This is especially true if the casualties are suffered by those less valued; in this case, poor whites, blacks, and Hispanics.

Once the United States withdrew militarily from Vietnam, any serious political debate about our foreign military commitments became a nonissue in American domestic politics. For years, pundits have explained that this is because most Americans are uninterested in foreign policy issues. The collapse of the Soviet Union in 1990 allowed the Pentagon to substantially reduce the numbers of troops stationed in Western Europe. However, this did not lead to a reduction in foreign deployments. Instead, they were mostly reassigned to new bases, particularly in the Persian Gulf region.

With his unilateral invasion and occupation of Iraq, George W. Bush may have unwittingly placed the issue of foreign troop deployments on America's political agenda once again. If Bush fails to steadily reduce America's military presence in Iraq and the casualties continue to mount, it's possible that the question of America's foreign military commitments will finally receive the kind of public discussion that it has always deserved.

"SMART" WEAPONS VS. "DUMB" GROUND TROOPS

World War Two ended abruptly when American nuclear bombs, theretofore secret, devastated two Japanese cities, killing tens of thousands. Some referred to this as a "triumph" of technology, and it spurred America's armament industry to a new round of weapons development.

As with previous wars, Vietnam became a virtual laboratory for the development of a new generation of weapons. One of the deadliest new weapons deployed there was a harmless-sounding weed killer, dubbed Agent Orange by the military. Millions of gallons of this herbicide were sprayed all over southern Vietnam to kill crops and vegetation used for concealment by the enemy. The human health effects, birth defects, cancers, and other chronic ailments from these exposures are now well documented for both Vietnam vets and the Vietnamese. The degree of knowledge of either the manufacturers or the Pentagon concerning the presence of deadly TCDD-dioxin in the herbicide is still a matter of debate.[8]

Since World War Two, western militaries have sought whenever possible to replace conventional ground troops with firepower and high-tech weapons. The attacker wants to inflict as much damage on the enemy as he can, while sustaining as few troop casualties as possible.[9] The U.S. military introduced another "wonder weapon" in the first Gulf War, which also may have caused chronic health problems for both Allied troops and Iraqis living in the battle zones.[10] For the first time, tank, artillery, and rocket shells were tipped with "depleted uranium" (see chapter 6). Its extreme density and pyrophoric nature enables it to punch and burn its way through conventional armor plating. When a DU shell strikes a target, up to 70 percent of the depleted uranium vaporizes into fine dust, which then settles out in the surrounding soil and water. Over half of the aerosolized particles are smaller than five microns, and anything smaller than ten microns can be inhaled. Once lodged in the lung, these particles can emit a steady dose of alpha radiation.

Another example of this preference for high-tech weaponry over the use of conventional ground troops was the aerial bombing of Serbia and Kosovo by U.S. and NATO warplanes in 1999. During the months of aerial attacks, which drove Serbia out of Kosovo and forced a change in their government, not a single Allied pilot was lost. Obviously, this sort of advantage only exists when an opponent lacks the requisite technology to fight back against the new weapons.

Since the first Gulf War, America's technological superiority over all potential opponents has allowed the Pentagon to drastically reduce the numbers of troops on active duty from 2.1 million in 1990 down to 1.4 million today. Guard and reserve units were downsized but not to the same degree. These reductions meant that recruiters had to sign fewer recruits. This helped the Pentagon avoid any discussion of a possible return to a socially disruptive draft. At the same time, the United States has maintained its foreign bases around the world, with significant reductions only in Western Europe and the Philippines.

NIXON CONFRONTS THE PEACE MOVEMENT

Richard Nixon was narrowly elected President in 1968, partly because he promised to seek "peace with honor" in the Vietnam War. Antiwar Senator Eugene McCarthy galvanized the peace movement partly with his pledge to abolish the draft in support of his presidential bid. Taking a leaf from his playbook, Nixon scored points against his eventual Democratic opponent Hubert Humphrey by labeling conscription inherently unfair and violative of "liberty, justice, and equality." On the defensive, Humphrey countered that Nixon's plan for an all-volunteer military was fiscally irresponsible and would cost an additional $8 to $16 billion annually.[11] Actually, Humphrey's estimate grossly understated the eventual cost of scrapping the draft. But if an idea's time had ever come, it was this one.

It's useful to recall that when Richard Nixon was inaugurated president in 1969, there were 3,460,000 people serving on active duty, with 550,000 assigned to Vietnam. Roughly 14 percent of the troops serving there were in combat units, which had about one officer for every ten enlisted. One analyst has pointed out that this unusually high officer–enlisted ratio reflected the intense scramble for postings to a combat zone, which had become a prerequisite for promotion in America's Vietnam-era military.[12]

THE NEW NIXON

An enduring stereotype about Richard Nixon is that he was a rigid and unimaginative politician. While these traits may have returned later in his presidency, a more flexible and creative Nixon appears to have surfaced during his 1968 quest for the White House. Joe McGinniss argues in his *The Selling of the President* that Nixon embraced new theories about how to best exploit television for public appearances and advertising. McGinniss paraphrases the ideas of media guru Marshall McLuhan in explaining Nixon's makeover: "The politician [who relies on TV] cannot make a speech; instead he must engage in intimate conversation. He must never press. He should suggest, not state; request, not demand. Nonchalance is the key word." [13]

Nixon applied these same "soft" techniques to turn around public opinion about scrapping the draft for an all-volunteer force. When he first introduced the issue, 62 percent of Americans polled still favored conscription, while only 32 percent supported a volunteer force. Most career military officers, staff members of the National Security Council, and the editorial board of the influential *New York Times* also favored a continuation of the draft.[14] Yet, within a year, Nixon had pulled off a public-opinion coup, making the all-volunteer concept seem inevitable. Of course, the continuing deterioration of the U.S. military situation in Vietnam also played a part.

One historian of the draft confirms how this was accomplished: "In the Nixon White House nothing was more important than selling an image. Any idea had to be packaged and sold like so much lipstick or hair coloring." [15] In this case, Nixon Chief of Staff Bob Haldeman enlisted legendary Oklahoma football coach Bud Wilkinson to develop a "game plan" to sell the public on draft reform.[16] A key part of their strategy was the selection of a highly reputable commission to "study" the issue and make recommendations for the future.

SELLING THE ALL-VOLUNTEER FORCE

Nixon's hatred of the antiwar protesters who regularly ringed his White House is well known. Yet he was shrewd enough to understand that after the Tet Offensive showed that America wasn't winning the war, they spoke for a majority of Americans.

Two months after taking office, Nixon announced the creation of a commission on the all-volunteer force to be chaired by former Defense Secretary Thomas Gates. He asked it to "develop a comprehensive plan for eliminating conscription and moving toward an all-volunteer force." He filled the commission with politically influential conservatives, including Nobel Prize–winning economist Milton Friedman and Alan Greenspan, later to serve as chair of the Federal Reserve Board. Heads of major corporations and universities were also named, along with Alfred Guenther, former Supreme Allied Commander in Europe, who provided military ballast. A black college president and a black female professor joined Roy Wilkins, NAACP head, presumably to provide a minority viewpoint. Wilkins provided a bit of historical asymmetry because thirty years earlier he had exchanged support for a peace-time draft for a commitment to desegregate the U.S. military. The commission was asked two questions: is an all-volunteer force feasible and, if so, is it desirable?

Nixon provided no insight into how he selected members of this panel. One might ask why he'd pick a neoconservative economist like Friedman, who's best known as the "father of monetarism," to lead this battle. According to the *Random House Unabridged Dictionary,* monetarism is "a doctrine holding that changes in the money supply determine the direction of a nation's economy." Eliot Cohen has written, "This dominance of economists in defense policy was not an isolated phenomenon. It was part of a much larger development: the rise of systems analysis, a mode of strategic thought derived from economics that was at its height during Defense Secretary McNamara's [tenure]."[17] An influential advisor to the commission was Martin Anderson, who later became an important economic advisor to Ronald Reagan.

One reason Friedman and another panelist, Thomas Curtis, were selected may have been because they had already published articles endorsing the positions that Nixon wanted the commission to take. Friedman had organized a national conference on the future of the draft in 1966, at which papers were presented attacking conscription as economically unsound and a threat to liberty. He later published an influential *New York Times Magazine* article, "The Case for Abolishing the Draft,"[18] which served as a conservative manifesto against the draft. Its basic themes would appear later to form the outline for the Gates Commission report. To Friedman, conscription imposes a hidden tax on young draftees by forcing them to work for less pay than they could command in the private job market. One error in Friedman's essay was his claim that the apparent monetary cost of the all-volunteer military "probably wouldn't" be higher and that the real cost would "almost surely" be less than the present system.

Friedman also argued that the draft abridges the constitutional rights of those drafted. In the opinion of one historian of the draft, "No one played a more important role in selling the idea [of the all-volunteer force] to members of government and to the public than Milton Friedman. He [always] argued that three-fourths of the opposition to the war was because of the draft."[19]

From its inception, the Gates Commission drew support from an unusually broad political spectrum: from conservatives like Barry Goldwater to leaders of the antiwar movement. Goldwater was one of the first politicians to stake out an antidraft position during his unsuccessful presidential campaign in 1964. One of his campaign videos labeled the draft as "wasteful and unfair." He also spoke in glowing terms about an all-volunteer military as "a good professional corps [with] real pride in its service."[20]

The National Council to Repeal the Draft, which was founded by such antiwar luminaries as Dr. Benjamin Spock, Coretta Scott King, and Senators George McGovern and Ernest Gruening, also applauded the Gates Commission's plan to end the draft. During this period, they published a popular book, *The End of the Draft*.[21] In its preface, antiwar Senator George McGovern, who was later steam-rollered by Nixon's reelection bid, sounded a theme which some antiwar advocates now argue the opposite way: "As to prevention [of future wars] the voluntary force might serve as some restraint on Presidents and generals prone to military involvements, because they couldn't automatically count on forced manpower to do the fighting."[22]

THE GATES REPORT: PREDICTABLE CONCLUSIONS

After nine months of hearings and studies, the Gates Commission announced its foregone conclusion. It declared that not only was peacetime conscription unnecessary, but it was also a threat to personal freedom. The first chapter, "Protecting the Free Society," sets a broad philosophical tone: "We unanimously believe that the nation's interests will be better served by an all volunteer force . . . and [it] will strengthen our freedoms. [This] minimizes governmental interference with the freedom of the individual." The draft, it explains, has "weakened the political fabric of our society and impaired the delicate web of shared values that alone enable a free society to exist."[23]

Despite the purple prose about threats to freedom, the commission was careful to prepare demographic studies to support its most important conclusion: there would be sufficient numbers of young volunteers to fill the ranks. Census projections showed that the postwar baby boom would result in eight-and-a-half million young men between the ages of 17 and 20 by 1980.

Nowhere in its report does the commission discuss whether or not America should maintain its massive network of foreign military commitments. It clearly assumed that our role as the world's policeman would continue. Its only task was to figure out how this could be done without the benefit of conscription. While some in the antiwar movement expected that our humiliating withdrawal from Vietnam would cause this issue to be placed on the public agenda, Nixon and his circle were having none of it.

The commission foresaw a need for only a moderate reduction in active-duty force levels. It calculated that if enlisted pay were boosted, at an annual cost of $2.7 billion, an active force of anywhere from two to three million volunteers could be recruited. For the reserves, which had been swamped by people like George W. Bush who were escaping the Vietnam War, it projected that between 900,000 and 1,000,000 reservists could be retained if their pay and benefits were increased. Five years later, selected reserve strength had dipped below 550,000.[24]

The influence of conservatives like Friedman can be detected throughout the report. One of his central beliefs is that freedom can only exist where capitalism and free markets are allowed to flourish. He has written, "the appropriate free market arrangement is voluntary military forces, which is to say, hiring men to serve . . . paying whatever price is necessary to attract the required number(s)."[25] In another antidraft essay, the buttoned-down economist becomes boldly impassioned: "The case for abolishing conscription and recruiting our armed forces by voluntary methods seems to me overwhelming. One of the greatest advances in human freedom was commutation of taxes in kind to taxes in money. We have reverted to a barbarous custom. It is past time to regain our heritage."[26]

ANSWERING THE OBJECTIONS

Any marketing plan for a new product or service normally contains a section where the seller is coached on answers to every objection of a potential buyer. Because the Gates Report was designed to be a historic document justifying an epochal change from a draft to a volunteer military, the commission felt it necessary to examine and refute every argument that would be raised against its recommendations. Some of the points discussed below were debated again in January 2003, when two black congressmen proposed a restoration of the draft (see below).

Objection #1: An all-volunteer force will be very costly, so costly the nation can't afford it.

Gates Report response. The AVF would actually cost less than the present system. They claimed that since draftees receive at least $2 billion less pay than they would if they were privately employed, this "cost" will be eliminated by an AVF. They also predicted that training costs would decline since there would be less attrition with a volunteer force.

2004 analysis (with benefit of thirty-one years' hindsight). Its prediction that the AVF would cost less than the mixed conscript/volunteer military was wildly off the mark. Recruiting costs alone, for all service branches, have ballooned to at least $3 billion per year. This includes only payroll for full-time recruiters, advertising, and other marketing costs. In 2004, the Army alone must recruit

73,800 new soldiers. Since between 15–20 percent of those who sign up will never report for active duty, this means that nearly 100,000 young men and women have to be convinced to sign on the dotted line. The total quota of recruits for all services in 2004 is 260,000.[27]

Second, the Army and, to a lesser extent, the Navy and Marines, suffered high rates of attrition, especially in the early years of the AVF. One out of three Army recruits failed to complete their first term during the late 1970s, causing training costs to skyrocket.[28] Even today, with each branch being more selective in terms of aptitude and qualification (virtually all recruits are now high-school graduates), attrition rates still hover between 15 percent and 20 percent, depending on the branch of service. By way of comparison, in 1973, the first year of the AVF, the total Pentagon budget was $81 billion. In 2004, it was approximately $445 billion, and even when inflation is considered, this is a very large increase.

Objection #2: The all-volunteer force will lack the flexibility to expand rapidly in times of crisis.

Gates Report response. "Preparedness depends on forces in being, not on the ability to draft untrained men." They argued that the reserves and National Guard units would be given new, expanded roles and would provide the backup to respond to crises. They also noted they were recommending standby draft registration, whereby all eighteen-year-old males would be required to register. President Ford terminated draft registration in 1975, and Congress didn't revive it until 1980. This followed President Carter's request for registration of both men and women. He wanted to show resolve in the face of the Soviet Union's invasion of Afghanistan. Women were dropped from the registration plan, and the Supreme Court rejected a challenge to exempting females.

2004 analysis. The *Gates Report* is partially correct: the old draft system was not designed to provide trained combat replacements on short notice. However, during the Vietnam War, very few reservists were used as replacement troops. President Johnson rejected Defense Secretary McNamara's request to call up 235,000 reservists for Vietnam duty in 1966, preferring instead to rely on increased draft calls. He no doubt realized that 75 percent of those in the reserves had joined solely as a means of evading Vietnam,[29] and he wasn't about to take the politically unpopular step of sending affluent whites like George W. Bush into a combat zone.

The Gates Commission realized that if the active-force numbers were reduced and foreign military commitments remained the same, then reserve units were going to have to take up much of the slack. Defense Secretary Melvin Laird explained the Total Force Concept in 1970 as follows, "Emphasis will be on consider[ing] the total force, active and reserve, to determine the most advantageous mix to support national strategy and meet the threat. The concept will be applied to all aspects of planning . . . and employing the Guard and Reserve Forces."[30]

The Army Reserve and National Guard were much more affected by the Total Force doctrine than were the Air Force, Navy, and Marine reserve units. This was because the latter service branches' reservists had already begun to train and operate with active units. One method developed by the Army to accomplish the difficult task of integrating reserve and active-duty units involved "roundout" brigades. Two active-duty brigades were matched with a roundout brigade from the reserves. Theoretically, this would produce an Army division, and five such divisions were eventually created.

The first Gulf War in 1990–91 was the first time that America fought a war using the Total Force Concept. President George H. W. Bush signed orders mobilizing reservists in phases; eventually 188,000 were activated. The Army was only allowed to mobilize combat-support and combat-service units—no combat units were used. The other services, by contrast, were allowed to mobilize some combat units.[31]

Even the three roundout brigades that had been considered the most combat ready were found to need extensive and time-consuming predeployment training. In the end, none were actually sent to the Persian Gulf. This set off an intense controversy between reserve and active-duty officers. According to a GAO postmortem, "The Army has not adequately prepared its National

Guard roundout brigades to be fully ready to deploy quickly. When [they] were activated, many soldiers were not completely trained to do their jobs; many non-commissioned officers were not adequately trained in leadership skills . . . many soldiers [also] had serious medical or dental conditions that would have delayed or prevented their deployment."[32]

Another analyst drew a similar conclusion about Army reservists as a whole: "The physical condition of reserve soldiers was less than adequate; up to 80 percent of some California National Guard units were unable to meet physical fitness standards . . . the overall success of [reserve] units must be qualified. [Their] problems were masked by the brevity and uniqueness of Operation Desert Storm."[33]

Today, with the active military scaled down to 1.2 million GIs from 2.1 million at the time of the first Gulf War, the role of reservists in actual combat has become more critical than ever. Put another way, the Army has shrunk its active force from sixteen divisions, at the time of the first Gulf War, to ten divisions today. Once George W. Bush decided to launch his unilateral invasion of Iraq on March 20, 2003, the Pentagon had no choice but to activate tens of thousands of reserve and guard members. Six months later, more than one-third of US troops in Iraq and Afghanistan and 85 percent of those in the Balkans were reservists. Of the 200,000 serving in or near Iraq, 150,000 were Army, and 36 percent of them were reservists. Of the 20,000 Air Force members assigned in the theater, half were from Air Guard or reserve units. Most of these troops were activated for up to eighteen months, with an average tour in Iraq of one year.[34] Many reservists and their families have begun to complain publicly that these extended tours work enormous hardships on people who had expected to train one weekend a month and at worst serve short periods of mobilization.

Objection #3: An all-volunteer force will undermine patriotism by weakening the traditional belief that each citizen has a moral obligation to serve his country.

Gates Report response. Using a draft to compel military service actually undermines respect for government. "A voluntary decision to serve is the best answer, morally and practically."

2004 analysis. It's difficult to evaluate whether the ending of conscription has caused patriotism and the general sense of civic duty to decline. Certainly after 9/11 there has been a sharp increase in patriotic rituals at public gatherings, sports events, and the like. There are many factors that contribute to a citizen's sense of public duty; performing military service is just one of them.

Objection #4: The presence of draftees guards against the growth of a separate military ethos, which could pose a threat to civilian authority, our freedom, and our democratic institutions.

Gates Report response. Draftees serve on the lowest rungs of the military. It is the attitudes of the career officers and noncommissioned officers that set the tone. Removing conscripts from the military mix would not have any effect on these issues.

2004 analysis. Once draftees were no longer part of the military, the social, ethnic, and racial composition of the enlisted ranks changed. It is indisputable that people serving in the armed forces today do not come from the middle and upper classes of American society. Today, just 4 out of the 535 members of the House and Senate have children serving in the military. It is uncommon today to find younger reporters, government policy makers, congressional staffers, or corporate decision makers who are military veterans. Once considered a key posting, legislators don't seek out assignment to the congressional armed services committees as they once did.[35]

Charles Moskos, a preeminent military sociologist, commented in 1988 that "Whatever one's value judgment of the [AVF], the irreducible fact remains that without a citizen-soldier component the most privileged elements of our youth . . . will not be found in the enlisted ranks."[36]

Objection #5: The higher pay required for a voluntary force will be especially appealing to blacks, who have relatively poorer civilian opportunities. This, combined with higher reenlistment rates, will mean that a disproportionate number of blacks will be in military service. White enlistments and reenlistments might decline, thus leading to an all-black enlisted force. Racial tensions would grow because of white apprehensions at this development and black resentment at bearing an undue share of the burden of defense. At the same time, some of the most qualified young blacks would be in the military, not in the community where their talents are needed.

Gates Report response. They rejected this claim as having "no basis in fact." They estimated that in the Army blacks would eventually constitute 19 percent of the force. If higher pay does make military opportunities attractive for blacks, then the appropriate response is to "correct discrimination in civilian life—not to introduce additional discrimination." Blacks who join have decided that the military is their best alternative. To deny them this opportunity would reflect either bias or a paternalistic belief that blacks are incapable of making wise career decisions.

2004 analysis. The commission's projections of black participation in the military were seriously flawed. Seven years into the AVF, blacks constituted 37 percent of all recruits and 32 percent of the total Army enlisted force.[37] In 2000, African Americans still accounted for nearly a third of all enlistees, while black women were nearly half of all Army enlisted females. The reenlistment rate for blacks also remains much higher than it is for whites or other groups. Except for the Marines (where it's lower), black representation in the other service branches has been roughly equivalent to their numbers in the general population. Some ask whether it's desirable to have a military whose composition, racially speaking, isn't representative of society as a whole.

The Gates Report makes no mention of a future role for Hispanics in the AVF. By the late 1970s, their numbers in both the active and reserve forces had increased, but their percentage in the military has generally remained below that of their numbers in the general population. This may be changing, however. According to the 2000 census, Hispanics have now passed blacks as America's largest minority. Due to a high birth rate, one in seven eighteen-year-old Americans is now Latino. This is expected to climb over the next fifteen years to one in five. Recently, military recruiters have been promising Hispanic noncitizen recruits an accelerated "fast track" to citizenship in exchange for military service. At the onset of the Iraq War in 2003, more than 37,000 noncitizens were serving in the US military. In the last seven years, the percentage of these recruits in the total force has increased from 3.1 to 4.3 percent.[38]

Objection #6: Those joining an all-volunteer force will be men from the lowest economic classes, motivated primarily by monetary rewards, rather than patriotism. The all-volunteer force will be manned, in effect, by mercenaries.

Gates Report response. "Our research indicates that an all volunteer force will not differ significantly from the current force of conscripts and volunteers." Then-current entrance standards could prevent an "undue proportion" of disadvantaged youth from being recruited. Why would "mercenaries" suddenly emerge just because pay and other benefits are improved? "Mercenaries are those who join solely for pay, usually to fight for a foreign power."

2004 analysis. Military sociologist Charles Moskos has criticized what he calls the "marketplace philosophy" contained in the *Gates Report*. He feels that it demeans the concept of military service as an obligation of citizenship. He thinks there are pitfalls in treating military service as just another "occupation." In his view, this reliance on financial incentives detracts from the military values of service and sacrifice.[39] Recruiters today rely more than ever on monetary rewards like college assistance packages and cash bonuses to sign up their quota of recruits. It could be argued that the 37,000 noncitizen soldiers described earlier are, in effect, "mercenaries."

One of the most glaring omissions in the *Gates Report* is how it overlooked the rich recruiting opportunities provided by 51 percent of the American population. Until 1967, women were prevented by law from constituting more than 2 percent of the enlisted population. Prior to the all-volunteer force, females served in separate military units, performing mostly nursing and administrative duties.

A Pentagon task force picked up on the Gates panel's myopia about women and implemented new policies that encouraged their enlistment. By 1990, females constituted 226,000, or 11 percent, of the Army enlisted force.[40] Today, women constitute roughly 15 percent of the Army and Navy while in the Air Force they approach 20 percent. In the Marines, their numbers stand at about 5 percent, since most Marines are combat troops and women are still excluded from these jobs.

Traditional attitudes about the "weaker" sex kept women out of many military jobs for years after the AVF was implemented. Congress had sanctioned this by adopting "combat exclusion" laws, which prevented females from being assigned to a long list of jobs, some of which were combat related, but many of which involved only combat support. President Clinton dropped many of these restrictions, so that today Army and Marine Corps women are prevented only from serving in infantry, armor, and some artillery units. In the Navy, nearly all jobs are open to women, except for submarine duty. The Air Force has women serving in nearly all jobs, including flying combat aircraft.

The struggle to open up most jobs in the military to women was made more difficult by recalcitrant elements within the armed forces. In 1992, an elite group of Navy combat pilots called the "Tailhook Association" (after the hook that catches jets on carriers) touched off a national scandal. Aviators attending its convention assaulted and groped females, both military and civilian, in what was apparently a time-honored tradition. Protests and publicity forced the Navy to discipline many of the "tailhookers," and other reforms led to a less-sexist environment for female sailors aboard ship.[41]

In 1996, a number of Army drill instructors were court-martialed for an epidemic of sexual abuse toward female recruits at several training bases. This led to an armywide survey of females GIs, which found that a large percentage of them had been sexually harassed one or more times while on duty. This was followed by the highly publicized adultery prosecutions of two female Air Force officers, Kelly Flynn and Crista Davis. Both were accused of sexual misconduct with consenting males, while higher-ranking male officers who were similarly accused (with consenting females) were let off the hook. (One was even promoted to Commander of all NATO forces.)

Objection #7: An all-volunteer force would stimulate foreign military adventures, foster an irresponsible foreign policy, and lessen civilian concerns about the use of military force.

Gates Report response. Decisions to use military force are based on many complicated factors. The financial and political costs, the moral burden of risking lives, and the risk of nuclear confrontation all must be considered. It's "absurd" to suggest that planners would ignore these factors just because all troops were volunteers. The fact that all enlisted are volunteers would have no effect on military leaders or the degree of control civilian leaders have over them.

2004 analysis. It's true that the presence of draftees isn't likely to make civilian or military leaders more prone to engage in foreign invasions. Highly trained volunteers, such as Green Berets, Rangers, or SEALs, would be the most likely to support such operations. Draftees also wouldn't have any influence on the evolution of foreign policy, "irresponsible" or not. The third part of the objection, however, may be affected by the absence of draftees. As I argued earlier, the general public may be more willing to accept casualties if they're inflicted on "volunteers." ("You signed up, didn't you? What did you expect?" goes the logic.) Also, if the dead or wounded are black, Hispanic, or poor white, there may be less public concern, at least in the corridors of power, where nobody knows them personally.

George Bush has used the fear of terrorism brought on by September 11 to rewrite the old rules about avoiding foreign wars. One respected historian, Arthur Schlesinger, has argued that with the invasion of Iraq, "Bush has replaced a policy aimed at peace through the prevention of war [with] a policy aimed at peace through *preventative* [emphasis added] war. He did this . . . without calling attention . . . or provoking a national debate over his drastic change of course."[42]

Objection #8: A volunteer force will be less effective because not enough highly qualified youth will be likely to enlist and pursue military careers. As the quality of servicemen declines, the prestige and dignity of the services will also decline and further intensify recruiting problems.

Gates Report response. They were impressed with the numbers and quality of those then choosing a military career. Once everyone serving has freely chosen to do so, it would enhance the military's prestige. Improvement in benefits coupled with intensive recruiting would allow the military to attract a force that is more experienced, better motivated, and with higher morale.

2004 analysis. It's clear that if pay and benefits, including enlistment bonuses, are set high enough, the American military can attract enough volunteers to keep at least 1.4 million on active duty. The unanswered question is how will such a military fare in a protracted war, when nearly every GI is serving primarily because of economic incentives? As someone once wrote, the ultimate purpose of a military is to *wage war*—not to provide skills training or finance someone's college education.

Objection #9: The defense budget will not be increased for an all-volunteer force, and the Department of Defense will have to cut back expenditures in other areas. Even if additional funds are provided initially, competing demands will, over the long term, force the DOD to absorb the added expense of an all-volunteer force. The result could be a potentially serious deterioration of the nation's overall military posture.

Gates Report response. Public attitudes about national defense would determine how large and strong our military should be. Since World War Two, there had been support for a large military because of concerns about national security. Relying solely on volunteers wouldn't affect these decisions. It's better for democracy to openly pay for a certain size military rather than using the "hidden tax" on conscripts to secretly finance a larger force.

2004 analysis. It is difficult today to understand why the Gates Commission would worry about the level of future military appropriations. Perhaps the deep divisions over the Vietnam War made the panel fear that postwar defense spending would be more closely scrutinized by Congress. In retrospect, they had no reason to worry. Military spending has continued on a steady, upward spiral since Vietnam, passing $445 billion in 2004.

On July 1, 1973, the ponderous machinery of the Selective Service System finally ground to a halt. Draft boards were disbanded and phone calls from anxious draft registrants went unanswered. Dog-eared draft cards quickly became an icon and relic of another era. Some in the antiwar movement, especially pacifists, hailed the ending of the draft as a victory. After all, one of their favorite protest buttons had been "Draft Beer—Not People!"

Over the next three decades, the American antiwar and anti-intervention movements paid little, if any, attention to the concerns of the rank and file of the all-volunteer military. A couple of pacifist groups, the War Resisters League and the Central Committee for Conscientious Objectors (CCCO), focused their attention on the relative handful of GIs who attempted to obtain discharge as conscientious objectors. In an average year, there would be fewer than a thousand CO applicants from the entire military. Since the first Gulf War and September 11, their numbers have declined even further. Only one national group, Citizen Soldier, and a handful of small groups and counselors scattered around the country continued to conduct outreach and agitate among active-duty GIs. Milton Friedman may have been right when he said that the vast majority of anti–Vietnam War sentiment was fueled by the specter of the draft. Replace white middle-class guys with less-visible blacks, Hispanics, and whites from unfashionable parts of town and the antiwar movement loses interest.

IS THERE A DRAFT IN OUR FUTURE?

At the end of 2002, as the national debate over Bush's threats to unilaterally invade Iraq intensified, two black Congressmen dropped a bombshell. US Rep. Charles Rangel (D-NY) and US Rep. John Conyers (D-MI) introduced the Universal Service Act, which would reinstate the draft. Their proposal would require two years of compulsory military or alternative public service from every American male and female, between the ages of eighteen and twenty-six. The president would determine the number of draftees to be called and the means for selecting them. There would be no deferments for college or graduate study, only for high-school students until they reached age twenty. Senator Fritz Hollings (D-SC) introduced a companion bill in the Senate.[43]

"If our great nation becomes involved in an all-out war," Rangel announced, "the sacrifice must be equally shared. For those who say the poor fight better, I say, give the rich a chance." Rangel explained that his main goal in offering the legislation was to have people debate the issue.

In a *New York Times* Op Ed Rangel wrote: "I believe that if those calling for war knew their children were more likely to be required to serve and placed in harm's way, there would be more caution and a greater willingness to work with the international community [on] Iraq."[44]

Defense Secretary Rumsfeld responded immediately, saying, "There is no need for it at all. The disadvantages of using compulsion to bring in the men and women needed are notable." He added that the draft wouldn't work because of a high attrition rate among those forced to enlist. Rumsfeld attacked Rangel's claim that Congress or officials might be more willing to support war when their family and friends wouldn't have to fight it: "I don't know anyone in this building [the Pentagon] or this administration who thinks that anyone should go to war lightly."[45]

A month later, the Pentagon launched a counterattack on Rangel's bill with a special report entitled "Conscription Threatens Hard-Won Achievements and Military Readiness." Trying to dispel the image of blacks as cannon fodder, it claims that 36 percent of African American soldiers perform jobs classified as "function support and administration," while another 27 percent serve in the medical and dental fields. The report continues: "These young men and women are high school graduates with above-average aptitude; they are not the 'poor and uneducated.' "

Opposition to the all-volunteer force, once widespread among the professional officer corps, is no longer politically correct. Clearly averse to even uttering the dreaded C- or D-words, every officer from the chairman of the Joint Chiefs of Staff on down endlessly repeats (at least in public) the same mantra: the AVF is the finest military the United States has ever had; there's just no need for an (ugh!) draft.

Resisting congressional pressure to send more active-duty troops to Iraq in August 2003, Rumsfeld requested new deployment studies to propose ways to use active and reserve forces in the most efficient manner possible. Some have suggested that he wants to earmark any additional defense money for new technology to modernize the arsenal, in the process giving fat contracts to corporate pals of the Bush administration. Another one of his pet projects has been "civilianizing" military jobs. Rumsfeld has also reaffirmed his support for another round of military base closings in 2005.

If the military situation in Iraq doesn't improve in the months ahead, it's likely that Congress will want to revisit the issue of force levels. A number of powerful congresspeople, including House Majority Leader Roy Blunt (R-MO), have grown more critical of the Pentagon's reliance on activated reservists to do much of the fighting. One skeptical Senate Armed Service Committee aide told the *Army Times*, "A lot of us feel that the Pentagon is dead wrong here. We feel the heavy reliance on the reserves is pushing the force to the breaking point. But, if there isn't any money, there won't be any extra people, as bad as that may be."[46]

To no one's surprise, Rangel's bold initiative has found no takers. The silence of his liberal colleagues in the Congress has been deafening. John Kerry, the Democratic presidential candidate, hasn't been willing to even discuss under what circumstances the draft should be an issue.

Draft Registration: What the Law Requires

In 1980, responding to President Carter's request, Congress reinstated peacetime registration of the draft. All men between ages eighteen and twenty-six who reside in the United States are now required to provide their names and current addresses to the Selective Service System (SSS). This includes citizens, legal residents, and even those living here illegally. Registration is supposed to take place during a sixty-day period, which begins thirty days before a registrant's eighteenth birthday. Registrants are also required to keep the SSS informed of their current address until their twenty-sixth birthday.

A lawsuit that challenged on Constitutional grounds the exclusion of women from draft registration was rejected by the Supreme Court in 1981. The Court held that male-only registration didn't violate due process and that courts should defer to Congress on issues of national security and military manpower.[47] In the early years of the program, from 1980–84, there was widespread resistance, with nearly twice as many people refusing to register as refused during the entire Vietnam War period, 1964–73.[48] Just before the Iraq War was to begin, in February 2003 the same ACLU lawyer who'd filed the original suit tried again to overturn male-only registration on behalf of five Boston students. In dismissing the case once again, the federal judge ruled that "customary deference" should be paid Congress on the issue.[49]

As mentioned, tens of thousands of young men refused to comply as antidraft groups sprang up to encourage resistance and provide counseling. In response to this resistance, Congress adopted the Solomon Act in 1983, which required colleges to demand proof of registration before providing students with any federally funded college aid.[50] This was later broadened to include all federally funded entitlement programs. Another law, named after controversial Senator Strom Thurmond, bars nonregistrants from all federal employment, even summer jobs for students.[51] The criminal penalties for refusal to register are quite severe: up to five years imprisonment and up to $250,000 in fines. However, only eighteen were ever prosecuted, and these were all in the Reagan era, before 1986.[52]

The States Get into the Act

Many state legislatures have also passed laws punishing young men who fail to register. At least thirty-three states now require proof of draft registration before they will issue a driver's license to any man between eighteen and twenty-six. Some states also deny admission to state-funded colleges or employment to nonregistrants. Many make registration a precondition for the receipt of any state aid. With this proliferation of penalties it's understandable that only a small percentage still hold out against registering.

Currently, there are five ways to register for the draft:

1) Complete a registration form at any post office
2) Complete a form and mail it to the SSS
3) Check "yes" on box #29 of a federal Student Financial Aid form (FAFSA)
4) Register at high school, if a teacher has been designated as a Selective Service Registrar
5) Register online, at www.sss.gov

How a Draft Will Likely Work

If Congress restores the president's authority to draft, which it could do in a few hours, SSS's current plan is to call its first draftees 193 days after receiving its marching orders. Congress could also decide to draft females, although some time would be needed for them to register. The first group to be called will be males who turn twenty years old during the current calendar year. SSS would organize a lottery drawing, which would randomly assign a number to each day of the year. The risk of being drafted would then depend upon how "high" or "low" the number assigned to one's birthday. If, say, December 15 was drawn as number 1, then everyone in the draft pool with this birthdate would be called before they moved on to the next number.

At present, only the national and regional SSS offices are operating, with about 2,000 local draft boards on standby status. If Congress voted to resume the draft, hundreds of military reservists who've already been designated would be activated to assist the permanent SSS staff. Although members of the 2,000 local boards have already been selected and trained, their identities are withheld until induction resumes. According to regulations, "to the maximum extent possible (board) members should reflect the ethnic composition of registrants within its jurisdiction."[53]

WINNING EXEMPTIONS

At least half of those who receive induction notices are expected to fail either the physical or the mental qualifying tests for military duty. The SSS plans to use the current network of Military Entrance Processing Stations (MEPS) to conduct the exams. Currently, the regulations recognize two categories of exemption, administrative and judgmental. Basically, the first category of exemptions are claimed as a matter of right.

Administrative Exemptions:

1) GIs serving on active duty or in the reserves
2) Military veterans
3) Certain public officials
4) Dual-nationals and certain aliens
5) Inductee whose father, mother, brother, or sister was killed or is MIA in a U.S. military operation

Documentation, but no hearing, is required for these exemptions.

Judgmental Exemptions:

1) Conscientious objectors (COs), who for religious or moral reasons are opposed to participating in war in any form (discussed below)
2) Hardship cases, where induction would cause severe hardship to others
3) Ministers and persons training for the ministry[54]

Personal appearance before a local draft board is mandatory only for those seeking CO status.

Note that anyone attending college, graduate, or professional school will *no* longer be eligible for deferments. Students will be deferred only until the end of the current semester of study. Those seeking judgmental exemptions will be sent to the MEPS for physical and mental screening *before* their claim is heard. If they're found unfit at the MEPS, then their exemption request is rendered moot.

Current regulations do not allow anyone to apply for a deferment or exemption until they've actually *received* an induction notice. This will likely create some problems for those claiming to be conscientious objectors, since these claims require careful preparation. Induction orders (which will be sent as mailgrams) will contain some language describing possible exemptions, but it appears that draftees will lack sufficient information to file a valid claim for exemption within the short time periods.

All inductees will be sent for physical and mental exams, even though some have exemption claims pending. If no such claim has been filed, inductees will be shipped from the MEPS to military training on the *same day* they pass their exams. An inductee with a pending claim will be given additional time to allow his draft board to rule on his claim.

Problems for Conscientious Objectors

There is currently no way for someone to indicate on their registration form that they consider themselves to be a CO. Therefore, it's recommended that the registrant write, "I'm opposed to participation in war in any form due to my ethical, moral, or religious beliefs," on the registration form. Photocopy this card before submitting it. SSS will send an acknowledgment once it receives the form, but it will not refer to any note. Form 3B will be enclosed to make any necessary correction in the registration. Registrant should send this back certified mail, return receipt requested, with the following notice: "You made a mistake by failing to mention that I have registered as a conscientious objector. Please correct your records." Keep all registered-mail receipts along with photocopies of all forms on which notes were written. This may help later to demonstrate that the registrant held CO beliefs prior to being called for induction.

Once called for induction, SS form 22 must be used to submit a claim for CO status. Supportive letters from teachers, clergy, and other respected citizens attesting to the sincerity of the claimant's stated beliefs are helpful. This will be followed by a personal hearing before members of the local draft board, at which time personal witnesses can be offered in support of the claim.

If the board denies a CO claim, review can be sought by the district appeals board. If they uphold the local board's ruling by a divided vote, an appeal may be brought with the national appeals board.

NATIONAL SERVICE: ALTERNATIVE TO THE AVF AND THE DRAFT?

The *Gates Report* paid scant attention to the possibility of a system of compulsory national service. In three short pages, they dismissed this as an alternative to either the AVF or conscription. Of course, they were writing in a period when *any* type of compulsory government service would likely provoke intense opposition.

By the early 1980s, however, the AVF was struggling to recruit and retain enough qualified volunteer soldiers. Attrition among non-high-school grads was particularly bad, with half of them failing to complete their first term of enlistment. The numbers for high-school grads were much better, with a 25 percent attrition rate.[55] Because of these problems, some scholars, such as Richard Danzig and Peter Szanton, revived the idea of national service. They described three different possibilities: first was a system that would fill the ranks of social-service and environmental programs if there were drastic cutbacks in their funding; second, as an employer of last resort for young people, similar to the way the Civilian Conservation Corps (CCC) and the National Youth Administration (NYA) programs operated during the Great Depression; third, as a means of filling the ranks should declining birthrates lead to recruiting shortfalls.[56] Since they regarded a return to conscription as highly controversial, they argued that a system of universal national service would "provide a way of sharing the burdens more broadly and permit youths who resisted military service on CO or other grounds to find an acceptable alternative."[57] They remained pessimistic about such a change however, noting that "national service is an [idea] whose time never seems to come."

DRAFT OF MEDICAL PERSONNEL

One chink in the solid wall of opposition to the draft within the Bush administration was a March 2003 announcement that the Pentagon was dusting off a

1987 law which allows for the drafting of thousands of health professionals in the event of a biological or chemical attack. The president, by proclamation, can order up to 3.5 million health care workers, male and female, to register for a draft within two weeks. The Pentagon would then advise the Selective Service on the numbers it needed in each of 62 different medical specialties. A separate draft lottery would be held for each of categories.[58]

Prospects for a (New) Draft

As the U.S. occupation of Iraq has dragged on past its first anniversary and casualties continued to mount, voices urging a return to conscription have become louder.

Just days after the Pentagon announced that 20,000 of its 135,000 troops in Iraq would have to stay at least an additional three months, moderate U.S. Senator Chuck Hagel (R-NE) told the Senate that the situation in Iraq may force a return to a draft. "Why shouldn't we ask all our citizens to bear some responsibility and pay some price?" Hagel, a Vietnam combat vet asked. He argues that restoring the draft would force "our citizens to understand the intensity and depth of the challenges we face."[59]

When the Army's top recruiting official, Lt. General Dennis Cavin, was asked by the *Army Times* in May 2004 if a draft was needed, he predictably responded, "Absolutely not, as long as we don't need a massive growth in end strength."

Although the Army has met its recruiting goals for every month so far in 2004, Cavin was cautious. "This is the first time in history we've had an all volunteer force during a prolonged conflict," he said. He praised the current "Army of One" campaign, stating, "It's about one Army, one set of values and a brotherhood being engaged in the Global War on Terrorism. These young people know exactly what they're getting into. They understand the likelihood that during their first enlistment, they will go into harm's way."[60]

10

The Return of the Poor, Bloody Infantry

George and Meredith Friedman

The individual soldier is the hardest thing to find on the battlefield; he is the smallest unit of warfare, and his intelligence makes him naturally stealthy. But, in general, he is also relatively harmless. Ever since the invention of artillery and the tank, the amount of firepower the individual infantryman could wield was limited. Even the machine gun, powerful as it was, could not fire an explosive shell and therefore was inherently inferior to larger explosive rounds.

But imagine that this limit was removed and the stealthiest element of warfare could bring to bear the deadliness of the most advanced weapon system. Imagine if enormous firepower were concentrated in the hands of single individuals, harder to kill than tanks. In other words, imagine if the revolution in weapons, sensors, and battle management were applied to the infantryman—a human system designed to engage the enemy at close quarters, seize terrain, and, in general, operate in close conjunction with weapons systems scattered globally. Such a transformation would be a return to an ancient understanding of war—the ancient logic of the infantryman, the logic of weapon against weapon and life against life.

In his current form, the infantryman has a number of weaknesses. First, if located, he can easily be killed by a wide array of weapons. Second, compared to everything else on the battlefield, his weapons are both weak and inaccurate. Infantry weapons lack enough range to project power adequately and they barely reach the limits of the individual's line of sight. During combat, individual soldiers are easily isolated from one another and their commanders. Commanders communicate with each other by radio, while the infantryman's means of communication is still a loud shout. Perhaps most important, the infantryman's knowledge of his surroundings is limited by what his eyes can see and his ears can hear. He usually has a pretty chaotic sense of what is going on around him; in fact, no one experiences the fog of war more intensely or personally than he does.

The traditional solution to this problem has been training—forging individuals into units, drilling them as realistically as possible on their responses to different situations, creating noncommissioned officers to hold the unit together while officers devise strategies. Sometimes this worked. Usually, victory went to the side whose cohesiveness and coherence collapsed least. Until the technical revolution of the 1980s started to percolate downward, until commanders started considering the implications of advanced technology on the grunt, the infantryman's fate appeared to change not at all.

But the same technology that has made the tank obsolete opens the door to a radically different future. The multispectral sensors, high-speed computers, and brilliant munitions (as well as the advanced materials used in the vain attempt to prolong the life of the tank) raise the possibility of a superior soldier or, to use a phrase from a study by former CINC South Paul F. Gorman, a *Supertroop.*

The idea for a superinfantryman did not originate with military men or engineers. Just as H. G. Wells was the first to imagine the tank, a science-fiction writer, Robert A. Heinlein, writing in 1959 about space warfare in the future, described a "Cap Trooper," dropped by capsule from an orbiting spacecraft to the surface of the planet. Heinlein envisioned the Cap Trooper wearing an armored powersuit, which multiplied his strength and speed tremendously. The helmet would be filled with sensing, communications, and data-management apparatus. He would be armed with a wide range of precision munitions, from antipersonnel devices to atomic weapons. A small number of such troopers would be able to devastate a city if needed.

The idea of a superinfantryman is no longer mere speculation. The U.S. Army has initiated a program known as the Soldier as a System (SAAS), in conjunction with the Marines and the U.S. Special Operations Command. The program, part of a larger thrust called Warrior's Edge, is intended to have two parts. The first, Block I, or The Enhanced Integrated Soldier's System (TEISS), will be deployed in 1999 and will be followed by a second phase, Block II, which is scheduled for deployment in 2010. These projects will involve a wide array of new systems, including advanced weapons for individual soldiers, computer networks at the platoon and company level, helmet-mounted sensors and displays, exoskeletons, and even chemical compounds to improve the ability of soldiers to learn—in short, Heinlein's Cap Trooper.

This new approach to the problem of infantry warfare is not confined to laboratories. Thinking about technology and the infantry has penetrated to the operational level. A report issued by the United States Army Infantry School at Fort Benning, entitled *Infantry 2000,* states:

> The future infantryman requires a system that integrates full body ballistic protection along with NBC [nuclear, biological, chemical], flame, laser and microwave protection. Enhanced productivity will be achieved if we can relieve climactic stress on the soldier. Lethality will be increased with an integrated full solution individual fire control system. It will use a helmet-mounted image display (HELMID) to provide point and shoot accurate fires which will be equally effective day or night or through obscurants and camouflage.

The SAAS program, and the needs described by the Army Infantry School, present a consistent and coherent vision of a revolution in infantry warfare. Until now, the infantryman has been fairly well limited to combat capabilities provided by biology. He could move, see, hear, and so forth only to the extent that his body permitted him to do so. Now the infantryman will be radically transformed, even enhanced, which will initiate a new era of ground combat.

THE INFANTRYMAN AND THE SENSOR/DATA REVOLUTION

Extending the range of vision in space and spectrum is the first task in creating an advanced infantryman. Such an extension has already taken place with the introduction of night goggles as near standard issue to U.S. combat troops. These goggles, which use available light, such as starlight, and enhance it thousands of times, make night vision and twenty-four-hour combat possible. At present, such sights, called I^2 (image intensification), have a number of limitations, particularly in trade-offs between acuity and field of vision as well as general clumsiness. But by gathering light through a lens and converting it into electrons, and passing the electrons through a phosphor plate, thereby multiplying them thirty thousand times, it has become possible for an infantryman to see on a moonless, cloud-covered night. The addition of other types of sensors will further enhance the infantryman's ability to see things hidden to the naked eye.

The revolution in sensor technology that made the nonballistic projectile possible offers even more dramatic possibilities for the infantryman. A report prepared for the U.S. Army by the National Research Council, *Star 21: Strategic Technologies for the Army of the Twenty-First Century,* published in 1992, includes the following set of expectations about the future of sensors:

> Passive optical and infrared systems provide information on direction (bearing) and on spectral distribution and intensity, range, range extent, velocity and direction. Millimeter-wave synthetic aperture radars provide high-resolution images that are responsive to the material properties of targets. These systems can be configured so that the active and passive components share the same optics and thus can provide pixel-registered images in a multidimensional space, which allows multidimensional imagery. Acoustic sensors can provide information regarding frequency and direction of detected signals.

Taken together, the wide array of sensors that were developed to locate targets for precision-guided munitions and cruise missiles allows for a vast and comprehensive sense of reality—providing an enhanced and extended sense of risks and targets. In addition, information from other sensor platforms, such as satellites, unmanned aerial vehicles (UAVs), manned aircraft, ground sensors, and so on, could be transmitted to the infantryman, extending his vision even farther.

The gathering of such data is already a technical reality, with relatively minor problems—including miniaturization, shared use of apertures, and designing data transmission systems large enough to handle vast amounts of complex, graphical traffic—still to be solved. The problem derives from the very success of these sensors—they provide so much data that it would be impossible for the infantryman to read it all in alphanumeric form, let alone to absorb it and act on it during combat. The situation is similar to that faced by fighter pilots, who must simultaneously fly their aircraft, locate threats, fire their weapons, and navigate.

Fighter pilots have solved this problem—not altogether satisfactorily—with the heads up display (HUD), in which all necessary data is displayed on the canopy of the aircraft or on the visor of the helmet. The data displayed is carefully structured to be absorbable by the pilot, in an environment where data overload has become a fatal problem. The Hughes Corp. is already developing a display unit for ground forces' helmets weighing two ounces, which will display graphics or text on the front of a helmet.

While HUD presents essential data within the pilot's field of vision—as if he were viewing a control panel without having to look down—it does not provide him with a fused sense of reality. He does not have something that he can grasp as effortlessly as if he were looking at something outside his window. Instead, the pilot is left to integrate the data. Warfare is spatial—with interactions of location, shape, motion. Grasping spatial relationships rapidly, intuitively, as a gestalt, without pausing for reflection or calculation, is a matter of life and death.

Imagine two swordsmen, dueling in the dark. One has sensors that display a simulated picture of his opponent, properly proportioned, and moving synchronously with the real figure. Now imagine the other swordsman having, instead of a picture, a series of gauges and readouts. To figure out where his opponent was and what he was doing, this other swordsman would have to read the data, integrate it, understand it, then execute his swordplay according to this flow of data. Who would win the fight?

Let us imagine a second scenario. Assume that the visual display was a bit off, while the data display was precise. Would it take longer for the swordsman with the picture to adjust for error than it would take the swordsman with precise alphanumerical data to read it, absorb it, and act on it? It is clearly easier to comprehend a picture—and compensate for errors—than to understand data.

The problem is no longer the gathering of data—indeed, there is a surplus of usable data. Nor is it a problem of rendering data as information—that too can efficiently be done. Rather, the key problem has been the management and display of information in a manner compatible with the normal sense and thought processes of soldiers.

The system must be designed so that each bit of information from a variety of sources is fused into a coherent image that can be taken in by the infantryman as if it were a single reality in the visible spectrum. Assume, for example, that the millimeter-wave radar spots a dug-in tank straight ahead. The infrared sensor detects a squad of enemy infantry at three o'clock. The acoustical sensor detects an aircraft engine overhead. An overhead unmanned aerial vehicle spots some armored personnel carriers off to the left. How could all of this data be usefully displayed?

The term *virtual reality,* which has come into vogue, revolves around the idea of managing data generated by a computer program and displaying it in such a way that it simulates ordinary reality as a human being experiences it. Usually, virtual reality involves encapsulating someone's head in a helmet and using a computer to generate images. But other sensory inputs can also be controlled. For example, sensors and servomechanism on the limbs and fingers can exert pressure and tactile sensation so that, after "seeing" an object, a person can "feel" and "pick" it up, actually experiencing its weight and texture. Much has been made of the entertainment value of such a construct, but it has considerable usefulness as a training device, in military and other contexts.

The U.S. Army has already committed itself to virtual reality for training purposes as part of its Force XXI concept. During the 1980s, a program called SimNet was initiated to train tank drivers and gunners in a virtual-reality environment. SimNet has evolved into a much broader initiative—the Distributed Interactive Simulation Environment—and a specific program intended to train infantrymen, the Close Combat Tactical Trainer (CCTT). Infantrymen will be placed in a room and outfitted with helmets that will cover their eyes. They will "see" a combat situation, from terrain to enemies, and they will carry weapons that will have the feel of the real thing. A camera will track the movement of their bodies and adjust the picture accordingly. They will feel as if they were in combat—except that they will be perfectly safe, and the simulation can be run over and over again.

Rensselaer Polytechnic Institute, working with Avatar Partners, has been awarded a contract by the U.S. Army to develop a full-scale artificial-intelligence environment, the Dismounted Infantry Virtual Environment (DIVE), which will include:

- An instrumented room with multiple video cameras for video-based tracking and orientation estimation, which will track the key body joints of a soldier without tethers, bodysuits, or other restrictive equipment.
- An ultralightweight, wireless, head-mounted display including spatial sonics.
- A high-speed, real-time image-generation system, capable of rendering body models of immersed users and combining those models with digitally created environments.
- Virtual weapons and software that will provide the user with the ability to "fire" at simulated targets, with simulated results that account for standard effects such as ordnance type, gun elevation, and wind.
- Networking capability to interconnect individual DIVE modules for squad/platoon-level exercises and to connect them to the Distributed Simulation Internet via standard protocol data units.
- Intelligent agents that respond to human voice commands to simulate an

entire squad or platoon under the leadership of a DIVE-immersed human commander.

Virtual reality is a system of data fusion with a presentation that is faithful to the normal experience of reality. That is what makes it such an exciting training tool. But virtual reality can have a more direct use. Instead of being generated by a program, the data could just as easily be generated by actual sensors scanning a literal and not a virtual reality. The interface between the infantryman and the system does not care where the input originated. It could have been a simulation of an infrared sensor—or it could have come from a real infrared sensor. Thus, the technologies being developed for simulations and training could, with different sensor sources, solve the problem of data fusion, not only in a training room but on the battlefield as well. An infantryman could be fitted with a completely opaque helmet—identical to those used in training—inside of which he would see as real images and icons the data that was being fed into the system by the sensors.

For example, he might see arrayed on his screen, in full relief resembling his own optical experience, an airplane thirty miles away, visible through enhanced optical television; enemy troops two hundred yards away and camouflaged, visible in imaging infrared; a camouflaged tank two miles away, visible only to radar; and a fortification visible in ultraviolet. Side-looking synthetic aperture radar located in an overhead satellite would note minefields, while nuclear, biological, and chemical sensors in a UAV would measure air quality and flash a warning if necessary.

The data available to the infantryman will not only be gathered by his own sensors but by those of the rest of the unit as well. Data will also flow from other data-gathering platforms—satellites, high-altitude UAVs, low-altitude remotely piloted vehicles, and ground-based sensors—all linked together in complex laser and electromagnetic nets. A flick of a switch will display the trooper's rear, another will allow the soldier to zoom in on a particular feature. The unit's commanding officer will be able to see the position of each of his men, plus call up a readout of each man's physical condition, available ammunition, and systems integrity.

This nonvirtual reality will, first, extend the infantryman's physical senses into distant spaces. The experience will be undistorted—he will understand what is happening around him as quickly as if he were using his own eyes and ears. Second, the old problem of command and control in combat, as well as some parts of the problem of unit cohesion, will be solved or, at least, eased. The commander's sense of where his men are and what they are doing will be greater than at any time since warfare became a large enough enterprise that it extended beyond the reach of a commander's eyes and voice.

For these developments to take place, the revolution in data management will have to be supplemented by a revolution in communications. The key to the operation of the system will be a high-speed computer, linked to a high-capacity data communication system that will be rugged enough and small enough to be carried in combat.

The U.S. Army's Communications Electronics Command (CECOM) is currently developing such a device, called the soldier's computer, which is planned for validation by 1996, and for introduction under The Enhanced Integrated Soldier's System (TEISS) program by 1999. It is intended to be a multiprocessor computer, with specific chips for such functions as graphics, communications, position location, and voice recognition. It would also have extensive storage capacity based on hard drives, CD-ROMs, and other more advanced memory media such as EEPROM. Indeed, so high are the expectations for the lightweight computer that CECOM hopes that its central processing unit (cpu) will have the same capacity as today's supercomputers, such as the Cray.

The memory will contain extensive mapping data, which, in conjunction with the data flowing in from sensors, will tell the soldier where friendly forces are, where enemy forces are, and his own precise location. In addition, a large graphic capability will match images gathered by sensors with images built into the memory, for target recognition and additional identify-friend-or-foe (IFF) capabilities.

The computer would also manage communications. In part, this communication would be standard voice communication between soldiers based on secure transmission systems such as SINGCARS. More important, it would also include the transmission of graphical data, which would require a cpu for formatting and interpretation.

In addition to being tied to a worldwide communications network, all computers in a unit would be linked together in a single data network, transmitting data via high-speed fiber-optic links (which have the advantage of being jam-proof) or line-of-sight photo-optic or laser links—with UAVs and satellites being used to relay even short-range communications for the sake of signals integrity. In large part, this system was in place during Desert Storm; however, it lacked sufficient capacity to carry the amount of traffic. As we discussed earlier, data caused one of the most severe logistical problems in the war. It will be necessary to develop satellites and UAVs with more data transmission capacity, or there must be a breakthrough in the way data, particularly graphical data, is formatted.

From the squad to the CINC, a commander will be able to view the battlefield from any level of resolution desirable, with data aggregated in any way useful. He would immediately have information available on casualties, ammunition expenditure, and so on, allowing him to make battle plans with enhanced precision. A CINC, for example, might view the developing situation from the standpoint of a particular brigade or focus in on a single battalion and, if desirable, analyze the deployment of a platoon or even a squad. He might generate a map showing the location of all fuel in the theater, from tankers to trucks. A platoon leader could monitor casualties and the precise deployment of his forces, as well as enemy troops, obtain information on the last time a soldier slept in order to gauge fatigue levels, and so forth. The soldier's computer could be the rock on which the next century's Army is built.

THE ART OF KILLING IN THE 21ST CENTURY

The purpose of all this, of course, is to kill the enemy. All of the data in the world, no matter how brilliantly managed and displayed, will be of no use if the individual infantryman can't act on it by destroying enemy soldiers. All these various sensors and data management systems must, in the end, converge on the individual soldier's weapon, his means of destruction. Indeed, there has been little or no progress in the weapons of individual soldiers since World War I. They have gotten lighter, less likely to jam, able to fire more rounds, but the machine gun, submachine gun, rifle, hand grenade, and light mortar are all old weapons with fresh veneer. The AK-47, M16, Galil assault rifle, and the rest have not changed their basic design in nearly thirty years.

The U.S. Army recently concluded that the conventional rifled personal weapon has reached the limits of its development. During the 1980s, the Department of Defense undertook the Joint Service Small Arms Program, looking for a successor to the M16, which had been introduced during the Vietnam War. After an eight-year, $50 million search, Program Manager Vernon Shisler announced, "It's now obvious that you can't get much better performance from bullet-type rifles. You can lighten the load using caseless or plastic-cased rounds and gain some improvements with optic sights, but you can't significantly increase performance."

It is difficult to imagine the conventional rifle surviving in the radically changed environment we have been describing. It is a line-of-sight weapon in a world of indirect fire. It fires a dumb, slow projectile in a world of brilliant, hypervelocity projectiles. It fires a nonexplosive projectile in a world of high explosives. In the end, the rifle-bearing infantryman is governed by the same principles that governed the spear hurler and the bowman—first see the target, then try to get your hands to direct your projectile toward it. The failure of the Joint Service Small Arms Program is merely official confirmation that the rifle is at the end of the line.

No matter what improvements are made to the rifle, it is not going to work any better. But the sensor revolution opens a new avenue for improving human control. The *Star 21* report predicts:

> Special helmet-mounted sensors could track the soldier's eye movement to aim personal sensors and weapons. For instance, a soldier might look at a building at a distance. A laser range finder and the navigation system could quickly deter-

> mine the building's exact location. The soldier could provide audio information about the building through a helmet-mounted microphone. All the real-time information could be stored in the soldier's personal computer or transmitted through the C³I/Rista network.
>
> The helmet and visor conceivably could be used to aim the soldier's personal weapons. Current weapons depend on tight hand-eye coordination for aiming. The problem is that the eye is accurate, but the hand is not. Eye-only aiming is certainly possible with emerging technologies.

The eyes survey a multisensor, multiplatform reality, select a target, and focus on it. A laser sensor would note precisely what the eye was looking at and determine, from a database created by sensors, the precise position of the target. The infantryman could then select a projectile to be fired at the target, blink twice, twitch a finger, or perform whatever action was programmed into the system, and the projectile would be launched at the target. The question that remains is, what sort of projectile would the infantryman be carrying, and how would it be launched?

The Block I plan of The Enhanced Integrated Soldier's System (TEISS) includes an element called the Small Arms Master Plan, which envisions the reduction of the current mix of weapons to three basic types: the sidearm, the individual combat weapon, and the crew-served weapon. The individual combat weapon will be fundamentally different from the rifle—much more powerful, with an explosive charge. Both it and the crew-fired weapon are intended to fire more than one type of munition—including grenades and explosive bullets. While certainly increasing the flexibility and lethality of the infantryman somewhat, the changes envisioned under the first phase of the system do not represent a quantum leap in the firepower of the infantryman, but merely an incremental improvement.

The future of infantry weapons can already be seen in the manportable antitank weapons currently in use, such as the Javelin, as well as in the new guided mortars. The Javelin can be fired by a single infantryman, who focuses on the target, locks the warhead onto the target point, and launches. He can fire and forget, as the Javelin will guide itself to the point the infantryman focuses on. Other weapons do not even need an initial lock-on. Once fired, they can locate the target themselves, or they can be guided to the target by the gunner or by another sensor platform, such as a UAV or satellite—there are multiple guidance choices. In each of these cases, both the inefficiency of hand-eye coordination and the tyranny of ballistics have been abolished. The problem remaining is wedding them to the individual infantryman, something that does not really require vast innovation or imagination.

The continued miniaturization of warheads and rockets allows more and more of them to be made man-portable—even without strength enhancement. Imagine a series of tubes (one to four) mounted on the back of the infantryman, made of a light, durable material, such as fiberglass insulated with aerogel. The infantryman would observe his surroundings with his and other sensors. The data would be collated and fused by his computer, which would display it graphically on his screen. His eye would then focus on the target, while his hands selected the type of projectile and warhead he was going to launch—which would depend on the type of target. A laser scanner inside the helmet would identify the target being focused on, the computer would use its gunner's primary sight (GPS) system to locate the target, provide a vector, and order the missile to launch.

The missile would have a two-stage engine, as before. The first stage, a powerful CO_2 motor, would propel the missile upward and away from the infantryman, without back blast. An internal gyroscope would order side thrusters to stabilize the missile at the appropriate angle for the second, explosive-rocket engine to ignite, delivering the missile to its target. The projectile and warhead could be a small, explosive bullet, a grenade, a hypervelocity antitank round, a high explosive, a shrapnel-laden mortar round—whatever was appropriate. A smart sensor would guide it to maneuvering targets. Once the projectile was fired, the infantryman would be free to get on to his next task—getting away from the launch point.

Whichever sort of round was fired, the infantryman would cease being the weakling of the battlefield. He would be able to carry with him the firepower of armored vehicles and have greatly increased range and accuracy. As a result of these developments, infantry warfare will cease to be the statistical game that it has been since the invention of gunpowder. It will no longer be a matter of vast numbers of soldiers firing enormous quantities of highly inaccurate projectiles in the hope that, by saturating a target area, something would be hit. The massed infantry armies of the past, necessary to produce the swarms of projectiles required to hit even a single target, will have become as obsolete as the tank.

Obviously, no matter how small projectiles get, the ability to carry a sufficient number will tax the physical capability of the infantryman. That infantryman will need to have substantial assistance, both in the form of robots to carry material and, more important, augmentation of his body's strength. In a way, this augmentation is one of the keys of modern warfare.

One of the virtues of the tank was its ability to mount a heavy gun, carry ammunition, and still move about the battlefield. The tank's weakness, its visibility on the battlefield, could be solved by the infantryman. But, in the end, the infantryman cannot begin to replace the tank unless he can field an equivalent amount of firepower—and that weighs a lot, no matter how much it is miniaturized.

At the same time he must still remain agile. This is an old problem, and the solution is an exoskeleton—a frame that fits to the outside of the body, senses the body's motions and exertions, and multiplies their power.

During the 1980s the Los Alamos National Laboratories was working on a project, code-named PITMAN, to produce an infantry battle dress that would use robotics to amplify human strength. The suit would be built around a computer chip that would memorize the motions of a particular infantryman. This could be done either by placing tiny sensors on his body, the conventional path, or as the chief engineer on the PITMAN project suggested, by attaching electrodes to his skull that could sense magnetic fields generated by the brain prior to and during motion—magneto encephalography—the more exotic approach.

Drawing on a power source, the exoskeleton would emulate and enhance human muscle motions, permitting not only lifting but rapid movement as well, providing strength and mobility at the same time. A man able to lift a hundred pounds, for example, would find that he might lift five hundred or a thousand pounds. The suit, weighing up to a ton, would bear its own weight and the weight of all equipment, including that of armor and projectiles and launchers.

The suit's frame would be made of a strong, lightweight material, such as a graphite epoxy. It would be surrounded by a rigid, advanced material that would protect the soldier not only from enemy projectiles (up to perhaps 20-mm rounds) but from chemical and biological threats. Ideas for this material include combining Kevlar (the current protection against ballistic threats) with a substance such as silk, for a lighter-weight protection. More creatively, projects are under way to bioengineer new materials to control the permeability of clothing so that they would normally be air permeable (and comfortable) but would become impermeable when in a dangerous environment. Under any circumstances, a sealed suit with an air circulation system along with bottled air for use when the outer atmosphere might be contaminated would provide a comfortable and safe environment for the infantryman in his exoskeleton.

The suit itself, essential to tie together the entire system, cannot really proceed until the power-source problem is solved—which, given the quantity of power required, is not an insurmountable problem, as it may be with electrothermal (ET) and electromagnetic (EM) guns. Thus, the infantryman would achieve the firepower that previously required a platform driven by a petroleum engine, along with an accuracy and range beyond anything that direct fire could achieve.

In changing the range of weapons the structure of command is dramatically changed. The chain of command was created to facilitate management of forces too large to be controlled by any single commander. Direct interventions by higher commanders into lower echelons had historically been undesirable because the senior commander could not possibly have sufficient information about the situation on the ground to make reasonable judgments. In the future, a company commander's data display will instantaneously be available at any higher command level. Thus a senior commander can view the situation from the standpoint of the junior commander. Micromanagement, previously a dirty word in the military lexicon, might carry different connotations. The commander could, in addition to managing the entire battle, control the movement of a critical spearhead formation. Whether he would wish to would depend on his personal management style.

But just as data flows become decentralized with the new technology, the possibility of a hypercentralization of command also becomes a possibility. Certainly, the rigid command structures of the mass armies of the last five hundred years will become more fluid, more ad hoc, depending on circumstances and even personalities. It should also be added that the function of the general staff, which had been developed in part to accumulate and manage data for the commander, would have to shift. An interesting evolution to observe will be the extent to which staff function at all levels will be changed by the new technology. With new means available for command and control, the responsibilities of commanders will increase—along with the pressures. We must not expect, of course, that the fog of war that Clausewitz described will be abolished, but it will certainly be driven back.

BEYOND TOTAL WARS

Three things distinguish the emerging infantryman—or more appropriately, "individual armor units"—from his predecessors:

- Relative invulnerability—The only defense of the traditional infantryman, who fought without any shielding, was to dodge the bullets. Wearing a protective "suit," the future infantryman will be invulnerable to traditional threats—nonexplosive ballistic projectiles, NBC threats, shrapnel. He will be vulnerable to armor-piercing rounds and direct hits with high explosives.
- Multispectral sensing—The traditional infantryman saw with his eyes. The future infantryman will see in spectra and at distances far beyond human

vision. Moreover, sensors on other platforms—UAVs, satellites, reconnaissance aircraft—will extend his visual capacity even farther.

- Non-line-of-sight weapons—Powered exoskeletons and robot ammunition caddies will permit the infantryman to carry large weapons loads. While it is not clear that there are any limitations on the weapons range, assume conservatively that the range of the individual weapon would equal that of a multiple-launch rocket system—about twenty miles—and that of the crew-served weapon would equal that of a Lance missile—about fifty miles. This would permit a small number of soldiers to lay down enormous firepower over a large area.

Consider—again arbitrarily—the makeup of a standard eleven-man squad in the twenty-first century:

1. **Squad leader**—He will carry a personal weapon and massive computing and communications gear that will enable him to communicate to any command echelon—from infantryman in the field to company commander.
2. **Programmer/telecommunication specialists**—Their primary job would be to calibrate weapons and personal gear for satellite grids and to reprogram projectiles for new targets and tasks. In combat they would serve as the target-acquisition team, using multispectral sensing devices to search for enemy air and land threats and targets, transferring data to appropriate weapons systems.
3. **Heavy weapons team**—Supplied with heavy-duty exoskeletons to aid in lifting and follow-on robots to aid in launching, they could simultaneously launch twenty heavy projectiles into combat, using the multimission projectile system.
4. **Personal weapons specialists (plain-vanilla infantryman)**—Armed with ordinary weapons launchers, they advance ahead of the groups to provide perimeter security for the specialist teams and do the dirty work.

Assuming sensor support from unmanned aerial vehicles, a single squad could secure an area twenty miles per side (four hundred square miles) and project explosive power over a radius of fifty miles (nearly eight thousand square miles)—although probably without sufficient ammunition in a target rich environment without substantial prior planning. Lest the mind boggle at these numbers, bear in mind that the gap between them and the amount of territory able to be secured by a modern-era squad is no more extraordinary than the range, mobility, and firepower of a Vietnam-era Air Cavalry company compared to its World War II equivalent or the mobility and firepower of an American armored battalion in World War II compared with a Civil War regiment. Such quantum leaps in capability have become commonplace in warfare since the industrial revolution.

Depending on the likely opposition and the quantity of terrain involved, larger numbers of troops may be needed—but it is impossible to imagine the need for five hundred thousand troops as in Desert Storm. First, the radical increase in mobility, firepower, and, above all, accuracy makes the firing line obsolete. Second, the decrease in manpower dramatically reduces the need for logistical support. Where thousands of artillery shells are to be fired in an hour, and tens of thousands of gallons of gasoline are going to be consumed in an afternoon, and thousands of meals need to be prepared and delivered, then thousands upon thousands of truck drivers, cooks, munitions specialists, are needed. However, when dozens of munitions fired by dozens of men moving in battery-powered suits are needed, a few men managing a few robots will be sufficient.

What we are seeing is the end of the GI. The GI, the stamped government-issue interchangeable warrior, becomes obsolete when masses of men are no longer required to fight wars. Ever since the invention of the musket, the purpose of training was to force men into a mold—to drill them, depersonalize them, until they became a unit, until they fired in unison to overcome the inaccuracy of their firearms. The archetypal old sergeant used to tell the recruits that if the Army had wanted them to think, it would have issued them brains, and indeed, too much imagination was the ruin of many a soldier, contemplating his probable fate on the firing line.

The model for the soldier of the future is not the GI of our large-scale wars, but the Special Operations trooper—the Green Beret, Special Air Source, Spetznaz, or, indeed, knight of old. The future soldier will be highly trained and skilled, but not in the rigid way of mass armies. He will have to master technologies that are esoteric in the extreme—communications theory, sensor technology, and so on. As with the Special Forces, the small size of the unit will require each man to become an expert.

Small-unit operations in the past were associated with low levels of destructive force. Small units in the future will be capable of tremendous destructive force. Soldiers will have to have a deep sense of unit loyalty and, simultaneously, a strong sense of personal independence. In a physical sense, the individual's level of isolation will dramatically increase. Visual contact with other troops may be impossible. The data links will keep the unit together—but when those fail, the mission will have to continue.

For the first time in five hundred years, we are about to see a dramatic decrease in the size of land forces, without a decrease in military power. Sociologically, this will mean that members of the military will once again constitute a social elite as they did in the Middle Ages—where the means of war were expensive, the skills esoteric, and the powers of those who mastered the skills great. Mass armies are, ultimately, democratic armies. Small armies, consisting of skilled and courageous men wielding enormous power, represent a challenge to democratic ideals. Meritocracy may well turn into aristocracy.

Modern war became total war because of the inaccuracy of weapons. Mass-producing weapons required near total mobilization of factories and soldiers. The distinction between civilian and soldier was obliterated. Everyone fought or worked, and everything was at risk. War became a social catastrophe more than a political one. Nuclear weapons, which placed absolutely everything in danger, were the logical conclusion of this process.

With precision-guided munitions, the number of men involved in arms factories and armies will decline precipitously—one projectile can be fired for every thousand previously needed. More important, the level of devastation will decline as well. The relatively light damage to Iraq in the six-week bombing campaign, compared, for example, to the damage to Hanoi in the Christmas bombing, is a foretaste of a more moderate sort of war. More precisely, in seeing the end of total war, we see an end to an era where war puts society's very being at stake. Regimes may rise and fall, but as in the premodern era, the life of ordinary men will go on.

Through most of human history, the city-state was the natural political institution. The nation-state emerged only after guns blasted down the city's walls and cities could not produce the cannon or the men for armies. This is what befell the last generation's great powers—Britain, France, Germany—so they coalesced into continental alliances or avoided politics altogether. The end point of the first global system, the post-World War II era, was the continental state—the United States, the Soviet Union, and China. But the weaponry does not require continents. It requires expertise.

With the new technologies of war, smaller nations and cities suddenly become important. Countries like Israel or Singapore, with a few hundred thoughtful scientists and skilled engineers, can produce the instruments of war—sensors, computers, precision-guided munitions, and so on—in the coming centuries. If nothing else, their ability to sell weapons to less gifted but larger nations gives them tremendous political power.

Land warfare is therefore making a quantum shift, not only in technology but also in the consequences of technology. The logic of the first global empire—the logic of mass armies, nation-states, total war—makes little sense in a world of precision-guided weapons. Certainly, the transitions will take generations to work themselves out—to senility, as inevitably happens. But just as Cervantes could see the absurdity of the knight at the dawn of the first global epoch, so we can see the end of the GI and the birth of the Supertroop—at the beginning of the second epoch.

Contributors

Christian G. Appy received his PhD in American Civilization from Harvard. He is also author of *Patriots: The Vietnam War Remembered from All Sides.* He currently teaches at the University of Massachusetts at Amherst.

Martin Binkin is a senior fellow in Foreign Policy Studies at the Brookings Institution, Washington, D.C.

Dan Fahey served in the Navy, including service in the Persian Gulf in 1991. He has researched the use and effects of depleted uranium munitions since 1993. He holds a Master's degree in International Relations from Tufts University and is currently enrolled in a PhD program in environmental policy at the University of California at Berkeley.

Louis Font was the first West Point graduate to refuse service in Vietnam. For the past 27 years he has practiced as a civilian defense attorney before military courts and boards.

Linda Bird Francke has been a contributing editor to *New York,* an editor at *Newsweek,* and a Hers columnist for the *New York Times.* She has collaborated with four women on their best-selling memoirs: Geraldine Ferraro, Rosalynn Carter, Jehan Sadat, and Benazir Bhutto.

George Friedman is on the faculty of Tulane University and chairman of Strategic Forecasting which specializes in global business intelligence.

Meredith Friedman is a freelance writer who has published on international affairs.

Charles Sheehan-Miles was a combat soldier during the first Gulf War from 1990–91. He is currently Executive Director of the Nuclear Policy Research Institute, a nonprofit advocacy organization founded by Dr. Helen Caldicott.

Servicemembers Legal Defense Network (SLDN) is a nonprofit legal watchdog and policy advocacy organization dedicated to ending discrimination against and harassment of military personnel affected by the "Don't Ask, Don't Tell" regulations and related forms of intolerance.

Notes

1: Military Recruiting

1. Eric Schmitt, "Soft Economy Aids Recruiting Effort," *New York Times*, Sept. 17, 2003.
2. Michael Duffy and Mark Thompson, "Secretary of War," *Time*, Dec. 29, 2003–Jan. 5, 2004.
3. Thom Shanker, "US in Huge Troop Movement," *New York Times*, Jan. 9, 2004.
4. David Lamb, "Marine Ranks Swell By More than a Few" *Los Angeles Times*, June 6, 2004.
5. Robert Dorr, "Army Recruiting: Sales Pitch Changes with the Times," *Army Times*, Jan. 19, 2004.
6. Whitney Joiner, "The Army Be Thuggin' It," www.salon.com, Oct. 17, 2003.
7. Thomas J. Cutler, *The Bluejackets Manual* (Annapolis: Naval Institute Press, 2002), p. 4.
8. "Military Advertising," *Advertising Age*, June 21,1989.
9. Gina Cavallero, "Recruiting Success: Patriotism Trumps Combat Fears," *Army Times*, Aug. 18, 2003.
10. Tod Ensign, *Military Life: The Insider's Guide* (New York: ARCO, Prentice Hall, 1990) p. 9.
11. Gina Cavalerro, "Recruiting Tool Becomes Popular Online Game," *Army Times*, Sept. 1, 2003.
12. David R. Segal, *Recruiting for Uncle Sam* (Lawrence: University of Kansas Press, 1989), p. 40.
13. *Recruiter Journal*, Sept. 2002, p. 14.
14. Vince Crawley, "Recruiters See Sharp Increase in Access," *Army Times*, Dec. 23, 2002.
15. Ibid.
16. Sgt. Peter Seaberg, "Letters to the Editor," *Oregonian*, Dec. 30, 2003.
17. "JROTC at a Glance," *National Catholic Reporter*, Mar. 28, 2003.
18. Interview with author, Jan. 22, 2004.
19. Interview with author, Jan. 26, 2004.
20. Sara Olkon, "Military Recruiting/The Iraq Factor," *Miami Herald*, Dec. 26, 2003.
21. Diana White, "The Two Year College Market," *Recruiter Journal*, Sept. 2003.

22. Joiner, "The Army Be Thuggin' It."
23. Enlistment/Reenlistment Document, Armed Forces of the United States, DOD Form 4/1, published Jan. 2001.
24. Ibid., statement for enlistment, sec. 4.
25. Interview with author, Jan. 25, 2004.

2: Military Training

1. Robert Roth, *Sand in the Wind,* (Los Angeles: Pinnacle Books, 1973), p. 95.
2. Ron Kovic, *Born on the Fourth of July,* (New York: McGraw Hill, 1976), p. 77.
3. Gustav Hasford, *The Short-Timers,* (New York: Harper & Row, 1979), p. 4.
4. Kovic, *Born on the Fourth of July,* pp. 78–79.
5. Ibid., p. 81.
6. Ibid., p. 84.
7. On "toilet training" see Roth, *Sand in the Wind,* p. 119. While there were, of course, major differences between basic training and Nazi concentration camps, the "welcoming ceremonies" of each might usefully be compared. Barrington Moore offers the following description of the Nazi camps: "Upon entering the camps the prisoners faced 'welcoming ceremonies' of a thoroughly brutalizing nature. . . . These traumatic rites of passage had two closely related effects. The first was straightforward degradation, the destruction of the prisoner's self-respect, the obliteration of whatever individuality and status he or she may have enjoyed in the outside world. Second, the camp officials 'processed' the prisoners to make them as much alike as possible by issuing them uniforms and numbers after confiscating all personal possessions.

"These actions were the beginning of a regime that deprived the prisoners of all but a minimum of food and minimum of sleep. As soon as possible, camp officials controlled nearly every moment of the prisoners' waking life, even to the point of giving them only limited and selected periods of time for urination and defecation" (*Injustice,* p. 65).

8. Robert Flaherty interview, 7 July 1982.
9. Rap Group Notes, 21 Feb. 1985.
10. Peter Barnes, *Pawns: The Plight of the Citizen–Soldiers,* (New York: Knopf, 1972), p. 93–8.
11. Gene Holiday interview, 8 May 1984.
12. Barnes, *Pawns,* pp. 86 and 101; *Time,* 10 Dec. 1965, p. 31.
13. Bo Hathaway, *A World of Hurt,* (New York: Taplinger Publishing, 1981), pp. 19–20.
14. Ibid., p. 8.
15. Barnes, *Pawns,* p. 131.
16. Roth, *Sand in the Wind,* p. 115.
17. Barnes, *Pawns,* pp. 101–2.
18. Ibid., pp. 103–4.
19. Peter Tauber, *Sunshine Soldiers* (New York: Simon & Schuster, 1971).
20. Ibid., p. 24.
21. Roger Neville Williams, *The New Exiles,* (New York: Liveright, 1971), pp. 103–14; Cortright, *Soldiers in Revolt,* pp. 10–15; Helmer, *Bringing the War Home: The American Soldier in Vietnam* (New

York: Free Press, 1974), pp. 36–39; Baskir and Strauss, *Chance and Circumstance: The Draft, the War, and the Vietnam Generation* (New York: Free Press, 1972), pp. 109–66.

22. Williams, *The New Exiles,* p. 140.
23. Kenneth Emerick, *War Resisters Canada,* pp. 83–84.
24. Stan Bodner interview, 17 Mar. 1981.
25. Barnes, *Pawns,* p. 111.
26. Robert Flaherty interview, 7 July 1982.
27. Hathaway, *A World of Hurt,* p. 14.
28. Robert Flaherty interview, 7 July 1982. For another account of a "blanket party" see Hasford, *The Short-Timers,* pp. 16–17.
29. Lucinda Franks, *Waiting out a War,* (New York: Coward, McCann & Geoghegan, 1974), p. 56.
30. Ibid., p. 57.
31. Roth, *Sand in the Wind,* pp. 99–100.
32. Ibid., p. 113.
33. Ibid., p. 99.
34. Ibid., pp. 102–3.
35. Willa Short and William Seidenberg, "A Matter of Conscience," (p. 83.) *Vietnam Generation,* Winter 1989.
36. Roth, *Sand in the Wind,* pp. 142–43.
37. Tim O'Brien, *If I Die in a Combat Zone* (New York: Delacorte Press, 1973), p. 59.
38. Bob Foley interview, 15 Sept. 1981.
39. Hasford, *The Short-Timers,* pp. 12–13.
40. Sandee Shaffer Johnson, *Cadences: The Jody Call Book #1* (Canton, OH: Daring Books, 1983), p. 139. Tauber, *Sunshine Soldiers,* pp. 129–30.
41. Barnes, *Pawns,* p. 99.
42. Goff and Sanders, *Brothers: Black Soldiers in the Nam* (Norato, CA: Presidio Press, 1982). Roth, *Sand in the Wind,* p. 138.
43. Emerick, *War Resisters Canada,* p. 84.
44. Gene Holiday interview, 8 May 1984.
45. Rap Group Notes, 10 Jan. 1983.
46. Photographs of the first two billboards appear in Maitland and McInerney, *Contagion,* p. 30. The Fort Dix sign is described in Citizens Commission of Inquiry, *Dellums Committee Hearings* (New York: Vintage Press, 1971).
47. Wallace Terry, *Bloods: An Oral History of the Vietnam War* (New York: Random House, 1984).
48. Luke Jensen interview, 24 Apr. 1983.
49. Mark Baker, *Nam: The Vietnam War in the Words of Men & Women Who Fought There* (New York: William Morrow, 1981).
50. O'Brien, *If I Die,* p. 45.
51. Tauber, *Sunshine Soldiers,* pp. 141, 204.
52. Barnes, *Pawns,* p. 136; Baskir and Strauss, *Chance and Circumstance,* p. 120.

53. Mark Sampson interview, 14 Mar. 1982.
54. Todd Dasher interview, 12 Jan. 1981.
55. Frank Mathews interview, 3 Sept. 1981.

Update: Army, Navy, and Marine Basic

1. Michael Valpy, "The Soldier Who Refuses to Fight," *Toronto Globe and Mail,* Feb. 7, 2004.
2. Matthew Cox, "True Grit," *Army Times,* Feb. 16, 2004, p. 8.
3. Greg Jaffe, "A Maverick's Plan to Revamp Army," *Wall Street Journal,* Dec. 12, 2003.
4. Lt. Col. Dave Grossman, *On Killing: The Psychological Cost of Learning to Kill in War and Society* (New York: Little, Brown, 1995), pp. 254–55.
5. Ben Shalit, *The Psychology of Conflict and Combat* (New York: Praeger Press, 1988).
6. Grossman, *On Killing,* p. 319.
7. Ibid, p. 191.
8. Rowan Scarborough, "Sergeants Ill Prepared to Train Women," *Washington Times,* June 15, 1997.
9. Tod Ensign, "A Lethal Behemoth," *Against the Current,* May–June 1998, p. 15.
10. "Sergeant Pleads Guilty to Sexual Harassment," *USA Today,* June 24, 1997.
11. "Drill Instructor Convicted," *USA Today,* May 4, 1997.
12. "Eleven Female Recruits Accuse DI's," *USA Today,* June 3, 1997.
13. Bradley Graham, "Army Shuts Sex Harassment Hot Line," *Washington Post,* June 14, 1997.
14. Jim Tice, "900 Detailed Recruiters Can Expect 4th Year," *Army Times,* Feb. 16, 2004, p. 17.
15. *The Fort Jackson Guide,* manual published by Public Affairs, (2002) p. 25.
16. Laura Bailey, "Night Live Fire Training Suspended," *Army Times,* Dec. 15, 2003.
17. " 'Warrior Ethos' Is All Talk," letter to the editor, *Army Times,* Jan. 26, 2004.
18. J.F. Leahy, *Honor, Courage and Commitment: Navy Boot Camp* (Annapolis: Naval Institute Press, 2002), p. 24.
19. Ibid., pp. 92–93.
20. Thomas Cutler, *The Bluejacket's Manual* (Annapolis: Naval Institute Press, 2002), p. 361.
21. Dick J. Reavis, *The Ashes of Waco* (New York: Simon & Schuster, 1995), pp. 264–5.
22. Leahy, *Honor, Courage and Commitment,* p. 78.
23. James B. Woulfe, *Into the Crucible* (New York: Ibooks, Simon and Schuster, 2003).
24. Note: Masculine language forms are common, even though women have served as regular Marines since the 1970s.
25. Woulfe, *Into the Crucible,* p. 147.
26. Thomas E. Ricks, *Making the Corps* (New York: Scribner, 1997), p. 102.
27. David Tarrant, "Forging the Warrior," *Dallas Morning News,* April 27, 2003.
28. The author has relied on the accounts in Woulfe's *Into the Crucible* for these descriptions.
29. Woulfe, *Into the Crucible,* p. 23.
30. Michael M. Phillips, "Semper Nice: Before Heading to Iraq, Marines Learn People Skills," *Wall Street Journal,* Jan. 6, 2004.

4: Women in the Military

1. Nelson DeMille, *The General's Daughter* (New York: Warner, 1992), p. 94.

2. Ibid., p. 4.

3. S. L. A. Marshall, *Men Against Fire* (New York: Morrow, 1947), pp. 55–56, cited in *Minerva*, vol. VIII, no. 3 (Fall 1990), p. 6; also Kenneth Karst in "The Pursuit of Manhood and the Desegregation of the Armed Forces," *UCLA Law Review* 38 (1991), p. 534.

4. Col. Frank A. Partlow Jr., "Womanpower for a Superpower: The National Security Implications of Women in the United States Army," *World Affairs*, vol. 146, no. 4 (Spring 1984), p. 303.

5. Capt. Carol Barkalow with Andrea Raab, *In the Men's House* (New York: Poseidon, 1990), p. 28.

6. *New York Times*, Feb. 14, 1996, p. D20.

7. Tom Wolfe, *The Right Stuff* (New York: Farrar, Straus, Giroux, 1979), p. 29.

8. Nancy Chapkis, "Sexuality and Militarism," in Eve Isaksson, ed., *Women and the Military System* (New York: St. Martin's, 1988), p. 110.

9. Remarks by a military guide during a tour of the "Women's Corridor" in the Pentagon.

10. *West Point 1991–1992 Catalog. One Hundred Ninetieth Year*, p. 135.

11. Femininity is described as "negative identity" by Erik Erikson in *Toys and Reasons: Stages in the Ritualization of Experience* (New York: Norton, 1977) and used by Karst in "The Pursuit of Manhood and the Desegregation of the Armed Forces," p. 504.

12. George Gilder, *Men and Marriage* (Gretna, LA: Pelican, 1986), p. 183.

13. Susan Faludi, *Backlash: The Undeclared War Against American Women* (New York: Crown, 1991), p. 290.

14. Gilder, p. 183.

15. *Marines: Recruit Training for Women*, p. 6.

16. Ibid., p. 9.

17. Ibid.

18. " 'Rape' Slogan Outrages Marine Corps Commandant," *Minerva's Bulletin Board*, vol. II, no. 4 (Winter 1989), p. 5.

19. Molly Moore, *A Woman at War: Storming Kuwait with the U.S. Marines* (New York: Scribner, 1993), p. 213.

20. Dr. David Marlowe, testimony before the Presidential Commission on the Assignment of Women in the Armed Forces, May 5, 1992.

21. U.S. General Accounting Office, *DOD Service Academies: More Actions Needed to Eliminate Sexual Harassment*, GAO/NSIAD-94-6, January 1994, p. 10.

22. Melanie Martindale, Ph.D., "Sexual Harassment in the Military: 1988," 1988–89 DOD Surveys of Sex Roles, Defense Manpower Data Center, Arlington, VA, September 1990, p. iii.

23. GAO report, p. 10.

24. Martindale, p. xiii.

25. Shirley Sagawa and Nancy Duff Campbell, "Sexual Harassment of Women in the Military,"

Women in the Military Issue Paper, National Women's Law Center, Washington, DC, Oct. 30, 1992.

26. 1990 Navy Women's Study Group, "An Update Report on the Progress of Women in the Navy," pp. 111–24.

27. Martin Binkin and Shirley J. Bach, *Women and the Military* (Washington, DC: Brookings Institution, 1977), p. 87. Binkin and Bach cite menstruation research which warned that half the crimes committed by women prisoners occurred during the week before their periods (premenstrual syndrome) and that women living in close quarters tended to synchronize their menstrual cycles, leading to possible "physical and psychological effect" on units with high proportions of women.

28. Ibid., p. 89.

29. Peter Lyman, "The Fraternal Bond as a Joking Relationship: A Case Study," in Michael S. Kimmel and Michael A. Messner, eds., *Men's Lives* (New York: Macmillan, 1989), p. 167. *Men's Lives* is an anthology of social science studies and articles about men and masculinity compiled for academic courses in women's studies in the 80s.

30. Ibid., p. 170.

31. Gary Alan Fine. "The Dirty Play of Little Boys," in *Men's Lives,* p. 177. The boys established their superior group identity as white heterosexual males by disparaging outsiders like blacks.

32. Lyman, p. 174.

33. John Stoltenberg, "Pornography and Freedom," in *Men's Lives,* p. 485.

34. Jill Neimark, "Out of Bounds: The Truth About Athletes and Rape," *Mademoiselle,* May 1991, p. 196.

35. Susan Brownmiller, *Against Our Will: Men, Women and Rape* (New York: Simon & Schuster, 1975), p. 107.

36. Ibid., p. 103.

37. Ibid., p. 110.

38. Neimark, p. 198.

39. Brownmiller, p. 105.

40. Marlise Simons, "For First Time, Court Defines Rape as War Crime," *New York Times,* June 28, 1996.

41. Carol Burke, "Dames at Sea," *New Republic,* Aug. 17 & 24, 1992, p. 20.

42. Barkalow, p. 48.

43. Burke, p. 18.

44. Sheila Coronel and Ninotchka Rosca, "For the Boys," *Ms.,* November/December 1993, p. 13.

45. U.S. House Committee on Armed Services, *Women in the Military: Hearings before the Military Personnel Subcommittee,* 96th Congress, November 15, 1979. The House subcommittee held four hearings in November 1979 and one in February 1980 on the expanded utilization of women in the floundering All-Volunteer Force. In 1979 not one service met its recruiting goal, including, for the first time, the Air Force. Without the infusion of 42,000 women into the services in 1979 alone, the All-Volunteer Force would have failed. "Women made the All-Volunteer Force work," says retired Admiral Louise Wilmot. "It's one of the things we're all very proud of. They cannot

now say, 'We don't want these women, or women are not equal partners because they can't do (a), (b), (c) and (d). We didn't make the rules. We've lived by them.' "

46. Richardson testimony at 1979 hearings, p. 193.
47. Testimony of Diana Danis at hearings before the Committee on Veterans Affairs, U.S. Senate, 102nd Congress, June 30, 1992, p. 140.
48. Barbara Franco testimony at Senate hearing, p. 241.
49. *Women in the Military,* Nov. 13, 1979, p. 23.
50. Ibid., Nov. 14, 1979, p. 70.
51. Ibid., Nov. 15, 1979, p. 119.
52. Ibid., p. 156.
53. Helen Rogan, *Mixed Company: Women in the Modern Army* (New York: Putnam, 1981), p. 243.
54. *Woman in the Military* testimony of Pvt. Sarah Tolaro, Feb. 11, 1980, p. 300.
55. Ibid., testimony of Lori Lodinsky, pp. 304–305.
56. Ibid., testimony of Specialist Jimi Hernandez, p. 300.
57. Ibid., testimony of Lodinsky, p. 302.
58. Ibid., testimony of Pvt. Tolaro, p. 304.
59. Ibid., testimony of Jacqueline Lose, p. 302.
60. Ibid., Congressman Antonio Won Pat, p. 302.
61. Ibid., Congressman Sonny Montgomery, p. 303.
62. Ibid., Congresswoman Marjorie Holt, p. 307.
63. Ibid., testimony of Gen. Mary Clarke, p. 337.
64. Ibid., testimony of Congresswoman Patricia Schroeder, p. 339.
65. Ibid., testimony of Congressman Montgomery, p. 343.
66. Ibid., testimony of Brig. Gen. Margaret Brewer, USMC, p. 341.
67. Ibid., testimony of Airman Marilyn Fields, p. 346.
68. U.S. Army Audit Agency, "Enlisted Women in the Army," Report HQ 82-212, April 30, 1982, p. 37.
69. Martindale, p. 34.
70. The military's special exception to legal avenues of redress from its members has been reinforced time and again by the courts. In 1953, in *Orloff* v. *Willoughby,* 345 U.S. 83 (1953), Supreme Court Justice Robert Jackson deemed the military "a specialized community governed by a separate discipline from that of the civilian." The judicial testing of Title VII thirty years later would not penetrate that "specialized community." In 1983 the Supreme Court, in *Chappell et al.* v. *Wallace et al.,* 462 U.S. 296 (1983), would let stand a lower court ruling that the protections of Title VII did not extend to a group of black sailors trying to sue the Navy for racial discrimination in duty assignments. Military justice was a stand-alone. "The special status of the military has required, the Constitution has contemplated, Congress has created, and this Court has long recognized two systems of justice, to some extent parallel: one for civilians and one for military personnel," Chief Justice Warren Burger wrote in *Chappell* v. *Wallace.* Cited by Judith Hicks Stiehm in *Arms and the Enlisted Woman* (Philadelphia: Temple University Press, 1989), p. 109, and by Karst in "The Pursuit of Manhood and the Desegregation of the Armed Forces," p. 565, note 247.

71. *Women in the Military* statement of Col. Thomas E. Fitzpatrick, post commander, Fort Meade, MD, Feb. 11, 1980, p. 318.

72. *DOD Service Academies: More Actions Needed to Eliminate Sexual Harassment,* p. 18. The GAO lists a total of ten articles under the UCMJ to which harassment can be attached, including bribery and graft (Article 134) for servicemen offering rewards for sexual favors and Dereliction of Duty (Article 92) for those engaging in sexual harassment to the detriment of job performance.

73. Jean Ebbert and Marie-Beth Hall, *Crossed Currents: Navy Women from WWI to Tailhook* (Washington, DC/New York: Brassey's [U.S.], 1993), p. 187.

74. Tamar Lewin, "A Case Study of Sexual Harassment and the Law," *New York Times,* Oct. 11, 1991, p. 24.

75. U.S. General Accounting Office, *DOD's Policy on Homosexuality,* GAO/NSIAD-92-98, June 1992, p. 10.

76. Randy Shilts, *Conduct Unbecoming: Gays and Lesbians in the U.S. Military* (New York: St. Martin's, 1993), p. 5.

77. Celia Morris, *Bearing Witness: Sexual Harassment and Beyond—Everywoman's Story* (Boston: Little, Brown, 1994), p. 189.

78. J. Harry, "Homosexual Men and Women Who Served Their Country," *Journal of Homosexuality* 19 (1–2), 1984, p. 117, cited in Theodore R. Sarbin, Ph.D., and Kenneth E. Karois, M.D., Ph.D., "Nonconforming Sexual Orientations and Military Suitability," Deputy Personnel Security Research and Education Center (PERSEREC), Monterey, CA, 1989, p. 23.

79. *Face to Face,* Connie Chung, CBS TV, Nov. 8, 1991.

80. B. D. Clark, "The 'Lesbian' Label to Hold Back Women," *Virginian-Pilot and Ledger-Star,* Sunday, Oct. 21, 1990.

81. Jane Gross, "Hiding in Uniform—Homosexuals in the Military," *New York Times,* April 10, 1990, p. A1.

82. Michelle M. Benecke and Kirstin S. Dodge, "Military Women in Nontraditional Job Fields: Casualties of the Armed Forces' War on Homosexuals," *Harvard Women's Law Journal,* vol. 13 (1990), p. 221.

83. Jim Lynch, "Witch Hunt at Parris Island," *The Progressive,* March 1989, p. 26.

84. Ibid., p. 23.

85. Jane Gross, "Navy Is Urged to Root Out Lesbians Despite Ability," *New York Times,* Sept. 2, 1990.

86. Benecke and Dodge, p. 223.

87. Shilts, p. 632.

88. Gross, "Hiding in Uniform," p. A1.

89. Shilts, p. 640.

90. Ibid., p. 637.

91. Cynthia Enloe, *Does Khaki Become You? The Militarisation of Women's Lives* (Boston: South End, 1983), p. 143.

92. Lynch, p. 24.

93. Shilts, p. 595.
94. Philip Shenon, "New Study Faults Pentagon's Gay Policy," *New York Times,* Feb. 26, 1997, p. A10.
95. "Rape in the Military," ABC News *20/20,* Nov. 15, 1996. The Navy men who gang-raped the mechanic reported on went free. The Navy dropped the charges against two of the men without a hearing and dismissed the charges against the third after a one-day hearing because of "insufficient evidence."

Update: Women in the Military

1. Lorraine Demi, "Military Family Violence, Hushed Epidemic," *Draft Notices* newsletter, May/June 2003.
2. Ibid.
3. Miles Moffeit and Amy Herdy, "Betrayal in the Ranks" (3 part series) *Denver Post,* Nov. 17, 18, 19, 2003.
4. Demi, "Military Family Violence."
5. Moffeit and Herdy, "Betrayal in the Ranks."
6. Eric Schmitt, "New Army Rules on Ways to Cope with Civilian Life," *New York Times,* May 15, 2003.
7. Moffeit and Herdy, "Betrayal in the Ranks."
8. Diana Jean Schemo, "Air Force Secretary Says Academy Leaders Could be Punished," *New York Times,* April 2, 2003.
9. Michael Janofsky, "Air Force Begins Inquiry on Rape Charges," *New York Times,* Feb. 20, 2003.
10. Diana Jean Schemo, "Air Force Academy Seeks to Prosecute Cadet," *New York Times,* May 15, 2003.
11. Diana Jean Schemo, "Rate of Rape at Academy Put at 12%," *New York Times,* Aug. 29, 2003.
12. Diana Jean Schemo, "Air Force Ignored Sex Abuse at Academy, Inquiry Reports," *New York Times,* Sept. 23, 2003.
13. Donna Miles, "Academy Introduces Sweeping Change," *Armed Forces Press Service,* Oct. 7, 2003.
14. www.usafa.edu/agenda.cfm.
15. Judith Graham, "Expelled Cadet to be Reinstated," *Chicago Tribune* Dec. 26, 2003.
16. Eric Schmitt, "Military Women Reporting Rapes by U.S. Soldiers," *New York Times,* Feb. 26, 2004 and "Reports of Rape in Pacific Spur Air Force Steps," *New York Times,* Mar. 9, 2004.
17. Jane McHugh, "Congresswomen Urge Punishment for Sexual Assaults," *Army Times,* April 12, 2004.
18. Miles Moffeit and Amy Herdy, "37 Seek Aid after Alleging Sex Assaults by U.S. Soldiers," *Denver Post,* Jan. 25, 2004.

5: Minorities and Gays in the Military

1. Richard M. Nixon, "The All-Volunteer Armed Force," radio address, October 17, 1968, quoted in Gerald Leinwand, ed., *The Draft* (Pocket Books, 1979), p. 106.

2. *Report of the President's Commission on an All-Volunteer Armed Force* (GPO, February 1970), pp. 15–16, 149.

3. A similar proportion of white men who entered the armed forces during the decade had also not completed high school. Data are from Defense Manpower Data Center; and Bureau of the Census, "Preliminary Estimates of the Population of the United States, by Age, Sex, and Race: 1970 to 1981," *Current Population Reports,* series P-25, no. 917 (Department of Commerce, 1982), table 1.

4. The derivation of these estimates is provided in Binkin and Eitelberg, *Blacks and the Military,* p. 66.

5. James A. Davis, Jennifer Lauby, and Paul B. Sheatsley, *Americans View the Military: Public Opinion in 1982,* NORC report 131 (Chicago: National Opinion Research Center, University of Chicago, April 1983), p. 43.

6. Milton Friedman, "The Case for Abolishing the Draft—and Substituting for It an All-Volunteer Army," *New York Times Magazine,* May 14, 1967, p. 118.

7. One of the strongest proponents for black participation has been Congressman Ronald V. Dellums of California, who chairs the House Armed Services Committee and is a member of the Congressional Black Caucus. See his article, "Dellums: Don't Slam Door to Military," *Focus,* vol. 3 (June 1975), p. 6.

8. In 1978 the Southern Christian Leadership Conference blamed black overrepresentation in Army penal facilities on inequities in the criminal justice system, specifically the low percentage of black officers and the predominance of prejudiced white officers from the South. Bill Drummond, "Army Concerned about Blacks' High Rates of Criminality," *Washington Post,* November 19, 1978, pp. G1, G2.

9. By 1979, for example, blacks made up 32.2 percent of Army enlisted personnel but only 6.8 percent of the Army officer corps (Binkin and Eitelberg, *Blacks and the Military,* p. 42). Much of the disparity resulted from a requirement that officers, with few exceptions, possess college degrees. In 1979 only 5 percent of all male college graduates age twenty to twenty-nine were black. Bureau of the Census, "Educational Attainment in the United States: March 1979 and 1978," *Current Population Reports,* series P-20, no. 356 (Department of Commerce, 1980), table 1.

10. Among the earliest to highlight the issue were Morris Janowitz and Charles C. Moskos, Jr., "Racial Composition in the All-Volunteer Force," *Armed Forces and Society,* vol. 1 (November 1974), pp. 109–23; and Binkin and Eitelberg, *Blacks and the Military* (Brookings, 1982), which drew heavily on Mark Jan Eitelberg, "Military Representation: The Theoretical and Practical Implications of Population Representation in the American Armed Forces," Ph.D. dissertation, New York University, 1979. Eitelberg's work is the most comprehensive and insightful examination of issues involving representation in the armed forces.

11. Binkin and Eitelberg, *Blacks and the Military.*

12. Clifford L. Alexander, Jr., "In the Army Now," *Washington Post Book World,* August 22, 1982, p. 3.

13. Nicholas Von Hoffman, "Black Gls: A Khaki Quota?" *Philadelphia Daily News,* July 30, 1982.

14. Carl Rowan, "No One's Worried about 'Grunts,' " *Atlanta Constitution,* July 2, 1982.
15. Roger Wilkins, "Right Issues, Wrong Questions," in Edwin Dorn, ed., *Who Defends America? Race, Sex, and Class in the Armed Forces* (Washington: Joint Center for Political Studies Press, 1989), p. 164. This book compiled the papers and remarks presented at the 1982 symposium. Wilkins's comment about the reaction of allies was aimed at the revelation by Lawrence J. Korb, then an assistant secretary of defense, that officials of some allied nations, most notably the Federal Republic of Germany, had expressed concerns over the growing number of black American servicemen in their countries. Lawrence J. Korb, "The Pentagon's Perspective," in Dorn, ed., *Who Defends America?* p. 23.
16. Michael R. Gordon, "Black and White," *National Journal,* June 4, 1983, p. 1182.
17. Office of the Secretary of Defense, *Military Compensation Background Papers, Compensation Elements and Related Manpower Cost Items: Their Purposes and Legislative Backgrounds,* 4th ed. (Department of Defense, November 1991), p. 43.
18. Derived from data provided by the Defense Manpower Data Center; and Bureau of the Census, "Projections of the Population of the United States: 1977 to 2050," *Current Population Reports,* series P-25, no. 704 (Department of Commerce, 1977), table 8.
19. For a discussion of the caucus's position, see Rowan Scarborough, "Caucus's Plan Could Hit Blacks Hardest," *Washington Times,* April 19, 1990, pp. A1, A8. Also see Edwin Dorn, "Assessing the Peace Dividend," *Focus,* vol. 18 (April 1990), pp. 3–4.
20. Quoted in Democratic Leadership Council. *Citizenship and National Service: A Blueprint for Civic Enterprise* (Washington, May 1988), p. 25.
21. Democratic Leadership Council, *Citizenship and National Service,* p. 25. Ironically, Governor Bill Clinton, who would become embroiled in the draft controversy during his presidential campaign, was a member of the governing board of the Democratic Leadership Council and one of the architects of its national service proposal. In effect, the council's report appeared at odds with Governor Clinton's credentials for president by asking, "how can [America's future] leaders be expected to grasp the complexities of defense policy without any first-hand experience with the military?" (p. 25).
22. Quoted in Scott Shepard, "Who Dies? Racial Makeup of Gulf Troops Revives Issue of Fairness," *Atlanta Journal,* December 17, 1990.
23. Office of the Assistant Secretary of Defense for Force Management and Personnel, *Population Representation in the Military Services, Fiscal Year 1990* (Department of Defense, July 1991), pp. 33, 41.
24. Richard L. Fernandez, *Social Representation in the U.S. Military* (Congressional Budget Office, October 1989), p. xii. Also see Fernandez, "A Poor-Man's Military? Not At All," *Washington Post,* December 18, 1990, p. 21.
25. Edwin Dorn, "Devil's Bargain in the Front Lines," *Los Angeles Times,* December 4, 1990, p. B7. Also see Lynne Duke, "For Many Blacks, Call to Duty Rings of Inequality," *Washington Post,* November 28, 1990, p. 1; and Shepard, "Who Dies?"
26. Juan Williams, "Race and War in the Persian Gulf . . . Why Are Black Leaders Trying to Divide Blacks from the American Mainstream?" *Washington Post,* January 20, 1991, p. B2. Williams,

a syndicated columnist, criticized these leaders for driving a "wedge between black America and its troops in combat as well as mainstream America."

27. Isabel Wilkerson, "Blacks Wary of Their Big Role in Military," *New York Times*, January 25, 1991, p. 1.

28. Ibid., p. 1.

29. James M. Perry, "Black Voters Are More Disapproving Than Whites of the Deployment of U.S. Forces to Middle East," *Wall Street Journal*, August 22, 1990, p. A10.

30. Williams, "Race and War in the Persian Gulf," p. B2.

31. Lynne Duke, "Gen. Powell Notes Military Enlistment Remains Matter of Individual Choice," *Washington Post*, November 28, 1990, p. A30.

32. Department of Defense, "Fact Sheet," Desert Shield 153, January 3, 1991.

33. Mark J. Eitelberg, "A Preliminary Assessment of Population Representation in Operations Desert Shield and Desert Storm," paper prepared for the 1991 Biennial Conference of the Inter-University Seminar on Armed Forces and Society, pp. 15, 17, 18; and Defense Manpower Data Center.

34. Les Aspin, chairman of the House Armed Services Committee, estimated that total casualties would be 3,000 to 5,000 with up to 1,000 deaths; Molly Moore, "Aspin War Would Start with Air Strikes, Escalate to Ground Battles," *Washington Post*, January 9, 1991, p. A15. The Center for Defense Information, assuming a 120-day campaign, predicted 45,000 U.S. casualties, including 10,000 deaths. Juan J. Walte, "One Estimate: 45,000 U.S. Casualties," *USA Today*, January 7, 1991, p. 8.

35. Eitelberg, "Preliminary Assessment," pp. 17, 32; and data from Defense Manpower Data Center.

36. Nearly a quarter of the combat deaths, according to one report, were the result of friendly fire. Eric Schmitt, "U.S. Seeks to Cut Accidental War Death," *New York Times*, December 9, 1991. p. 12. See also Eitelberg, "Preliminary Assessment," pp. 28, 31.

37. Even in the event of stronger Iraqi resistance, it is unlikely that blacks would have suffered casualties in the same high proportion as their presence in ground combat units because they tend to be clustered in units that have traditionally had less hazardous duties. For example, in 1990 blacks accounted for 23 percent of soldiers assigned to infantry, armor, and combat engineer skills, which in previous wars have accounted for over 93 percent of Army battle losses. But they fill 44 percent of artillery positions, which have accounted, at most, for 7 percent of casualties. See *Planning Factors*, Student text 101-2 (Fort Leavenworth, Kans.: Army Command and General Staff College, June 1985), p. 4–25; and data from Defense Manpower Data Center. Thus if history is a guide, it could be expected that black casualties would have amounted to 22 percent of the casualties taken by ground combat units, a percentage smaller than that of blacks in the combat arms or in the ground forces, but still much larger than in the military-age population as a whole.

38. For example, in August 1991 the *New York Times* was once again reporting that blacks stood to lose the most from the renewed force reductions. Lee A. Daniels, "With Military Set to Thin Ranks, Blacks Fear They'll Be Hurt Most," *New York Times*, August 7, 1991, p. 1. Also see James E. Ellis, "Where Troop Cuts Will Be Cruelest," *Business Week*, June 8, 1992, pp. 72–73.

39. Mark Shields, a liberal political and social commentator, lamented that the military buildup on the Arabian peninsula had not touched the Washington establishment. "This noisy, contentious city turned mute because almost without exception no Washington dinner party guest—liberal or conservative, Democrat or Republican—personally knows a single one of the 1.8 million enlisted Americans serving in our armed forces." Mark Shields, "Bellicose Hypocrites," *Washington Post,* November 2, 1990, p. 25. See also John Kenneth Galbraith, "(Class) War in the Gulf," *New York Times,* November 7, 1990, p. A31; and Richard Lacayo, "Why No Blue Blood Will Flow," *Time,* November 26, 1990, p. 34. Finally, the *Boston Globe,* in an editorial opinion, called for a revival of conscription "for reasons of social and economic fairness." "It's Time to Think about the Draft," *Boston Globe,* February 4, 1991, p. 10.

Various groups that opposed the military intervention were quick to join the crusade in hopes the threat of conscription would reignite the "Hell no, we won't go!" rallying cry of the 1960s' campus counterculture that had been widely credited with hastening the end of U.S. involvement in Southeast Asia. See, for example, Michael deCourcy Hinds, "Confrontation in the Gulf: Anti-war Effort Buds Quickly, Nurtured by Activism of 60's," *New York Times,* January 11, 1991, p. A1; and Anthony DePalma, "War in the Gulf: On Campus: A War again Stirs Anguish, But of a Quieter Kind," *New York Times,* January 20, 1991, p. 18A.

40. Data from Defense Manpower Data Center. This assumes that the smaller group of volunteers would have the same racial distribution and that conscripts would be provided by a stochastic, or lottery, system with few exemptions and deferments, which in theory would provide a representative cross section of the eligible population. It should be noted that blacks would be underrepresented in a randomly selected draft population because they would be less likely to meet minimum entry standards. For example, blacks make up about 15 percent of 18-year-old men, but under existing entry standards only 11 percent would be *eligible* for military service. See Fernandez, *Social Representation in the U.S. Military,* p. 78.

41. Ibid., pp. 64–65.

42. "Prepared Statement of Dr. Ronald Walters" in *The Impact of the Persian Gulf War and the Decline of the Soviet Union on How the United States Does Its Defense Business,* Hearings before the House Armed Services Committee, 102 Cong. 1 sess. (GPO, 1991), p. 135. Walters, a professor of political science at Howard University, suggested that a limitation be placed on the number of enlistments that could be accepted from certain "economically impacted communities" (p. 135).

43. The close connection between voluntary enlistments and civilian employment opportunities has been verified in countless econometric studies. For example, see Charles Dale and Curtis Gilroy, "The Effects of the Business Cycle on the Size and Composition of the U.S. Army," *Atlantic Economic Journal,* vol. 11 (March 1983), pp. 42–53.

44. Testimony by Christopher Jehn, assistant secretary of defense for force management and personnel, in *Hearings on National Defense Authorization Act for Fiscal Years 1992 and 1993—H.R. 2100 and Oversight of Previously Authorized Programs,* Hearings before the Military Personnel and Compensation Subcommittee, House Armed Services Committee, 102 Cong. 1 sess. (GPO, 1991), p. 394.

45. An important measure of the quality of prospective volunteers is the score obtained on the Armed Services Vocational Aptitude Battery (ASVAB). This entry test is used both to measure general military trainability in a single index common to all services and to assess vocational aptitude for job categories specific to each service. Qualification for entry into a service is based on scores obtained on one portion of the battery, called the Armed Forces Qualification Test (AFQT), which place applicants into categories ranging from very high trainability (category 1, 93d to 99th percentile) to very low trainability (category V, 9th percentile and lower). The services have found that entrants scoring below the 31st percentile (categories IV and V) require more training and present greater disciplinary problems than those in the higher groups, and those scoring in category V are disqualified. *Test Manual for the Armed Services Vocational Aptitude Battery,* DOD 2304.12AA (North Chicago, Ill.: U.S. Military Entrance Processing Command, July 1984), p. 2.

46. "Choice" recruits, in the eyes of the services, are high school graduates with above-average aptitudes for military skills. Those who have completed high school are considered more likely to complete their initial obligation, and those with high test scores are considered easier to train. The Army, for example, establishes recruiting goals for this category of volunteers, dubbed GSMAs (seniors or high school graduates who score in the top half of the population of test takers).

47. For an excellent discussion of service entry standards and their sensitivity to external factors, see Mark J. Eitelberg and others, *Screening for Service: Aptitude and Education Criteria for Military Entry* (Office of the Assistant Secretary of Defense for Manpower, Installations, and Logistics, September 1984).

48. Office of the Assistant Secretary of Defense for Manpower, Reserve Affairs, and Logistics, *Profile of American Youth: 1980 Nationwide Administration of the Armed Forces Vocational Aptitude Battery* (Department of Defense, March 1982), pp. 24, 77. A spread of one standard deviation means a cutoff score that included the top 50 percent of whites would include only 16 percent of blacks. This is based on the assumption that the scores of blacks and whites are distributed normally and that the standard deviations of each distribution are the same.

49. "Propensity," the inclination to consider military service, has been measured since 1975 by the Youth Attitude Tracking Study (YATS), sponsored by the Department of Defense. The study gathers information about the characteristics, values, aspirations, and activities of young people in the military's traditional recruitment target population. For a description of the methodology, see Peter F. Ramsberger, "Characteristics of Youth and Propensity for Military Service: Findings from the 1990 Communications and Enlistment Decisions/Youth Attitude Tracking Study," FR-PRD-91-15, Human Resources Research Organization, Alexandria, Va., October 1991, app. A.

50. This has been apparent in survey data. In 1992, for example, 36 percent of 16- to 21-year-old male respondents indicated they would be "less likely to enlist" in response to the question, "With the budget cuts in the Defense Department, the military may not recruit as many new people as before. How does this affect your attitude towards enlistment?" Data from Department of Defense in Defense Manpower Data Center, "1992 Youth Attitude Tracking Study," memorandum, n.d.

51. Bernard Adelsberger, "Drawdown May Tip Racial Scales," *Army Times,* December 23, 1991, p. 45.
52. David Binder, "Army Head Favors Volunteers," *New York Times,* February 11, 1977, p. A14.
53. "An Examination of the Use of the Armed Forces Qualification Test (AFQT) as a Screen and a Measure of Quality," report to the Secretary of the Army and the Chief of Staff (Department of the Army, July 1980), p. iii. This study, known as the Lister report after Army General Counsel Sara E. Lister, was carried out during Secretary of the Army Clifford Alexander's term. It is no secret that the military leadership was at odds with the secretary on many issues, including this one.
54. "Examination of Use of Armed Forces Qualification Test," pp. III-11, IV-6. For a discussion of criterion-referenced systems, see W. James Popharn, *Criterion-Referenced Measurement* (Prentice-Hall, 1978).
55. Alexandra K. Wigdor and Bert F. Green, Jr., eds., *Performance Assessment for the Workplace* (Washington: National Academy Press, 1991), p. vii.
56. Ibid., pp. 11, 179.
57. Ibid., p. 179.
58. John P. Campbell, "An Overview of the Army Selection and Classification Project (Project A)," *Personnel Psychology,* vol. 43 (Summer 1990), pp. 232–33. This seven-year research effort initiated in 1983 was conducted by the Army Research Institute for the Behavioral and Social Sciences and a consortium of three research firms. The summer 1990 issue of *Personnel Psychology* is devoted to a description of the project and summarizes its findings.
59. "Examination of the Use of the Armed Forces Qualification Test," p. III-30. Bias in testing is a complex, highly technical question on which it is difficult to obtain a consensus, even about its meaning. For an overview of the literature, see Mark J. Eitelberg, "Subpopulation Differences in Performance on Tests of Mental Ability: Historical Review and Annotated Bibliography," technical memorandum 81–3 (Directorate for Accession Policy. Office of the Secretary of Defense, August 1981).
60. For a general discussion of cultural bias in standardized testing, see Robert L. Green and Robert J. Griffore, "The Impact of Standardized Testing on Minority Students," *Journal of Negro Education,* vol. 49 (Summer 1980), pp. 238–52.
61. Nancy Guinn, Ernest C. Tupes, and William E. Allen, "Cultural Subgroup Differences in the Relationships between Air Force Aptitude Composites and Training Criteria" (Lackland Air Force Base, Tex.: Air Force Human Resources Laboratory, September 1970). See also Lonnie D. Valentine, "Prediction of Air Force Technical Training Success from ASVAB and Educational Background," Lackland Air Force Base, Tex.: Air Force Human Resources Laboratory, May 1977.
62. R. Darrell Bock and Robert J. Mislevy, "The Profile of American Youth: Data Quality Analysis of the Armed Services Vocational Aptitude Battery." University of Chicago, National Opinion Research Center, August 1981, p. 51.
63. Department of Defense, Office of the General Counsel, "Does the ASVAB Test Meet Applicable Legal Requirements Prohibiting Use of Tests That Discriminate on the Basis of Race, Color, Religion, Sex or National Origin?" Memorandum, September 1977, p. 6.

64. "The All-Volunteer Force and the End of the Draft," special report of Secretary of Defense Elliot L. Richardson (March 1973), p. 13, as quoted in Martin Binkin and John D. Johnston, *All-Volunteer Armed Forces: Progress, Problems, and Prospects,* Committee Print, Senate Committee on Armed Services, 93 Cong. 1 sess. (GPO, June 1973), p. 52.
65. Office of the Assistant Secretary of Defense for Manpower, Installations, and Logistics, *Defense Manpower Quality,* vol. 2: *Army Submission* (Department of Defense, May 1985), p. xii. Fiscal year 1991 data are from Defense Manpower Data Center.

An Overview of "Don't Ask, Don't Tell, Don't Pursue, Don't Harass"

1. C. Dixon Osburn, *A Policy in Desperate Search of a Rationale: The Military's Policy on Lesbians, Gays and Bisexuals,* 64 UMKC L. Rev. 199 (1995).
2. DADTDPDH does not address gender identity. For information on military rules and regulations see the section on transgender issues in this guide.
3. *Policy Concerning Homosexuality in the Armed Forces: Hearings Before the Senate Comm. on the Armed Services,* 103d Cong., 707 (1993) (statement of General Colin Powell) [hereinafter Powell Statement]. "[H]omosexuals have privately served well in the past and are continuing to serve well today." *Id. See also,* Memorandum from Secretary of Defense Les Aspin to the Secretaries of the Military Departments, *Policy on Homosexual Conduct in the Armed Forces* [hereinafter Aspin Policy Memorandum] (Jul. 19, 1993). "[T]he Department of Defense also recognizes that individuals with a homosexual orientation have served with distinction in the armed forces of the United States." *Id.*
4. Dep't of Defense Directive 1332.14, *Enlisted Administrative Separations* [hereinafter DoDD 1332.14], para. E3.A1.1.8.1.1 (1994); Dep't of Defense Instruction 1332.40, *Separation Procedures for Regular and Reserve Commissioned Officers* [hereinafter DoDI 1332.40], para. E2.3 (1997). "A member's sexual orientation is considered a personal and private matter, and is not a bar to continued service . . . unless manifested by homosexual conduct. . . ." *Id.*
5. *See* Dep't of Defense Directive 1304.26, *Qualification Standards for Enlistment, Appointment, and Induction* [hereinafter DoDD 1304.26], para. E1.2.8.1 (1994).
6. *See* Powell Statement, *supra* note 3. "We will not ask, we will not witch hunt, we will not seek to learn orientation." *Id.*
7. *See* Aspin Policy Memorandum, *supra* note 3, attachment *Policy Guidelines on Homosexual Conduct in the Armed Forces; see also* DoDD 1304.26, *supra* note 5. *Applicant Briefing Item on Separation Policy.* "The Armed Forces do not tolerate harassment or violence against any service member, for any reason." *Id. See also,* Memorandum from Under Secretary of Defense for Personnel and Readiness [hereinafter P&R] Rudy de Leon to the Secretaries of the Military Departments, *Guidelines for Investigating Threats Against or Harassment of Service Members Based on Alleged Homosexuality* [hereinafter de Leon Investigating Harassment Memorandum] (Aug. 12, 1989).
8. Memorandum from Secretary of Defense Les Aspin to the Secretaries of the Military Departments, *Implementation of the DoD Policy on Homosexual Conduct in the Armed Forces* [hereinafter Aspin Implementation Memorandum] (Dec. 21, 1993). "[The new policy] provides that investigations into sexual misconduct will be conducted in an evenhanded manner, with-

out regard to whether the alleged misconduct involves homosexual or heterosexual conduct." *Id.*

9. *See* Pub. Papers William J. Clinton, 1993, vol. 1, p. 1111. President Clinton pledged that the policy would provide for "a decent regard for the legitimate privacy and associational rights of all service members." *Id.* Then Senator William Cohen understood that the small amount of privacy under the current policy was intended to prevent the military from prying into people's private lives. *See, Policy Concerning Homosexuality in the Armed Forces: Hearings Before the Senate Comm. on Armed Services,* 103d Cong. 787 (statement of Senator William Cohen).

10. Exec. Order No. 12,968, 60 Fed. Reg. 40,245 (Aug. 7, 1995).

11. Exec. Order No. 13,140, 64 Fed. Reg. 55,115 (Oct. 12, 1999). *See also,* Manual for Courts-Martial (2000) rev. [hereinafter MCM], part III, Military Rule of Evidence 513.

12. *See also,* MCM, part II, Rule for Court-Martial 1001(b)(4).

13. *See* Evaluation Report: *Military Environment With Respect to the Homosexual Conduct Policy,* Office of the Inspector General of the Department of Defense, Rept. No. D-2000-101 (Mar. 16, 2000).

14. DoDD 1332.14, *supra* note 4, para. E3.A4.1.4.3: DoDI 1332.40, *supra* note 4, para. E8.4.3.

15. DoDD 1332.14, *supra* note 4, para. E3.A4.1.3.2.2; DoDI 1332.40, *supra* note 4, para. E8.3.2.2.

16. Communications with Chaplains regarding "spiritual matters" are protected. However, discussing sexual orientation may not be considered a spiritual matter. Please see the section on Chaplains in this Guide.

17. *See* Dep't of Defense Reg. 5200.2-R, *Personnel Security Program* [hereinafter DoD 5200.2-R], para. C2.4.3.4.3 (1996).

18. *See* DoDD 1332.14, *supra* note 4, para. E3.A1.1.8.1.1; DoDI 1332.40, *supra* note 4, para. E2.3.

19. *See* DoDD 1332.14, *supra* note 4, para. E3.A4.1.1.1; DoDI 1332.40, *supra* note 4, para. E8.1.1.

20. *Id.*

21. *See* DoDD 1332.14, *supra* note 4, para. E3.A4.1.3.3.4; DoDI 1332.40, *supra* note 4, para. E.8.3.3.4.

22. *See* de Leon Investigating Harassment Memorandum, *supra* note 7.

23. *See* DoDD 1332.14, *supra* note 4, para. E3.A4.1.1.3; DoDI 1332.40, *supra* note 4, para. E8.1.3.

24. *See* Office of the Under Secretary of Defense (P&R), Report to the Secretary of Defense: *Review of the Effectiveness of the Application and Enforcement of the Department's Policy on Homosexual Conduct in the Military* [hereinafter Under Secretary of Defense (P&R) 1998 Report], at 11, 12 (Apr. 1998); *See also* Memorandum from Under Secretary of Defense (P&R) Rudy de Leon to the Secretaries of the Military Departments, *Implementation of Recommendations Concerning Homosexual Conduct Policy* [hereinafter de Leon Implementation Memorandum] (Aug. 12, 1999).

25. *Id.*

26. Dep't of Defense Instruction 5505.8, *Investigations of Sexual Misconduct by the Defense Criminal Investigative Organizations and Other DoD Law Enforcement Organizations* [hereinafter DoDI 5505.8], para. 4.2 (2000).

27. *See* DoDD 1332.14, *supra* note 4, para. E3.A4.1.1.3; DoDI 1332.40, *supra* note 4, para. E8.1.3.;

see also, Under Secretary of Defense (P&R) 1998 Report, *supra* note 24, at 11,12; *see also,* de Leon Implementation Memorandum, *supra* note 24.

28. *See* Under Secretary of Defense (P&R) 1998 Report, *supra* note 24, at 12.

29. *See id.*

30. *See* de Leon Implementation Memorandum, *supra* note 24.

31. *See* Under Secretary of Defense (P&R) 1998 Report, *supra* note 24, at 12.

32. DoDD 1304.26, *supra* note 5, *Applicant Briefing Item on Separation Policy; see also,* Aspin Policy Memorandum, *supra* note 3, attachment *Policy Guidelines on Homosexual Conduct in the Armed Forces.*

33. *See* DoDD 1332.14, *supra* note 4, para. E2.1.7; DoDI 1332.40, *supra* note 4, para. E1.1.12.

34. 10 U.S.C. §654 (f)(3).

35. 10 U.S.C. §654 (b)(1).

36. *See* DoDI 5505.8, *supra* note 26, para. 1.2. *See also,* Under Secretary of Defense (P&R) 1998 Report, *supra* note 24, at 9.

37. *See* MCM, part IV, paras. 51(e)(4), 59(e), and 90(e), respectively.

38. *See* DoDD 1332.14, *supra* note 4, para. E3.A1.1.8.4.

39. *See* DoDD 1332.14, *supra* note 4, para. E3.A3.1.3; DoDI 1332.40, *supra* note 4, para. E5.4.

40. *See* DoDI 1332.40, *supra* note 4, para. E4.1.

41. *See* DoDD 1332.14, *supra* note 4, para. E3.A3.1.3.5.1.

42. *See* DoDD 1332.14, *supra* note 4, para. E3.A3.1.3.5.7.2; DoDI 1332.40, *supra* note 4, para. E3.3.3.

43. *See* DoDD 1332.14, *supra* note 3, para. E3.A3.1.3.5.5.

44. *See generally,* DoDI 1332.40, *supra* note 4, para. E3.3.3.

45. Members of the board can be challenged for cause, however, if defense counsel can show bias or susceptibility to outside influence. *See* DoDI 1332.40, *supra* note 4, para. E5.1.

46. *See* DoDD 1332.14, *supra* note 4, para. E3.A1.1.8.3; DoDI 1332.40, *supra* note 4, para. E7.2.2.2.

47. *Id.*

48. *See* DoDD 1332.14, *supra* note 4, para. E3.A4.1.4.3; DoDI 1332.40, *supra* note 4, para. E8.4.3.

49. *Id.*

50. *Id.*

51. *See* DoDD 1332.14, *supra* note 4, para. E2.1.7; DoDI 1332.40, *supra* note 4, para. E1.1.12.

52. *See* DoDD 1332.14, *supra* note 4, para. E3.A4.1.3.3; DoDI 1332.40, *supra* note 4, para. E8.3.3.4.

53. *See* MCM, part III, Military Rule of Evidence 305(d)(1).

54. *See* MCM, part III, Military Rule of Evidence 305(d)(2).

55. *See e.g.,* COMMANDER NAVY LEGAL SERVICES COMMAND INSTRUCTION 5800.1E, §1103 (2002).

56. *See* MCM, part II, Rule for Court-Martial 506(a).

57. *See* DoDD 1332.14, *supra* note 4, para. E3.A4.1.3.2; DoDI 1332.40, *supra* note 4, para. E8.3.2.

58. 10 USC §654(f)(2).

59. 10 USC §654(b)(2).

60. *See, e.g.,* Air Force Manual 52–103, *Chaplain Service Readiness Manual,* attachment 10. The quoted language is part of the Covenant and Code of Ethics for Chaplains of the Armed Forces as prescribed by the National Conference on Ministry to the Armed Forces.
61. Service members should inform a chaplain that the communication should not be disclosed to third parties. "A communication is 'confidential' if made to a clergyman in the clergyman's capacity as a spiritual adviser or to a clergyman's assistant in the assistant's official capacity and is not intended to be disclosed to third persons. . . ." MCM, part III, Military Rule of Evidence 503(b)(2).
62. *See* U.S. Const. amend. IV.
63. *See* Dep't of Defense Directive 1325.2, *Desertion and Unauthorized Absence,* para. 4.1.2 (1990). Desertion may also be proven by intent of a person leaving or going to a foreign country under certain circumstances. *See id.*, at paras. 4.1.1 and 4.1.3.
64. *See* MCM, part II, Rule for Court-Martial 302(b)(3); *see also,* UCMJ, Art. 8.
65. *See* U.S. Const. amend. IV.
66. *See generally,* VA Pamphlet 22-90-2, *The Montgomery GI Bill-Active Duty* [hereinafter VA Pamphlet 22-90-2], Dep't Veterans Affairs (2001).
67. Any person subject to the UCMJ can prefer charges against any other member subject to the Code. MCM, part II, Rule for Court-Martial 307(a). However, the common practice is only commanders, through the aid of command legal officers, prefer charges.
68. *See* MCM, part A2, §938.
69. *See* 10 USC §1034.
70. *See* U.S.Const. amend. IV; *see also,* 10 USC §1034.
71. *See* 10 USC §1034; *see also,* Dep't of Defense Directive 7050.6, *Military Whistleblower Protection* (2000).
72. 10 U.S.C. §654(e); *see also,* DoDD 1304.26, *supra* note 5, *Applicant Briefing Item on Separation Policy;* DoDD 1332.14, *supra* note 4, para. E3.A1.1.8.4.7.2; DoDI 1332.40, *supra* note 4, para. E2.3.3.
73. *See* DoDD 1332.14, para. E3.A4.1.1.1; DoDD 1332.40, para. E8.1.1.
74. *See* DoDI 5505.8, *supra* note 26, para. 6.3.
75. *See* DoDD 1332.14, *supra* note 4, para. E3.A4.1.1.1; DoDI 1332.40, *supra* note 4, para. E8.1.1.
76. *See* DoDD 1332.14, *supra* note 4, para. E3.A4.1.3.1; DoDI 1332.40, *supra* note 4, para. E8.3.1; *see also,* DoDI 5505.8, *supra* note 43, para. E1.1.2
77. *See* DoDD 1332.14, *supra* note 4, para. E3.A4.1.3.3; DoDI 1332.40, *supra* note 4, para. E8.3.3.
78. *See* DoDI 5505.8, *supra* note 26, paras. 1.2, 4; *see also,* Under Secretary of Defense (P&R) 1998 Report, *supra* note 24, at 9.
79. *See* MCM, part IV, paras, 51(e)(4), 59(e), and 90(e), respectively.
80. *See* MCM, part IV, para. 58 (UCMJ Art. 132).
81. *See* MCM, part IV, para. 31 (UCMJ Art. 107).
82. *See* MCM, part IV, para. 83 (UCMJ Art. 134 (Fraternization)). Note that only commissioned or warrant officers may be charged with fraternization. *Id.* Enlisted members can be charged with violating applicable service regulations. *See* MCM, part IV, para. 16 (UCMJ Art. 92).

83. *See* MCM, part IV, para. 16 (UCMJ Art. 92).
84. *See generally,* 10 USC §513.
85. 10 USC §802(a)(1).
86. 10 USC §802(b).
87. *See* DoDD 1332.14, *supra* note 4, para. E3.A1.1.5.5.
88. *See* DEP'T OF DEFENSE INSTRUCTION 1336.1, *Certificate of Release or Discharge from Active Duty* [hereinafter DoDI 1336.1], para. 3.3.1 (2002).
89. *See* DoDD 1332.14, *supra* note 4, para. E3.A1.1.6. Entry level separation is not available for officers.
90. *See* DoDD1332.14, *supra* note 4, paras. E3.A1.1.8.3, E3.A2.1.3; DoDI 1332.40, *supra* note 4, para. E7.2.1; *see also,* Aspin Implementation Memorandum, *supra* note 8, attachment *Overview, Directives Implementing the New DoD Policy on Homosexual Conduct in the Armed Forces.*
91. *See* DEP'T OF DEFENSE DIRECTIVE 1332.28. *Discharge Review Board (DRB) Procedures and Standards* [hereinafter DoDD 1332.28], para. E3.3.6 (1983).
92. *See* DoDD 1332.14, *supra* note 4, para. E3.A1.1.8.3; DoDI 1332.40, *supra* note 4, para. E7.2.2.2.
93. *See generally,* VA Pamphlet 22-90-2, *supra* note 66.
94. *Id.*
95. The short form is called Member Copy 1 and the long form is called Member Copy 4. *See* DoDI 1336.1, *supra* note 88, para. 3.2.1.1.
96. For the Air Force, the code is 2B or 2C. *See* AIR FORCE INSTRUCTION 36-2606, *Reenlistment in the Air Force,* table 3.2 (2001).

6: Veterans and Toxic Exposures

1. Raul Ramirez is a pseudonym for a Mexican American veteran interviewed by the author who did not want his real name used.
2. Enriched uranium is uranium in which the U235 content has been increased from 0.7 percent to 90 percent.
3. The Royal Society, *The Health Hazards of Depleted Uranium Munitions,* part 1 (London, 2001), p. 2. R. Pengelley, "The DU Debate: What Are the Risks," *Jane's Defence Weekly,* 15 January 2001.
4. J. Middleton, "Elimination of Toxic/Hazardous Materials from Small Caliber Ammunition—An Overview," International Tungsten Industry Association, December 2000 newsletter, p. 5, http://www.itia.org.uk.
5. P. Bolté, "The Tank Killers—Tungsten v. Depleted Uranium," *National Defense,* May–June 1983, p. 44.
6. Joint Technical Coordinating Group for Munitions Effectiveness (JTCG/ME), Ad Hoc Working Group for Depleted Uranium, *Special Report: Medical and Environmental Evaluation of Depleted Uranium,* vol. 1 (1974), pp. 1, 2.
7. Ibid., p. 96.
8. Reed C. Magness, "Environmental Overview for Depleted Uranium," CRDC-TR-85030 (Aberdeen Proving Ground, MD, October 1985), pp. 10–12. In a response to Mr. Duncan Smith in

the UK Parliament on 2 February 2001, Mr. John Spellar, UK Minister of Transport, stated that DU is used in balance weights in the Tristar helicopter, Wessex helicopter, and C-130 aircraft.

9. US Army Center for Health Promotion and Preventive Medicine, Radiological Sources of Potential Exposure and/or Contamination (Aberdeen Proving Ground, 10 December 1999), pp. 114–20.

10. P. Richter, "Old-Fashioned Hide-Outs Fuel High-Tech Weaponry," *Los Angeles Times,* 17 March 2002, p. A1; M. L. Wald, "U.S. Refits a Nuclear Bomb To Destroy Enemy Bunkers," *New York Times,* 31 May 1997, p. A1.

11. US Army Environmental Policy Institute, *Health and Environmental Consequences of Depleted Uranium Use by the U.S. Army, Technical Report* (Atlanta: AEPI, 1995), p. 25.

12. M.E. Kilpatrick, "No Depleted Uranium in Cruise Missiles or Apache Helicopter Munitions—Comment on an Article by Durante and Publiese," *Health Physics* 82(6) (June 2002): 905; Chief of the Radiation Protection Division, Air Force Medical Operations Agency, e-mail message, Subject: "Cruise Missiles," May 6, 1999; Head of Radiological Controls and Health Branch, Chief of Navy Operations, e-mail message, Subject: "NO DU in Navy Cruise Missiles," August 4, 1999.

13. M.E. Danesi, *Kinetic Energy Penetrator Long Term Strategy Study* (Picatinny Arsenal, NJ: US Army Armament, Munitions, and Chemical Command, 1990), appendix D, vol. 1 pp. 2–2, 4–5.

14. Ibid., appendix D, vol. 2, pp. 3–4.

15. Ibid., appendix D, vol. 1, pp. 2–5.

16. Dan Fahey, *Case Narrative, Depleted Uranium (DU) Exposures,* 3rd ed. (The Military Toxics Project, The National Gulf War Resource Center, Swords to Plowshares: 20 September 1998), p. 107.

17. The Office of the Special Assistant to the Deputy Secretary of Defense for Gulf War Illnesses, *Depleted Uranium in the Gulf (II)* (Washington, DC, 2000), pp. 102–106.

18. See, e.g., General Hugh Beach, "The Military Hazards of Depleted Uranium," ISIS Briefing Paper No. 78, January 2001, para. 18, 19, http://www.isisuk.demon.co.uk/0811/isis/uk/regpapers/no78long_paper.html#16.

19. Corrosion rates in soil are highly variable depending on locations and environments, but penetrators may completely disintegrate into particulate matter within five to twenty years. The Royal Society, *The Health Hazards of Depleted Uranium Munitions,* part 2 (London, 2002), p. 21; United Nations Environment Programme, Post-Conflict Assessment Unit, *Depleted Uranium in Serbia and Montenegro: Post Conflict Environmental Assessment* (Geneva, 27 March 2002), p. 27; United Nations Environment Programme, Balkans Task Force, *Depleted Uranium in Kosovo, Post-Conflict Environmental Assessment* (Geneva, March 2001), pp. 27–28, 30–31. See also, Umberto Sansone, Pier Roberto Danesi, Sabrina Barbizzi et al., "Radioecological Survey at Selected Sites Hit by Depleted Uranium Ammunitions during the 1999 Kosovo Conflict," *The Science of the Total Environment.*

20. See, e.g., Tab F, "DU Use in the Gulf War," of DoD's 2000 report on DU: Office of the Special Assistant, *Depleted Uranium,* pp. 99–104; http://www.gulflink.osd.mil/du_ii/du_ii _tabf.htm.

21. James F. Dunnigan and Austin Bay, *From Shield to Storm* (New York: William Morrow, 1992), pp. 284–86.

22. See Dan Fahey, "Science or Science Fiction? Facts, Myths and Propaganda in the Debate Over Depleted Uranium Munitions," (self published) 12 March 2003, p. 10.
23. US Army Armament Munitions and Chemical Command message to Army Central Command Headquarters, Subject: "Depleted Uranium (DU) Contamination," March 7, 1991.
24. U.S. Army testing found normally 10–35 percent (but up to 70 percent) of the round oxidizes into dust upon impact with a hard target. Twenty percent is commonly used to determine the amounts of dust created by an impact. Office of the Special Assistant, *Depleted Uranium,* 203.
25. U.S. Army Center for Health Promotion and Preventative Medicine (CHPPM), *Depleted Uranium—Human Exposure Assessment and Health Risk Characterization,* no. 26-MF-7555-00D (15 September 2000), R-2.
26. See e.g., Scott Peterson, "The Trail of a Bullet," *Christian Science Monitor,* 5 October 1999, http://www.csmonitor.com/atcsmonitor/specials/uranium/. See also Dan Fahey, *Don't Look, Don't Find: Gulf War Veterans, the U.S. Government and Depleted Uranium, 1990–2000* (Lewiston, ME: Military Toxics Project, 30 March 2000), pp. 14–19, http://www.ngwrc.org/Dulink/dont_look_dont_find.htm.
27. Ibid., pp. 14–15.
28. US Army Regulation 40–5, "Preventative Medicine," 15 October 1990, ch. 9, 9–6 a(2).
29. The Office of the Special Assistant to the Deputy Secretary of Defense for Gulf War Illnesses, *Annual Report* (Washington, DC: US Department of Defense, 8 January 1998), p. 30.
30. US General Accounting Office, "Army Not Adequately Prepared to Deal with Depleted Uranium Contamination," GAO/NSIAD-93-90, January 1993, pp. 15–16.
31. U.S. General Accounting Office, "Army Not Adequately Prepared"; see also Col. Robert G. Claypool, U.S. Army Medical Corps, letter to Headquarters, U.S. Army Chemical School, "Subject: Depleted Uranium (DU) Safety Training," 16 August 1993.
32. U.S. General Accounting Office, "Army Not Adequately Prepared," pp. 7, 37.
33. U.S. Army Armament, Munitions and Chemical Command, memo from Depleted Uranium Recovery Team to Senior Command Representative AMCCOM-SWA, "Vehicle Assessment Report, Depleted Uranium Contamination" (14 May 1991).
34. U.S. General Accounting Office, "Army Not Adequately Prepared," p. 5.
35. F. Hooper, et al, "Elevated Urine Uranium Excretion by Soldiers with Retained Uranium Shrapnel," *Health Physics,* Vol. 77, No. 5 (November 1999) 513. Of note, between 1993 and 1998, the Department of Defense told five consecutive U.S. federal investigations of Gulf War veterans' illnesses that only 35–36 veterans were exposed to DU in friendly-fire incidents; in 1998 pressure from Swords to Plowshares Veterans Rights Organization, the Military Toxics Project, and the National Gulf War Resource Center forced the Pentagon to admit that approximately 104 veterans were exposed to DU in friendly fire incidents. See Fahey, *Don't Look, Don't Find,* p. 4–6.
36. U.S. Department of Veterans Affairs, Baltimore VAMC, *Department of Veterans Affairs Program for the Follow-up and Monitoring of Gulf War Veterans with Imbedded Fragments of Depleted Uranium,* draft, (23 September 1993), p. 11, http://www.gwu.edu/~nsarchiv/radiation/dir/mstreet/commeet; shmeet3/brief3.grf/tab_h/br3h1a.txt.
37. R.H. Gwiazda et al. "Detection of Depleted Uranium in the Urine of Veterans from the 1991

Gulf War," *Health Physics* 86 (1) (January 2004): 12–18; M. McDiarmid et al., "Health Effects of Depleted Uranium on Exposed Gulf War Veterans" *Environmental Research* 82 (2000): 172.

38. The Office of the Special Assistant to the Deputy Secretary of Defense for Gulf War Illnesses, "Meeting with Dr. Melissa McDiarmid and her staff on October 15, 1999 to discuss the Baltimore DU Follow-Up Program and the Extended Follow-Up Program," undated; Akira Toshiro from the Hiroshima, Japan, newspaper *Chugoku Shimbun* (4 April 2000), http://www.chugoku-np.co.jp/abom/uran/us_e/000404.html.

39. Alexandra Miller et al., "Transformation of Human Osteoblast Cells to the Tumorigenic Phenotype by Depleted Uranium-Uranyl Chloride," *Environmental Health Perspectives* 106 (1998): 469; F. Hahn, R.A. Guilmette, and M.D. Hoover, "Implanted Depleted Uranium Fragments Cause Soft Tissue Sarcomas in the Muscles of Rats," *Environmental Health Perspectives* 110 (2002): p. 51.

40. U.S. Institute of Medicine, *Gulf War and Health,* vol. 1, *Depleted Uranium, Pyridostigmine Bromide, Sarin, Vaccines* (Washington, DC: National Academy Press, 2000), p. 142.

41. On several occasions, A-10s shot DU munitions either within the 20-km exclusion zone around Sarajevo or near Han Pijeak, which was the headquarters of the Bosnian Serb Army. North Atlantic Treaty Organization, "Briefing by NATO Acting Spokesman Mark Laity and Statement by Ambassador Daniel Speckhard, Chairman Ad Hoc Committee on Depleted Uranium" (Brussels, Belgium: 24 January 2001).

42. U.S. Department of Defense, news briefing by Mr. Kenneth Bacon, 4 January 2001.

43. Angela Ashton-Kelley, U.S. Air Force 11th Wing, letter to Dan Fahey, 31 January 2000.

44. A-10s conducted 112 strikes with DU rounds against eighty-five targets in Kosovo, ten targets in Serbia, and one target in Montenegro. United Nations Environment Programme, Post-Conflict Assessment Unit, *Depleted Uranium in Serbia and Montenegro: Post Conflict Environmental Assessment in the Federal Republic of Yugoslavia* (Geneva, 27 March 2002), p. 168.

45. United Nations Environment Programme/United Nations Centre for Human Settlements (Habitat)/United Nations Centre for Human Settlements (Habitat), Balkans Task Force, *Depleted Uranium in Kosovo, Post-Conflict Environmental Assessment.* (Geneva, March 2001), p. 28–29, 36, 48.

46. P. Roth et al., "Assessment of Exposure to Depleted Uranium," *Radiation Protection Dosimetry* 105, nos. 1–4 (2003): 157–61: 160; Office of the Special Assistant to the Deputy Secretary of Defense for Gulf War Illnesses, Medical Readiness, and Military Deployments, *Information Paper: Depleted Uranium Environmental and Health Surveillance in the Balkans* (Washington, DC: U.S. Department of Defense, 25 October 2001); Nick D. Priest and M. Thirlwall, "Early Results of Studies on the Levels of Depleted Uranium Excreted by Balkan Residents," *Archive of Oncology* 9 (4) (2001): 240.

47. United Nations Environment Programme, *Depleted Uranium in Bosnia and Herzegovina* (Geneva, 25 March 2003), pp. 35–36, 42; Luigi di Lella et al., "Lichen as Biomonitors of Uranium and Other Trace Elements in an Area of Kosovo Heavily Shelled with Depleted Uranium Rounds," *Atmospheric Environment* (2003).

48. The Office of the Special Assistant to the Deputy Secretary of Defense for Gulf War Ill-

nesses, "Meeting with Dr. Melissa McDiarmid and Her Staff on October 15, 1999 to Discuss the Baltimore DU Follow-Up Program and the Extended Follow-Up Program," undated.

49. M. Kilpatrick, statement at NATO press briefing, Brussels, 10 January 2001, http://www.nato.int/docu/speech/2001/s010110b.htm. Dr. Kilpatrick is director of the Office of the Special Assistant to the Deputy Secretary of Defense for Gulf War Illnesses, Medical Readiness, and Military Deployments.

50. Col. Frank O'Donnell, expert meeting on "Depleted Uranium in Kosovo: Radiation Protection, Public Health and Environmental Aspects," Bad Honnef, Germany, 20 June 2001, author's notes.

51. Dennis Gray, "US Military Says Depleted Uranium Shells in Iraq Pose No Health Dangers," *Associated Press*, 6 May 2003.

52. US Department of Defense, "Briefing on Depleted Uranium," 14 March 2003, http://www.defenselink.mil/news/Mar2003/t03142003_t314depu.html.

53. U.S. General Accounting Office, *Hazardous Waste: Information on Potential Superfund Sites*, GAO/RCED-99-22 (Washington, DC: Government Printing Office, Nov. 1998), p. 170; Michael Orey, "Uranium Waste Site Has a Historic New England Town Up in Arms," *Wall Street Journal*, 1 March 2001.

54. Peter Pae, "Friendly Fire Still a Problem," *Los Angeles Times*, 16 May 2003; Paul Wachter, "Fought for Freedom with Marines He Loved," *The State* (South Carolina), 25 May 2003; Pamela Hess, "Iraq War-Related U.S. Deaths Now 147," *United Press International*, 12 May 2003.

55. Rory McCarthy, "Friendly Fire Kills Two UK Tank Crew," *The Guardian* (UK), 26 March 2003; Rory McCarthy, "British Soldier Killed by US Jet," *The Guardian* (UK), 29 March 2003; Audrey Gillan, " 'I Never Want to Hear That Sound Again,' " *The Guardian* (UK), 31 March 2003.

56. See Dan Fahey, "The Use of Depleted Uranium in the 2003 Iraq War—An Initial Assessment of Information and Policies," (24 June 2003).

57. Ian Bruce, "Fewer than 10 Gulf War Troops Had Uranium Poisoning," *The Herald* (UK), 5 February 2004.

58. US Air Force, CENTAF Assessment and Analysis Division, "Operation IRAQI FREEDOM—By the Numbers," 30 April 2003, p. 11.

59. Mr. Ingram, in response to question 150356 from Mr. Hancock, UK Parliament, 2 February 2004, column 747W. Mr. Ingram stated: "To date eight military vehicles have been identified as having been hit by depleted uranium (DU) munitions within the southern sector of Iraq under British military control. All these vehicles have been clearly marked. Arrangements are currently being negotiated with the US for a contractor to collect and securely store these military vehicles."

60. UK Ministry of Defence, "Depleted Uranium—Middle East 2003," 6 June 2003, http://www.mod.uk/issues/depleted_uranium/middle_east_2003.htm.

61. Sarmad Sufian, "U.S. Used Nuclear Waste" *Weekly Independent* (Pakistan), vol. 1, no. 23, 29 November–5 December 2001, front page; Uranium Medical Research Centre, "Afghan Field Trip #2 Report," undated, http://www.umrc.net/downloads/destruction_effects.pdf; Republic of

Iraq, Ministry of Higher Education and Scientific Research, "Conference on the Effects of the Use of Depleted Uranium Weaponry on Human and Environment [sic] in Iraq," 26–27 March 2002, posted at the Web site of the International Depleted Uranium Study Team, http://www.idust.org/; Leuren Moret, letter to the Honorable Jim McDermott, 21 February 2003, http://traprockpeace.org/LettertoMcDermott.pdf.

62. US Department of Defense, "Briefing on Depleted Uranium," 14 March 2003, http://www.defenselink.mil/news/Mar2003/t03142003_t314depu.html.

63. Dennis Gray, "US Military Says Depleted Uranium Shells in Iraq Pose No Health Dangers," *Associated Press*, 6 May 2003.

64. World Health Organization, *Depleted Uranium: Sources, Exposure and Health Effects* (Geneva, 2001) p. 57; Royal Society, *Health Hazards*, part 2, p. 27.

65. Christina Giannardi and Daniele Dominici, "Military Use of Depleted Uranium: Assessment of Prolonged Exposure," *Journal of Environmental Radioactivity* 64 (2003): 227–36: 233.

66. D.E. McClain et al., "Biological Effects of Embedded Depleted Uranium (DU): Summary of Armed Forces Radiobiology Research Institute Research," *The Science of the Total Environment* 274 (2001): 118.

67. See, e.g., David Hambling, " 'Safe' Alternative to Depleted Uranium Revealed," *New Scientist*, 30 July 2003; Sean Rayment, "Army's New Tank Gun Will End Use of Controversial Uranium-tipped Shells," *The Telegraph* (UK), 21 September 2003.

68. See Dan Fahey, "The Development and Use of Depleted Uranium Munitions," in *The International Legal Regulation of the Use of Depleted Uranium Weapons: A Cautionary Approach*, ed. Avril McDonald (Den Haag: Asser Press, forthcoming, 2004).

69. T. Gander and C. Cutshaw, eds., *Jane's Ammunition Handbook*, 9th ed., 2000–2001 (Surrey: Jane's Information Group Limited, 2000), p. 226; Anthony H. Cordesman, "The Military Balance in the Middle East—The Southern Gulf by Country: Part XII," Center for Strategic and International Studies, 30 December 1998, p. 14.

70. C. Foss, ed., *Jane's Armour and Artillery, 2000–2001*, 21st ed. (Surrey: Jane's Information Group Limited, 2000), p. 76; Gander and Cutshaw, *Jane's Ammunition*, p. 231–32.

71. "Pakistan Joins DU Producer Nations," *Jane's Land Forces*, 9 May 2001, http://www.janes.com/defence/land_forces/news/; "Pakistan Ordnance Factories Launches Rs 4 Billion Upgrade Plan," *South-Asian Defence News*, December 2002.

72. U.S. Department of Defense News Briefing, "Sec. Rumsfeld and Gen. Myers" (16 January 2002), http://www.defenselink.mil/news/Jan2002/t01162002_t0116sd.html. 73. Melissa Fleming, Senior Information Officer, International Atomic Energy Institute, e-mail to author, 28 July 2003.

74. See Lewis Walker, Deputy Assistant Secretary of the Army, "Memorandum for Director, Army Environmental Policy Institute," 13 December 1992.

75. U.S. Army Environmental Policy Institute, *Health and Environmental Consequences*, p. 4.

76. Public Law 103–160, "National Defense Authorization Act for Fiscal Year 1994," passed 30 November 1993, section 271.

77. See Medical Reference for Gulf War-Related Research, "Environmental and Occupa-

tional Health: Depleted Uranium," http://www.gulflink.osd.mil/medsearch/Environmental Occupationa/DepletedUranium/DepletedUranium_home.shtml, visited 20 January 2004.

78. H.R. 1483, *Depleted Uranium Munitions Study Act of 2003*, sponsored by Rep. Jim McDermott (WA-7), introduced 27 March 2003.

79. The Honorable Bob Filner and the Honorable Ciro Rodriguez, letter to the Honorable David Walker, Comptroller General of the U.S. General Accounting Office, 3 December 2003.

80. Senator Russell Feingold, letter to the Honorable Arlen Specter and the Honorable Bob Graham, 30 December 2003.

81. U.S. General Accounting Office, "Gulf War Illnesses: Understanding of Health Effects From Depleted Uranium Evolving but Safety Training Needed," GAO/NSIAD-00-70, March 2000.

82. International Coalition to Ban Uranium Weapons, www.bandepleteduranium.org/, site visited 10 February 2004.

83. Martin Williams, "First Award for Depleted Uranium Poisoning Claim," *The Herald* (UK), 4 February 2004.

84. Personal interview with author, Dec. 2003.

Gulf War Illnesses

1. CNN.com, "The Unfinished War: A Decade Since Desert Storm," http://www.cnn.com/SPECIALS/2001/gulf.war/facts/gulfwar/.

2. Patrick J. Sloyan, "Head of Gulf War Illness Panel Had Ties to Chemical Supplier," *Newsday*, November 27, 1996.

3. Philip Shenon, "New Look Urged on Gulf War Syndrome," *New York Times*, December 10, 1996.

4. "The Gulf War," *Frontline*, PBS, http://www.pbs.org/wgbh/pages/frontline/gulf/syndrome/chrono.html.

5. Philip Shenon, "Half of Gulf-Illness Panel Now Calls Gas a Possible Factor," *New York Times*, August 19, 1997.

6. National Center for Infectious Diseases, *Traveler's Health*, http://www.cdc.gov/travel/diseases/leishmaniasis.htm.

7. US Department of Defense Military Health System, *Unexplained Illnesses Among Desert Storm Veterans, A Search For Causes, Treatment and Cooperation*, http://www.tricare.osd.mil/pgulf/arch8.html.

8. CNN.com, "Troops from Iraq Can't Donate Blood," October 23, 2003, http://www.cnn.com/2003/HEALTH/10/23/iraq.blood.ap/.

9. US Department of Defense Military Health System, *Unexplained Illnesses.*

10. University of Virginia Health System, *Yellow Fever/Reed Commission Exhibit*, http://hsc.virginia.edu/hs-library/historical/yelfev/tabcon.htm l.

11. *UT Southwestern Team Traces Gulf War Illnesses to Chemicals: Three Primary Syndromes Identified*, press release, UT Southwestern Medical Center, January 8, 1997.

12. Thomas D. Williams, "Soldiers Medical Testing Faulted," *Hartford Courant*, September 22, 2003.

13. "Bragg Investigation Put on the Fast Track," CBSNews.com, August 23, 2002, http://www.cbsnews.com/stories/2002/08/29/national/main5202 73.shtml.

7: Military Justice

1. *Chappel v. Wallace,* 462 U.S. 296 (1983), at 300.

2. Keith E. Bonn, *Army Officers Guide,* 49th ed. (August 2002).

3. This is the provision on unlawful command influence as stated in the *Manual for Courts-Martial* (2000), rule 104. Similar language is found in Article 37, UCMJ, 10 U.S.C. Sec. 837.

4. Article 37, UCMJ, 10 U.S.C. Sec. 837. This provision was an attempt by Congress soon after World War Two to eliminate "unlawful command influence." In 1986 the U.S. Court of Military Appeals emphasized that unlawful "command influence is the mortal enemy of military justice." *United States v. Thomas,* 22 M.J. 388, 393 (C.M.A. 1986).

The abysmal record of the Pentagon and the military courts in challenging unlawful command influence is shown by facts found in recent cases. An example is *United States v. Rico Gore,* 58 M.J. 776 (NCCA 2003), a Navy case. In this case, a Navy commander intimidated an enlisted defense witness under his command. He told the witness that he "wasn't going to testify." The commander would not allow anyone else in the command to testify for the defense during the sentencing phase of trial either. At trial, the military judge made a specific finding that the commander "took it as a personal affront" that the military defense lawyer had interviewed the witness and had made plans for the sailor to testify on behalf of the accused. The military trial judge courageously dismissed the entire case "with prejudice," that is, the case could not be tried again. On appeal, the Navy Court of Criminal Appeals found that indeed unlawful command influence had occurred, but held that the appropriate remedy was a new sentencing hearing, rather than dismissal of charges. This case is currently on appeal to the U.S. Court of Appeals for the Armed Forces.

Not found in the record of this case and so many others is any explanation of why the commander was never charged criminally with obstruction of justice and unlawful command influence. If commanders were put on trial for such gross violations of law, illegal command influence and control would quickly be eradicated.

It is unconscionable that more than fifty years after the outlawing of illegal command influence and control, commanders are allowed to get away with violating the UCMJ.

5. *O'Callahan v. Parker,* 395 U.S. 258 (1969), at 298. The *O'Callahan* decision and others sharply limited the jurisdiction of the military to matters occurring on military property, unless there was a service connection between the alleged crime and the military.

6. In 1987 the *O'Callahan* decision was overruled by the Supreme Court in *Solorio v. United States,* 483 U.S. 435 (1987). Now, it is common for members of the military to be tried for alleged offenses that took place in the civilian community hundreds or even thousands of miles from base, post, or ship, and while the service member was off duty.

7. See *Manual for Courts-Martial* (2000), Rule 503: "If . . . a request is made, an enlisted accused may not be tried by a [special or general] court-martial the membership of which does not in-

clude enlisted members in a number comprising at least one-third of the total number of members."

8. For decades the maximum punishment at trial by special court-martial was six months in prison. Congress amended Article 19, UCMJ, 10 U.S. Code, sec. 819, in 1999 to provide for a longer sentence. This was accomplished without any public congressional hearings.

9. *Parker v. Levy,* 417 U.S. 733 (1974).

10. Title 10, U.S. Code, Section 825a (2003), Public Law 107-107, 115 Stat. 1124.

11. The UCMJ provides for the power of subpoena in military courts "similar to that which courts of the United States having criminal jurisdiction may lawfully issue," but the military does not live up to this law (Article 46, UCMJ, 10 U.S.C. sec 846). The *Manual for Courts-Martial* provides that both the prosecution and the defense shall have "equal opportunity to obtain witnesses and evidence, including the benefit of compulsory process" (MCM (2000), Rule 703). The *Manual* explains, however, that "The defense shall submit to the trial counsel [prosecutor] a written list of witnesses whose production by the Government the defense requests" (Rule 703, discussion). The military's refusal to follow the UCMJ concerning the subpoena of witnesses by the defense is an area which is long overdue for exposure, investigation, and reform.

12. Article 25, UCMJ, 10 U.S.C. Sec. 825.

13. According to Article 25, UCMJ, "Any commissioned officer on active duty is eligible to serve on all courts-martial for the trial of any person." Nonetheless, the service branches as a matter of regulation or practice or both, usually refuse to appoint chaplains, doctors, nurses, and other support personnel for jury service.

14. In *United States v. Moore,* 28 M.J. 366 (C.M.A. 1989), the U.S. Court of Military Appeals applied the Supreme Court's recent decision in *Batson v. Kentucky,* 476 U.S. 79 (1986).

15. In 1997 CAAF held that the proferred reason given by a prosecutor for peremptory challenge of a court member cannot be "unreasonable, implausible, or [one] that otherwise makes no sense." *United States v. Tulloch,* 47 M.J. 283, 287 (CAAF 1997). See also *United States v. Hum,* 58 M.J. 199 (CAAF 2003).

16. Each year the highest-ranking lawyer in each branch of the military service, the Judge Advocate General, publishes a report that contains "Military Justice Statistics." The annual reports of the judge advocate general of the Army, Navy, and Air Force are published on the official Web site of the U.S. Court of Appeals for the Armed Forces.

17. Critics of the military judicial system have included insiders and participants in the system. See Luther C. West, "A History of Command Influence in the Military Judicial System," *UCLA Law Review* (1970): 1–156. West is a US Army lieutenant colonel, ret., who spent many years as a staff judge advocate. See also Kenneth J. Hodson, "Military Justice: Abolish or Change?" 22 *Kan. L. Rev.* 31 (1973). Major General Hodson is a former judge advocate general of the Army and former chief judge of the Army Court of Military Review.

18. See Kevin J. Barry, "A Facelift (And Much More) For an Aging Beauty: The Cox Commission Recommendations to Rejuvenate the Uniform Code of Military Justice," *L. Rev. M.S.U.-D.C.L.* 58 (2002). Captain Barry, USCG (ret.), served on active duty in the Coast Guard for over twenty-five years, including as a chief trial judge and appellate military judge.

19. For a frightening example of military judicial misconduct, see *United States v. Quintanilla,* 56 M.J. 37 (CAAF 2001). In that case an Army judge engaged in a variety of unprofessional actions, including confronting witnesses outside the courtroom, engaging in extrajudicial communications, and apparently attempting to cover up his egregious conduct. While this case presents an extreme example, many military judges consider themselves to be the commander of the courtroom and take charge accordingly.

8: Policing America

1. Eric Schmitt, "Wider Military Role in US is Urged," *New York Times,* July 21, 2002.
2. Samuel Adams, quoted in Michael C. Desch, *Civilian Control of the Military* (Baltimore: Johns Hopkins University Press, 1999), p. 23.
3. US Constitution, Article IV, Section 4.
4. US Constitution, Article I, Section.
5. US Constitution, Article II, Section 8.
6. Matthew C. Hammond, "The Posse Comitatus Act: A Principle in Need of Renewal," *Washington University Law Quarterly,* 75 (1997): 953.
7. *The Federalist Papers,* ed. C. Rossiter, (1961) Bobbs-Merrill pp. 258–60.
8. Daniel Levitas, *The Terrorist Next Door.* (New York: Dunne / St. Martin's Press, 2002), p. 53.
9. Joan Jensen, *Army Surveillance in America.* (New Haven: Yale University Press, 1989), p. 32.
10. Howard Zinn, *People's History of the United States.* (New York: HarperCollins, 1991), p. 205.
11. Jensen, *Army Surveillance,* pp. 33–34.
12. 18 US Code, Sec. 1385, as amended, 1994. Although the original statute mentioned only the Army, the Air Force was added by statute in 1956, and the Navy and Marines were incorporated by DOD regulation in 1991.
13. Richard Boyer and Herbert Morais, *Labor's Untold Story* (New York: UE Press, 1971).
14. Timothy J. Dunn, "Waging War on Immigrants," in *Militarizing the American Criminal Justice System,* ed. Peter Kraska (Boston: Northeastern University Press, 2001), p. 78.
15. Paul Chevigny, *The Edge of the Knife: Police Violence in America* (New York: Knopf, 1995), p. 124.
16. Standing Rules of Engagement for US Forces, 1994, quoted in Col. Charles J. Dunlap, Jr., "The Thick Green Line," in Kraska *Militarizing the System,* p. 35.
17. Bill Toque and Douglas Waller, "Warriors without War," *Newsweek,* March 19, 1990, p. 18.
18. Jensen, *Army Surveillance,* p. 178.
19. Ibid., p. 177.
20. "Federal Military Interventions in Domestic Disorders" in *U.S. Military under the Constitution* (New York: NYU Press, 1991).
21. Ted Morgan, *Reds: McCarthyism in the Twentieth Century* (New York: Random House, 2003), pp. 141–43.
22. Page Smith, *Democracy on Trial* (New York: Simon and Schuster, 1995), p. 428.
23. Michael Linfield, *Freedom Under Fire: U.S. Civil Liberties in Time of War* (Boston: South End Press, 1990), p. 96.
24. David Cole, *Enemy Aliens* (New York: The New Press, 2003), p. 102.

25. Smith, *Democracy on Trial,* p. 31.
26. Linfield, *Freedom Under Fire: US Civil Liberties in Time of War* p. 92.
27. *Hirabayashi vs. U.S.,* 320 US 320 (1944).
28. *Korematsu vs. U.S.,* 323 US 214, at 241.
29. *Personal Justice Denied,* Report of Commission on Wartime Relocation and Internment of Civilians CWRIC, (Seattle: University of Washington Press, 1997).
30. "Racial Profiling, Post-9/11," Tamy E. Coke, in *Lost Liberties,* ed. Cynthia Brown (New York: The New Press, 2003).
31. Linda Greenhouse, "Supreme Court Denies Detainees," *New York Times,* January 6, 2004.
32. Philip B. Heyman, *Terrorism, Freedom, and Security* (Cambridge, MA: MIT Press, 2003), p. 155.
33. Jensen, *Army Surveillance,* p. 255.
34. US Senate Judiciary Committee, *Military Surveillance of Civilian Politics,* 87-312, 1973.
35. Jensen, *Army Surveillance,* p. 243.
36. Christopher Pyle, "Military Spying Unmasked," *Washington Monthly,* January 1970.
37. Jensen, *Army Surveillance,* p. 245.
38. "Federal Military Intervention," p. 141.
39. Ward Churchill and Jim Vander Wall, *COINTELPRO: The FBI's Secret Wars* (Boston: South End Press, 1990), ch. 4.
40. *Laird vs. Tatum,* 408 U.S. 1 (1972).
41. David Caute, *The Great Fear* (New York: Simon and Schuster, 1978), p. 403.
42. Nancy Chang, *Silencing Political Dissent* (New York: Seven Stories Press, 2002).
43. Ruth Wedgwood, "Rule of Law and War on Terror," *New York Times,* Dec. 23, 2003.
44. Chang, *Silencing Political Dissent,* p. 115.
45. Ward Churchill and Jim Vander Wall, *Agents of Repression* (Boston: South End Press, 1988), ch. 4–12.
46. *U.S. vs. Red Feather,* 392 F. Supp. 916 (D.S.D. 1975).
47. *U.S. vs. Jaramillo,* 380 F. Supp. 1375 (D.NEB, 1974).
48. *U.S. vs. McCarthur,* 419 F. Supp. 186 (D.N.D. 1975), aff'd sub nom, 541 F 2d 1275, (8th Cir., 1976).
49. Jensen, *Army Surveillance,* pp. 257–58.
50. Arnold S. Trebach, *The Great Drug War* (New York: Macmillan, 1987), p. 168.
51. 10 U.S. Code, Sec. 371–380, as amended, 1994.
52. Trebach, *Great Drug War,* ch. 5.
53. Ted Carpenter, "Collateral Damage," in *After Prohibition,* Timothy Lynch, ed. (Washington, DC: CATO Institute, 2000), p. 148.
54. Paul B. Stares, *Global Habit,* Washington, DC: Brookings Institution, 1996), p. 69.
55. Micheline Maynard, "Drop in Business Clients Seen After Cancellations," *New York Times,* Jan. 3, 2004.
56. Reuters dispatch, printed in *New York Times,* Nov. 29, 2003.
57. Alfred McCoy, *The Politics of Heroin* (New York: Lawrence Hill, 1991), p. 449.
58. Paul Williams, *Al Qaeda: Brotherhood of Terror* (New York: Alpha/Pearson, 2002), p. xiv.

59. Peter Kraska, "Militarization of the Drug War" in *Altered States*, ed. Peter Kraska (New York: Garland Press, 1993), p. 167.
60. Trebach, *Great Drug War*, p. 169.
61. P. Reuter, *Sealing the Border* (Santa Monica: RAND Corp., 1988).
62. Dunn, "Waging War on Immigrants," p. 69.
63. 10 U.S. Code, Section 381–86.
64. Peter Kraska and Victor Kappeler, "Militarizing American Police," *Social Problems* (Feb. 1997).
65. Kraska, "Militarization of the Drug War," p. 159.
66. James W. Button, *Black Violence: Political Impact of the 1960s Riots* (Princeton: Princeton University Press, 1978), p. 133.
67. Ron Ridenhour and Arthur Lubow, "Bringing the War Home," *New Times*, June 1975, p. 20.
68. *Domestic Support Operations*, U.S. Field Manual 100–19, July 1, 1993.
69. Operation Urban Warrior Homepage, www.defenselink.mil/specials/urban_warrior/.
70. R.W. Glenn, *Marching Under Darkening Skies* (Santa Monica: RAND Corp., 1998).
71. *Military Operations in Urbanized Terrain*, Marine Corps Warfighting Publication. 3–35.3, April 16, 1998.
72. Mike Davis, "LA: The Fire This Time," *Covert Action Info Bulletin*, spring 1992.
73. See www.Army.mil/features/strykeroe/.
74. Dick J. Reavis, *The Ashes of Waco* (New York: Simon and Schuster, 1995).
75. John George and Laird Wilcox, *American Extremists* (Buffalo: Prometheus Books, 1997), p. 252.
76. James Ridgeway, "General Alarm," *Village Voice*, Sept. 24, 2003.
77. Stephan Labaton, "Report on Initial Raid," *New York Times*, Oct. 1, 1993.
78. Ellen Ray and William Schaap, ed., *Covert Action*, (New York: Ocean Press, 2003), pp. 64–65.
79. Williams, *Al Qaeda*, p. xiv.
80. Stephen Jones, *Others Unknown: Tim McVeigh and the Oklahoma City Bombing*, (New York: Public Affairs, 2001), p. 130.
81. Ibid., pp. 150–51.
82. Ibid., p. 160.
83. Williams, *Al Qaeda*, p. xv.
84. Eric Larson and John Peters, *Preparing the US Army for Homeland Security* (Santa Monica: RAND Corp., 2001), pp. 247–50.
85. David Cole and James X. Dempsey, *Terrorism and the Constitution* (New York: The New Press, 2002), p. 120.
86. David Cole, "The Course of Least Resistance," in *Lost Liberties*, ed. Brown p. 17.
87. Noam Chomsky, *Hegemony or Survival* (New York: Metropolitan Books, 2003), p. 206.
88. Seymour Hersh, "The Other War," *The New Yorker*, April 12, 2004.
89. Detention, Treatment, and Trial of Certain Non-Citizens in the War Against Terrorism, 66 Fed Register 57833, Nov. 13, 2001.

90. Barbara Olshansky and CCR, *Secret Trials and Executions: Military Tribunals* (New York: Seven Stories Press, 2002), p. 12.
91. Ronald Dworkin, "The Trouble with Tribunals," *New York Review of Books,* April 25, 2002.
92. Jess Bravin and David S. Cloud, "Bush Policy on Detainees Is Dealt a Setback," *Wall Street Journal,* Dec. 19, 2003.
93. Linda Greenhouse, "Justices to Hear Case of Citizen Held as Enemy," *New York Times,* Jan. 10, 2004.
94. Louis Fisher, *Military Tribunals* (Hauppauge, NY: Novinka Press, 2003), p. 4.
95. *Ex Parte Quirin,* 317 U.S. 1 (1942).
96. Neil Lewis, "US Negotiating to Release Many Held at Guantánamo," *New York Times,* Jan. 10, 2004.
97. Jim Garamon, "DOD Announces Military Commission Review," *Armed Forces Press Services,* Dec. 30, 2003.
98. Chang, *Silencing Political Dissent,* p. 72.
99. Jensen, *Army Surveillance,* p. 261.

9: Filling the Ranks

1. Col. Robert Heinl, Jr., "The Death of the Army," *Armed Forces Journal,* June 7, 1971; reprinted in *Vietnam and America,* Marvin Gittleman ed. et al. (New York: Grove Press, 1995), p. 326.
2. Ibid., pp. 328–29.
3. James Lewes, *Protest and Survive: Underground GI Newspapers During the Vietnam War* (Westport, CT: Praeger, 2003),
4. Tom Wells, *The War Within: America's Battle Over Vietnam* (Berkeley: University of California Press, 1994), p. 269.
5. Eliot A. Cohen, *Citizens and Soldiers: The Dilemmas of Military Service* (Ithaca, NY: Cornell University Press, 1985), p. 165.
6. George Q. Flynn, *Conscriptions and Democracy* (Westport, CT: Greenwood Press, 2002), p. 256.
7. Ibid.
8. Michael Uhl and Tod Ensign, *GI Guinea Pigs: How the Pentagon Exposed Our Troops to Dangers More Deadly Than War* (New York: Playboy Press, 1980), chs. 7–10.
9. Frank Barnaby, *The Automated Battlefield* (New York: Free Press, 1983).
10. *Metal of Dishonor: Depleted Uranium,* Ramsey Clark, Helen Caldicott, Michio Kaku, Dan Fahey, Victor Sidel, Tod Ensign, et al. (New York: International Action Center, 1997).
11. Flynn, *Conscriptions and Democracy,* p. 237.
12. Joel Guyer, "The Soldiers' Revolt" *International Socialist Review* (Aug.–Sept. 2000):, p. 1.
13. Joe McGinniss, *The Selling of the President* (New York: Trident Press, 1969), p. 32.
14. *The All Volunteer Force, After a Decade,* William Bowman, Roger Little, G. Thomas Sicilia, eds, (Washington, DC: Pergammon Brassey's, 1986), p. 11.
15. *The Draft: 1940–1973* George Q. Flynn, (Lawrence: University of Kansas Press, 1993).
16. Ibid., p. 239.

17. Cohen, *Citizens and Soldiers,* p. 167.
18. "The Case for Abolishing the Draft and Substituting for It an All Volunteer Army," *New York Times Magazine,* May 14, 1967, p. 118.
19. Flynn, *The Draft,* p. 265.
20. James Robbins, "Neo-Conscription," *National Review,* Jan. 9, 2003, ???
21. Thomas Reeves and Karl Hess, *The End of the Draft* (New York: Random House, 1970).
22. Ibid., preface, p. xvi.
23. Gates Commission, *The Report of the President's Commission on an All Volunteer Armed Force* (New York: Collier Books / Macmillan, 1970), pp. 5–10.
24. Bowman, *The All Volunteer Force After a Decade,* p. 206.
25. Milton Friedman, *Capitalism and Freedom* (Chicago: University of Chicago Press, 2002), p. 36.
26. Ibid., p. 42.
27. Jim Tice, "Recruiting is Robust" *Army Times,* Oct. 13, 2003.
28. Bowman, Little, et al. *All Volunteer Force after a Decade,* p. 28.
29. *Gates Report,* p. 95.
30. Martin Binkin, *Who Will Fight The Next War?* (Washington, DC: The Brookings Institution, 1993), p. 117.
31. Ibid., p. 108.
32. *GAO Report,* quoted in Binkin, *Who Will Fight?,* p. 127.
33. Jeffrey A. Jacobs, *The Future of Citizen Soldier Force* (Lexington: University of Kentucky Press, 1994), p. 89.
34. Vince Crowley, "Reserves to Keep Big Roles in Hot Spots," *Army Times,* Oct. 13, 2003.
35. "In Non-Draft Era, Citizens Become Military Illiterates," Gannett News Service, Mar. 23, 2001.
36. Binkin, "Who Will Fight?" p. 81.
37. Ibid., p. 71.
38. Vince Crawley, "Noncitizen Soldiers: Lawmakers Want to Speed Naturalization," *Army Times,* Sept. 23, 2003.
39 Brent Scowcroft, ed., *Military Service in the United States* (Englewood Cliffs, NJ: Prentice-Hall, 1982), pp. 140–41.
40. Binkin, "Who Will Fight?" p. 6.
41. William McMichael, *The Mother of All Hooks* (New Brunswick, NJ: Transaction Books, 1997).
42. Arthur Schlesinger, Jr., "Eyeless in Iraq," *New York Review of Books,* Oct. 23, 2003.
43. Clair Schaeffer-Duffy, "Conscription Returns to Public Discussion," *National Catholic Reporter,* March 21, 2003.
44. Charles Rangel: "Bring Back the Draft," *New York Times,* Dec. 31, 2002.
45. Darryl Fears, "Draft Bill Stirs Debate Over Military," *Washington Post,* Feb. 4, 2003.
46. Rick Maze, "DOD Resists Force Increase" *Army Times,* Sept. 23, 2003.
47. *Rostker vs. Goldberg,* 453 US 57 (1981).
48. Stephen M. Kohn, *Jailed for Peace* (Westport, CT: Greenwood Press, 1986), p. 104.
49. *Schwartz* vs. *Lewis Brodsky* 03-10005-EFH, May 29, 2003.

50. Basic Draft Registration Information pamphlet, Center for Conscience and War, Washington, D.C. (1992), p. 1.

51. "Teacher's Guide to Selective Service," SSS, Arlington, VA (2002), p. 5.

52. Kohn, *Jailed for Peace,* p. 105.

53. "Teacher's Guide to Selective Service," p. 23.

54. Ibid., pp. 24–25.

55. Bowman, Little, et al., *The All Volunteer Force,* p. 24.

56. Richard Danzig and Peter Szanton, *National Service: What Would It Mean?* (Lexington, MA.: Lexington Books, 1986).

57. Ibid., p. 9.

58. Mark Libbon, "Selective Service Wants Doctors, Nurses Ready," *Newhouse News Service,* March 21, 2003.

59. "Senator Says U.S. May Need Compulsory Service," Agence Francais Press, April 20, 2004.

60. Jim Tice, "Return to Draft Not Needed, Lt. General Says," *Army Times,* May 10, 2004.

Index